The
Nurse's
Story

Carol Gino

aah-ha! Books© Inc.
New York

THE NURSE'S STORY

REVISED EDITION
Published by aah-ha! Books, Inc.
http://www.starwater.com

PRINTING HISTORY
Linden Press Edition published September 1982
An Alternate selection of Book-of-the-Month Club,
(Nurses Book Club)
Serialized in the Daily News, October 10th, 11th, & 12th 1982
Bantam edition / October 1983

aah-ha! Books are published by aah-ha! Inc.
Its trademark, consisting of the words aah-ha! Books and logo,
is registered in U.S. Patent and Trademark Office
Library of Congress Catalog Card #96-095308

ISBN 1-889853-03-8
ISBN 0-553-23667-9

PRINTED IN THE UNITED STATES OF AMERICA

0 2 4 6 8 9 7 5 3 1

I walked back into her room and closed the door behind me. I turned off the alarm on the respirator, detached her and started blindly to do her dressings. I refused to look at the monitor. And then, for the first time, I held her small body tight against me. I hugged her, rocking. After I had lain her down and fixed her bed, I straightened the entire room. Finally, I looked at the monitor. Straight line.
. . . I opened the chart to see what the doctor had written. It read: "Patient died while on respirator. Pronounced dead at 6:45 A.M."

"She knows the front lines of nursing through and through . . . her stories . . . are almost invariably unsettling. But she is always honest. In public and in private hospitals alike, people die daily in ways we don't want to imagine; and when the rewards no longer compensate for the pain and frustration, tough, caring people like Gino are lost to the profession. A graphic, hard-line testimonial.'

-Kirkus Review

"The Nurse's Story does make one a believer in second chances."

-Denver Post

"The Nurse's Story . . . speaks with honesty, vigor, eloquence and sensitivity to the essentially human daily experience of Every nurse, tales that are so intertwined in the mysteries of life and death that they are rarely admitted and heretofore never publicly told even as myth"

- Dolores Krieger, Ph.D., R.N.
Professor of Nursing, New York University

Gritty and honest . . it has a fierce compassion."

-Martha Lear
Author of HEARTSOUNDS

"Riveting, wrenching. Few nurse's have experienced the range of cases this dedicated woman describes: cancer, burn unit, emergency ward, birth, brain damage . . . The writer is a vigorous optimistic, caring woman. And she exudes frankness . . ."

-Los Angeles Times

Original Author's Note

Throughout my nursing career I've made a tacit agreement with my patients that I would never hurt them or their families while they shared their vulnerabilities with me. I told them that they could trust me, that I would protect their privacy, that I would protect them. And I can't betray that promise.

So I've changed names and other identifying characteristics, often made composites, disguised hospitals and circumstances. Particulars never mattered to me; any one of my patients could have been my mother, my father, my sister, my children . . . or me. And I've chosen a fictitious name for the book's narrator, because she is not only me: she is many of the nurses it's been my privilege to know.

But I have always kept to the essential truth as I am able to see it.

In a time when so little seems to have meaning, when people search for values, and many people lead lonely lives; when few of us get to meet real live heroes and see true dignity in human beings, I've been lucky. Through nursing, through my patients, I've been given a rare gift. To thank them, I'd like to share it with my readers.

C.G.

*~ For my mother and father
and all the rest of us ~*

Author's note - 1997

It's been over ten years since I first wrote "The Nurse's Story" and in that time much has changed, in nursing, in the medical system and in my life. Still, as I read it over again from the perspective of time and experience, I see a love here that for me has never been matched.

The nurse in this book is not only me, but when Teri Daley's experiences were my own, and when her patients were mine, like Yves and Rachael and Robin and Steve....and of course, Melody, I found myself amazed at how much of each of them had stayed alive within me over all this time. I remember how each looked and sounded, I still remember the touch of their skin, the way they smelled, the sound of their voices, their essence. And I can see now that it was in helping these special people and watching them fight their battles, that I was inexorably molded and eventually armed for my own life's journey.

Now, from this vantage point, I can sometimes laugh at the young nurse in this book: she's so angry, so passionate, so self righteous even, but I am grateful that with all her flaws, she took me to very deep places in my heart which helped prepare me for the difficulties that I would encounter in my own life.

It was that young nurse in me with the fervent optimism and anger at injustice who allowed me to survive and help my daughter through my grandson's death from Sudden Infant Death Syndrome. The knowledge I garnered from all those years spent on hospital wards, at bedsides, loving and caring for all my "patients," which helped me develop the ability to stay strong for my family when they really needed me.

I write this note to all of you, especially those of you who are caretakers; whether nurses, doctors, mothers, or wives, to let you know that even after all this time, what I've learned best are the lessons I learned as a nurse.

Most important of all, my patients taught me that Life was a very special gift to be lived to its fullest and that only when we welcome life completely - with both its joys and tragedies - can we let it go with grace at the time of our own Death.

I believe with all my heart that nursing is a calling, and that especially in this time of corporate agendas in the health care system, with all the changes that will be invented and enforced, the most important thing to remember, and the most healing component of that system is still the "caretaker," the nurse who is willing to risk loving her patients - because then healing will take place no matter what the outcome.

I also know now, without a doubt, that caring for others is the greatest gift of all....and when done with love and compassion, it heals the healer as well.

I offer this to you with love,
Carol Gino

PROLOGUE

THE LITTLE GIRL'S SCREAMS MADE ME FURIOUS. I wanted to slap her. She was lying in a "monster crib," a chrome basket covered with a large plastic bubble to keep her from climbing out.

She was a beautiful baby, chubby, with wispy cornsilk curls. But her fair pink skin was now blotched from her crying and rubbing on the sheets. Each of her little arms was trapped, taped to a green-paper-covered board and hooked to the mattress by huge safety pins. Each of her legs was tied with gauze at the ankle and pulled tight to the side of the crib. Spread-eagled.

Above the disposable diaper, her small chest heaved from the force of her screams. I could see the fluid drip slowly from the intravenous bottle overhead, down the tubing, and through the IMED, or drop regulator. The machine monitored the rate and amount of solution to be infused and would warn of any malfunction with a high-pitched, insistent beep. A light in the upper right-hand corner of the box-shaped computer winked like a red eye when it was working properly.

I watched myself watching the child. I was sitting in the corner of the small darkened hospital room, the light from the slightly cracked bathroom door molding shadows on the wall which crowded me into the high-backed vinyl chair. I leaned back and thought about what the evening nurse had told me at report: "Beth Casey. Two years old. Fever of unknown origin; possible meningitis; isolation. Seizures."

Beth began to toss her head back and forth, still screaming and crying. I shut my eyes tight to try to blot out the sound, but when I opened them she was sneaking her blond head sideways and down her arm, trying to bite the tubing that carried the fluid through the needle into her vein. When I jumped up to stop her, I pushed her head away with more gentleness than I wanted to.

She looked terrified as I stood by the crib.

"Beth, what's wrong?" I asked, trying to soothe, as I lowered the side rail of the crib.

The tossing of her head got more frantic, and suddenly her gray eyes flickered and rolled upward. Only the whites showed. Before I could grab the tongue blade fastened to the wall by adhesive tape, her teeth came down hard on the side of her tongue. Almost instantly, her legs began to tremble in an exaggerated chill, and violent tremors ran upward until they had her body in an arch that threatened to crack her back.

I struggled to unpin one of her arms so that I could turn her on her side, but both flew up and away from the mattress, pulling hunks of sheet with them. The boards slammed down hard only once before the force of her jackknifed arms broke them. The IV needle ripped out, leaving a ragged tear. She was having a grand-mal seizure.

I strained to reach the call bell for help, but Beth was coughing, choking on saliva and blood, from her bitten tongue, that had reached the back of her throat. Quickly, I grabbed the tubing from the wall suction machine and pushed the switch on. I shoved her on her side with my free hand, hoping the secretions would run out of her mouth. Then I tried to push the clear-plastic tubing past her clenched teeth toward the back of her throat. I couldn't. She was gurgling, her lips turning blue, as I forced the tubing down one of her tiny nostrils. Instantly, a large amount of pink frothy fluid was sucked up the tubing toward the glass bottle on the wall. My hands trembled as I tried to stop the bleeding from the wound in her arm the IV needle had left.

Beth's body relaxed long enough for me to tear the taped syringe of Phenobarbital off the chrome headbar of the crib and give an injection in her thigh before her muscles stiffened again.

As the second seizure started, I managed to fit the gauze-covered tongue blade between her teeth and push the blankets against the bars of the crib to keep her from hurting herself. The tremors hit again, less violently than before, and lasted only seconds before she relaxed. She was white and pasty-looking. Her lips were colorless. I placed my stethoscope on her chest and listened to the speeding gallop of her heart, fast but regular.

God, was I hot! Encased by the nylon uniform I wore under the sterile yellow paper gown, I could feel the perspiration running down between my breasts, itching my skin.   I tore the green filter mask from my face so that I could breathe more easily and bent closer, parting Beth's eyelids with my fingers to see her widened pupils. She moved her head away slowly and opened her eyes, still dazed.

There was blood smeared all over Beth's face: it trickled from her nostril because I hadn't had time to lubricate the tubing, and she was still dribbling blood from the cut on her tongue. The bed was a mess. Her arm had bled profusely and she had urinated past her diaper. I knew I should change the sheets, but I didn't want to move her for fear the seizures would begin again.

My palm felt the heat of Beth's soft belly. I wondered if she really did have meningitis, or if it was *just* a seizure disorder. Just a seizure disorder? If she was one of my kids, would I think *just?* Maybe I would. . . after all, epilepsy isn't terminal, and with medication most people can live normal lives. Meningitis can cause permanent damage, and it can be terminal. Another theory of relativity.

"Beth, Beth?" I whispered. She wasn't alert yet. As I stared at her, I could feel my eyes fill. What's happening to me? I wondered. I never used to fall apart like this. And her screaming or crying never would have annoyed me or made me angry before. I would have played with her, petted her, hugged and kissed her. I would have walked with her for hours, no matter how many machines she was attached to. I would have held her and rocked her. Up until now, I would have done anything and everything to help her be less frightened, but all I could do now was sit in a chair watching her. I wouldn't harm her—even now, I was at least competent; but all the special, all the *me*, was gone from my nursing tonight.

The smell of Beth's urine burned my nose, bringing me back, and I knew I had to clean her up. Only then did I notice the blind red eye and hear the constant beeping of the IMED as the liquid from the bottle poured through the torn tubing and made a large sticky puddle on the floor. I pushed the off button, and the bleating stopped. Then I threw a sheet on the floor so I wouldn't slip, and pulled the side rail of the crib up until I heard it click. The noise startled Beth and she opened her eyes. I smiled at her and pushed back her wet curls. I wanted to kiss her, but I felt my eyes fill again. Suddenly I was outside myself again; watching me again as I bent to clean the floor. Teri, I told myself, cut it out! Are you losing your mind tonight? You're supposed to be a professional. I bent down and pulled some sheets, a washcloth and a towel from under the brown Formica cabinet. Then I went to fill a stainless-steel basin with water.

Beth jumped, her eyes widening momentarily, when the side rail clicked as I lowered it. Her forehead felt hot, so I reached into the drawer of the cabinet for the glass thermometer. I turned her over and inserted it, rubbing her back as I waited for it to register. Even before I removed it I could see that her fever was over 103. Working fast, I tore the foil wrapper on a Tylenol suppository with my teeth and inserted that. Then I washed her and changed her bed, gently moving her limp body from side to side. The phenobarb had knocked her for a loop.

I had to call the doctor to restart Beth's IV, and although she was sleeping, breathing regularly, I was still afraid to leave her alone even for a few minutes. I looked into the hallway, but it was deserted, so I stood in the doorway calling out occasionally. Finally, frustrated, I rang the call bell.

After more than an hour, I saw one of the floor nurses at the far end of the hall and motioned to her. She was an older woman, about four foot ten and heavy. One hip was thrown out to the side, making her limp. Her dyed brown mop with bangs looked inappropriate over her coarse and wrinkled face. When she smiled, one gold tooth flashed. Ronnie Berdger, LPN, announced her blue-and-white plastic badge.

"What the hell is happening around here?" I asked her, "I've been ringing for an hour."

"There are only two of us on, and a cystic kid went out," Ronnie said apologetically, breathing hard. "They're still working on him. Though God only knows why,"she added, as she rubbed an alcohol sponge up and down her hands, trying to clean them. She shook her head. "The kid's been breathing like he's got a pillow over his face for years. . ."

"I need the doctor for an IV," I said more civilly, and when she nodded I added, "Do you think you could cover me so I can get something to eat later?" I knew she thought I was a crazy person, moaning about getting away from one patient when she had twenty, but even though I felt guilty I couldn't stay on the floor without a break that night.

"Do what I can," Ronnie said with more grace than I would have. She limped down the hall, peering into the rooms as she passed. She would have scared the hell out of me if I was a sick kid and caught her gazing at me over a flashlight in the middle of the night. Yet I found myself smiling at her good-natured answer.

After she disappeared, I went back into the room to sit. I tried to read but found the silence, broken only by machines, oppressive. The skin on the back of my neck prickled when I felt a shadow over my shoulder, and I jumped. But nothing was there, so I leaned back again and tried to force myself to relax. For the thousandth time I wondered why, in every hospital, there was so little staff on this shift. . . .

Night leaves a hospital a deserted camp, with only a skeleton crew to watch for signs of invasion, as Death sneaks quietly and Disease rummages. Darkness covers an aneurysm, the silent grenade, and a man can blow from sleep to death without a sound . . . one missed buzz, as coma stuns another . . . taunting us with creeping fear and brutal dreams of unseen struggles, unheard screams. There are so few of us on guard at night, and we run one step in front of our own lurking panic.

I shook my head hard and looked at my watch. Two A.M. Only three hours into the shift. Five more to go. I stood up, paced around, and finally walked aimlessly into the small steel-and-porcelain utility room that connected Beth's room with the one next to it. As I stared through the glass panel into the other room, all I could see was a pile of flannel blankets, a monitor and a huge blue-and-gray metal respirator. I couldn't see the child, who I knew lay in the bed, but as I watched the bellows squeeze inexorably up and down my mind went back to Melody.

Melody was the first person I ever gave to Death. I took her off a respirator long before euthanasia was a recognized ethical dilemma. Poor little Melody would have been more than happy to settle for seizures.

My legs were stiff and my unseeing eyes still focused inward when I heard Beth moan and remembered where I was. I walked quickly out of the utility room. Beth seemed restless, but her eyes were still closed. In her sleep she turned over onto her stomach, put her thumb into her mouth and began sucking it greedily.

I walked over to the crib, then walked away again, around the room, pacing, thinking. It must have been horrible for her to have been tied down like that, not to be able to suck her thumb. Stuck in this small room in a strange place without anyone familiar to comfort her, and not understanding any of it. Only knowing that every new person caused her pain.

I was starting to hope that the doctor would not get the message to restart her IV. It would at least give Beth a while longer to suck her thumb, and if I had to call him to remind him it would give us even more time.

As I walked toward the window, I stopped suddenly and thought: give *us* more time? Shit! I was supposed to *fight* to get the damn stuff restarted. I knew that if we were dealing with bacterial meningitis, antibiotics were imperative. The more quickly we stopped the infection, the less damage done. So whose side was I on? Mine, obviously, not hers.

But if, I thought, it's viral meningitis, we might be sticking her for nothing. I looked over at the little girl. I was smart enough to know that sticking her with needles for an IV wasn't going to kill her . . . not sticking her could. I had to get the doctor as quickly as possible.

I walked over to the doorway again and looked down the dim hallway. Still deserted. I could hear the hiss, hiss of a respirator, the soft whimpering of a child crying for his mother, and an occasional loud bang as something fell on the floor. I wanted to leave the room to check on the crying child, but couldn't. Not because of Beth—she was still sleeping—but because she was an isolation case and I had been told firmly that she was the only one I was to touch that night. If it was meningitis, it would be disastrous to spread it on a pediatric ward. Trapped, I walked back into the room and closed the door behind me. If I couldn't help, I didn't want to hear anything.

I squeezed my arm through the bars and touched Beth's stomach lightly. She was cooler. Then I stuck my finger into her diaper: she was wet, so at least her fever hadn't dehydrated her. When she woke up I would change her.

I sat down in the high-back chair again, very quietly. I didn't want to do anything to awaken her. I couldn't listen to her cry again . . . and if I picked her up and held her, if I patted her butt and stroked her back for any length of time, if I let myself smell her hair and kiss her cheek, I would be sucked into loving her. I knew I couldn't afford it. Not tonight.

All at once, Ronnie pushed open the door noisily and enthusiastically announced, "Go to lunch. I'm here to cover." She was dressed in sterile gear, including gloves and paper boots.

My eyes darted to Beth. She had pulled her legs under her stomach and was rocking frantically, butt in the air. I put my finger to my lips, grabbed Ronnie by the hand and dragged her into the small tiled bathroom, closing the door behind us before I spoke.

"Jesus! Am I flaky tonight." She patted my shoulder as I told her about Beth.

"Kid somebody special?" she asked.

"Nope, just another kid. But for some reason my nerves are shot. Maybe I didn't get enough sleep today." The excuse sounded feeble even to me.

Beth was rocking more gently as we walked out. I tore off the paper gown, rolled it up and threw it into the red plastic hamper. Before I left the room, I scrubbed my hands hard.

On my way to the elevators I saw a priest and several people standing outside the room at the end of the hall. The cystic kid that Ronnie had told me about must be in there. In the doorway, a young woman was crying on an older man's shoulder, and the priest was talking in whispers to a distraught-looking father. I dreaded walking past them, dreaded looking more closely at their pain. In my white uniform, I felt partially responsible for the defeat. I walked quickly, staring at the gray polished floor as I tried to quiet the squeaking of my shoes, to make myself invisible. I decided to take the stairs to get off the floor as quickly as possible.

Downstairs, the long corridor was especially dreary in the dim light, and I hesitated before walking through the eerie shadows. No one was in sight. The hall was dotted with the varnished wooden doors of administrative offices, radiation rooms, labs, and medical-records rooms. I looked over my shoulder constantly.

The thick smell of formalin oozed from under the door to the morgue, forcing my thoughts back to Elmwood Hospital, where I had first started working as a nurse. Once, I had accidentally walked in on an autopsy, just as someone was throwing a woman's liver onto a stainless-steel meat scale. I had frozen at the sight. No one noticed me, and the pathologist in his bloody white lab coat laughed as he removed the other organs and threw them on the scale, shouting the weight with the impersonality of a butcher. On the white enamel table lay a young woman, cut open like a chicken, blobs of yellow fat exposed through the long bloodless slice that ran from chest to pubis. The pathologist finally looked up and asked, "What lab are you looking for, honey?" He seemed not at all surprised to see me there and acted as though my uniform was armor.

"Hematology," I stammered, and he continued to cut and weigh as he gave me directions. I nodded, stunned, and left to find the other lab.

Afterward I went to lunch. And as I stood on the long line with giggling, chattering nurses waiting to be served, I kept seeing the young woman on the enamel slab. When my turn came to be served, I looked at the large stainless-steel tray of corned-beef hash complete with potatoes that looked like blobs of yellow fat, and thought of the stainless-steel scale. I walked away from the counter immediately.

Though it had been years since my horror burned that experience into my brain, I still shuddered whenever I walked past a hospital morgue.

Now, the lights shone brightly as I turned the corner onto the green Astroturf carpeting which ran along the hall outside the coffee shop and cafeteria.

I stopped in front of the large glass windows of the closed coffee shop to look over the book titles on the paperback display rack and was shocked for a minute when I saw my reflection. I moved closer as I ran my fingers over my cheeks. They looked almost hollow to me. I knew I had gotten thinner lately, but I hadn't noticed until now that even my new uniform was loose. I reminded myself, as I took one last look, to go easy on the eyeliner. The dark brown of my eyes and the black of my lashes made my eyes look huge. When I reached up to fix my hair, it felt straighter than usual and I could see that it had lost its shine. It looked sort of dusty black. Have to get a perm, I thought as I grabbed a lipstick out of my pocket. I put it on as I walked slowly down the long empty corridor. The silence was deceptive. It seemed so far from the sufferings on the wards above.

I heard the clatter of dishes and smelled the bacon cooking before I opened the heavy wooden door to the cafeteria. As I walked in, I noticed several scattered groups of people sitting around long tables, talking and laughing a little too loudly.

I wasn't hungry, but I had to eat. Reluctantly, I went up to the counter to buy a hamburger and French fries from a grouchy old lady who always looked as though she was doing you a favor when she made it for you. I smiled at her; I tried to break her down with my smile. Then I tried to outrun her grouch with some pleasantries. She didn't buy it.

"One dollar," she rasped as she plunked my order onto the counter.

I lifted my tray and carried it over to the large metal soda machine. Struggling to balance the tray between my hip and the ledge of the machine, I fished through my pocketbook to find a quarter. After I deposited it, I watched as the cup fell crooked and my coke washed foamily over the outside. I got it upright in time to capture half.

When I scanned the room again, with its white stucco walls, shiny high-glossed floor, white Formica table tops and glaring fluorescent lights, it struck me as *too neat*. Neat and clean and sterile-looking. Then, with relief, I noticed the bent, half-full tinfoil ashtrays. Cigarette butts smashed with speed and tension.

Somebody laughed and I focused again on the same motley groups of people. I couldn't figure out why they seemed so motley on this particular night. It should have been my first clue. I decided I didn't want to sit with anyone. Another clue. I liked people; also, I hated to sit alone. But I continued to ignore the flickering warning light going off in my head, and told myself that I was just beat.

Finally, after standing for what seemed like an eternity, I walked over to a long empty table and sat down. But I couldn't get comfortable. So I got up and walked over to a smaller table. Still no good. Restlessly, I searched the room until my eyes fixed on a large red neon exit sign. It seemed to beckon directly below to a tiny table with only two chairs.

Once there, I sat with my back toward the room. I stared into the corner, pulled out a book from my purse, and hid behind it. Slowly, it began to seep into my consciousness that even for me this was strange behavior.

Maybe I'm tired, I thought again, or maybe I just don't want to be *on*. I had been working a lot lately. Loved three patients who had just died on me. Three in a row. Gave it all I had, and still they died. Oh, well, I thought, the hell with it.

I put down my book. Absently I picked up a French fry, dunked it in some ketchup, but on the way to my mouth my hand stopped. . . French fry frozen . . . ketchup dripping . . . and I suddenly knew: I didn't want to be a nurse anymore.

For twelve years I had loved it, and now I thought, *I'll never be able to do it again.*

Puzzled, I looked around me, as though someone else had said it. And silently I asked, "How come?" "What happened?" Automatically I answered, "You don't believe in it anymore." Still confused, I wondered what it was that I didn't believe in. Then slowly I began chewing on my French fry while my whole life was changing.

Within minutes, I started to get really pissed; as though someone had put something over on me. Nursing had been my life for twelve years. And now, without warning, suddenly it was different. The passion I had for medicine, the belief I had in medicine, were gone. I *knew* they were gone. And what had happened to them? I lost them while I was chewing on a French fry?

I felt miserable as I stared into my plate. I wanted fireworks. I wanted music. I wanted big black horses pulling white marble coffins. This was no ordinary passion; this passion had saved my life. When I had nothing left to believe in, when I had outgrown religion, when my husband had walked out on me, when I had two kids to support and didn't know how, when I had nobody to love enough and when nobody loved me enough, there had always been nursing.

And then in a flash, without my even knowing it, it had changed. I miss it already, I thought, as my mind raced on. Sure, I'll probably be able to take care of patients again, might even be able to hug and kiss them, because they'll still be people, but it will never be the same. I thought I'd be able to change something. Save people. But, one after the other, the people I came to love because I was taking care of them, because I took responsibility for them, went and died anyway. I had watched them suffer. Sure, I had helped relieve some of their pain; but still they died . . . *after* I'd given it all I had.

With instant clarity, I knew I'd never be able to repeat, with the same kind of passion, anything else I did. And so I was angry. Outraged because I was almost too grown-up ever to *love* anything that much again . . . ever to *trust* anything that much again . . . ever to let it be everything in the world to me.

I slumped down in my chair. It was so tangible, my loss, that I wanted people to come up to me and tell me how sorry they were.

I turned my head, looked over my shoulder. Only a few people remained. Everyone else had gone back to the floors. I lit a cigarette and smoked it slowly, stalling. When I put it out on the Styrofoam plate, I held it until it burned through.

Blindly, I pulled my makeup mirror out of my pocketbook and as I looked at myself I said, "Jesus, Teri, you were playing Don Quixote all those years. You were fighting windmills. Do you know how *crazy* that makes you?" I shook my head, laughing at my own absurdity, and closed the mirror. I could feel the lump in my throat as I thought, Oh, but do you know how lucky that makes you? You were fighting for something you believed in, and sometimes you did win, then you believed in it more. That was a terrific present. There's so little to believe in anymore and you believed and trusted nursing totally.

Then my mind flew back . . . years. I remembered standing in a hospital corridor looking out the huge plate-glass windows as the red sun came up in the red, red sky, making everything in the hospital lobby pink. The smell from the operating room came sneaking through the doors; came running up my nose screaming *Hope*. We were going to *Save* people! We were going to do *Big* things! At the beginning of that day, my first working day, I stood by the elevators, thinking, I'll never be this happy again. This is where I belong. Somebody should have turned me into salt.

I stood, picked up my tray and walked over to the trashcan. And as I scraped the tray and watched the cup and plate fall into the garbage pail, I thought, goddammit! How come it slipped away so quietly? If it had even spurted a little, like a cut artery, I might have been able to wrap a tourniquet around it or apply some pressure to it and save some of the hope, some of the belief, some of the passion. But instead it sloughed off like dead skin, causing no more pain than a peeling suntan. It didn't even hurt.

I heard nothing and saw nothing as I left the cafeteria, and I walked with my head down, scuffing my shoes against the floor. I felt as though I must look different, the way I did after the first time I had sex; I had expected to have green spots or something. This time, I was sure I looked like a skeleton. Nursing had beat the hell out of me. I kept getting up as it knocked my teeth out, scratched my eyes out and tore holes in my heart, but I had loved it as I never loved anything before and as I'd never love anything again. No man or woman ever meant to me what nursing did, and whenever I heard the word "passion," while everyone else thought it meant sex, I thought it meant nursing.

No one was in sight as I got off the elevator and walked slowly down the hall to Beth's room. The rest of the night seemed endless. I paced, got the doctor to restart the IV and did little else. Beth had no more seizures, and her fever was normal by 6 A.M. I dragged my body around the room tidying up, talking to Beth when she woke, still not able to stay close enough to hug or kiss her. If the phenobarb hadn't snowed her so much that she didn't cry, I probably would have cried with her.

As the end of the shift approached, I motioned to Ronnie, who came over to the door long enough for me to tell her that I wasn't coming back.

When I gave report on Beth to the day nurse, I was aware that I was jumping from one thing to another without my usual precision. I waved and walked out the door, with the nagging feeling that I had forgotten something. Even after I checked for my glasses, my keys, my sweater—they were all there—the feeling that I had left something behind remained.

As I walked down the long white hospital corridor toward the elevators, I stared intently at the shiny polished floors. *Remember this*, I told myself. Then I took a deep breath, filled my head with the smell of alcohol, and thought how strange it was that some people preferred the smell of flowers. Right then, I knew I had to freeze everything and store it in my brain for later. So I was cramming, filling myself with the smell of baby powder, ether, disinfectant, even the smell of sickness, and fixing it in my head. I just knew I was never coming back.

I heard the voices of children crying, "Nurse . . . nurse," as though from some faraway war zone, and walked right through, dazed, to the elevators. There were several other nurses waiting to leave at the same time, and as the doors opened everyone piled in. I waited. Their chatter and laughter, the thought of being crowded into a small space with other people, made me uneasy. I didn't want to have to smile or speak to anyone.

Waiting for the next elevator, I leaned against the wall and watched absently as a nurse down the hall ran from a room in the Coronary Care Unit. She looked frantic. I heard her call to me, but I couldn't hear what she said. Instantly alert, I knew what she wanted. But instinctively my whole body rebelled. I could feel my head shaking a silent no even as I pulled my anchored feet slowly forward. I looked around, not believing what was happening. As I reached the door to the room she had run from, I knew I had been right.

An elderly man lay flat in the bed, his eyes staring upward, his skin stark white with already bluing lips. "I don't want to do this," I heard myself say as I pushed my fingers hard into the side of his neck to check his carotid pulse. I felt none. I leaned down and placed my face next to his nose and mouth to feel his breath, and when I felt nothing I muttered, "Damn!" There wasn't any chest movement. I shoved my fingers into his slackened jaw to see if anything had lodged in his throat. It felt clear. I didn't have time to look for a stethoscope, so I couldn't listen to his heart, but I was willing to bet it had stopped. The few seconds it took to do all this seemed like hours, and I looked again to see if anyone else had arrived. No one.

I had no choice but to start pumping. I wanted to run. No one knew who I was. I wasn't responsible for him; I wasn't even covered if something went wrong. What do I care, goddammit, if one more poor sick human being goes to his grave without heroics . . . mine, anyway. Jesus Christ, somebody else save this poor bastard—I don't want to help anyone anymore.

I pulled the footboard off the bottom of the bed and struggled to shove it under his body for support. I was getting panicky as I knelt on the bed and placed my hands, one over the other, on his lower chest. One, two, three . . . I pumped. No one around yet. It must be at least two minutes, I thought . . . I'll have to do mouth-to-mouth resuscitation, "I'm not going to do it," I said aloud as I heard the loudspeakers calling the code. I had hated breathing for an adult ever since I saw a man vomit into a nurse's mouth on one cardiac arrest; the thought alone gagged me. I jumped off the bed, put one hand behind the old man's head and tried to pull his jaw forward to get his tongue out of the way. I pinched his nose to keep the air I was going to blow into his mouth from escaping from his nostrils instead of going into his lungs. Soon there will be other people here, I assured myself as I bent down and placed my mouth over his. But as soon as I felt the cold and clammy touch of his skin on my lips I knew I couldn't do it. I backed away from the bed just as the Code Team came running into the room.

Within seconds the room was filled with people. The anesthesiologist quickly and deftly pushed the metal airway down the man's throat and hooked an "ambu" bag on. The large black balloon filled and forced air into the man's lungs as I watched his chest rise and fall. Someone asked me to jump on the bed again and start pumping, but I recoiled in horror, mumbling something about being a "private nurse." I was out the door and on my way back to the elevators, all the time hearing the one. . . two. . . three. . . breathe. . . as the ambu bag was squeezed.

As I waited impatiently for the elevator, pushing the red button again and again, afraid that something else would happen that would keep me from escaping, I wondered who the man was on whose chest I had pounded, what his life had been, what his prognosis was and whether he would make it back this time. And if he didn't . . . how much of it was my fault?

The air outside was so cold it stung my cheeks and made my

eyes tear. I walked quickly, almost ran, moving away from the hospital, moving against the wind, looking behind me . . . afraid that at any minute I would be vacuumed back, swallowed alive. When I reached the car the door lock was frozen, and as I held the lighter to try to thaw it my hands shook so badly I almost dropped it. Finally, after several frantic pulls and a few hard kicks, the door opened. I slid in and collapsed on the front seat. My smoky breath fogged the windows as I turned the key in the ignition, but I managed to drive out of the parking lot without once looking back.

CHAPTER 1

When I was seven years old my grandmother died. One rainy day, I was standing, nose pressed against the window-pane in her large bedroom, waiting for her to get out of her white uniform. Gram was a nurse who worked in Harlem, drove around in a blue Packard, and carried a gun in her black doctor's bag. Mom, Dad and I had lived with her ever since she had divorced my grandfather years before.

I was trying hard not to blink at the huge drops crashing on the foggy pane in front of my eyes when Gram broke through my concentration by saying, "Teri, I have to go away." She was sitting on her bed, thick orange cotton stockings half pulled down.

"Why?" I asked. I could see she wasn't angry.

"Because I'm sick," she answered softly.

I walked toward her. "I could get you an aspirin," I offered.

She shook her head. "I have a lump," she explained as she took my hand and ran it across her breast over her pink satin slip. I felt something hard. "I have to be operated on," she added more gently, "and I won't be able to come back."

"Gram, don't go away," I said, crying as I hugged her, "I'll be good. And if you're sick, I'll take care of you."

She kissed me and held me tight, but when I looked at her again I knew that nothing I could say or do would make it different.

"Now," she said firmly, tears glistening in her blue eyes, "remember that I love you and I'll miss you as much as you miss me." I nodded and sniffed until she held a handkerchief to my nose and ordered, "Blow." Then she added, "Don't forget: Never go out of your way to hurt anyone, but trust yourself and try to do what makes *you* happy." After one more tight squeeze, she winked and said, "Go play."

I watched from the doorway as Gram slowly got into bed and lay down, her back toward me. For the first time, I noticed the graying roots through her auburn hair and how bent her back was. When she turned her head to look over her shoulder at me, I saw dark circles under her eyes. She looked pale and tired as she waved me away. Impulsively, I ran to the bed and kissed her cheek. It was very soft.

They didn't tell me right away, and they never let me see her. I never saw them in black; it was all very secret. For days my mother was closed in a room, and as I paced up and down the long hall outside I could hear her crying. When I put my ear to the large oak door, I heard her say, "They let her bleed to death."

A friend of Gram's cried, "No, no, she died in shock."

Then my mother sobbed, "But, my God, she was only fifty-two!"

All that day, as people entered or left the room, I tried to see my mother through the crack in the door, but someone always pushed me away.

Finally I walked outside, opened the front gate and looked down the street toward the bus stop. I could almost see Gram, running as usual, tall with the sun bouncing off her short curly hair, eyes sparkling with laughter, as she raced to me mumbling something about having to go to the bathroom. But when I blinked, she had disappeared.

On one leg, I hopped over the cracks on the cement walk until I reached the front stoop. I sat staring at the large green bush covered with enormous blue and white pompons. Gram loved those flowers. "But," I thought, "she didn't love me enough to stay."

Then I remembered the Easter Sunday, just weeks before, when I was all dressed up waiting outside for my mom and dad to get ready for church. It had rained and the sun had painted a beautiful rainbow over a large puddle. When I tried to sneak up and grab a color, I slipped and landed flat in the mud. "Sloppy! Clumsy!" my mother had shouted as she scooped me out of the water. Then Gram had appeared and I ran to bury my face in her clean flowered skirt. She never flinched as she lifted me and felt my muddy hands around her neck. My eyes were still shut tight, my face hidden in her shoulder, when I heard her say softly to Mother, "Mud washes off much more easily than insults."

Now, suddenly, I *hated* her for dying and leaving *me;* and I hated my mother and father for letting it happen, for not making her stay. She had gone and I didn't know where.

In a fury, I got up, ran over to the pompon bush and started to tear the flowers off, one by one.

My next big separation came fifteen years after Gram died. And it was then that my unconscious, not knowing death from divorce, spun me headlong into nursing.

" . . . and they lived happily ever after," ended all the fairy tales my father had read me as bedtime stories. So for years, each Saturday as I washed the blinds, scrubbed the bathrooms, dusted and vacuumed, I waited impatiently for the time when I would be spirited away by some wonderful prince who would save me from housework, protect me from danger and take care of me forever.

Finally, when I was sixteen, at my first dance, it happened. The casting was perfect. Shawn was tall, with finely chiseled features, blue-black hair and catlike crystal-green eyes which made him look more pretty than handsome. He was wearing a Navy dress uniform, and by the time he asked me to dance it was already too late. I was prepared to be transported to the castle immediately.

I had memorized all of Aesop, all of Grimms . . . and in not one of them did the prince, after he married, have a drinking problem; in not one did he disappear periodically, leaving the frightened princess with two screaming children she couldn't support.

Even after years with Shawn, I had such an elaborate denial system—in other words, I still believed so strongly in the happily-ever-after ending—that I hung on and kept trying to spin straw into gold.

"One last chance?" Shawn asked. And so we gathered up the last five years and packed everything into the back of his white station wagon—away from New York, away from the rat race, away from all the pressures that Shawn hated, to a place he believed was Shangri-la.

Ohio . . . Back to nature, back to grass, back to where Shawn grew up.

Four-year-old Niki crawled all over me for ten hours; we had to stop the car six times so that she could pee and get something to drink. The baby, Spinner, wiggled and cried while my arms ached from holding him. Finally, when my nerves were as tight as guitar strings, Shawn pulled up in front of an old cedar house fixed on the side of a hill, in the center of a patch of barren brown land.

"Home," Shawn said proudly. Stricken, I couldn't believe we were seeing the same thing.

Shawn got out of the car and picked up Niki, throwing her over his shoulder playfully. Then he walked around to open my door. I was so stiff I felt as though my hinges had rusted. I could hardly unbend my legs. Spinner started to whimper, and I shoved his thumb into his mouth, hoping Shawn wouldn't see.

We walked through the dry wilted weeds covering the path. The weatherbeaten front door creaked noisily as soon as Shawn touched the handle. "There are no locks on the door," he told me apologetically, "but I can do that in no time."

Inside, from where I stood, I could see a huge old room with wooden floors and peeling lavender walls. As we walked through, our footsteps echoed. Even Niki was quiet, eyes wide.

"The ceilings are high," I said, groping for something uncritical to say. Shawn just looked at me; then he put Niki down and she began to stomp loudly through the living room into the dingy, barnlike dining room . . . beige walls, also peeling.

"Oh, Shawn," I wailed, "it's scary. It's so big and empty . . . and ugly." There were several holes in the walls with lumps of plaster underneath: dribbled oatmeal on an old man's chin.

I followed Shawn into the grimy kitchen. "I hate it," I said softly, and Shawn turned, dark brows knit disapprovingly over his eyes, and took Spinner out of my arms. He walked away, rocking the baby gently.

All the white enamel counters sloped downward and were badly pitted and chipped. Thick green slime covered the bottom of the sink, except for where the dripping faucet had carved a rusty exclamation mark.

On the verge of tears, I asked, "Do we *have* to live here?"

Shawn just motioned me to follow him up the stairs. On the second floor were three more enormous rooms, all with dusty gashes in the old wooden floors and scaling, flaking paint hanging off the walls.

"I didn't see all this when I looked at the place," Shawn said, shaking his head and running his hand around the inside of one of the larger jagged holes in the wall. "The furniture must have covered most of it." Suddenly he looked so overwhelmed, I knew I'd have to cheer him up or he'd start drinking again.

"It will probably look fine with some new paint or wallpaper," I said, moving closer to him and leaning my head on his shoulder.

"We can pick up some furniture at the Salvation Army," he said, sounding a little more hopeful, "and maybe some curtains, cheap."

Later, when the car had been unloaded, Shawn and I sat together on the bottom step of the stairs.

"It's a few days before I have to start working at the phone company," Shawn said softly. "By then I can do most of the cleaning up."

I nodded. I was exhausted at the thought of setting up another new home. We had done it so many times before.

Shawn unpacked some sandwiches and handed me one. We sat chewing soundlessly.

"Wish I had a beer," he said casually, but I almost choked. He caught my look, and, exasperated, shouted, "Teri, you promised you wouldn't get hysterical about this. I told you I wouldn't drink anymore. I was just wishing out loud."

"I know," I said softly, trying to keep the panic level in my voice down. "It's just that if you leave me and the kids here . . . I don't know anybody or anything."

Shawn jumped up from the step, green eyes glaring, like a cat's, and growled, "You have no faith in me."

For the next three weeks, Shawn and I painted, cleaned and wallpapered. He seemed happy and I was getting used to the place. But the night of his first paycheck was disaster. He was defeated again: though the pressure in Shangri-la was less, so was the pay.

"It'll be okay," I said, leaning over in bed to hug him that night. He hadn't wanted to make love to me since we moved, so when he pulled me close and kissed me hard I tried to remember to do everything he liked in bed so that he would make love to me more often. Later, I lay awake a long time with a lump in my throat, wondering why I still felt so lonely.

The following morning, Shawn left for the Laundromat to wash Spinner's diapers and never came back. That night I jumped out of bed a thousand times. Every time I heard a car door slam, I jumped up. Every time I heard someone talk outside, I jumped up. When the door blew open, I leaped out of bed ready to forgive Shawn anything he had done, as long as he'd not abandon me and the kids again. But it was only the wind. By morning I was exhausted and scared to death.

"Where's Daddy?" Niki asked, rubbing her sleepy eyes. She started to crawl into bed with me, but I bolted up.

"Gone again," I answered with an insensitivity I wouldn't dare use on anybody but my own kids.

"Who's going to feed me breakfast, then?" she asked.

I had to cook Niki's oatmeal with water because I was trying to save the remaining milk for Spinner. "Mommy, this stuff is lumpy and gooey," she complained, stretching the gluey cereal in as long a string as she could before it broke away from the dish. Ugh! I thought, but I was too depressed even to yell at her.

After several minutes, Niki put her spoon down and sat with her head in her hand, imitating my pose. Then she reached over and touched my arm. Frowning, she asked, "What are we going to do, Mommy?"

The next night I sat for hours on the tattered blue velvet couch we had bought from the Salvation Army, trying to decide. How the hell could he do this to me again? I fumed. What am I supposed to do here, with no money, two kids, no car and no food? I didn't even have a phone. I had no profession, no training, and I wasn't emotionally prepared to live alone. I was haunting myself with questions, when my eyes started to burn. Within minutes I started to sneeze madly.

I watched numbly, unbelieving, as the large black iron grate in the middle of the living room spewed forth soot and smoke like a wounded locomotive. In seconds I couldn't see my hand in front of me. That damn coal furnace, I cursed, as pictures flashed through my mind of me running from room to room trying to decide which of my children to save first.

I circled the black grate as though it was a snake pit, listening to the clanking and banging from the cellar below. When the smoke kept coming, I knew I'd have to go down. I was wide awake, my heart beating like a primitive bongo. "Please, Shawn, come back," I pleaded in an angry whisper, and then because I was desperate, willing to try anything, I knelt on the floor and prayed. But right in the middle of my big bargain with God there was a huge thunderclap from the furnace that scared the hell out of me. Jumping up, I remembered one of my father's famous little chestnuts: "Pray to God, but row for shore."

I took a deep breath and started to walk carefully down the narrow wobbly staircase. The smell of cold dank air hit me, and cobwebs crawled over my face as I tried to find the light switch. There was none. The creak of my feet as they hit one step after another was like something out of Alfred Hitchcock.

At the bottom of the stairs a cold wind hit me, and I wrapped my sweater closer around me. The cellar door had blown open. As my eyes adjusted to the dark, I could see that snow covered everything. Niki's stuffed animals, piled in the corner of the basement, had an eerie glow; Shawn's bicycle had been transformed into a crouching Abominable Snowman.

I can only stay scared for so long before I get mad, and now I was furious. I stamped through the water from the melting snow and groped my way along the wet, mold-covered wall until I found the light socket. The string gone, I had to stand on my toes and screw in the bulb. Serves him right if I get electrocuted, I thought as I felt the water up around my ankles. As the light went on, huge red rings clouded my view of the immense black furnace. The Iron Monster. Gingerly I reached down and tugged at his jaw. With a grinding screech, the gargantuan mouth opened wide.

I couldn't figure out what had made all that noise: only a few red embers remained of the fire inside. "Crap!" I said aloud, and started to search the cellar until I found a shovel. I lifted it with both hands and moved toward the darkened coalbin. Snow covered that too. Suddenly, as I watched, several pieces of coal seemed to jump from the top of the pile. I stopped short when I heard what sounded like scratching against a blackboard, more jumping coal, the sound of scurrying. And while I just knew the next thing I would see would be a mummified human hand stretching up from the debris, I wasn't prepared for the squeak that came from the large gray animal that ran over my feet, darting frantically, trying to escape my shovel.

"Shit! Shit! Shit!" I screamed, "I *hate* rats!" That made me feel better. Hollering always made me feel less alone. But I was very shaky after that. The only thing that kept me down in the cellar was knowing that my parents would kill me if my kids froze to death. Because I was more afraid not to do it than to do it, I spent the next six hours fighting that lousy furnace. The shovel was leaden, and with more than three pieces of coal on it I could hardly lift it. Several times when the coal was wet, the fire went out. Several times when the fire went out, I cried. Eventually, I had to burn some of my books and one of the wooden kitchen chairs to restart it.

Finally, back upstairs, exhausted, I checked the kids and found them both sleeping peacefully. So I threw myself down on the couch again and tried to figure out what I was going to do the next day. I was practically out of food, and almost all of Spinner's diapers were in the back of Shawn's car.

My mind started to drift when a sudden movement caught my eye. A lady in an old-fashioned long woolen dress was pacing up and down in front of me. She seemed to be searching for something along the baseboard of the wall opposite me. Bent over, really *looking*. She wore a very dusty rust-colored cape; her hair was piled on top of her head, wisps falling around her smudged, dirt-streaked face.

I sat straight up, thinking that I had fallen asleep and was dreaming, but when I poked myself in the eyes I found they were wide open. I blinked several times to make sure, then pinched myself hard. She was still there. As I stared more closely, I could see that in her hand she carried a lamp—a long-ago lamp. The flickering light cast shadows on my wall, and for a minute the outline of someone's arm reached toward the lady. I shook my head hard to clear it, and then called in a soft voice, "Excuse me, ma'am?" She never looked toward me; she never answered. She just kept pacing, checking out my baseboard.

What puzzled me more than who she was, what she was looking for or how she had gotten into my house was that I wasn't the least bit frightened. *Me*, who was scared to death of everything.

I rubbed my eyes again. I really *was* awake! Fascinated, I watched for a while longer. Finally, when I couldn't keep my eyes open another minute, I pulled the red-and-blue afghan up over my shoulders and lay down again. The furnace was heating the house nicely and there was no more noise from downstairs. I fell asleep instantly, a peaceful, dreamless sleep, and woke in the morning more rested than I had been in ages.

It was a sunny day, so bright as the powdery snow fell that Niki and I had to squint to see. Everything white and clean enough to be a winter postcard. Niki sang "Jingle Bells" and I stopped several times to grab some new snow to sprinkle into Spinner's mouth just to see him make a funny face. I felt almost happy as we walked to the corner phone booth. It was the first time we had been out in days.

While Niki sat in the snow holding the baby, I called home collect and asked my father to come pick us up.

"Are you sure you know what you're doing, baby?" he asked, concerned.

"Yes," I told him firmly. "I'm going to be a nurse."

CHAPTER 2

Poor Mr. Rugby. When I descended on him that first day at Unemployment, he was totally unprepared for me. He probably thought it was going to be just another day.

He was sitting at his large metal desk running his fingers through his graying hair and sifting through this impressive pile of papers when I walked over and plunked myself down on a chair directly opposite him. He was a skinny little man who looked as though his dark-brown wool suit was wearing him. His knuckles were newspaper-print dirty, and the end of his ballpoint pen was chewed to shreds.

"Yes, dear?" he said absently as he looked up over his bifocals.

I flashed what I thought was a dazzling smile and told him, "I want to be a nurse."

He looked at me as though I hadn't finished, put the end of the pen in his mouth and nodded his head up and down without saying a word.

"I was told that Unemployment ran a program to train practical nurses," I continued as I dropped my dazzling smile, "and I want to get in as soon as possible."

He stopped nodding, removed his pen from his mouth deliberately, squinted his dark small eyes and said dryly, "So does everyone, my dear. You missed the deadline." He began to shuffle through his papers as he mumbled past his pen, "This is April and the course starts in July." It had sounded like a dismissal, but I didn't move, so he said more emphatically, "We are already filled."

Fini. Ended. My whole life, my big dream shot to hell. I couldn't let him do it to me, so I said more forcefully, "Look, you don't understand. I have to be a nurse. I have two little kids I have to feed or they'll starve. And nursing is the only thing I want to do."

Sensing my panic, he stopped chewing on his pen long enough to say, "I'm not trying to be unkind, my dear, but there are others in the same situation."

I understood his point, but all those other people weren't me and all those other children weren't mine.

I sat there desperately groping for something else to convince him with, pictures of two children with bloated, malnutritioned bellies flashing through my mind. Then skeletons of the same two children at a later stage of starvation. My children. Relax, I told myself. My little Italian mother would no sooner let my children starve than she would stop making novenas for my salvation.

Motivated by my fear, I insisted, "Mr. Rugby, you've got to listen to me. I get along really well with people. I've always gotten fantastic marks in school. And in these programs you run, you have to have people who succeed, don't you? Isn't that how you get funded?"

At this point he must have realized I wasn't going to let up, because he removed his glasses to look at me more closely. This response was all I needed.

"Really, Mr. Rugby," I persisted, "you can give me a test and if I get over a ninety-five, then you can let me in. Okay?"

He leaned back in his chair and took a deep breath. "You're setting pretty high standards for yourself, young lady, but that still doesn't tell me if you can function within a hospital. Have you ever *worked* in a hospital?"

"No," I said, "but I used to help my father clean pheasant and deer after we went hunting when I was a little kid." Evidently that didn't reassure him.

"You've never even been an aide?" I shook my head. "Then how do you *know* that you want to be a nurse?"

"I just know," I said firmly.

"Marks aren't enough," he said decisively.

"So," I bargained, "if I can get a job as an aide and a ninety-five, *then* can I be in your program?"

Mr. Rugby closed his eyes, rested his head in his hand and let out a long hard sigh. When he lifted his head again, he looked at me as though straining to see something.

"Have you ever considered getting a job as a saleswoman?" he asked seriously, but the corners of his mouth turned up just a little.

"Does that mean yes?" I asked, trying to keep my voice from jumping happily.

"That means yes."

"Yippee!" I hollered. "What's the toughest hospital to get a job in around here?"

"New Hope," he answered, almost excited in spite of himself. "It's a little community hospital, run by the good sisters. If you're hired, you'll be trained properly."

I knocked my chair over as I vaulted up and planted a kiss on poor Mr. Rugby's forehead. He looked stricken and confused as he buried himself in his papers again.

I walked regally down the hall of 2 North at New Hope that first day, my green nylon uniform a coronation gown, my white nylon cap a crown. More aware of the way I stood than I had been since my Communion, I presented myself to Miss Cann, the head nurse on Surgery.

"Hi," I said, trying to smile, "my name is Teri Daley. I'm your new aide."

Miss Cann was a tall husky young woman with craggy, heavy features and a very large jaw. Her narrow brown eyes and untweezed dark eyebrows contrasted sharply with her pasty acned skin. When she stood straight, a foot taller than I, and spoke, all my enthusiasm withered. She had a voice so deep it sounded like a man's.

"Yes, my pretty," she said as she winked at a tall light-haired woman in a green aid's uniform who was sitting alongside the desk, "we've been expecting you. Haven't we, Alexis?"

Alexis nodded, and Miss Cann reached over and pulled lightly at my hair, which hung down onto my collar.

"First, *we* must wear a net, to keep *our* curls off *our* collar. "Then," she continued as she picked up one of my hands and stared at my fingernails, "*we* must wear only clear nail polish. And," as she looked with raised eyebrows at my blue eye shadow and pulled at

one of my earrings, "*we* mustn't wear dramatic makeup or jewelry."
Then she rummaged through one of the desk drawers and pulled
out a blond hairnet. When she handed it to me she said, "By
tomorrow I will expect you to have a black one to match your hair."
She grabbed me by the shoulders, turned me toward the bathroom
and ordered, "Go wash your face and then Alexis will show you
around."

I was totally deflated by the time Alexis reached for my hand
and pulled me away from the nursing station, where Miss Cann was
now getting report. "Not to mind," Alexis said in a gentle voice with
a trace of an English accent, "Cann's crackers." She put her arm
around my shoulders. She was as tall as Cann but not as heavy, with
the sturdy body of women in Flemish paintings. The kind of body
that a little kid can hide in. Her face was clear, with pink
windburned cheeks, a small upturned nose, blue-gray eyes
surrounded by thick light lashes, and a sunburst of yellow hair only
partially restrained by her large-holed hairnet. She was about my
age, yet her whole presence soothed, unruffled, protected. Whew! I
thought, saved again.

"You're rather a compact little waif," Alexis said with
amusement, then added more seriously, "better lift slowly to start."

In the clean-utility room, between the metal shelves stacked
with gleaming stainless-steel enema cans, water pitchers and
washbasins, surrounded by brown rubber tubings, stacks of gauze
bandages and piles of disposable razors and scissors, Alexis taught
me how to take vital signs—temperature, blood pressure and pulse.
I was fascinated that all this seemed so easy for Alexis. After she let
me practice, using her as my patient, she said, smiling, "Okay. On
to real people."

Two North was large and new. Immaculate in a freshly painted,
recently decorated way. Beige and airy, light with big windows and
green potted plants lining the halls. I felt a mounting excitement as
Alexis showed me around the unit and men waved and called to us
from their rooms.

We pushed the utility stand, with its stainless-steel trays,
thermometers soaking in alcohol, blood-pressure cuff, stethoscope
and recording charts, down the hall.

As Alexis and I walked into the first semiprivate room, she

motioned me toward the patient in the bed by the window. He was a young man with an ulcer. I watched everything Alexis did and tried to copy it exactly.

"I did it!" I said with great satisfaction, and she laughed as we moved on to the next room.

There my patient, a man of about sixty with wavy gray hair, was sleeping. I stood by the bed and cleared my throat several times to try to awaken him, but he never moved. Helplessly I motioned to Alexis, who smiled and gently called, "Mr. Marcus?"

He opened his mouth without opening his eyes, and I was immensely relieved. At the time, it seemed like such an intimate gesture, waking him, that I was glad he couldn't see my face or he'd know how embarrassed I was. I put the thermometer under his tongue so gently that it almost dropped out, and as he tried to push it back I reached out to take his pulse. When his hand hit mine, his eyes shot open.

I was really flustered, but I tried to be charming. "Hi, Mr. Marcus. My name is Teri Daley. How are you today?" I asked all in one breath. His answer was muffled as he tried to talk past the thermometer.

I was getting frantic as I tried to feel his pulse and count his respirations, because each time he moved or coughed I got all mixed up. I could hear Alexis pushing the cart down the hall.

I started to leave the room several minutes later, repeating the numbers over and over in my head to keep from forgetting them, when Mr. Marcus asked softly, "Could I please have the urinal, dear?" The numbers I had just captured flew from my mind like freed birds.

I found the urinal under Mr. Marcus' bedside stand and handed it to him, but before I could turn to go he had thrown off the sheet and whipped out an amazing penis that looked like a thick tan slug. I didn't know whether to stand fast or disappear. I had never seen a stranger's penis before, and I was fascinated as well as horrified. Mr. Marcus chattered as though everything was normal while I tried to ignore the sound of his urine, like machine gun bullets, hitting the side of the metal urinal. I tried to be cool and not giggle nervously, so I focused on his belly button.

"Thank you so much, Teri," Mr. Marcus said kindly, and I

marveled at the dignity with which he handed me the urinal. I took it with both hands, smile frozen on my lips as I felt the warmth penetrate the container. I was embarrassed again.

Once inside the bathroom, I took a deep breath and rested against the door before I tried to pour the urine gently down the inside of the toilet so it wouldn't make any noise. Then I almost fainted. The water in the bowl turned a bright orange, and I was certain that Mr. Marcus was dying of some dreadful disease. I didn't smile as I returned his urinal.

It took immense effort not to tear down the hall after Alexis. But when, through stammers and stutters, I explained what I has seen, she just smiled reassuringly and told me, "He's on a pill called Pyridium. It's a bladder analgesic and it colors urine."

God! Did I feel dumb—and slow. Alexis had finished all the other vital signs while I was doing Mr. Marcus.

"Ease along," was Alexis' response to my apologies. We sat in the nursing lounge and had a cup of tea before we gave out water and straightened all the beds. Alexis kept teaching and leading me around, helping me and reassuring me throughout the shift. By the end of the night, I knew we would be friends.

During the next few weeks, things did get a lot easier for me, barring some snags. One day when Alexis was off and I was the only aide on, the hospital instituted a change of equipment from reusable to disposable. No one remembered to mention it, and when I passed out the water that day I put ice in all the urinals, mistaking them for water pitchers. I discovered my error when my first patient poured ice water all over his testicles. I was humiliated and he was enraged because he thought it was a practical joke.

"It wasn't a joke, honest," I protested with a lump in my throat, then blurted, "It was just . . . dumbness." Minutes later, I ran through the ward like a maniac, emptying the urinals that I had just filled.

Still, after just a few days I loved coming to work, hearing the sound of forty men calling, "Nurse, nurse," and meaning me. It almost made me forget how many times Shawn had turned his back on me in bed, how many times he had run away. I practiced being absolutely charming, and both Mr. Marcus and his roommate, Mr. Rizzo, told me that nobody smiled as much as I did emptying bedpans.

The first time Miss Cann told me to take a rectal temperature I was too afraid to tell her I had never done it before. Alexis was off, so there was nothing for me to do but forge ahead.

Mr. Rizzo had fractured his spine and was in a full body cast—plaster from nipples to knees, except for his crotch. He had to lie on his back, and when I pulled down the sheet I realized that I would have to lift his penis and testicles to reach his rectum. That means I have to touch him, I thought, horrified. Stop acting like a girl, I scolded myself, and act like a *nurse!* With that, I lifted more enthusiastically than I would have if I had known what I was doing. Mr. Rizzo was too embarrassed to cry out, but I caught a fleeting wince crossing his face. After I had kept my head under the sheet for several minutes to watch the thermometer register, he said, "You searching for gold, honey?" I smiled and shrugged, still hanging on to the thermometer, as he ran his fingers through his hair, patiently waiting for me to finish in ten minutes what everyone else could do in three, blindfolded. When I was finished I made a big production of washing him. We both survived, but I was too embarrassed to speak to him for the next couple of days.

My second temp was Mr. Marcus, who had become one of my favorite patients. I stood next to him hesitantly because I didn't want to hurt him. He had been bleeding rectally the last few days, and as yet no one knew why.

He smiled gently and held out his hand. "I can do that, dear," he said, as he inserted the thermometer himself and then chatted to me so that I could keep my head above the covers.

"Hey, Teri," he said apologetically as he pulled the sheet up, "I didn't know you were Italian, or I never would have told you all those dumb Italian jokes. . . ."

"No problem, Mr. Marcus," I told him, staring at my watch, checking the second hand, and worrying about the thermometer sliding up and getting lost because I wasn't hanging on to it. "I never minded them." Then, surprised, I asked, "Who told you I was Italian, anyway?"

Mr. Marcus' pale skin flushed as he smiled. "Nobody. I just *saw* you talking in the hall today."

I laughed. "My husband, Shawn, used to say that if they tied my hands I wouldn't be able to say a word."

"You're married?" he asked as, to my relief, he handed me the thermometer. "You look like a kid."

"No," I said, suddenly afraid I had told him too much, afraid I hadn't been professional, but he was waiting expectantly, so I knew I had to answer him. "Not anymore. I'm separated." When he raised his eyebrows I added, to legitimize myself, "I have children, too, so I'm not as young as I look."

I began to leave and Mr. Marcus stopped me. "Wait a minute," he said as he reached over into his bedside stand. "I have something I'd like to give you."

He handed me a small black obsidian elephant with twinkling green jade eyes. "Why?" I asked him.

He motioned for me to sit on the bed. I knew that wasn't allowed, but he looked so eager to talk that I couldn't say no to him. Leaning back against his pillow, he got a faraway look in his eyes as he spoke.

"That little elephant, Teri," he said softly, "belonged to my wife, Katie. She died over a year ago."

I was touched but still puzzled. "Why me, Mr. Marcus?" I asked again. "Maybe you should keep it for good luck."

He dismissed what I said with a nod. "You would have had to know her to appreciate this, but Katie wanted life on her terms, too." He brightened as he added, "When she was young, she smiled just like you."

"Thanks, Mr. Marcus," was all I could say as I flew out of the room to show Alexis.

She smiled and looked happy for me, but warned, "Don't show the Drone. No gifts allowed."

I slipped my little elephant quickly into my pocket and promised myself that for as long as I worked as a nurse I would carry it.

New Hope Hospital allowed its aides to do more in the way of treatments and procedures than the other Long Island hospitals, which would work to my advantage later when I went to nursing school.

One night Miss Cann floated me to a female unit where one of my patients was going down for a D and C in the morning. The head nurse explained what to do, then introduced me to Mrs. Reeves, my pre-op patient. She was a heavy dark-haired woman, cheerful but nervous.

After supper I gathered my equipment to take into the treatment room. In the middle of this room, which was tiled in white with corkboard ceilings, was a long enamel table, complete with iron stirrups. I dropped my eight disposable razors and a package of two hundred and fifty gauze pads on the counter and walked down the hall to get Mrs. Reeves. Her smile was gone. She looked as though she was about to be executed, which immediately made me feel guilty. I couldn't begin to reassure her, because I was afraid I was going to kill her.

In the room, I smiled weakly and patted the table. She struggled onto it with difficulty and finally was able to lie down. Even with the overhead fluorescents, I needed more light, so I pulled the treatment lamp to the foot of the table and turned it on. Her knees were clamped together and she still wore her underpants.

"Mrs. Reeves," I said, trying to sound matter-of-fact, "while I go and fill this pan with warm water, why don't you remove your panties, okay?"

She gave me a half smile and as I turned toward the sink, I could hear her struggling—huffing and puffing. I put my basin on the stand next to the table and tried to act blasé as I asked her to separate her legs. When she did, I didn't handle it well. I had never looked straight into another woman's vagina before, and I found it frightening. She looked different from me. I was sure I didn't have all that extra skin. At the time I was under the impression that all women were built the same. But as soon as I got over my initial horror, all I worried about was how I was going to get around all those corners and under and over all those crevices without chopping off pieces of her.

I put on gloves and soaped her bottom with about a pint of greensoap, holding my breath in case she smelled. Then I started doing a quarter of an inch at a time; soap, shave, rinse.

"Don't cut me," Mrs. Reeves kept repeating nervously.

"I have never *cut* anyone in my life," I answered, in my best professional tone. Not adding that I had never before shaved anyone, either.

The head nurse had said, "Shave it close," and I took her at her word. That woman's hair probably didn't grow back for years; there wasn't even peach fuzz left when I got finished. And when I wiped Mrs. Reeves with the iodine solution that was used as an antiseptic, her vagina looked like a "Paint the Dots" picture. It had taken me three and a half hours; I had used all eight razors and had barely ten gauze pads left. But I never cut her.

The first enema I gave was one of the biggest disasters of my career. It was Mr. Marcus again—diagnostic tests showed he had an abdominal tumor, and the doctors were taking him down to operate on him the following morning. Miss Cann had ordered me to give the pre-op enema, and I ran frantically to Alexis for instruction. She told me exactly what to do and then warned, "You'd better use gobs of lubricant; the man also has huge hemorrhoids."

Alone in the white-tiled utility room, my hands shaking, I slowly unwrapped the large shiny stainless-steel enema can. I was in a frenzy before I even began. Even half full, that can seemed to hold more water than any human being could in an entire lifetime. I checked the temperature on the inside of my wrist, as I had my kids' bottles, scared to death that by some fluke I would burn away Mr. Marcus' intestines. Then, remembering what Alexis had said, I pushed the long orange tubing, which looked to me like a garden hose, halfway into the jar of Vaseline.

When I reached his room, Mr. Marcus was sitting up in a chair waiting for me. I puttered around for a long time, stalling, not knowing what to say, then finally padded the bed with Chux (large green plastic-lined blotters) and asked him to lie down.

"Don't worry about it, Teri," Mr. Marcus said gently. "We'll get through this."

I nodded and pulled the curtains around us, but as I stepped behind him my hands began to tremble violently again. When I looked, Mr. Marcus had pulled his pajama bottoms down. Sprouting from his rectum, a clump of purple grapes grew. Hemorrhoids? I had never seen anything like it before. I took a few gentle blind stabs, and Mr. Marcus moaned involuntarily. Without saying a word, he covered my hand with his and guided the tubing in.

"I hope it's not cancer," he said, in a voice that trembled.

"Me too," I answered, concentrating as I raised the enema can above my head. Alexis had told me to hold it shoulder high but because her shoulders were so much higher than mine, I made the adjustment.

As soon as I unclamped it, the force of the water propelled the Vaseline plug out and ejected the tubing from Mr. Marcus' rectum. And before I could stop it, the rubber hose popped, jumped and leaped like a crazy writhing snake, shooting water all over the bed, Mr. Marcus and me.

I mopped him up, afraid that I was going to cry, and ran out to get Alexis. But Miss Cann intercepted me. And she, like my father when he made me get back on the horse I had fallen off, made me go back in to Mr. Marcus.

"One more time," he said, smiling good-naturedly. I thanked him and apologized a thousand times. But we finished that enema, and I think of it as one of the monumental victories of my early career.

The weeks flew past, and the best part of my day was always work. I dreaded my days off, because then I was overwhelmed with the responsibility for my children and my guilt over them. I was living with my parents, and my mother and I hassled constantly over how to bring them up. Often, I acted much more like her daughter than their mother, and didn't like myself for it. I was living in her house, which meant living by her rules. I hated *it* after all the years I had been on my own, but I needed the help and the safety or I never could have gone to work or applied for school. So I was obligated to be more civilized than I really felt. Besides, to be even a little fair, my mother *was* knocking herself out taking care of *my* kids.

Alexis and I spent all our time during work together, and yet she made no move toward seeing me outside. When I asked her about it, she took a deep breath, lit a cigarette, nodded and said, "I don't socialize, I'm a hermit." When I looked hurt, she added, "I must spend time by myself in order to do a proper job here. At home, I surround myself with beautiful things. I paint, write poetry and read. I can't allow anything in this world to invade that and still maintain my own peace of mind."

I figured she wasn't married because she didn't wear a ring and never mentioned anyone special. When I asked where her family was, she said only, "Europe." So after that I chattered to her about my life and she seemed to enjoy listening, but I accepted the fact that she never volunteered anything about her own.

Toward the end of that week, one day after we had fixed Mr. Marcus' bed and straightened his room, I took his temperature. As I held the thermometer up to the light, the red line of mercury pushed past 102 degrees, and, startled, I looked at Alexis. She put her finger to her lips and wet a washcloth to place over Mr. Marcus' closed eyes. When I picked up the dirty sheets to throw them into the hamper, I noticed for the first time the strong odor of infection.

Once outside the room, Alexis immediately reported his condition to Miss Cann, then we went into the lounge for our break. Alexis poured us each a cup of coffee from the large yellow enamel percolator and sat next to me on the couch. I was upset about Mr. Marcus. He had looked terrible to me in the last few days; he hadn't teased or spoken much.

"Hey, Alex, what's happening with Marcus?" I asked.

She put her head back against the sofa and she said, "Possibly the cancer. Possibly a rotten infection. Or possibly, the man is just weary. . . ."

"Well, the doctors will probably fix him up," I said. I finished my coffee, crushed the cup and threw it into the garbage. Alexis sat up, raised her eyebrows and said nothing.

At that time, I believed a doctor could just lay his hand on the head of a sick man and heal him . . . touch a dead man and have him walking.

"Will you be home more, Mommy?" Niki asked excitedly when I told her I was starting school the following week. She was splashing around the bathtub, my mother washing her back, when I ran in waving my acceptance letter. It had been three months since I began working at New Hope and lately I had been holding my breath, waiting to hear from Mr. Rugby.

Mother looked up and smiled as she scooped Niki out of the tub and began to dry her so vigorously that her whole body shook. Niki asked again, "Will you be home for supper now, Mom?" "No kiddo," I said unhappily. "School is from three in the afternoon until eleven at night, the same as work."

I tried to ignore her look of disappointment, but when she threw her arms around my mother's neck and said, "Well, Gram will be here, anyway," I felt rotten.

I walked into the kitchen, where Spinner was smashing slobbered cookie all over his high chair, and tried to find a clean spot on his face to kiss. He babbled at me happily, and as I aimed for his forehead he smeared wet lumps of cookie through my hair. "I don't care what anybody says," I told him, making a face. "Motherhood is just not what it's cracked up to be." He frowned as though he understood, then with renewed intensity destroyed another cookie.

After supper, I put Spinner to bed and watched TV with Niki. Then I went downstairs into the paneled basement to try to read, but I was too wound up. I was really excited about learning nursing but still more than a little afraid. There seemed to be so much I'd have to know. Miss Cann, after my initial impression of her as an ogre, had surprised me by letting me help with Mr. Marcus' dressings, even showing me how to apply his colostomy appliance. Since the operation he had gotten much weaker, and I found myself wishing I knew enough to really help him. The doctors had put him on antibiotics for a suspected infection, but they hadn't helped and he had developed pneumonia. He was put into a private room and I saw him only if Miss Cann asked for my help.

That night when I went to bed, I kept thinking about school. And Mr. Marcus. Tomorrow I'd take him some flowers.

"Too bad," Alexis said as we stood in Mr. Marcus' room and she arranged my flowers in a water pitcher. "The day nurse said he dehisced and the doctors had to rush him to emergency surgery."

"Dehisced?" I asked, puzzled, as I stared at his empty bed.

"Sutures came apart; incision opened. They had to take him

down and resuture—stitch him back together."

For the rest of the week, Mr. Marcus was in Intensive Care.

As I rode to work the day he was scheduled to come back to the floor, the air was so crystal clear it made waves in front of my eyes. The trees were a brighter green than usual, and only a few fluffy white clouds, like gliding doves, crossed the clear blue sky. I was truly happy to be going to work doing something I loved, something essential. It filled me up, used me up, took advantage of all I felt I had to give . . . and gave me back more. I smiled, knowing that now I had a reason to smile. I was supporting my kids, paying off old bills, helping sick people and being grown-up. It was a terrific feeling. Nothing could ever make me feel worthless again. Nothing could ever make me feel a failure, as my marriage had, again.

I practically skipped into Two North, gave out water, took vital signs and answered call lights. It was suppertime when Miss Cann approached me to ask, "Teri, before you go to supper, would you help me with Mr. Marcus?"

Miss Cann and I went into Mr. Marcus' room. His face was so much thinner since I had last seen him that his skin was transparent. Tiny red veins ran like long-legged spiders over his eyelids, and his lips were blue. He was having a hard time breathing.

Miss Cann motioned me to stand across the bed from her. I held Mr. Marcus' head up, because he was so weak, while Miss Cann untied the strings on the back of his gown. He tried to smile but kept coughing and clearing his throat. His eyes stayed closed.

When Miss Cann pulled down the top sheet, I could see that Mr. Marcus' gown was dirtied with greenish pus and old blood straight across the front. As we tried to remove it, the gown stuck to him in places. And as Miss Cann washed him I stared at his enormous swollen belly.

It was the first time I had seen retention sutures, like double-headed white plastic spoons, which held together the ragged edges of his too taut stomach. His incision, an angry red zipper, swelled dangerously with his slightest cough, and between the spoons there ran a constant dribble of light-brown fluid. Miss Cann placed some fresh white gauze over his wound before we put him into a new gown.

"First," Miss Cann said when it was time to change the sheets, "we will turn him toward you, Teri."

I used the draw sheet as a hammock to pull him over on his side. He grunted every time he breathed. I reached over with my free hand to push the hair off his forehead, but his face was so pained that I quickly looked away, out the window. Miss Cann began to strip the old sheets from her side of the bed.

Outside, twilight dusted over the watercolor pink-and-blue sunset as a winged squadron of blackbirds zoomed back and forth across the purple horizon. Chasing each other, teasing each other . . . flying in line . . . down . . . under . . . above . . . apart. The window framed the picture and I watched as though they were playing just for me.

Miss Cann lowered the bed a little more in order to smooth the sheets; she wanted no wrinkles to cause him bedsores. Mr. Marcus moaned again; any movement caused him pain. With the top of the bed almost flat, I placed my arms around him and held him closer. Affectionately, I stroked his cheek and pushed back the wet gray hair. I could feel Mr. Marcus' body against mine, closer to me than anyone but Shawn had been, his belly separated from mine by only a sheet and my thin nylon uniform. I could feel his warmth against me. I concentrated on watching Miss Cann pull the sheet—hospital corners, army bed, bounce-a-coin tight—when I felt the warm turn wet.

I was certain Mr. Marcus had lost control and urinated. I knew he would be embarrassed if I indicated in any way what had happened, so I didn't say a word as the wet penetrated my uniform, seeped through my underwear and ran down my legs. "Poor man," I thought, the effort of his breathing must have been too much. The room was getting darker, but neither Cann nor I could reach the overbed light. I found myself wishing she would forget all the crazy bed fixing and let Mr. Marcus sleep.

By the time she said, "Okay, Teri, turn him on his back and help lift him over the lump made by the sheets," the liquid was running into my shoes.

A sudden silence forced me to stare at his face. Mr. Marcus wasn't having any more trouble breathing. I strained to see some movement of his chest, but couldn't. As I looked up, I could see his open eyes, fixed, unseeing. A dark stain oozed through his gown. I let go and reached up to turn on the light.

His skin was gray, his cheeks were sunken, and the stain on his gown was mahogany. When Miss Cann ran to get the blood-pressure cuff, I was left alone with Mr. Marcus.

Gently, I reached over and touched his cheek. Then I pulled up the sheet to cover him. In my head, I could still see how he smiled and hear him laugh. I moved closer and held his hand.

It wasn't until Miss Cann got back that I remembered to look down at my uniform. It was dark red.

After she tried to get vital signs and couldn't, she closed Mr. Marcus' eyes. I stood, still glued to the floor, until she said, "get out of your uniform and into an OR suit. Ask Alexis."

I walked out to the desk, where Alexis was charting tempera-tures, and just stood. She took one look at me and asked, "Mr. Marcus?"

When I nodded she pushed her way past me into the linen closet. She handed me a set of cotton clothes, gray-blue, and asked, "Want help?"

I shook my head and walked into the bathroom.

I stood for a while staring down at my uniform, then slowly unzipped it and let it drop to the floor. I looked at my white cotton slip. It was a mess: a bright-red circle of blood crossed the front where Mr. Marcus' belly had touched mine. I pulled my slip carefully over my head, trying to keep the blood from smearing across my face. Then I sat on the toilet and slid my shoes off; my pantyhose stuck in spots to my legs. By the time I removed my underpants, the blood was sticky on my stomach and my fingers too. I started to wash.

"It got into all the cracks," I whispered as I scrubbed, first with soap, slowly, then with Betadine, harder and faster.

Finally, after scrubbing until my skin was red and sore, I balanced with one foot on the toilet bowl, the other knee on the edge of the sink, and looked into the mirror. It was gone. All the blood was gone. I couldn't see it anymore. No one else would know. But I knew I could never forget it. Because in some strange way, as in all the stories my father told me about Indian manhood rights, I was changed now. I knew I wouldn't get Mr. Marcus' infection . . . that wasn't the problem. It was Death . . . *it* had touched me . . . *it* had gotten into all the cracks.

I bent down, reached into the pocket of my uniform and lifted out my good-luck elephant. I stared at it a long time. Then I put my soiled clothes into the plastic bag Alexis had given me and walked out of the bathroom.

The rest of the night dragged, and as I left to cross the parking lot a pouring rain fell. I walked slowly to my car, letting the storm drench me. It was then, between the lightning and the thunder, that I cried.

CHAPTER 3

Lilith, when I first saw her, was slumped in a small student desk in the corner of the large white room that was going to be our classroom for the next eleven months. The room was filled with women, all "heads of household" in nursing school on a federal grant for a second chance. The instructor was a black woman from Equal Opportunity, and the name of this moon shot was "Manpower." Through Unemployment, we were being trained to join the work force of the nation as licensed practical nurses. A few of us were inspired; all of us were desperate.

Nervous and excited, I moved through the blur of faces, toward an empty chair next to the woman in the corner, who looked shy and nonthreatening. "Hi," I whispered as I squeezed myself into the small wooden seat. I crammed my sweater behind me and jammed my pocketbook in front of me.

"Hi," she whispered back. She looked young, and blinked these perfectly round eyes, the kind that porcelain dolls had years ago. Exquisitely clear; bluejay blue. She had smooth scrubbed skin without wrinkles, full lips and short hair, both bright orange. And a smile that looked like a toothpaste commercial.

"My name's Teri Daley," I said as I moved my desk closer. She looked up, surprised, then murmured, "Lilith Hayes," flashed me an Ultrabrite, and glanced quickly down again.

Never one to be put off by lack of encouragement, I said, "Good. Let's be friends."

"Okay," she said slowly, as though deliberating, and nodded her head up and down.

That settled, I glanced around the room: mostly middle-aged women, dowdily dressed. I searched their faces for sparks of intelligence and found what I recognize now as exhaustion. At the time I just figured they weren't a very sharp group.

Mrs. Smith, the instructor, was a tall, very attractive woman who looked like a mechanized mannequin in her uniform. There was not one wrinkle, not even over her full, pointed bust. All her movements were so choppy and erratic that I could almost hear the knock in her motor. When she spoke, it was with an affected Southern drawl, as though someone had inserted a tape and played it at the wrong speed.

As she stood at attention in front of the large portable blackboard, I fought a mad urge to salute. She began by telling us what we could expect before we would be allowed entry into the sanctity of a hospital.

Our initial instruction, for three months, would take place in the classroom. For the remainder of the eleven-month course, theory would alternate with clinical practice for two-week periods. That meant we would have classroom instruction in "Surgical Procedure for Nursing Care of the Patient with Gallbladder Surgery," for instance, and then be rotated onto a surgical floor to practice what we had learned on a real patient. This part of the course was divided, like medicine itself, into several areas: medicine, surgery, obstetrics, geriatrics, pediatrics. There would also be classes in "Anatomy and Physiology," "Nutrition," "Disease Process and Treatment," "Practical Nursing Skills," and "Nursing History."

"God knows why, in an accelerated course to get women off the street, they'll waste time on history," Lil whispered, and I just shrugged.

We would take a lot of tests. We would fix a lot of beds. And we would have to do a lot of role playing so that we could develop empathy, the ability to put ourselves in a patient's position. We would do dressings and resuscitations on a big rubber doll called Mrs. Chaste. And Mrs. Smith smiled when she told us we would have to practice giving injections by sticking oranges.

There was a long list of clinical procedures that we were expected to have mastered by the time we were to take our licensing exams. During the eleven months, on the floors of the hospital, it was our job to find the patients who would afford us the practice we needed. A clinical instructor would supervise us the first time in each area. After that we were on our own.

Immediately after Mrs. Smith gave us the itinerary, before I could lean back and relax, we were into anatomy, and she was talking about "sails" of the lung.

Puzzled, I asked, "What *are* sails of the lung?" I thought maybe they were a new anatomical part. Mrs. Smith looked daggers at me.

Lilith blinked sympathetically and then poked me. "Ma'am," she said to Mrs. Smith, "she just misunderstood you." Then she turned to me and giggled, "*Cells*, dopey. *Cells* of the lung."

After that, all through school, Lil was considered a Goody Two Shoes and I was considered a smart-ass.

At dinnertime Lil offered to take me out to check the area for places to eat. She drove an old yellow taxi that she had picked up for a hundred dollars. The back seat was a library, unindexed—hardcover books from floor to roof. The back doors were held shut with fishing tackle tied from handle to handle.

A few blocks from school we jumped out at a deli and I bought us dinner. We sat in the car and told each other a little about our whole lives while we chomped on corned-beef sandwiches and drank Coke out of a quart bottle. Lil told me that she was divorced and that she and her three kids lived with her father. She was thirty-six years old, twelve years older then me. I couldn't believe it. She looked incredibly young.

After we ate, we sat leafing through our new textbooks. Lil was carefully paging through a nutrition book as I skimmed my book on nursing history. Suddenly, I froze; I couldn't believe my eyes. There *she* was again: the Lady with the Lamp. Only next to her, instead of my baseboard, there lay a group of bandaged, bleeding wounded soldiers. She wore the same grimy rust-colored outfit, and her hair was still loosely pinned on top of her head. The lamp she held illuminated the deep lines of pain carved on the faces of the soldiers. But underneath the picture, in bold italics, "*Florence Nightingale: Crimean War*" poked fun at me. "So that's what she was looking at," I said.

Suddenly my entire denial system disintegrated: what had happened was completely irrational. In an attempt to pull myself together, I blurted the whole story out to Lil. And she, with a bored yawn, said, "It's and old picture. You probably saw it when you were young and just stored it in your subconscious until you needed it." Then she brushed some crumbs from her lap and turned back to her book.

We never spoke of it again, because Lil was afraid of anything that couldn't be explained rationally and I was afraid I was insane. Still, not being one to leave a stone unturned or a strange woman pacing through my mind without permission, I continued to try to find some explanation *I* could accept. I even discussed it with a sophisticated lady shrink. She assured me I wasn't crazy, and asked me what *I* thought it was.

"Imagination," I said, still secretly thinking I was nuts. I leaned back in my chair and stared straight into her eyes for the telltale sign of compassion that I thought I would find. I didn't.

Instead she asked in a matter-of-fact voice, "What, my dear, *is* imagination . . . if not an extension of your own reality?"

I still wasn't satisfied. Yet at that time I didn't question my belief in God, saints or guardian angels . . . and I had never even *seen* them.

"Oh yes, I've traveled all over the world," Lil told me as we drove home from school that first night. "Even slept in the rice paddies in Japan under Shinto shrine one of the times I ran away."

I was fascinated by her. She seemed so well read, she recited poetry; and now, to find out she had been *everywhere* while her husband was in the Air Force . . . I sighed, totally impressed.

"But don't you sometimes wish you could go back and be married again?" I asked earnestly as we pulled up in front of my parent's house.

"Ugh!" she said, and then whispered softly,

" *The Moving Finger writes and, having writ,*
Moves on; nor all thy piety nor wit
Shall lure it back to cancel half a Line,
Nor all thy tears wash out a Word of it."

"Wow!" I said. "What's that from?"
Lil lifted her hand and placed it across the bottom of her face, pretending a veil. The street lights helped with shadows as she whispered in an exaggerated accent, "Zeez is from zee *Rubaiyat of Omar Khayyam.*"

I laughed and could have listened to her for hours, but I saw my mother flash the porch light and knew I had to go in. I jumped out and watched as the yellow taxi, sputtering smoke and roaring like a dragon, zoomed away.

My mother, in a faded rose flannel bathrobe, was sitting at the round Formica table, her head in her hand, as I walked into the large kitchen.

"How were the kids tonight?" I asked cheerfully.

"Okay," she answered, sounding tired. The house was a mess.

I looked around and noticed that the dishes from supper were piled in the rack, something Mother never did, and that there was still cookie sludge on Spinner's high-chair tray.

Guilt pangs, as tangible as stomach cramps, hit me as I thought of her working all day taking care of *my* kids.

I took my sweater and threw it over the back of the chair, asking, "Where's Daddy?"

"He's upstairs with Niki." Mother got up slowly, dishrag in hand, to wipe the dishes. "She didn't want to go to sleep, so he read her a story. Maybe he dozed off too."

Just then my father, sleepy-eyed and with his straight black hair sticking up on one side, came down the stairs. He smiled a greeting.

"Hi, Daddy." I smiled back. "Thanks . . ."

"No problem, baby. How did school go?" He kissed me on the cheek and put his arm over my shoulder. While I told him about school, my mother served us tea and finished cleaning up. When she finally sat down, she looked as though she was going to fall over.

Hoping to cheer her up I said, "You don't have to drive me anymore, Ma. I got a ride with Lil." She just nodded.

"I'm going to take a bath and go to bed," she said, looking at my father, and then at me. "Don't forget to take Niki to the bathroom before you go to sleep. If we have to keep washing sheets the cesspool is going to back up again."

"Ma, I did take her last night. I can't know if she has to go twice, and I can't wake her up every couple of minutes to ask her. I'm doing the best I can." Some people act penitent when they feel guilty, I act angry. Mother shrugged, then kissed us both good night. Dad and I sat for a long while talking before he followed her.

Later, as I sat alone thinking about the kids, and Shawn, I felt overwhelmed and miserable. How had I made such a mess of everything? Knowing that kind of thinking could do me in, I tried to focus on school, on all the new things I'd be learning. And then when I thought about Lil I found myself smiling. Maybe it could even be fun.

A chill made me realize that it was getting cold; my mother had turned the heat down to night temperature. I quickly rinsed my cup, checked the doors and walked quietly upstairs to the room I shared with the children. I undressed in the half-dark, the only light the moon shining through the open blinds. Then I went over and carefully sat on the bed next to Niki. Her fine dark-brown hair was damp as I pushed it off her forehead. I watched her eyes flicker under her eyelids, long dark lashes typing her dreams on her tan baby-fat cheeks. She looked so sad and serious, even when she slept, that I found myself depressed again, remembering how Shawn could always make her smile more than I could. Taking a deep breath, I tucked the covers around her solid four-year-old body and bent to kiss her. Then I got up quickly and walked over to the crib.

Spinner was lying on his stomach, rocking, his butt up in the air, the thick fuzzy blue of his sleeper waving back and forth. I rolled him over and put my hand into his sleeper bottom to feel his diaper. He was soaked. I tried to change him without waking him completely, but in minutes he was cooing and giggling. Big grin. I picked him up and kissed him too hard. When he started to cry, I whipped him out of the room, almost smothering him, holding his head on my chest so he wouldn't wake Niki or my parents.

"Shut up, kid," I whispered, "or you'll get us creamed."

He laughed, looked straight into my eyes, and then slammed one very small palm right in my face. He obviously wanted to play my father's game, which went, "Nice, nice" and then, when you least expected it, "Boom." Two pats and a slap. Terrific. I carried him quietly downstairs to the finished basement, turned the heat up, and sat on the couch rocking and hugging Spinner until it got warm.

He kept wiggling around, trying to get off my lap, but it was too cold to let him crawl around the asphalt-tiled floor. Finally I let him walk along the top of the couch, holding tight to his sleeper. He ran his hands over the rough dark paneling, and as it scratched he made a face and screeched, "Ouch!" Then he laughed. He was definitely not sleepy. I picked him up and walked over to turn the radio on, low. Nothing on in the middle of the night.

I rummaged through the record cabinet with one hand, struggling to hold Spinner with the other, and pulled out an opera record of my father's.

I put it on, turned it louder, and when there were no shouts of protest from upstairs I started to dance around the room, holding Spinner, singing to him. He laughed. The music got happier-sounding; we danced around so fast that his head swung back, and we laughed so hard that I was covering our mouths to keep us from waking everyone. Spinner pulled away from the hand I held over his mouth, put both arms around me, and kissed me smack on the lips. Suddenly I started to cry. I wanted so much for my kids to have a perfect life, to really be taken care of . . .

The next morning I woke up with more energy than I had had in a very long time—enough even to feed Niki and Spinner breakfast while Mother slept. Through the morning, until after lunch, I cleaned the house; I managed to finish just in time to iron my blue-and-white striped uniform.

At two-thirty on the dot, Lilith beeped the horn. Cinderella's taxi. I kissed my mother and the kids and was outside struggling to open the car door within minutes.

"Hi," I said, plopping my pile of books on top of Lil's.

"Did you read last night?" she asked, looking at me as though the answer I was about to give was the most important in the world. Her uniform was freshly washed and dried, but not ironed.

"I looked over some of the stuff," I answered. "What about you?"

"Didn't get a chance last night. Just collapsed when I got home, and this morning I had to be up for work by six."

"You're *working* too?" I was surprised. I had quit my job at New Hope.

"Oh yes," she answered, nodding and blinking, "I clean people's houses from seven until two."

I thought she was a real heroine, working *and* going to school. As we drove, we talked.

"My husband was such a creep that I packed all my kids into the car and rode up from Florida with only chocolate bars for us to eat," Lil said. "No money. No shoes on. In fact, I didn't even get a chance to throw on a pair of underpants."

"What did he do to you?" I asked, thinking, *No underpants?*

"He screamed at me constantly," she said, blinking like a *femme fatale* in silent movies. You'd never make it in my house, I thought. My family, like most of the Italians I knew, didn't know shouting from talking; but I was so used to it that it held no terror. Only silence frightened me.

We pulled in front of the large white barn that had been converted into the temporary learning quarters for Manpower, and Lilith tried unsuccessfully to smooth some wrinkles out of her uniform.

"Look really bad?" she asked, biting her bottom lip and looking bewildered.

"A steamroller could take them out in no time," I teased, but when I saw her worried look I added, "Tomorrow, if you can pick me up five minutes earlier, I'll iron it for you."

She thanked me and we ran into class, just in time. It was like that all through school; the closest we got to being on time was just about making it. During the three months before we got into a hospital, we studied together every chance we had. Our marks were very good, though Lilith's were always better than mine. She won with incredible grace, saying always, "I don't know how this happened." I didn't either, but I just kept trying to beat her.

CHAPTER 4

It was a dark gray day, heavy with rain-filled clouds, as Lil and I drove along Southern State Parkway.

"There she is," Lilith announced, sounding a lot like Columbus and pointing ahead to two huge brick smokestacks spitting black smoke into the already gloomy sky. "Meadowland Sanitarium."

"It looks more like a crematorium," I said, sliding down in my seat and covering my eyes. Lil giggled.

Both Lil and I had previous hospital experience, so it had been decided by the powers that our initial clinical practice should be in psych. This was our first day at a mental institution. A state psychiatric hospital. All I knew about crazy people was what I had read in textbooks. I had never even met one.

"Invaluable experience," was how it had been presented by Mrs. Smith. Frightening, was how I saw it.

"The trouble with medicine," Lil said regretfully, "is that in order to learn we have to practice on real people." She sighed with resignation just as we pulled past the immense stone pillars that guarded the driveway to the grounds.

We drove slowly down the narrow dirt road, looking across the dry brown grass and naked trees, trying to find Building 64, Admissions. As we rode past tall cracked brick buildings, past smaller stone houses, pebbles hit our windshield like bullets. Meadowland looked like a deserted university campus . . . except for the bars on the windows.

We found the building and parked. As we walked up the sidewalk toward Admissions, a crowd of men and women, different ages, stopped and stared at us, expressionless. They looked poverty-stricken, all dressed in Bowery-bum clothing.

"Why?" I asked Lilith. She had worked in another institution years before as an aide.

"State issue," she answered as she smiled at a very pale, very thin girl about fifteen years old.

"They can't keep their own clothes?" I whispered, moving closer to Lil.

"Nobody can keep track. Most of the patients can't remember what belongs to them," Lilith answered distractedly, patting the girl's stringy light-brown hair. The child moved closer, purring like a kitten each time she was petted.

After several minutes, I grabbed Lil's hand and pulled her forward and up the steps. At the top, on either side of the entrance, a stone lion snarled. Each was covered with graffiti; each had green mold covering his fangs and an open mouth full of discarded candy wrappers and old cigarette butts.

I shivered and held tighter to Lil's hand as we walked into a large square lobby. Empty—no furniture, scuff-marked tile floor, faded tan stucco walls without one decoration; and, in every corner, more crumpled paper, candy wrappers and stomped-out cigarettes. Two large narrow windows, cut high, coaxed light through the bars, which cast shadows on the walls and made the entire room a dingy cage.

"Creepy," I whispered to Lil. "Where is everyone?"

Lilith walked up to a heavy wooden door and kicked hard. There was an audible scurry behind it and then the sound of keys clinking, scraping in the stubborn lock. Finally the door was opened by a big gray-haired black woman in a tinted blue cotton uniform. She didn't smile as she said curtly, "Hurry in. I ain't got all day." She locked the door behind us and added, "I hope that's the last of you." Lil and I were late as usual.

We followed the woman silently through another locked door, until we reached the elevators. There she placed her key in a special slot marked "3". I stood behind her making faces, but Lil just stared ahead wide-eyed. She knew, better than I, that without our own keys we were as defenseless as the patients.

Once on the third floor, Lil and I followed large blue arrows pointing to the male ward. Mrs. Smith greeted us with raised eyebrow and tapping foot, then dismissed the other students, who had already gotten their assignments. To Lil she said, "Go to the female ward." Then, turning on me, with a voice that matched the snarling lions at the entrance she roared, "And whenever you're ready, you can find your patient in there." She flung a piece of paper at me and pointed to a large room down the hall. I glanced at the note as I walked the corridor slowly, but all it said was, Fredrik Haner, 30 years old, paranoid schizophrenic."

At the doorway of the immense barren dayroom, I stiffened. About thirty patients, all males, most in "state issue," sat, stood, paced and ran around in circles. I walked numbly into the room, feeling like a target in my blue-and-white uniform, white stockings and polished shoes. I wandered past the long, heavy wooden benches lining the walls, past an old man staring straight ahead, past a young boy rocking back and forth excitedly.

Then a young man with a blond crew cut walked quickly up to me, placed his hand firmly on top of my head, bowed his, and said gently, "Jesus loves you."

Suddenly I heard a terrific racket coming from the hall behind me. Before I could turn around, a young black boy was thrown into the dayroom past me. Behind him, taking mile-long strides, came the attendant, Mr. Suggs. He was enormous and bald—Mr. Clean right down to the gold earring. Immaculate in his starched whites, wielding a ring of keys bigger than God's.

As he slammed the paddle he held into the open palm of his left hand, I jumped. And as soon as he entered the room, silence fell like a tarpaulin.

A muscular young man with hair like a weed garden stood on top of one of the benches, and as the big man approached he ambushed him. Mr. Clean grabbed him and threw him like a rag doll onto the bench. Some of the men began to sing aloud, and others began madly pacing. One little old man got off his bench and peed in a corner of the room. With one swing, Mr. Clean knocked him to the floor. I was more afraid of the orderly than of the patients.

There was no one to show me what to do; no one to help me. I was outraged . . . and scared out of my mind. I leaned against the woodwork and waited until Mr. Clean finished his morning routine. I figured that sooner or later he'd notice me.

I was wrong. Eventually, I had to walk into the middle of the dayroom to talk to him. As I did, several men walked up behind me. When one patted me on the shoulder, I almost jumped out of my skin. "Yes?" rasped Mr. Clean, as though he had no idea what I was doing there.

I fought hard to be charming as I said, "Fredrik Haner is my patient today."

"Fine, dear," Mr. Clean said, looking past me. Then as an afterthought he pointed toward a young man who was looking out a window, leaning his face against the bars. "There's your boy."

Fredrik turned to look at me when I introduced myself, but then turned back to stare out the barred window again without saying a word. He was tall, and his black straight hair was separated by grease into thick strings, as though his fingers had been run through it constantly. He had dark thick eyebrows which met over his long fine nose and framed the most peculiar eyes that I had ever seen. They were a light turquoise blue . . . so light that they looked as though someone had dropped one tablespoon of blue tint into a clear lake and then tried to match the color. With his long full lashes and clear olive skin, he was almost beautiful.

"What's your name?" I asked him, and when he stared without answering, I said, "Can you tell me?"

Fredrik smiled. "I can and I cannot," he said quietly.

"Are you Fredrik?"

"I am everything."

He spoke for a few minutes in word salad, his conversation a crossword puzzle, with delusions and hallucinations confusing the clues. Finally he said, "Do you know if my mediruler will block my mind today?"

I was dumbfounded, but he looked as though he would wait forever for an answer, so I figured I should take a shot at it. I had read about neologisms, or new words, that were a combination of real words. If, I thought, "medi" means medicine, then a mediruler could be a doctor. Now . . . a mind block was something else. This is worse than algebra, I thought, as with a real stroke of brilliance— or maybe just luck—I remembered ECT. Shock therapy. It causes temporary memory loss. That could be it. Here goes, I said to myself, and then aloud, "Fredrik, do you want to know if your doctor is going to send you for a treatment today?"

He tossed his head back and looked at me as though I were a simpleton. "Is that not what I asked?"

Yippee! I felt as though I had just gotten the answer to *Password.* "I'll find out," was all I said, but I felt like a tremendous success.

We talked for a half hour. I was getting more confused by the minute. I couldn't even think of a question to ask him. Occasionally, one of the other men would come over to touch me, then walk away. Others stood and stared at me. I was afraid, but then I began to realize that their behavior, though odd, was not dangerous; that my own idea of insanity was much more threatening than anything they were doing. So I relaxed.

At eleven-thirty Mr. Suggs and a smaller attendant, Mr. Allon, decided to go to lunch. "Can we leave her here?" Mr. Allon asked Suggs, pointing at me.

"Sure," Suggs said. He handed me his keys and I was afraid not to take them.

"We'll only be gone about a half hour," he said, his gleaming teeth in such a wide smile that he looked evil.

Panic-stricken, I tried to glue myself together with reassurance. They must think I'm very capable, I said first. Then I looked around the dayroom. All the men seemed quiet and relaxed. But what if . . . Don't be a hysteric! I scolded myself. My next thought was, I wonder how many minutes are left in this half hour. I glanced at my watch: twenty-nine.

As soon as Suggs left the ward, a bony elderly gentleman came over and sat on the bench next to Fredrik and me. He smiled and held out his hand. "Name's Zachary, ma'am," he said. "I want to welcome you aboard."

When I smiled at him he ran his hand across his chin over his grubby white stubble. "Boy," he said wistfully, "I sure wish I could shave."

"Yes," I said sympathetically. "That would be nice."

Gray eyes twinkling, he asked, "*Can* I shave?"

I didn't know the routine on the unit, so I stalled. "Well, I don't have a razor or it would be a wonderful idea." I had read in several books that it was important to encourage psychiatric patients to keep up their appearance.

"I know where they are," he said helpfully.

"You do?" I was surprised. I thought all insane people needed help with the activities of daily living, but Zachary seemed quite self-sufficient.

"Sure," he said cheerfully, pointing toward a thick wooden door in the hall. "Supplies are kept in that closet."

"It's probably locked," I said, standing up next to him.

The old man tapped my pocket. "You've got the keys," he reminded me gently, as though I had forgotten. He seemed like an awfully nice man.

"But I don't know which key it is," I told him, smiling. I looked at my watch: twenty minutes to go.

"Let me be of service," Zachary said, bowing low. He pointed to a key that looked like all the rest. He made complete sense to me, and if he knew what key to use it was probably part of the procedure.

To be sure, I asked, "Do they usually let you shave?"

Zachary's brow wrinkled. "Only between eleven and twelve. Before lunch," he said, and then added emphatically, "And only after we sign the book for 'sharps'." Pretty complicated, I thought; thank God he knows what he's doing. I was still wary, but Zachary's concern for the rules, for doing everything just right, reassured me.

Hanging by the closet door, on a thick string, was the black book. Zachary opened to the middle and showed me the page marked 'sharps'. Next to his name, 'razor' was scrawled.

I looked over to the bench where I had left Fredrik. He was lost in a conversation with some invisible force, lips moving, head nodding. He had no idea I was gone.

Zachary carefully signed the book with my pen as I struggled to unlock the door. When he had finished, he turned to me and offered, "Let me assist you."

With one quick turn, he had the closet open. There on the top shelf was a cardboard carton marked "Razors," just as he had promised. I stood on tiptoes to reach and then handed Zachary one.

"We have no shaving cream," I told him, rummaging through the other boxes on the shelf.

"We have to mix that ourselves," Zachary explained, grabbing a small package from the shelf. "It's powder. We have an automatic machine that whips it into cream."

Someone tapped me on the shoulder and I turned quickly. There stood a young man, pretzel thin and tall. He had dark circles under his eyes and skin so pale that he looked as though he had been made in a lab just hours before. On his head was a painter's cap. Before I knew what was happening, Zachary grabbed the young man's hat off his head and smacked him across the chest with it. "Drid," he said solemnly, "how many times have I told you to remove your hat in the presence of a lady?"

Drid hung his head. "Sorry, ma'am," he said in the gentlest voice I'd ever heard. "I was just wondering if I could also have this opportunity to shave?"

I looked at Zachary. He nodded vigorously up and down and then said firmly, "Just make sure he signs the book."

I reached into the closet for another razor and more packets of powder and handed them to Drid. When he smiled, I saw that all his front teeth were missing.

A stocky blond man with exceptionally ragged clothing and a sparse blond beard approached us. Around his neck hung about twenty strings of beads. When he held out his hand Zachary said, "This is Twill. He doesn't talk."

I reached into the closet again, pulled out another razor, handed it to Twill, and when Zachary stiffened I said, "Sign the book."

The old man winked at me and said, "There you go, girl. You're really catching on." I was thrilled.

By the time I locked the closet, I had handed out six razors. "Now what?" I asked Zachary.

He checked the closet door to make sure it was locked. A real stickler for rules, that old man. "Now," he said, "we go whip up the shaving cream."

Zachary led me down a rectangular white-tiled lavatory toward the grimy freestanding sinks. Along each wall hung a stainless-steel panel, like a fun-house mirror, which waved and stretched us as we passed. Several men squatted over seatless toilets, their urine running in streams over the rim, down the bowl and across the cement floor toward the sunken metal drains in the middle of the room. I tried to look away, embarrassed, but the men didn't seem to notice as I walked gingerly over the small yellow puddles. I stayed right on Zachary's heels, Twill followed me, three men followed him, and Drid sauntered in last.

Zachary carefully showed me how to work the shaving cream machine and then pointed out the key that I would need to turn it on. All the other men waited patiently, holding their razors tight in anticipation. They watched as I tore open several packets of powder and emptied them. When I added a few extra packets, just to make sure (like an Italian cook), Drid and Twill nodded at each other and smiled. Zachary stood by, concentrating on my every action. Finally, when I put my key into the lock and turned it, he explained gently, "You'll have to add water." I did just as he said, and right before my eyes the damn stuff started to grow like dough. It bubbled and erupted like white lava all over the shelf, then spread down the tiles and ran over the sinks onto the floor and toward the toilet bowls. I stood too stunned to do anything. Then I heard Twill giggle, Drid chuckle and all the other men break into gales of laughter. Zachary even flashed a broad grin.

Suddenly one of the men bent down and picked up a handful of whipped foam and threw it at Twill. Before I could stop him, Twill flung some back. I watched shocked as Drid bent down and grabbed a handful.

"Stop!" I hollered. "You're making a mess." But they were laughing so hard they couldn't hear me. Like children playing in the snow, they hurled this stuff until every one of them, and the entire bathroom, was covered in white goo. Through the shrieks and gleeful shouts I finally yelled, "*Cut it out!*" But their laughter was contagious and I found it impossible to sound serious.

My back was to the door when suddenly all six men stiffened, frozen in position like enchanted snowmen.

"What the *hell* is going one here? What the *fuck* is this nonsense?"

When I turned to explain, Mr. Suggs, his lip curled in disdain, shouted, "You—get over here!" He pointed to an invisible spot at his feet and I started to walk toward him, a panoramic view of my life passing before my eyes.

Suddenly I heard Drid growl, a low, throaty sound. I turned in time to see Twill spit viciously onto the floor. Mr. Suggs grabbed me by my uniform and shoved me behind him as he moved toward the patients.

"Give me those razors," he ordered, holding out his hand. I watched, horrified, as all six men slowly drew the razors behind them and moved backward against the stainless-steel mirrors, eerie melting wax figures in some ghostly dance.

Suggs turned toward me, red-faced, eyes wide with fury. "Look what you've done."

Suddenly I was angry. I felt betrayed. I was furious with myself for not realizing the danger, for trusting the patients, but more furious with Suggs and Smith for putting me in a situation that I wasn't prepared to handle.

Like a whirling dervish, I turned to the six men and stomped toward them, crying, "I trusted you. This isn't fair and now I'm going to be in trouble." Tears running down my face, I pointed to Suggs and continued to yell indignantly. "I didn't trust *him*, but I trusted you guys. I believed *you* and did what *you* asked." I waved my finger in front of Zachary as I sniffed and asked, "Do *you* think this is fair?"

I was a big believer in fairness and justice then. Luckily, those patients were saner than I was. Everything was quiet for what seemed like a long time before I heard Zachary say, in a low voice, "Drid?"

Drid, his painter's hat askew, walked slowly toward Mr. Suggs and held out his razor. Twill followed, and then the others. Zachary was last, and just before he handed over his razor he bowed toward me and winked.

I turned to Mr. Clean and asked, "What will happen to them?"

"They will be punished," he answered, very self-righteously.

Outraged again, I sputtered at him, "You should be locked up!"

Mrs. Smith was called away from her coffee break to come and get me. Exasperated again, she asked, "Can you never function within a system?"

I tried to explain, but she was more concerned that her own job was in jeopardy than she was by my damaged idealism. She informed me that I would have to defend myself to the head psychiatrist the following day.

The next morning I reported to a small shabby office. At the cluttered desk sat a heavy dark-haired man going through an enormous pile of official-looking papers.

I studied him as I waited to be noticed. He was about sixty years old, his hair pasted to the side with sweat. He wore a blue plaid sport jacket and under it a yellow shirt and a green knit vest; for convention's sake he wore a madras tie, askew. When he looked up through thick dark-rimmed glasses to greet me, I could see his brown eyes twinkle.

He pushed back the seat, stood, and indicated a chair opposite for me. "Dr. Nathan Davidson," he introduced himself. "I'd like to hear how *you* see what went on yesterday."

I wasn't frightened any longer and told him my story, complete with tears and outrage. When I was finished he said, "Try never to take on more responsibility than you feel prepared to handle, and remember that the phone is always close enough to check policy. But, more important, know that your compassion is a wonderful tool, if you learn to use it properly."

As he stood to indicate that our meeting was over, he reached out for my hand and said, "The real power to help change things is with education. Get your degree. Then you can come back and run a ward as you would like to."

"But what will happen to those men?" I asked him.

"There can be limit-setting with kindness," he answered. And he smiled.

CHAPTER 5

Spinner was a year old and it was time for my annual gyneco-logical checkup. As I soaked in the bathtub, I thought about how much I hated the indignity of lying flat on my back like a sick frog. And aside from that humiliation, Dr. Jansen, my gynecologist, was an arrogant know-it-all. He was tall and thin with curly grayish hair and olive skin that made him look healthy even in winter. I couldn't stand him, but he was an excellent doctor.

As I jumped out of the tub and started to dry off, I knew I had never really forgiven him for his sarcasm after Spinner's delivery.

I had been lying in my hospital bed crying because my marriage was falling apart, because I didn't know what kind of life my new baby was going to have, and because I was overwhelmed by the responsibility for all of us. Besides, Spinner had been premature and was lying in the nursery in an incubator, and my stitches hurt.

Dr. Joel Jansen had clattered through the swinging doors to my room, had seen my tears, and had quickly decided to exit, saying only, "Postpartum depression."

I tried to stop him with "I feel terrible."

"What do you expect? You just had a baby," he said, still walking toward the door.

He was so pompous I wanted to kill him. His marriage wasn't falling apart. He had plenty of money and his poor wife was home watching his spoiled-brat kids. His bottom hadn't been sawed apart and his baby wasn't turning blue in some crappy plastic box. He could afford to be smug. But I was furious. I sat up straight and hit him with "You have a crummy bedside manner."

He hit me back with "Babies shouldn't have babies." Then he

left without even looking at me.

I had been so outraged I had gotten well and gone home.

I decided as I left for my appointment that this time I would handle Dr. Jansen differently. No tears. If he gave me any grief I would just tell him he was fired.

I made it through my physical by counting the holes in the ceiling tiles and trying to ignore everything that was going on below my waist. Including Dr. Jansen. I followed his commands like a robot, not saying a word.

Afterward, as I waited nervously in his office, I stared at the paneled walls covered with gold-framed diploma's and browsed over the medical books and magazines that crammed his walnut bookshelves. Then I sat, hands folded in my lap, eyes exploring the large oil painting in front of me: a vase of very peculiar-looking white flowers. Next to it, smaller, was a watercolor print of a very young girl holding a bouquet of yellow daisies. Ah, I thought, the good doctor's added dimension.

Dr. Jansen breezed through the door, and as he passed me to sit at his desk I noticed the clean smell of his white lab coat and his cologne. After he had finished with the details of my physical, he leaned toward me and asked, "How have things really been going, Teri?"

"Well," I stammered, "I'm living back home with the kids. Shawn ran away again . . ." And then, because it had been so long since I had really spoken to a man, and because Dr. Jansen looked so concerned, I unloaded everything.

"Why the hell did you decide to have a baby?" he asked sharply, but his eyes, the color of willow buds, somehow softened the edges of his harsh words.

"I guess I just wanted it to work so much . . ." I began, and then poured out the rest of my hopes, fears and disappointment. Several times he held my hands because they were shaking, and he even mopped my tears off my cheek.

When I settled down a little, he asked softly, "Why do you want to be a nurse?"

"I need something to make me feel valuable, some way that I can help other people with their pain," I said with the fervor of an evangelist. "I'm tired of trying to stop Shawn from drinking himself to death and ruining me and the kids. It's too hard for me to deal with all the emotional pain. I want something simple, like medicine, where there are cures and I can stop pain with a pill or an injection. And, besides, I need to do something essential, to save me."

Terrific insight I had at the time. Nursing *without* emotional pain—a concept a lot like a featherless bird. I don't remember now, but I'm sure that even at twenty-four I still believed in the Easter Bunny.

Before I left, Dr. Jansen asked me out to lunch. Before I accepted, I asked him who had painted the reproductions on his wall.

"The picture of the girl is a Renoir." He got up and pulled an art book off his shelf.

I pointed to the painting of the vase and asked, "And that, Dr. Jansen?"

"Van Gogh. The name of the painting is *White Roses*. And please call me Joel."

I studied him as he leafed through the pages of the book, showing me pictures he particularly liked and talking about the artists enthusiastically. When he wasn't playing doctor he was an attractive man.

"Would you like to learn about art?" he asked, smiling. When I nodded he asked, "And music?" When I nodded again he asked, "Anything else?"

"Yes, I'd like to learn medicine, too."

Though I couldn't hear it then, the soft strains of My Fair Lady began playing in the background.

Lil and I had just finished clinical practice in surgery, which I had found challenging and exciting. The operations and treatments that were done really seemed to work, and I began to see some of the magic of medicine. But now we were back in the classroom, and as much as I loved learning nursing skills in the hospital I hated being back in school. I stormed and balked at book study; I felt we could do that at home. Besides, without patients, real people, to connect all the knowledge to it seemed boring, so one night Lil and I decided to cut class and go to the movies.

Only the night light in the kitchen was on by the time Lil

dropped me off. Everyone was asleep. As I tiptoed past the table I could see a note from my mother telling me what the kids had done that day . . . and a letter from Shawn. I picked it up, turned out the light and stumbled upstairs in the dark. Niki and Spinner were sleeping soundly when I pushed open the door to check them, so I walked into the bathroom to read my letter. It had been nine months since I had heard from Shawn, and my hands shook as I tore open the envelope. The postmark read Biloxi, Mississippi.

Hi Hon,

As you can see I've decided to go to missile maintenance school to try to get my life in some sort of perspective. I miss you and the little guys and hope when I'm finished training we can work something out. I'll start sending you $110 every two weeks and maybe you can put a little away so that when I get out we can buy a car. It's not bad here, except that it's been raining for the last three days. Guess this must be the rainy season—if it isn't it's a damn wet dry season.

Well Babe, got to go. Remember I love you and the kids.

All my love forever,
Shawn

I sat on the john and began to cry. I couldn't believe he was going to make me try again. He knew even better than I that I couldn't walk away from him as long as he said he needed me. Crap! I was just about getting over being in constant pain about the kids not having a father. How could he do this to me?

During the following months, letters from Shawn kept coming and I began to answer them, with mixed emotion. I knew I still loved him, figured I would always, but I was scared. Afraid to get my hopes up again; afraid to have them smashed. When he asked if he could come to my graduation, I reluctantly agreed—as long as he was still not drinking. Niki asked about him every day, and he enclosed a special note for her in each letter. Mother urged me to try one more time, "for the sake of the children", and my father sat tight-lipped, not offering any opinion.

I was seeing Joel a few times a week at this time, which helped me maintain some sanity. Often when we met he brought me a print of a famous painting and talked about the artist, or brought me a record of classical music and taught me about the composer. At other times he answered all my questions about medicine. He was good to me and I was learning to care about him. I didn't love him yet, but I found him exciting, and he helped fill some of the space Shawn had left in my life. The art, music and medicine made me feel happy and alive. When he wanted to make love to me, I responded easily. For the first time, I felt valuable as a woman. We talked for hours, really enjoying each other; not too much about his life, a lot about mine.

When I told him Shawn was coming back and I was going to consider living with him again, Joel was kind and reassuring. He reminded me that he would be around if I needed him, but said he would understand if I chose not to see him.

As time went on, even clinical practice began to disappoint me; I was learning little more there than I already knew from working. We got lots of theory, but as students we seldom got to take care of the sicker patients. We had to observe staff nurses from a distance, and after having worked on a regular floor as an aide I missed having the intimacy of knowing the patients well.

Among the specialties, medicine depressed me: there seemed to be too many patients with terminal diseases. Technically, surgery seemed a bigger challenge, and most of those patients got well. My experience in obstetrics had been limited to watching one delivery and spending one day taking care of a new mother. Each day I found myself looking forward to graduation more anxiously. I wanted to work on a floor of my own, with patients of my own.

The one area I had decided not to work in after graduation was pediatrics. My rotation there had been too painful, even though I treasured the memory I had of it. Both Lil and I had been scheduled for the two weeks before Christmas . . .

One step off the elevator and I could see the difference from the other floors I had been on. Instead of the dull beige or green of the adult wards, Peds was decorated all in primary colors. Navy tile floors with red-and-yellow painted walls; storybook cutouts, fairy-tale characters and animated animals dancing along the woodwork, made the place look more like a nursery school than a hospital ward.

For the first week and a half, Lil and I worked in a four-bed room together. We fed, changed diapers, fixed beds and played with the kids. The sickest of my patients was four-day postoperative appendectomy patient, a small boy who whined a lot but was healing nicely. The others had croup, diarrhea or broken bones. Lil loved the fact that the kids weren't really sick, but I found I didn't like Peds at all. To me it felt more like baby-sitting than nursing, and I felt pretty awful taking care of other people's children while someone else was taking care of mine.

Then, on my last day of clinic, so many of the staff called in sick that Lil was transferred back to Medicine and I was assigned a ward with the terminal children.

Pat, a pretty redheaded nurse with freckles, gave me a long report, explaining everything in intricate detail.

In the first bed was Derek, a five-year-old boy with an inoperable brain tumor. They had opened him up and found that his tumor had infiltrated too many vital areas to be removed, and so they were just hoping for a slow growth to give him some time.

Tammie was a three-year-old with cystic fibrosis who was recovering from pneumonia. This time she would probably go home; we could keep her alive for as long as we could keep the glue in her lungs from turning to plaster.

Sally was a four-year-old with leukemia. This was her second run of chemotherapy, and everyone was hoping for a remission. She had a good chance if the chemo didn't destroy her.

"The only one you really have to watch," Pat told me as she handed me a metal chart, "is Kerri Levine, the eight-month-old. She's got biliary atresia, and six months ago the doctors gave her only a few months to live."

"What is it?" I asked, hoping Pat wouldn't think me a dope.

"Kerri was born with an abnormal closure of her bile ducts," she explained, "so that the bile backs up into her system." She shrugged. "I don't know much more than that. She's very jaundiced and her level of consciousness has been changing lately. She's much sleepier for much longer." When she saw how panicky I was she reassured me, "I'll be here all night, so you can call if you run into trouble. They're so short-staffed that I'm going to do a double."

Pat was no older than I, but she had an air of efficiency that came from experience. "How long have you worked here?" I asked her.

"For about three years," she said, smiling. "I love it. By the way," she added, "Kerri's parents are with her all the time. They do most of the care." She shook her head. "They're lovely people."

By the time I walked into the room I had three pages of notes shoved into my pocket. Derek, chubby and cheerful, with a blue baseball hat on his shaved head, was struggling to fit a wrong piece of puzzle into place. Bald skinny Sally leaned over the red plastic chair Derek was sitting in and tried to reach across the small wooden table to help him, but she wasn't big enough.

"I can do it myself," he insisted, frowning.

"I wath trying to show you," Sally lisped indignantly, then shrugged and sat down next to Tammie, a frail, blue-lipped child who was carefully coloring. As I got closer to the table I noticed that Tammie wheezed when she breathed and that her fingertips were wide and flat. "Clubbing," the books had called it—a symptom of severe pulmonary disease.

In the far corner of the room a young woman was standing in front of a small white metal crib. I whipped up my courage and walked over to her.

"My name is Teri Daley," I said, not knowing whether to smile or not, and settling for what must have looked like a smirk.

The woman nodded, didn't smile, and turned toward the baby, who had started to cry. She struggled with the latch and I moved forward to help her, but stopped at the sight of the child's tears. They were yellow-green.

"It's okay, Kerri," the young woman whispered softly as she bent to kiss the baby's cheek. Kerri stopped crying and stared. The whites of her big blue eyes were bright yellow. Shocked, I didn't move an inch. The woman turned the key on a musical pink teddy bear and said to me, "My name's Ellen."

"Ow . . . ow," came Kerri's squeaky voice from the crib as she reached up to grab the teddy. When the music stopped, she frowned and wrinkled her nose. Both Ellen and I laughed: Kerri had such an old-lady expression and voice. It was weird—she looked like a little alien, greenish skin with yellow eyes and long light lashes. Her light hair was so fine and straight that it looked as though it had been painted on, like a tan Halloween cap, complete with widow's peak. Her small ears came to a point like a leprechaun's. She reached up to rub her tiny turned-up nose and smiled to show two little teeth. When she kicked excitedly as Ellen wound the teddy again, the pink flannel blanket fell off and exposed the biggest belly I had ever seen on a child. Worse than those pictures of starving children–as though she were nine months pregnant.

"She's beautiful, isn't she?" Ellen asked, lifting the baby carefully out of the crib.

"Yes, she is," I said, wondering why I too felt that way.

Kerri's head bobbed and flopped as Ellen tried to support it. She walked over and sat in the bright-orange vinyl chair. I sat opposite her as she talked.

"The doctors don't know how this happened," she explained. "I have another child, Denise, who's nine, and she's fine. Paul and I didn't think we could have any more children." She guided Kerri's pacifier into her mouth as she asked, "Do you know my husband?"

"No," I said.

"Well, I'm sure you'll meet him tonight. His name is Paul. He's great with Kerri"she said, wiping the baby's chin with a diaper. I noticed a strong acrid smell whenever I leaned closer to Kerri, but Ellen didn't seem to mind.

She talked for a long time, and whenever she mentioned Paul, though she said nothing sentimental, it was easy to see how fond she was of him. She told me they had been married for twelve years and he had worked two jobs for all but the last four. Then, with the money they had managed to save, Paul had bought a small camera shop. It meant working long hours because they couldn't afford to hire anyone, and with the time Ellen had to spend at the hospital she was no help.

I looked often at Kerri as she slept in her mother's arms, and was instantly angry with myself for having even a twinge of jealousy. I would have loved a wonderful relationship, but not at the price of Niki or Spinner. That's how I figured the fates worked: they gave you one, they took one away.

Ellen kept talking, fast, as though there were feelings she had to get rid of. She told me how guilty she felt about all the time she spent with Kerri; about how she resented spending time with Denise. She knew that her other child, her healthy child, was lonely and frightened, but she was so overwhelmed that any small demand from Denise annoyed her. She threw the words at me as though awaiting judgment, but all I could do was tell her how terrible I thought the whole situation was. I felt inept, and was certain that an older, wiser nurse would have known exactly the right thing to say to make everything better.

When the supper trays came up I left Ellen to help Derek, Sally and Tammie. I cut their meat and poured their milk, thankful to be able to do something I felt competent at. Later, Pat came in and told me to go down for dinner before evening care had to be done.

After dinner, as I rode the elevator up from the cafeteria, the doors opened on the main floor. A tall man with curly dark hair sprinted across the lobby into the elevator just before the doors slammed shut, and called out, "Pediatrics—third floor." He was carrying a large package. I smiled at him, wondering who he was going to visit.

At the entrance to Peds he shivered as the melting snow ran down his neck and under his raincoat collar. Like a Saint Bernard, he shook his head from side to side, and the water flew off his hair in a heavy spray.

"Brother! Is it cold out there today," he said aloud, shifting his package from one arm to another to remove his coat. He stopped at the white counter of the nursing station and smiled a big greeting to Pat. "It's really snowin' out there tonight."

She looked up from the chart she was reading, then stood up and walked over to him. "Hi, Paul," she said, touching his arm. "How are you today?"

"Depends," he said seriously. "How's my girl doing?"

Pat looked apologetic when she said, "Not any better . . . Just about the same."

Paul nodded and handed Pat the package. "Cake and cookies for you girls and the kids," he said. Then he turned and walked down the hall toward Kerri's room. I was right behind him as he reached the doorway.

Derek, Tammie and Sally all shrieked and giggled when they saw him. Paul walked over to the table and knelt down between Sally and Tammie. Derek jumped up to get closer.

"Okay," Paul said seriously, "cover your eyes."

Wiggling excitedly, they all did. Paul reached into his pockets and pulled out puzzles, crayons and flashlights.

When he told them to look, they laughed happily and then each in turn threw his arms around Paul and gave him a big kiss.

"One more surprise," he said, beginning to unwrap a long colorful tube. The kids watched, rapt. It was a huge cloth Walt Disney calendar. As Paul pinned it to the bulletin board, I noticed that December 25 had a big red felt X on it.

Present time over, Derek ran over to a small orange plastic car, jumped in and pedaled over to Paul. "Watch it, mister, or I'll run you over," he teased.

"Great car you got there, Derek," Paul said, kneeling next to the boy. "You're doing terrific."

Sally came slowly over and put her arm around Paul's shoulder. "I really mithed you," she lisped.

He kissed her forehead and then spoke to Tammie, who was hanging back, "Hey, sweetheart, how are you today?"

Derek answered for her. "She's sicker. The nurse said she has to have another needle for her 'fection."

Tammie hung her head as though she had done something wrong. Paul sat on the closest chair and pulled her up on his knee.

"The person who has to have an extra needle," he said, "has to have an extra present." He searched in his jacket until he found a big multicolored lollipop. When he handed it to Tammie she smiled shyly. Then Paul looked at Derek and Sally and winked. "Sorry, kids, maybe next time."

All this time, Paul hadn't looked at Ellen. I had the feeling he was deliberately avoiding her and Kerri. I glanced at her; she looked sad—not angry, as I might have been. Kerri was asleep in her arms.

Finally, Paul walked over and bent to kiss Ellen on the lips. "Hi, Hon," he said. "You look tired." And with a new seriousness, "How's the baby?"

At the sound of Paul's voice, Kerri's eyes opened and a big grin spread over her face. She held her arms out to him but winced from the pain, and the smile disappeared as quickly as it had appeared. Paul knelt down in front of them. "Hi, Rabbit," he said, planting kisses all over Kerri's face. With her enormous yellow-tinged blue eyes the baby searched his face. He lifted her gently out of Ellen's lap and began to rock her, humming a lullaby into her ear. Kerri's small hand rested on her father's cheek as he sang.

Ellen stood up slowly and stretched. She introduced me to Paul and then walked to the closet to get her coat. She waved goodbye to Derek, Sally and Tammie and came back to kiss Paul and Kerri. "I'll give Denise a kiss for you," she said to Paul. At the doorway she stopped and said, "If anything changes . . ." But Paul put his finger to his lips to keep her from continuing.

Paul sat and tried to give Kerri a bottle while I helped Tammie undress for bed. Derek and Sally had gone down the hall to help the candy-striper decorate the big Christmas tree.

" . . . 'Tis the Season to be Jolly'," vibrated through the open door as I pounded on Tammie's back doing postural drainage, trying to help her cough up some of the mucous plugs that were making it hard for her to breathe. Out of the corner of my eye I watched Paul. Kerri was having trouble drinking. She kept choking. Paul held her up and patted her. Often she rubbed her huge belly and whimpered. When she kept wiggling uncomfortably, Paul put her back in the crib and covered her with the pink floral blanket I had given him. He sang until she fell asleep.

Derek came racing into the room with a handful of tinsel and jumped onto Paul's lap, throwing the silver strands around his neck. "Mister, you look just like a Christmas tree," he teased. When he tried to remove the tinsel, he found it had tangled around Paul's gold chain. "Is that a cross, mister?" he asked as he studied the golden ornament hanging from the necklace.

Paul tilted his head and smiled. "No, Derek, this isn't a cross. It's a Chai."

"What's it for, mister?"

Paul smiled and tugged at the boy's baseball cap. "It's for life, buddy . . . for life."

Derek climbed off Paul's lap and hit the hall again, then hollered back to Paul, "Jamie wants something. His light's on, and I can't see nobody."

"Who's Jamie?" I asked Paul, wondering if I could help. "He's a fourteen-year-old kid who got hit by a car a couple of months ago. Got casts all over so he can't move much now, but he's gonna do okay. Main trouble is that the kid's lonely. His old man split last year and he lives alone with his mom. She works, so she doesn't have much time to visit." Paul moved toward the door, then looked back at Kerri, who was still sleeping peacefully. "I usually stop in to see him—shoot the bull awhile. Makes the holidays easier." I watched as Paul slowly walked across the hall.

Tis the season to be jolly—with decorated Christmas trees, holly wreaths and mangers. With hanging tinsel, silver balls, sick and wingless angels.

Later, with Tammie tucked in bed and Derek and Sally still down the hall, I went to offer Paul a cup of coffee. He was sitting in a chair next to Jamie's bed, staring at the television. I stood at the door, not wanting to interrupt, as I heard Jamie's cracked deep voice ask, "Is Kerri better?" Both the boy's legs were in casts hanging from ropes on pulleys, and his right arm was in a cast and suspended from an IV pole by gauze.

Paul absently shredded the edges of the newspaper he held as he answered, "Not really, Champ. Little kid's having a hard time of it." Both seemed intent on the television.

Jamie bit his full bottom lip and then scratched the end of his freckled nose. His voice quickened just a little when he said, "My mom just called and said she had to work Christmas Day. So she can't come till late."

Paul glanced sideways at Jamie and suddenly brightened. "How about if I bring some flicks, cartoons maybe, for a real Christmas show?" Jamie turned and smiled broadly as Paul continued, "And maybe some pizza, balloons, hats, noisemakers—the whole works!" Then Paul added quietly, "As long as we all gotta be here anyway."

"Gee, that would really be great, Paul."

Derek and Sally had come up behind me, and when they heard what Paul had said they came squealing and giggling into the room. "Cartoons, mister?" Derek shouted. "Yippee! A party. Yippee!" I tried to quiet them as Derek climbed onto Paul's lap. He lost his balance and started to topple, but Paul grabbed him quickly.

"Careful, buddy," he said gently, steadying the boy on his knee. Derek was pretty wobbly and his eyes had rolled strangely. Paul looked concerned as he soothed and hugged, whispering plans for the party. Derek finally seemed to settle down, resting his head on Paul's chest. Quietly, he asked, "Promise, mister?" Paul gave him a tight squeeze.

By this time, Sally, who was feeling ignored, tried to climb up on Paul, too. He bent down and with one sweep of his arm lifted her onto his other knee. She perched there, a pale princess, as she prissily smoothed the wrinkles out of her light-blue bathrobe. Then she leaned back, head on Paul's shoulder, eyes half closed, smiling.

They watched TV, all three of them, sitting next to Jamie for over a half hour before Paul said, "Okay, you kids. You're gettin' heavy." He slid them carefully off his lap and onto their feet. "Have to check Kerri again," he told Jamie as he stood to leave. Then he ruffled the boy's blond hair and said, "Keep countin' the days. We've got a date for a party."

Jamie waved his left hand and smiled. "Thanks a lot, Paul."

"Me too, me too," Sally said, walking alongside Paul.

"Right, mister," Derek cheered, tearing ahead of us.

I tucked Derek and Sally into bed, then went out to the desk to write my charts. When the shift was over, I felt better than I had for weeks. I had worked like mad, my feet and back ached from lifting the kids and running around, but I felt as though I had done real nursing for the first time since I had come to Pediatrics.

As I left, I stopped in to say good night to Paul. He was sitting in the dark, rocking Kerri. He smiled and thanked me for my help.

Weeks later, when I was doing clinic in the Emergency Room, I took a break and went upstairs to Peds to find out what had happened to the kids.

Pat was on. She told me that Derek and Jamie were still there; that Tammie and Sally had just gone home. That Kerri had died on Christmas Eve . . . and that Paul had come in Christmas Day, dressed as Santa, to give the kids a party.

CHAPTER 6

On graduation day I was the happiest person in the entire world. Shawn came up the night before, and as soon as I saw him, I knew he would always be very special; that I could never love anyone the way I loved him. He looked so proud when Mrs. Smith placed the starched white-winged cap on my head that for the first time in months I felt that the kids and I belonged. We were a family again.

The only rain cloud in my otherwise sunny day was that Lil and I wouldn't be together as much. Shawn and my parents snapped pictures of Lil and me holding our candles, arms around each other, and I knew by the empty feeling in the pit of my stomach how much I was going to miss her. She had gotten a job in a nursing home, and Joel had set up an interview for me at Elmwood General Hospital with the directress of nursing. Because of my marks and my previous experience, I was sure I would be hired.

Mother looked very relaxed, relieved that Shawn and I would have a place of our own soon. My father always preened at my accomplishments.

During our celebration dinner, Shawn told us that he had graduated with honors and that several interviews at the local defense plants had already been set up for him. I was certain he wouldn't have any trouble getting a job; he never did.

It was the best of all possible worlds for me–until we got into bed. Shawn had complained the night before that he was tired from traveling and I had accepted it, but as we made love again I realized that something was missing for me. In the months we had been separated, I'd gotten used to Joel's sensuality, his easy attitude. We had fun. With Shawn, sex felt sneaky. I found myself irritated that Shawn, whom I was married to, treated our lovemaking as something to be hidden, while Joel, whom I wasn't married to, treated sex as though it was good and right. I told myself to give it time . . . and tried to spin more straw.

The first week Shawn was home we spent every day doing something with the kids. We went out to eat, shopping to buy them shoes, and even took them to the movies. Shawn wrestled with Spinner and played house with Niki. Mother, who was fond of Shawn—probably because he was brave enough to try to take me on—cooked all his favorite meals. Bribery. And my father, who was desperately trying to understand him, often called him "son" with difficulty.

The days went well, and though sex was not great, I was satisfied.

The day I was hired at Elmwood, for the Obstetrics Floor, I was so thrilled that I called Joel from the hospital lobby to thank him.

The interview had been a cinch, and Obstetrics in a community hospital would be slow enough to give me time to learn well. I would have preferred Surgery, but for my first job I was willing to take anything that offered experience.

I've never been a morning person, so getting up in time to be at work by 7 a.m. almost did me in. I survived by reminding myself that it was temporary: in a few weeks, after the orientation period, I would be working evenings. When I was introduced to the nurses on OB by the directress who had hired me, I smiled and tried to appear pleasant and helpful.

Mrs. Angelo, the head nurse, was a short, middle-aged RN whose false teeth clicked as she spoke. She had a studied warmth and an overly professional manner. When she reached out to greet me, I was impressed by how cold her hand was.

"Please do not," she told me in ice-covered words, "be afraid to ask questions." She explained the day schedule and then had one of her aides show me around the floor. I felt as though I were an impostor, dressed in my white uniform, cap and shoes. As though people would automatically assume I knew what I was doing. The two nurses I had seen when I first arrived seemed to have disappeared.

During lunch, because I was uncomfortable sitting by myself in the cafeteria and no one had invited me to join them, I called home to speak to Shawn. "Framington Aviation called," he said cheerfully. "I start working the beginning of next week." Things were looking up.

Niki's sixth birthday; time for another party. Not a kid's party, an Italian-relative party. Children, the pivot of Italian culture; their being, a cause for celebration; their birthdays, a victory! For me the whole thing was a pain in the ass. I was off, but Shawn was working. I raced around all day, trying to get everything together. Mother was out for the day shopping, fortunately, and Shawn would be home by five to buy Niki's cake and help me with dinner.

I cleaned away the better part of the morning, then ironed Niki's clothes and washed her hair. By afternoon, Spinner was so cranky I threw him into his crib and closed the bedroom door to protect myself from his screams. Niki asked two hundred times, "When's my party?"

By five o'clock the spinach was soaking, the roast and potatoes were in the oven, my hair was curled and my makeup was on. Spinner was finally asleep, Niki was watching cartoons and I fixed myself a cup of tea to try to relax before the ambush.

Almost immediately, I found myself thinking about the hospital. The entire week and a half I had been working, no one had been more than polite to me. Neither of the other two nurses, Holly and Ernestine, had asked me to have lunch with her. I knew I was pulling my own weight, even though it took me longer than it should to pour medications. I lived in abject terror of making a mistake, so I even checked the dosage of the laxatives at least three times. Often, Joel and I had coffee in the Delivery Room during my lunch hour because I hated to eat alone, but other than that I hadn't seen him.

By five-thirty, I started to get nervous about Shawn. He was a half hour late, and every time I heard a car door slam I held my breath. Mother called, and I told her we were set. Except for Niki's cake, which Shawn was picking up.

At six, my father walked in the front door. I was helping Niki into her new pink party dress, being rougher than I should have been because of my worry over Shawn: he hadn't even called.

"When's Daddy coming home?" Niki asked.

"Soon," I snapped, brushing her hair so hard she whimpered.

By the time Niki and I went downstairs, my mother was home. My father had taken Spinner with him to pick up the cake. My parents had developed a complete emergency plan for any disaster.

Somehow we all got through dinner, my parents deliberately playing with Niki to take her mind off Shawn, and for once Mother was discreet enough not to ask questions.

The relatives arrived, and my father shook hands in greeting and chattered warm welcomes, covering for Shawn by saying he was working late. Mother passed around goodies and made everyone comfortable. We waited as long as we could before lighting the candles on the birthday cake, but finally did-without Shawn.

By nine o'clock everyone had left and I tried to keep Niki interested in her new toys and away from "Where's my Daddy?" But she was sulky, mad at me because I hadn't waited for Shawn.

"I know he wants to be here for my cake," she kept repeating. Then later, with quivering lip, "I want to wait up for *my daddy* . .."

Finally she fell asleep sitting up on the living-room couch. She had begged to stay dressed, and now her pink bow was tilted to the side of her sleeping head. I sat on the chair across from her, seething, and it was then I really understood that I could forgive Shawn almost anything except the pain he caused my kids. How many more nights like this would they have to go through if I stayed with Shawn? And what about *me?*

At midnight, I carried Niki upstairs and put her to bed, dressed. I didn't want to wake her up and have to answer any questions.

Then I got undressed, put on a nightgown, lay on the bed, and waited. Each time a car door slammed, I jumped up and looked out the window, just as I had for the last six years. After an hour, I dragged a chair over to the window and sat.

It was four in the morning by the time I saw Shawn stagger from the car. I didn't know whether to burst into tears of relief or into an untamed fury. But as soon as he walked into the room and I looked into his glazed green eyes, I knew he was past caring. I crawled into bed without saying a word, and in a few minutes Shawn lay down next to me. Seconds later, he was snoring. I was livid. I lay there, my stomach sick from the smell of alcohol, trying to cover my nose with the sheet, trying to fall asleep and refusing to think about what I was going to have to do. After a while I could feel the tears running down my cheeks.

In Shawn's sleep he turned and threw his arm around me. Like a pole vaulter I sprang out of bed, grabbed an encyclopedia off the shelf and hit him with it. He covered his head with his arms as the book came down again, but never said a word. For the rest of the night I slept with Niki, and by the time I woke up he was gone.

Getting through work that day was almost impossible. I kept refusing to think about what my next move would be, and for the first time since I started working I was happy that everyone ignored me. When Joel came onto the floor to make rounds, he took one look at me and dragged me into the treatment room. "What's wrong?" he asked as I stood in front of him teary-eyed. I couldn't talk for fear of falling apart. "Call me if there's anything I can do," he said, concerned. "I'll be at the office late tonight."

I nodded again and walked out ahead of him straight into a patient's room. Since I had been nursing I had found it easier to keep myself together when I was doing something for someone else. I took a lot of blood pressures that day and gave a lot of bed baths. As long as the patients talked to me, I didn't feel so lonely.

Shawn came home at exactly four o'clock, and the first thing he did was apologize to Niki for missing her party. He told her he had to work late and couldn't find a phone. She hugged him and with old-lady practicality said, "I'm happy you came home tonight, Daddy." Just by the way she looked, I could tell how crazy she was about him, and my heart sank. Shawn walked toward me slowly and hesitantly planted a kiss on my forehead. He started to explain, but I told him, "We'll talk later." I couldn't discuss anything while Spinner was playing London Bridge through Shawn's legs and Niki was gazing up at him adoringly. Shawn reached down, picked the baby up, threw him into the air and kissed him as he caught him.

I wanted to pulverize him again. How could he keep doing this to us? Mother and Dad steered clear of any confrontation at dinner but were cooler than usual. Shawn bathed both children and put them to bed while I tried to decide what I was going to say to him.

That night, with the glow from the moonlight illuminating Shawn's perfect profile, I lay in bed not knowing where to begin. I could see his green eyes glisten as he stared at the ceiling, and his cheeks looked wet. "What's wrong?" I asked him softly, "I mean, what's really wrong?"

"I'm tired of all the pain," he whispered. "The pain I'm in, and the pain I cause. And I'm tired of all the fighting."

It frightened me to hear him talk like that. He sounded whipped, beaten, more than depressed. Despondent. As though what he really was saying was that he was tired of living. He was twenty-eight years old and already too tired? It was the first time I could get outside myself far enough to feel bad for him. I knew so little about him. He allowed so little intimacy, and yet I had the feeling he was unbearably lonely . . . and I knew I couldn't help him anymore. I reached over and touched his arm as I would a frightened child or a sick patient, but even then I knew I really hadn't forgiven him for the things he had done. That I never could, not while I needed him at all.

"Why do you stay married to me, Teri?" he whispered, still not looking at me.

"Because of the kids," I answered, believing it was true. What I really should have said, if I had known, was: *Because I loved you first and that always counts for something. And maybe I still love you. Because whatever you do, I'm not sure it isn't my fault. Because I'm afraid for the children; and of the children. Because my mother and father may croak if we split again. Because I'm afraid to be alone and you're better than no one. What if no one will ever love me even as much as you do? And because as silly as it sounds, divorce is against my religion, which isn't as important as that it's against my principles to give up on anyone. And most of all because, though it looks like you're the one making a mess of this whole thing, I feel I'm the one who's failed.*

"Just because of the kids?" Shawn asked softly.

"Yes," I answered.

THE NURSE'S STORY   87

For the next week, I was wretched. Shawn and I went to work, were civil to each other, talked politely to my parents and played with the kids. When we slept, we squeezed onto opposite sides of the bed, not wanting any physical contact.

I had urged counseling several times before to give our marriage a better shot, but Shawn had always refused. Now he decided he would be willing to see a psychiatrist, so I suggested Dr. Davidson. When he made the appointment for Friday, only two days away, I knew how desperate he was; I also knew how afraid he was.

Friday morning I woke up in better spirits than I had been in for days. With relief in sight, I kissed Shawn goodbye and wished him luck before I left for work.

That day, OB was very busy with several new deliveries. Mrs. Angelo was off, and with her gone, Holly and Ernestine were friendlier. I assumed it was because I was a fast and careful worker and they appreciated my help. When, over coffee, I finally expressed my relief to Holly, she straightened me right out in a burst of candor.

"Oh, it's not that," she said, surprised. "It's that Mrs. Angelo and Mrs. Jansen are friends." She looked apologetic and embarrassed as she added, "Everyone knows about you and the doctor."

"Knows what?" I asked, more outraged than if I were innocent.

Holly tripped over the chair as she flew from the nursing station. "I thought you knew. . . ."

During lunch break, I went downstairs to call Shawn. The phone rang and rang, but no one answered. Maybe he's still at Dr. Davidson's, I thought. But I was nervous.

That afternoon it took all the restraint I had to keep me from the phone booth. The few times I tried to call, there was no answer. By the time I got off work I was frantic.

Shawn usually picked me up, but even before I walked out to the parking lot I knew he wouldn't be there. I ran the half mile home.

There, in the kitchen, on the table, was a note scrawled in black pen.

Dear Teri,
You and the kids can do better than a bastard like me.
I'm sorry.

Love,
Shawn

I read it numbly, knowing this was how it had to be, glad I hadn't had to do it . . . and then I thought about Niki. Spinner was too young to really know his father, and anyway he had always been my father's boy, but Niki was different. With her, no one could ever replace her father.

I told my parents after dinner. They were solemn but accepting. Later, as I tucked Niki into bed, she asked quietly, "Isn't Daddy coming back?"

"I don't think so," I told her as I hugged her tight. She didn't say anything.

Then, during the night, she called out to me that she felt sick, and we just made it to the bathroom before she vomited. I slept with her, but it didn't seem to help, and by the time I woke her in the morning she was still too sick to eat.

During the weekend I wandered around the house in slow motion, doing mindless tasks. I couldn't get my mind unfogged enough to think, and even the kids' voices seemed to be very far away. I called Lil, but her father said she was double-shifting and couldn't get back to me before Monday. When I called Joel, his service answered, so I hung up. Then I called Dr. Davidson to explain why Shawn hadn't kept his appointment.

"If I can ever be of help to you, please don't hesitate to call," he said in a voice so kind I wanted to cry. But I wasn't ready to talk to anyone yet.

By Sunday afternoon I was dry-eyed and determined. When the phone rang and my father came upstairs to tell me to pick it up, I was shocked to hear Shawn's voice. Usually, when Shawn disappeared, I had to track him down like an Indian scout.

"Teri . . . honey?" he said, in a very shaky voice. "I don't know what got into me. I'll go to Dr. Davidson this time, if you'll give me another chance."

I held the phone tight as the tears rolled down my cheeks, but I couldn't answer. Struggling, he said, "I can't think of life without you and the kids. I know there's something wrong with me. Help me, honey . . . please?"

I was shaking my head before any sound would come. Then I heard myself whisper, "No, Shawn. Not ever again." He was still pleading as I put the receiver down.

Then I fell apart. Broke down. I cried hysterically, holding my hand over my mouth to try to stifle the sobs, and then in sheer frustration I screamed. I heard the crack of my father's hand on my face before I felt it.

"Stop it, baby, stop crying," he repeated over and over. Then his arms were around me and he was stroking my hair as he soothed, "Shh . . . shh . . . You'll be fine . . ."

CHAPTER 7

The following week I started the evening shift, 3 to 11 p.m. A nurse and an aide were sitting at the L-shaped desk reading charts as I walked onto the floor. The nurse was Mrs. Wilson, a tall, skinny black woman. The aide, who wore a pink uniform and had long red kinky hair, told me her name was Joann. She was young and very pretty.

The evening schedule was less harried than the day. There was only one meal to serve, visitors left early, and most of the scut work like transporting blood specimens to lab and patients to X-ray was already done. There seemed much more time to talk to and care for the patients.

After Wilson and I made rounds, checking to make sure that each of the patients was in good shape, no bleeding or pain, she put me on the medication cart for the night. She warned me to check the doctors' orders very carefully because each had his own special protocol. "They act like prima donnas if we get them mixed up," she said dryly.

When Wilson scheduled me and Joann for dinner together I was surprised. It would be the first time I had eaten with anyone since I had started working. I couldn't figure out why Wilson acted differently toward me than the other nurses had.

Later, I heard her fighting with the Delivery Room nurse, Mrs. Thomas, saying, "What's it my business as long as she does her work?" They looked uncomfortable as I walked up to ask Wilson a question.

When Joel arrived to make rounds on his patients, I noticed that he spoke more professionally to Mrs. Wilson than he had spoken to the others. And she was cool but polite to him. In contrast, Mrs. Thomas, a heavy lady with scant brown hair, practically cooed when she greeted him.

Wilson and I were sitting together at the desk. "Just what that man needs," she grumbled, "another mother."

"Don't you like him?" I asked, wondering if she believed the same about Joel and me as the others.

She looked sideways at me, large dark eyes intent, and said, "That man has a job to do, and I have one. 'Like' has nothing to do with it." Then she stood, her gangling body resting on her arms as she leaned on the desk. She bit her full bottom lip with her wide teeth and added quietly, "We'll do fine, you and me, as long as you do your work and expect no special treatment." There it was, right out front. I was much more comfortable with her.

When Joel came out of the Delivery Room and tried to talk to me, I didn't want to alienate Wilson, so I told him I'd meet him after work at the office. He looked puzzled but agreed.

Later, Wilson called me into a patient's room.

"Feel this," she ordered, and placed the palm of my hand on a still-unconscious woman's lower abdomen. "The top of the uterus," she instructed, "is called the fundus. Can you feel it?" When I shook my head, she put her hand over mine and pushed down harder. The woman moaned but didn't wake up.

"Yes," I answered, "I can feel it now."

"Okay," she told me as I followed her to the desk. "Don't let any of these women bleed to death. Keep checking their funduses and don't forget to look under their buttocks. Remember, any heavy bleeding will pool underneath them, so you won't be able to see it unless you turn them over. Do you understand? Again, I have to repeat, it only takes minutes for a woman with a boggy uterus to hemorrhage and go into shock. So if you feel a soft fundus, massage

hard under the navel until it firms up and you feel a definite lump."
She grabbed her pocketbook from under the desk as she said,
"I'll only be downstairs for a half hour. If you have any trouble, ring
the cafeteria."
I remembered everything Wilson told me—until the elevator
doors closed. Then I forgot. I went into the medication room to start
to pour my pills but had to keep bouncing out to see if any of the
patients' buzzers were on. Joann was flitting from room to room
fixing beds and giving back rubs.

After taking forever to dispense my medications, I went to the
end of the hall to check our two new postpartum patients. The
shades were drawn in the clean pink room so that the patients could
rest. I walked over to the bed closest to the window. There a young
blond girl, not yet fully awake, was mumbling something unintelli-
gible. Her hair was stringy from sweat and labor, but even without
makeup she was a knockout. I checked between her legs with a
flashlight, trying not to disturb her, then I took her blood pressure to
make sure there was not internal bleeding. I gently washed her face
with a damp washcloth and wet her cracked lips with a piece of iced
gauze before I moved on to the other patient.

She was a middle-aged black woman who seemed much more
awake. "May I get out of bed to go to the bathroom?" she asked,
her voice still thick from the anesthesia. Groggily she tried to lift
herself to a sitting position.

"Not yet, I don't think so," I said, smiling. She fell back and lay
down. I lowered the chrome bed rail, pulled back the crisp clean
sheet and searched for her fundus. Right, I thought, as I jammed my
palm into her soft belly; just like a hard rubber ball. Her eyes were
closed as I took my flashlight to check her bleeding. In the shadows,
between her legs, spread what looked like a bloody hunk of meat or
liver, only it had several long fingers. I quickly pulled up the sheet
without touching or moving the thing. Frantically, I looked over my
shoulder to see if Joann or Wilson was around. Nothing. I was
grateful the woman's eyes had been closed so she couldn't see the
horror and confusion on my face. Maybe it's extra afterbirth, I
thought, but deep in my heart I was certain it was some terrible
congenital monster . . . the unformed twin of the child she had just
delivered.

I wanted to run to the phone and page Wilson, but I was afraid the woman would wake up again and look between her legs, would see what I had seen. I thought about picking it up with my fingers and plopping it into a paper bag, sneaking it away while the woman slept. But what if the thing was attached to her and I pulled it away? Like an uncorked bottle, she'd probably bleed to death.

I was nailed to the floor by my panic, so I didn't hear Wilson come up behind me. When she touched my shoulder, I leaped into the air. Then, as I held my breath, I pulled back the sheet carefully to show her what I had found. She frowned and looked at me quizzically. I pointed nervously to the grotesque object, not daring to say a word, not daring to touch it.

Wilson tried to look serious, but her eyes sparkled with amusement as she lifted the thing up. "Sorry," she said, "I forgot to tell you. We ran out of icebags, so I filled one of the brown surgical gloves with cubes and put it on her stitches to try to reduce the swelling."

Both of us laughed as we walked back to the desk.

By the time I gave out my sleeping pills, the shift was over. I thanked Mrs. Wilson, and for the first time since I had started working at Elmwood I didn't dread coming back.

Joel opened the office door, and before I had a chance to say anything he pulled me to him and kissed me. Classical music was playing in the background and all the lights were dimmed.

I pulled away and said, "I have to talk to you."

He rubbed his hand across his face and walked toward his desk. Then he sat down, lit a cigarette and took a long deliberate drag. "What's the problem?" he asked, annoyed.

I was surprised by his attitude. "Joel," I started, "Mrs. Thomas was giving Wilson a hard time about us." When he didn't react, I told him what Holly had said.

There was a long silence as Joel got up to make us coffee. He put mine in front of me and, without looking up, said, "I guess it's time to straighten something out." There was nothing soft or warm about him now. "Catherine and I have been married over twenty years," he said in a voice that made this sound like a prepared speech. "We were together when we didn't have a pot to piss in or a window to throw it out of. She worked to help me through medical school and I would never leave her."

"Do you love her?" I asked. This was the first time he had ever spoken about his wife. He had never offered, and I had always been too afraid to ask.

"I'm not sure I've ever been in love. I don't even know if I'm capable of it," he said softly, pensively. "But Catherine and I have been together for a long time, long enough, in fact, for her to prefer watching TV to talking to me." He had slumped slightly and leaned on the back of his chair. "I don't want you to misunderstand," he added. "Catherine is a good woman . . ."

"What about us, Joel?" I asked. "And what will happen if she finds out?"

He sat, leaning forward to speak. "I've fooled around before, and I will again," he said, almost apologetically. "It's my nature. But I enjoy being with you. You're pretty, bright, and you make me laugh." He reached over and touched my hand. "And I enjoy making love to you." He lit another cigarette and handed it to me. "Teaching you is fun because you learn so quickly, and the other things we share Catherine doesn't want from me."

I liked him better for not saying anything unkind about his wife and felt I understood him better now. Still, we hadn't settled the situation at work. "Joel," I asked hesitantly, "what should we do about the hospital?"

"Teri, we'll be as discreet as possible. But my private life is my business. You'll have to handle it as best you can. I've admitted nothing; I'll deny nothing. You can do as you wish."

What I wished, more than anything else, was that I could have my own goddam Prince and live happily ever after; without having to handle the guilt over hurting another person for my needs and without having to handle the judgment of other people. But I was giving to the kids at home; giving to the patients at work; compromising my own values in order to live in my parents' home, and feeling terribly depleted. Joel was the only part of my life that was for me. And I still needed someone. Someone who would hug me, talk to me, and care about me. I wouldn't need it forever; just for long enough to stop my hurting over Shawn; just for long enough to get strong enough to learn to believe in me.

By the time I had been working OB six months, I had learned a lot. Now it took me only one razor and five gauze pads to do a prep or a shave. I could give an enema blindfolded, and I recognized a boggy uterus with one feel. I was a whiz at bed fixing and back care. So Mrs. Angelo decided to start training me for the Delivery Room so that I could cover for the regular nurses when they were off.

Mrs. Wilson looked resigned when she told me to report to Mrs. Thomas in Delivery. "One of Dr. Jansen's patients and two of Dr. Young's are in labor. They think this is a good time to start you," she said.

As I walked through the heavy doors, I had a picture of myself holding my nose and jumping into some very cold water.

Mrs. Thomas, running around as though there was a fire, barely acknowledged me. I could hear women crying. I really don't want to be here, I said to myself.

With a wave of her hand, Mrs. Thomas ushered me into the doctors' lounge so I could change into Delivery Room greens. Then she handed me a chart and a piece of graph paper. "Can you time contractions?" she asked, looking as though she smelled something awful.

"I believe I can," I answered, as politely as I could.

"And would it be too much to ask you to take a fetal heartbeat?"

"I can manage that too," I answered civilly.

"I don't suppose you do rectals?"

"No," I said, less politely.

"Well, how are you going to know how far she's dilated?" she snapped.

"By asking you," I said pleasantly. She was infuriated that she had been put in the position of having to teach me; I wasn't happy about it myself. And in the meantime, unknowing, three women were going to have babies anyway.

"You better take Dr. Jansen's," she said. "He'll be more understanding when you make mistakes." Not *if*, mind you, but *when*. "The girl has had her enema, but she still needs to be prepped," Mrs. Thomas added, throwing open the closet door to display soap, razors, gauze and towels.

I walked into Labor Room No. 1, a white-tiled cubicle large enough to hold one metal stretcher-bed and one metal chair. Lisa Monroe, Dr. Jansen's patient, was sitting up in bed chewing her nails. She had long dark hair, shiny and obviously clean, which fell to her shoulders and practically covered her small, little-girl face. Her enormous brown eyes were half filled with tears as she asked me, "What are you going to do to me now?"

I guessed her to be about sixteen, but the age written in on the chart I was holding read eighteen. She's the same age I was when I had my first baby, I thought, smiling to reassure her. "I just have to shave your bottom. It's a little unnerving, but I won't hurt you." I introduced myself and asked her to lie down as I placed a Chux under her butt. I had to walk out a few times to get warm water and some towels, but finally we were set. As I started to prep her, I asked, "Are you happy about having a baby?"

"That's a funny question to ask me now," Lisa said, laughing.

"Why? Lots of girls have very mixed feelings about it." I looked up at her, smiled and admitted, "I know I did."

"Really?" she said, surprised. Then she hoisted herself up on her elbows to see what I was doing. "Ugh!" she said. "I'd hate to have to do *that* for a living."

I smiled again and said, "See what I mean about feelings? People are different. I don't mind this at all."

"Weird," she said, and then stiffened as a contraction hit. I glanced at my watch to time it.

"Let me know when it passes," I said, standing up to give my back a rest until her pain passed.

She nodded and then threw her arm over her head until she could talk again. "Whew!" she whispered, teary-eyed. "They're getting worse. Can I have something for pain?"

"Sure," I told her. "I'm almost finished."

Mrs. Thomas peeked in long enough to tell me, "The doctor ordered some Demerol, Scope and Lorfan, when you're finished with her." She didn't say a word to Lisa, as though she didn't exist.

As I was cleaning up, Lisa answered my question. "I'm really happy about this baby," she said. "You see, I spend so much time by myself; I'm looking forward to the company."

"And your husband?" I asked her. "How does he feel?"

She shrugged. "Well, he doesn't care one way or another, as long as I'm okay."

I excused myself to get Lisa's medicine, and returned just as another contraction began. She bit her lip as I placed my fingertips on her abdomen to time it. I watched her stomach start to rise like a wave and I felt it get harder as the pain increased. Then as her abdomen relaxed again it got softer and the pain diminished until it was gone. Though strong, her contractions were still pretty far apart. I took Lisa's blood pressure and timed a few more contractions before I asked her to turn over so I could give her a shot. "Now I can sleep until it's over?" she asked, like a trusting child.

"I hope so," I answered, "but if not, don't worry, I'm sure your doctor will order something more."

As soon as Lisa started to doze, Mrs. Thomas did a vaginal exam on her. "Only two centimeters," she said, annoyed. "She's got a long way to go." I knew that nurses were not allowed to do vaginals then, but I was afraid to say anything for fear Mrs. Thomas would chop my head off. I thought about asking Joel, but then realized that part of the problem I had with the other nurses was that they thought I would act as a spy. I decided not to make waves until I knew what the accepted practice was in this particular area.

I pulled the chair next to the bed and held Lisa's hand through the bars. When the next contraction hit, she tossed and turned but didn't cry out or moan. I felt better.

As I sat watching her I kept thinking how much like her I had been when I had Niki. I wondered what her husband was like; what her marriage was like. Then I wondered if the script was the same for all of us. It seemed so long ago to me now, when I had my first baby. . . .

I was going to be somebody's mother . . . I was never going to have to be lonely again. I would have someone to hang out with and something to do all day while Shawn was gone. I was sure that becoming a mother, the sheer process, would make *me* into a mature adult.

I read everything I could get my hands on about fetal development and could visualize every stage. I started to speak to "it," quietly, of course, so no one would think I was nuts, and spent a lot of time each day looking at my naked belly in the full-length mirror on the back of the bedroom door. I felt healthy, and only a few times did I even get nauseated.

When I started to show, I was proud of how my body looked. Every afternoon as I watched my soap operas I'd lie on the couch patting my newly swollen belly. God! I felt terrific, growing another real person—a new person who couldn't exist if it weren't for me.

I had a sense, then, of being complete, being essential, that I was never to know again until the first time I jumped on a dying man's chest and helped bring him back to life without brain damage; or the first time I helped a patient die without pain, without panic. There has been nothing else in my life, not love, marriage or any accomplishment, that has ever made me feel whole in that way. Except nursing.

Not until I landed in the Labor Room of the naval-base hospital did it finally penetrate my plaster brain that this was *for real,* that there was no turning back, and the realization shattered what little control I had. "I'm only eighteen," I sobbed. "I shouldn't be having a baby."

I lay there on the stretcher in the half-lit room and concentrated on the deep scratches in the walls. *Sound-proofing.* . . so the screams can't be heard, I thought, and *scratches* from some poor woman's nails as she tried to escape this cage. I held on to my scapulas and started some Hail Marys. The nurse came in after a few minutes and held a cup with two little red pills out to me. "Lover boy disappeared," she announced matter-of-factly as she turned to pour some water into a paper cup.

I stopped thinking about Shawn as the medication started to work and thought, Oh, good, I'll be able to sleep now.

I was in a thick fog when a young girl, also dressed in white, came in, sat next to me and started talking softly. I could hear somebody scream, again and again—bloodcurdling screams of panic and pain. I thought it was a young girl in the next room. Someone held me by the shoulders, shook me and cut through the fog to shout, "Stop!" at me.

"That's *me* screaming?" I asked, surprised. The young girl nodded. I tried to lie quietly, but at the end of every Hail Mary, when the pain got really strong, I'd scream, "Damn it to hell." She'd push me down in bed and I'd try to be quiet again.

The rest I saw through a tunnel, as though it were happening to someone else. The bright fluorescent lights, the nurses and doctors in green, the sound of a suction machine, the straps across my thighs and wrists and then hearing Dr. Gayer again, "Watch her, she's trying to knock the baby off her chest with her chin." The fast ride down the corridor and the feel of the cold sheets, then nothing.

I woke to rough towels on my skin as a pretty young nurse washed me. "I'll give you a quarter to use softener in those towels," I said, thinking I was making sense. She laughed. Every now and then I broke through the fog and asked, "Did I have my baby? How is it?"

The nurse smiled and said, "Yes and she's the prettiest baby in the nursery." Then I knew it was a girl.

"Let me see her?" I asked.

When she brought the baby over, I was shocked. The kid looked like a stranger; like nobody I knew. I had expected to recognize her. "I'm sorry," I said, "I think you brought me the wrong baby. I think this baby's mother is Korean." The baby had a haystack of black hair and slanty eyes, and this *was* a naval hospital . . .

The nurse looked at me curiously and just smiled as she said, "She's yours."

I unwrapped the baby slowly. Her face was pretty for a Korean kid whom I didn't know: little nose, full cheeks and what looked like a saber mark over one of them ("Forceps," the nurse explained), but her body was funny. Short with skinny legs and arms, big hands and feet, and hair hanging off each shoulder.

"Lanugo," the nurse explained. "Happens on preemie babies. Babies who are born a bit early haven't had a chance to shed it yet."

"You sure this baby is mine?" I asked again, wondering why I didn't feel that warm flush known as maternal instinct. In fact, I was a little afraid of this baby. What if she didn't recognize *me?* Somehow, I thought we'd know each other instantly. I stuck my finger into her mouth to be sure she didn't have a cleft palate, God only knows why, and she started to choke. The nurse grabbed her away from me and shot me a glance that could have pierced my heart. I was too tired to explain.

The next time I opened my eyes, I saw at the foot of my bed a man who looked like a tall skinny Groucho Marx in an officer's uniform. I rubbed my eyes and pulled my ponytail out from behind my head. Then I pushed myself up onto my elbows to stare at him.

"Who are you?" I asked, afraid he might be a dream.

"I'm Colonel Roper," he said, "the doctor who runs this hospital." He looked down at his folded hands. "I'm here to apologize."

"For what?"

Without a word, he handed me a small mirror. I had cuts on my forehead and a large blue bruise on my cheek, and my lips were badly swollen. He reached over and pulled up one of the long sleeves on the white hospital gown I was wearing to show me several bites on my arm. And when he lowered the sheets I saw long ragged scratches on both my legs. I looked like a war veteran just back from active duty.

"My God! What happened to me?" I forgot all about my sore bottom.

"We gave you too much Scopolamine," he answered, and explained, "It's a drug used to produce amnesia, to help women forget the pain of labor." He shook his head and continued, "You, unfortunately, had an adverse reaction. It happens."

I pulled my sleeve up again to look at the bites. They were familiar impressions, exactly like the bites I had made in juicy red apples as a little kid. "*I* did this? I did this to myself?"

He smiled slightly and nodded. "And that, my dear, is nothing compared to what you did to the nurse."

Though he said it gently, without judgment, and even smiled to reassure me, I was mortified. I was also afraid to ask which nurse.

"And the scratches on my legs?" I asked. "I did those too?"

It was incomprehensible to me that so much time had passed that I had no recollection of. First I was frightened, then I felt robbed. Anything could have happened during that period. I could have done anything, but, more important, the thought that others knew things about me that I didn't—that I could never remember no matter how hard I tried—was scarier than any feeling I had ever had.

They could accuse me of anything and I could never defend myself. Because I had no perceptions, I had to accept theirs. It made me feel crazy.

Throughout my nursing career, the knowledge of how fearsome that feeling was made me explain to all my patients, in great detail, everything that they did or had done to them while they were receiving medication that could alter or block out perceptions. I tried to give them back some of the control they had been forced to forfeit. On an even more expansive level, it helped me understand the fear of any of my psychotic patients.

After the colonel reassured me again that it was his fault and not mine, he left. I lay in bed a long time trying to shake the feeling of fear; the feeling of being totally alone. . . .

Lisa brought me back to the present by sitting upright just as Joel walked into the room. I was getting a terrible headache.

"Hi," he said to me, and to Lisa, "Lie down, dear, so I can examine you." She didn't understand through her medicated fog, so he pushed her down by the shoulders and instructed me to hold her as he prepared to do another vaginal.

He struggled to get into his sterile gloves without touching the outside, so as not to contaminate them. "Squeeze some Phisohex on my glove," he told me. "We use that here instead of lubricant." I held Lisa as she squirmed. Joel fished around till he was satisfied. "Six centimeters," he said, and I understood that to mean that she was progressing well. I was amazed that when he examined her most of his forearm was thrust into her vagina. Joel turned to me and instructed, "She's in active labor. I want the fetal heart tones monitored every five minutes, and I want to know if anything changes rapidly."

Lisa was still lying down, but she was much more restless than before. Every few minutes I placed the large bell-shaped fetoscope onto her rocklike abdomen and listened to her baby's heartbeat. It was regular. Her contractions started coming much faster after a while, between two and three minutes apart, and they lasted longer. She cried out when her membranes ruptured, and Joel came in to examine her again. "She's already eight centimeters," he said.

"She's moving pretty quickly." I felt as though I were sitting on a keg of dynamite, not knowing what to expect next. My head was pounding by the time I got the courage to ask, "What am I suppose to watch for now, Doctor?"

He was dressed in a green scrub suit with scrub cap. As he pushed it back off his forehead he smiled, but it was the smile of a stranger. "She should progress to full dilation from here, relatively quickly. She may have some nausea, she may even vomit. That's perfectly normal."

At that point, Lisa let out a loud cry. "Can't we give her any more medicine?" I asked Joel. Every time she thrashed and screamed I got more nervous and upset.

"She's had enough for now. She won't remember any of this anyway," he said as he patted her hand and shushed her quiet. "She'll start to feel some rectal pressure soon. When she starts bearing down, call me." As he left the room he reminded me, "Keep checking the fetal heart for any change."

I nodded my head; it hurt. I understood more now that Joel had explained but was still nervous about what could happen that I didn't expect. Also, knowing she couldn't remember the pain didn't make me feel better. She was still having it.

I sat for another hour, watching her like a hawk, taking blood pressure and fetal heartbeats almost constantly. My head was pounding and my back was breaking from leaning over the bed. Lisa was thrashing around and whining except when she had a contraction; then, she screamed. I wondered how long this could go on. Joel came in and examined her again. "She's fully dilated," he said. "Give her some more medicine."

I ran out of the room, glad for the break, and it was then I realized that no one had told me to go for supper. It was almost ten o'clock. In another hour, thank God, I'd be going home. But wasn't there anything I could do in the meantime to help Lisa get rid of that trapped animal look in her eyes?

When I came back to give her a shot, Joel left quickly. I had just pulled my chair over to the side of the bed again when Lisa started to grunt and bear down with more force than before. As I looked between her legs, her vagina opened and I caught a glimpse of something black. As the pain receded, so did the black thing. Could that be the baby's head? I went to the doorway and gasped, "Dr. Jansen."

He came right away and when Lisa started to bear down again he saw what I had seen and hollered, "Thomas, the stretcher. *Caput!*"

She hollered back, "I'm busy now, Doctor."

He ran out to get the stretcher himself, and when he came back with it he said, "Help me move her over, quickly." Lisa was flailing and dazed from the medication, so we had to keep shouting at her, but finally we pulled her onto the stretcher and Joel rolled her full speed into the Delivery Room.

He called for the nurse anesthesiologist and then asked me and Thomas, who had entered the Delivery Room, to wash her down and drape her. With a lot more shouting we helped her slide onto the table, and then Thomas and I together lifted her legs at the same time and slid them into the stirrups. Thomas told me to wash Lisa's perineal area while Joel was scrubbing, and she would apply the hand grips and the wrist restraints. All of this was being done at a speed faster than anything I had ever seen except during a cardiac arrest. By the time I began scrubbing Lisa's bottom with Betadine, I was practically blind from my headache and tension. Every time she had a contraction now, that black hairy thing, which I found out was the top of the baby's head, kept showing. I was afraid the baby was going to pop right out and I was going to blind it with detergent.

After we put green drapes over all of Lisa's body except her bottom, Joel pulled a round stainless-steel stool between her legs and sat down. "Bear down one more time, Lisa," Joel shouted, "and then we'll put you out." The anesthesiologist held the mask just above her face. She began to push hard, and as soon as Caput appeared Joel nodded toward the top of the table, and the anesthesiologist placed the mask over Lisa's nose and mouth. The black thing receded again. Joel turned to Thomas and me and said, "Forceps!" Then he grabbed a scissors, placed it in the side of Lisa's vagina and cut. The crunch made my mouth water. Thomas handed me something wrapped in white cloth, partially opened, and whispered for me to hand it to Joel. He pulled the long metal object out of the wrapper as I held it, but as soon as he looked at it he screamed, "What the hell are these?" and flung them onto the floor.

Thomas was right behind me, and when she handed him the right forceps he thanked her. I didn't know whether to cry or scream. My head was really pounding, my heart was racing, and all I wanted to do was run. By the time I looked up again, Joel had the metal clamp around the baby's head, pulling it out, the forceps biting into the baby's cheeks. Pulling with both arms, he turned the head slightly and freed the shoulders. The rest of the baby practically flew out. I held my breath. A boy!

Joel held the baby by the heels. Hanging upside down, still attached to Lisa by the translucent yellow umbilical cord, it looked like a blood-streaked white rubber doll. Joel flicked the bottom of the baby's feet, but its whole body just flopped and its dangling arms swung back and forth loosely. It didn't cry. Even through the thick cheesy vernix covering I could see that the baby was cyanotic—the same bluish-gray color as Mr. Marcus after he had died.

"Suction!" Joel shouted. Mrs. Thomas handed him a small rubber aspirator, which he inserted into the baby's nostrils and mouth. I could hear the slurping of the mucus. The anesthesiologist called out the time as she watched the seconds click away on the large wall clock.

"Come on, you little bastard, breathe!" Joel said as he slapped the baby's butt, hard. Nothing. On the next slap there was a noise like air being let out of the stretched end of a balloon. And on Joel's third slap the baby let out a loud cry of indignation and instantly pinked up.

Joel stood up, clamped the cord, and placed the baby across Lisa's draped abdomen. Then the anesthesiologist took over the baby's care and Joel sat again to stitch Lisa's episiotomy.

It amazed me for years after that before a baby takes his first breath he's the exact same color as a man after he takes his last. I know the explanation physiologically, but I haven't really been able to figure out whether that means a man comes full circle from birth to death, or half circle; the other half being in the space after the last breath and before the first.

After Mrs. Thomas showed me how to clean the baby and put silver nitrate into his eyes, we put an identification bracelet on his ankle. Then together we checked it three times against the bracelet on Lisa's arm. When Mrs. Thomas placed the baby's foot on the inkpad and made his footprint on his birth certificate, she also made a print of Lisa's thumb. She helped me wrap the baby and put it in a heated crib to take to the nursery.

I left the Delivery Room without looking at Joel. Deliveries were supposed to be an exhilarating experience. Most of the nurses loved them. But I was really upset. Remembering how painful the experience of childbirth had been for me made me aware I couldn't effectively handle the needs of other women in labor. I had identified so completely with Lisa that I couldn't separate my fear from hers. Instead of being calm and reassuring, all I wanted was for her to have enough medicine to take my panic away. Women in labor needed my empathy, not my sympathy. They needed my ability to understand *their* feelings.

Also, beyond my memories, there remained the fact that I hated what I saw as an archaic and barbaric procedure. Women treated like pieces of meat: knocked out, thrown on a table, hands tied, to have their babies pulled from them while their legs were up in stirrups, strapped apart, and some doctor was hacking at their bottoms. I made up my mind then that I would never work the Delivery Room again, even if it meant losing my job.

CHAPTER 8

"In the animal kingdom," my father started, and I knew I was in trouble, "when the mother bird sees that one of her fledglings is capable of flying, but refuses to leave the nest, she nudges it out."

We had finished dinner, the kids were in bed, and my mother, more silent than usual, was doing the dishes. My father and I were having a man-to-man talk, sitting in the TV room. He was slowly blowing smoke rings from his cigar as he spoke.

"You want me to move?" I asked him, shocked.

"Your mother and you have different philosophies. You have a right to bring your children up as you see fit." I was nodding, waiting for the sword of Damocles to fall, when he got up and started pacing. He looked pensive as he added, "And your mother has a right to run her house as she sees fit."

"But, Daddy," I protested, "We haven't even been fighting much lately; nothing like we use to."

"The fact remains," he said firmly, "that your children are being brought up by *your* mother—her way. We had our chance with you. Niki and Spinner are yours."

I was horrified. Didn't he know how frightened I was? Shawn had left only months ago. Niki still had stomach-aches all the time, and I couldn't cook for her the way my mother did. Besides, how could I work and watch Spinner?

"Get an apartment," my father suggested firmly, "and I'll help with the rent until you can get settled."

The details, like where I was going to live or how I was going to manage, seemed not to concern him. "You'll be fine," he assured me, as he had a million time before.

Strangely enough, I didn't get angry with him. But later, when I saw my mother, who had until that time done practically everything for me, I acted as though she had betrayed me. And when she looked guilty I said, "*You* can tell the kids."

The next day when I spoke to Lil she suggested that we live together; if we both got jobs at night, maybe my parents would still let the kids sleep at their house. Lil's own kids would remain with her father. I bypassed my father and had the deal okayed by my now repentant mother.

Lil came over early Saturday morning carrying a bundle of newspaper classified ads for unfurnished apartments.

"I circled the most promising ones," she said as we sat at my mother's kitchen table.

Mother was scooting around making the kids' breakfast, and when she called them in from the TV room to eat she insisted that Lil and I eat, too.

"Hi, Aunt Lil," Niki said softly. She didn't smile as she walked over and stood next to Lilith's chair. Lil reached over and stroked her hair. Spinner came whirling behind Niki and flung himself on Lil's lap, using her hair to pull himself high enough to kiss her smack on the lips. She giggled as he chattered like a magpie. He hadn't spoken at all until he was almost three, but when finally he did he jabbered constantly.

"I wan an Ingu mushin, an Ingu mushin, please," he said to my mother. Niki walked up to him and with pointed finger said, "English muffin."

I wanted to get started, so I gulped down my coffee and pancakes while listening to my mother scold the children. "Don't play with your food" was quickly followed by "Don't spill your juice," which was quickly followed by "Eat with your fork," which was followed by "Sit. Don't kneel at the table," which invariably was followed by my screams—at either my mother or the kids.

By the time Lil and I were out the door I couldn't wait to find an apartment. We looked all day and found nothing. The apartments were either too small, too expensive, too dirty or in the wrong school district.

Late in the afternoon we stopped at a small coffee shop to get something to eat and revise our plans. We sat in a corner booth.

"How many left?" I asked Lil as she took dainty bites of her cheese-burger. She was running her finger down the list we had made before we left home.

"That's it," she said, chewing slowly.

"You must be kidding," I said.

"The only thing left is the house your mom suggested and you said you didn't want to live that close," Lil said as she crunched on a pickle.

"Well," I said, sipping my shake, "it *is* a couple of miles away–and we can't lose anything by just looking." We had seen twenty-three apartments, and none of them right.

The house for rent was a gatekeeper's cottage, in back of a large cedar house. The landlady pointed down a long narrow driveway lined with a sentry guard of large trees.

We got back into the car and Lil drove the twisted gravel road until we found a clearing where we parked. The cottage was small, white-shingled, and looked like the houses children draw. Matchbox square with a black-and-red patched roof. Red-trimmed windows everywhere. We walked around through the screened porch on the side of the house, where we found the door.

Inside there was a living room and a tiny kitchen, too small to eat in. "We could always put a table and chairs in this corner of the living room," Lil said, pointing. The bathroom was an enlarged pink tiled closet with all-new blue fixtures. Through the door on the far wall of the living room, at the foot of the stairs, there was a boiler room which held a washer, a dryer and a laundry table. Upstairs there was a large center hall almost as big as the living room; at one end of it, a small room with eight windows; at the other end, a larger room with two windows, one looking out onto a boat-filled canal.

We signed a two-year lease before we left, and told the landlady that we planned to move in at the beginning of the month.

As soon as we got back in the car, I got cold feet. "Are you sure we're going to make it?"

"Certainly," Lil said, nodding and blinking. "What choice have you?" When I moaned, she said sweetly, in the exaggerated voice she used to make fun, "Besides, my child, it's time you moved away from the bosom of your family to pursue a life of your own." When I made a face, she said, "Think of it as an adventure."

Lil couldn't understand how I felt, because she hadn't grown up Italian. The transition from my parents' home to a separate apartment, without the vehicle of marriage, was my passage from Italian girl to liberated woman. Unheard of—a *divorced* woman, living *alone*. If it had not been for Lil's help and Joel's just being there, I could never have done it. My dependency hung like a prehensile tail.

It wasn't until I grew up that I realized what a service my father had done me. Like that fledgling, I would certainly never have voluntarily jumped to what I considered my doom.

Neither of my parents looked as thrilled as I thought they would. That night at supper Mother kept gazing at the children, teary-eyed, as she clicked her tongue, "Tsk . . . tsk . . ."

"Jesus, Ma, please cut it out," I said while we were doing the dishes. "I'm not taking them to Africa; we're moving a couple of miles away. They'll be staying over here five nights a week."

"It's just that they're such little angels," she whispered.

I almost dropped the dish I was wiping. "Ma," I said, "they are *not* little angels. In fact, sometimes they're pretty creepy."

"Don't say that," she snapped, looking as though she were going to kill me. "You're their mother!"

"What has that got to do with it?" I shouted, but still I felt guilty. She was so concerned about my not being able to take care of them, I got scared.

"Don't forget to give Niki her vitamins," she instructed. "And the vaporizer has to be run so that Spinner doesn't get bronchitis." And the list went on ad infinitum. I was getting so nervous I wanted to choke her. I didn't realize then how difficult it was for her. She was having her own separation pangs. After all, she had practically been their mother for the last two years.

During the weeks before we moved, Joel offered me money to buy furniture. I refused at first, but when he explained that he'd be using it, too, I accepted. "Besides," he insisted, "there's so much I'm not able to do for you that this will bring me pleasure."

Lil sewed curtains for all the windows, and we went shopping. We chose a green velour couch, a gold leather Danish-modern chair with wooden arms and a gold ottoman to match. I picked out walnut end tables and two white-and-gold ceramic lamps for the living room. Then we bought a convertible couch for the upstairs hall in case we decided to give each of the kids a separate room. With the money we had left, Lil and I bought a double bed. My parents gave each of the kids a single bed and a dresser. By the time my mother donated her extra towels, sheets, pots and silverware, Lil and I had a completely furnished house. And I was finally getting excited about my new life.

CHAPTER 9

Dante's Purgatory: medical surgical nursing at night. Hot fetid smells. Muffled cries. Suffering. Faded floors and walls. Too many patients and not enough staff. Darkness and the tangible sound of fear. There was no question that I was necessary here. So I took a deep breath, packed all my hopes, dreams and idealism in the strong knapsack of my needs, threw it over my shoulder, and set off across the ward to begin to *save* people.

The pace on this floor was much more frenzied than OB, and for the first few months I was a nervous wreck. The patients were all pretty sick, and each night I was responsible for at least twenty of them. Fresh postoperative patients, healing hearts and brittle diabetics filled the rooms. There were always treatments to do, dressings to change, pain medicines to give. Fortunately, the nursing assistants on the floor were helpful and competent. There were many nights, while I was learning, when they saved both me and the patients by keeping track of what I was supposed to do and reminding me.

Lil got a job on the surgical floor across the hall. It was great being with her again, and it was a really good feeling for both of us to be working with other nurses who were so happy to have our help that they were willing to teach us anything.

The kids seemed to be adjusting well, and the only thing that gave us any trouble was that five nights a week before we went to work we had to drag them over to my parents' house to put them to sleep. And every morning on the way home we had to pick them up. I enrolled Spinner in nursery school so that I could sleep during the day and taught Niki to walk to school on the days I was home. Lil and I tried to get the same days off, but she usually double-shifted the rest of the time. On the days she worked only one shift, she would come home to sleep for five hours, then race out to shop for her father and kids, visit them, give them money, and be back at the house in time to drive with me to work. She was always tired.

But the days we had off together were magic. After I cooked us breakfast, Lil would lie on the couch and read to me for hours. Everything from newspapers to Plato's *Republic*. She was fervently anti religion, telling me always, "Organized religion is a panacea for the masses." Then she would point out the damage the church did to poor people. "There are people," she would say, shaking her hand in a fury, "who are starving, and when they go to church for comfort a self-righteous priest passes around a basket they have to put their last coins in. After mass, he goes back to the rectory to eat good food while they go home and offer an empty stomach up to God."

Lil seldom raised her voice; in fact, much of what she said seemed without emotion, like flowers planted in cement. But when she spoke of religion or abortion she grew trees in very fertile soil. She was as pro-abortion as she was anti religion.

"Stop saying I'm pro-abortion," she used to say, "I happen to be pro-choice, and *your* Catholic Church doesn't allow for that kind of freedom." Everything she said made perfect sense to me . . . and all of it was against everything I had been brought up to believe.

Whenever I got Niki into her green plaid uniform, Lil would say, "I can't believe you allow your own child to be brainwashed by sending her to Catholic school." I would put my finger to my lips to silence her. On no other issue would I do that, but I was afraid Niki already felt different from the other kids because she had no father; I didn't want to alienate her more.

At work and with everyone else, Lil came across as docile as a lamb and as passive as a pussycat. She was always kind and gentle; "sharp" and "dynamic" weren't words that anyone but me would use to describe her. She was different with me. Funny, exciting to be with. I learned more from her than from anyone else.

Every weekend we were off, she would shake me awake, saying,

"Come on, get up. You're stuck in molasses and we're going to miss the day."

So Lil and I and the kids would all pile into the yellow cab and spend the day in New York visiting the Museum of Natural History or the Metropolitan Museum of Art to get "some culture." A trip like that always made me feel marvelous. While I was learning, I was also getting rid of some of the guilts I had over having to leave my kids while I worked.

The night supervisor, Mrs. O'Reilly, had been one of Joel's OB nurses. I almost groaned aloud the first night I saw her. She was a heavy middle-aged woman with snow-white hair. Pretty, but somehow sad-looking. Months passed while I tried to ignore the many times she floated me to another floor when it was someone else's turn to go; I didn't complain when she refused my requests for time off; and I even managed not to scream when I had to work three weekends in a row.

Allison McKenna, the other licensed practical nurse I worked with, made life on the unit almost fun. She was a frail blond girl, about twenty-eight, who was divorced and had a little boy. She lived at home with her parents and was taking night courses at a local college to become an RN. Every night after we checked our patients (we had fifty between us) and made the work schedules out for the two aides, we'd sit and look through her books. And in the five minutes between patient calls she'd teach me whatever she was learning. Any night it was quiet for a half hour or more, we'd look up a disease, study it, and challenge each other to see who remembered more about clinical symptoms and current treatment.

One night after I had made rounds on my side of the hall, I saw Mrs. Pact's light on. She was an elderly lady who had come down with pneumonia after having surgery to remove a cancerous lesion of her lung.

As I walked into the room and turned on the light, I could see that she had been crying.

"What's wrong, Mrs. Pact?" I asked her, sitting on the side of her bed.

"I can't sleep," she whispered. "I must need a sleeping pill."

"Now, come on," I said, smiling at her, "you're not crying

because you need a pill. You know I'd give you that in a minute."
I reached over and held her bony little hand. "Can't I help?"

"Well," she said, sniffling into the tissue I held over her nose,
"the doctor told me that my pneumonia is clearing up, but two days
ago they took another X-ray to make sure my other sickness hadn't
come back." She couldn't bring herself to say "cancer," though she
did know her tumor had been malignant. "And he promised," she
continued, her eyes filling, "that as soon as he got the report back he
would let me know what it was."

"And you haven't heard?" I asked her, my own heart sinking.
They probably would have raced right in if it was good news, I
thought, but what I said was, "Well, maybe the report just hasn't
come back yet."

Mrs. Pact nodded, but I could tell she didn't believe me.

"I'll come right back with your pill," I told her, touching her
finely wrinkled cheek.

Out at the desk, after I got Mrs. Pact's sleeping pill, I checked
the chart. Allison walked up behind me and looked over my
shoulder. "What's up?"

"Just want to see if the X-ray report on Pact is back yet," I told
her. She leafed into the yellow section of the chart past my fingers,
and there it was. We both read it silently.

I was stunned. The chest X-ray was negative: no disease. And
the date of the report was two days before.

"Well, thank God," Allison said as she plunked herself down on
one of the hard metal desk chairs.

"Those creeps," I muttered as I ran down the hall to tell Mrs.
Pact.

When I got back to the desk I told Allison, "She didn't even
swallow that pill before she was asleep, poor thing. Imagine making
her worry two whole days for nothing."

Allison shook her head. "Dr. Bruno's going to have a fit if he
ever finds out you told her," she said, making an ugly face at me.
"No diagnosis, dearie . . ."

"I didn't *tell* her her diagnosis," I said, making a face back. "I
just showed her the chart."

"Oh God!" Allison wailed as she flung herself down on the
desk.

At 4 a.m. Lil called from 3 North and asked me to come across and have coffee with her. Things were quiet on my ward, and Allison said she would call if she needed me.

Mrs. Stevens, Lil's aide, was sitting with her feet up and a blanket behind her head, but when I approached she opened her eyes long enough to greet me. Lil was hunched over her desk, busily transferring doctors' orders onto the Cardex. She never heard my approach, so when I touched her shoulder she jumped. "Jeez! When did you get so quiet?" she asked.

"You're crazy," I told her. "I practically stomped down the hall. You must have been preoccupied."

She held out the order book for me to see and said, "Look at this crazy bastard. He ordered an aspirin suppository for a patient with a colostomy."

I sat down at the desk next to her. "So, did you give it?"

"Of course I gave it," she said and then teased, "I'm not the one who refuses to follow doctors' orders." She stuck her tongue out at me. "But you should have seen how shocked I was when I tried to shove the suppository into his sewed-up rectum. The guy didn't even have a pinpoint hole left."

"I'm sure he was at least as shocked as you were," I said as I reached for the tea she had made me.

She poured herself a glass of milk and continued. "You should have seen the face he made when he had to swallow it!"

"What do you mean?" I asked, puzzled.

"Well," she said, looking sympathetic and blinking, "even though I smashed it as much as I could, it still was pretty lumpy."

"Lil, you didn't make him *eat* a suppository?"

She stopped with her glass halfway to her lips. "I did something wrong?"

"Why didn't you just put it into his stoma?" I asked. In a colostomy, a part of the intestine is brought out through a small slit in the abdomen, rolled like a doughnut and stitched down. The hole in the doughnut is called a stoma; it serves the same purpose as an anus.

"I didn't know I could do that," she said, her eyes filling with tears. "Did I hurt him?"

"No," I said, laughing now, "but if you were going to make him swallow it, why didn't you just give him an aspirin?"

"Oh," she said. She blew her nose noisily and then tucked her tissue into her sweater sleeve. "I hate nursing. I can't stand having to think, and I hate all this responsibility."

"Don't worry," I tried to reassure her. "Aspirin is only aspirin, and a suppository is only a wax base. No harm done. He probably won't even mention it." But Lilith jumped up from her seat and ran down the hall to check him, just in case.

When Lil and I walked to the car that morning, she was still devastated. She was walking more slowly than usual, looking at the pavement, as she said, "I may never be able to sleep again after what I did last night. I can't believe I'm so stupid sometimes."

"It has nothing to do with stupid, Lil," I said. "In fact, I only knew because I read it from one of Allison's books. Let's face it, there's tons of stuff we didn't learn in school. Most of what we did learn was basic theory; it hardly helped when we reached the floors. Nursing is on-the-job training, and it's impossible to know everything. There's too much and it changes too quickly."

"I hope the doctor doesn't have a fit," she said, shaking her head.

"Why?" I asked. "You figure he's never made a mistake?" She just shrugged.

"Hey, buddy," I said, putting an arm around her shoulder, "you're just human, you know. And no matter how hard you try, as long as you're human you're going to make some mistakes. In most other business, some waste is built into the budget."

"How come we never heard about mistakes in school?" she asked as we slid into her car.

"We did. They told us not to make any, the stakes are too high," I said, smiling gently. "C'mon, the premise of a perfect human being is faulty. It doesn't exist. Don't feel guilty."

She looked as though she felt a little better, though she said, "I still can't believe it. God knows what I might do next." Then, "Are you sure I didn't hurt him?"

I winked at her and whispered, "Don't be such a crazy. Forgive yourself."

As we drove away, I felt better because I had helped Lil feel better. What I didn't realize at the time was that I was able to be that objective only because it was Lil's mistake, Lil's patient. Later, I understood: guilt comes with the territory.

One night when Allison was off and I was scheduled to work the floor with a float nurse, Spinner got sick. Lil was the only nurse on her unit, so she couldn't call in, and if I called in, my unit would be impossible for one or even two float nurses to handle. Fifty-five patients you don't know means real danger.

Spinner's fever was 104 degrees, his cheeks were red hot and his little body was shaking as I wrapped him in a big quilt to take him over to my mother's. He cried the whole way over. Lil drove, and as I held him the heat from his body warmed my legs like a hot-water bottle.

"Did you give him aspirin?" Lil asked, looking worried.

"Of course," I said irritably. "And I started him on penicillin. There's really nothing more I can do."

When we got to my mother's she was waiting with the door open. She snatched him out of my arms and held him to her.

"Don't worry about him," she tried to reassure me as my father took Niki up to bed. "I'll take care of him. Remember, I brought you up."

"Thanks, Mom," I said, leaning forward to kiss her goodbye. Spinner was whimpering like a wounded puppy, and when I tried to kiss him goodbye he grabbed onto my neck and started to scream, "Mommy . . . Mommy, don't go! Don't leave me!" He hung on me as my mother tried to pull his arms from around my neck.

"Shh . . . Shh . . ." I whispered, but he wouldn't let go.

"Teri," my mother said firmly, "just go. Don't drag this out." She tore him away from me and practically pushed me out, but before she closed the door I could hear Spinner still screaming, "Mommy . . . Mommy! Please don't go. . . ."

Someone could have bludgeoned me to death that night and I would have felt less pain.

"Mrs. O'Reilly, I have to call the attending on Mr. Corona," I said through the static on the phone. "He's bleeding like mad. He's a new admission in to rule out ulcers or esophageal varices."

"No," she said. "Call the house doctor." Then she hung up.

When I rang again, she didn't answer.

I couldn't hold back any longer, so I stomped down to the nursing office, ready for war. My patient is bleeding out fresh blood into a bucket and she refuses to let me *bother* the attending doctor, his very own personal physician? No way.

She was sitting at her desk when I got to the doorway. "The house doctor isn't doing *it*," I told her furiously, "whatever *it* is. This man is forty-two years old and he's vomiting so much blood that if we don't get somebody to open him up fast there won't be anybody left to save."

She glanced up from her Cardex and said dryly, "If Dr. Laki, the house doctor, doesn't see any reason to call the attending, I don't."

"Look," I said, fuming, "it's been four hours. The iced saline isn't helping, the Levine tube is draining frank blood, bright red, and his pressure is dropping."

Mrs. O'Reilly looked down, pretending to concentrate, and then said mockingly, "Teri, the judgment you use cannot always be considered the best."

Now I was even more furious with her. I just knew by the way she had said it that she was referring to my personal life. She was trying to con me; get me off the track. She didn't want to call the attending because she was afraid he'd have a fit. She had a reputation for running interference, and most of the doctors loved her for it. My judgment wasn't bad, hers was. She was playing secretary for the big boss instead of nurse.

"My personal life is none of your business," I told her very coldly, "and you're confusing an important issue with bullshit." She looked shocked, but I went on, "This patient *is* your business, and it is your job to evaluate my *nursing* judgment. That's all I'm asking you to do. And you can't do it from this desk. So get your ass up to the ward and check that man out. Because if you don't, I'm going to call the attending myself, with or without your permission."

Mrs. O'Reilly was so mad she looked purple, but she ran up the stairs after me.

Mr. Corona was lying in a pool of blood. A torrential gush of bright red jetted from his mouth and nose, around the narrow tube that Dr. Lake had inserted to drain the blood in his stomach.

"What is this?" Mrs. O'Reilly demanded of Dr. Laki, who was

standing impotently holding a full basin of red liquid.

"I was of the opinion . . . it would stop," he said weakly.

Mr. Corona's eyes darted between us, and his stark white face was taut with panic. He kept frantically trying to sit up, but kept falling back. As I ran over to hold him and take his blood pressure, I could hear Mrs. O'Reilly in the hall, calling the attending and urgently explaining the situation.

"Get him ready for the Operating Room," she whispered when she came back. But at that point she could have shouted, because Mr. Corona's blood pressure was so low he was out cold, in shock.

His attending doctor was in and operating within a half hour. Three quarters of Mr. Corona's stomach had to be removed, but he would survive.

Mrs. O'Reilly called to thank me during morning report, and I heard a tacit apology in her voice. With Mr. Corona taken care of, I could afford to feel bad for her. She had an enormous amount of responsibility. Together, we laughed with relief, glad that the attending doctor was one of the really good ones who answered a call quickly.

On the way out of the hospital that morning, I stopped by the Recovery Room to check on my patient. I got there just as he was waking up and his doctor was explaining what he had done.

"Thanks so much, Doctor," Mr. Corona said, with still-slurred speech from the anesthesia, "for saving my life."

One night when Allison's side of the floor had so many patient call lights on that it looked like Times Square, I offered to give her patients their pain medicine.

"Thanks," she said as she sprinted down the hall again, "but most of them are on four-hour schedules and they're not due yet." Both our sides were full of post-operative patients or cancer patients.

"How far away are they?" I called after her.

"Well, most of them were medicated between three and three and a half hours ago," she answered back.

When she came back to the desk I asked her, "Why don't you call their doctors?"

"What, are you kidding?" she said. "That's a last-ditch

maneuver. Even if I could get past the supervisor. The last few times I tried, she refused and told me to talk to the patients to help the time pass for them. And tonight there's no way I can do that. Besides, most of the times I did get through to the doctors they either hollered because I woke them or sounded so sleepy they told me to give whatever I'd been giving. I'm too hassled tonight to deal with it."

"Allison," I said, grabbing her uniform to keep her from running down the hall again, "this is ridiculous. Those people aren't addicts, they're having pain. The longer we make them wait, the more afraid they're going to be. You know how fear makes pain worse. By the time they get it, it won't even help."

"Okay, smart-ass," she teased, "what do you want to do about it?"

"Let's give them their pain medicine early."

"I can't do that," she said, shaking her head. "If we get caught, I'll lose my job."

"Well, then, just chart it for the time it's due and still give it early. By the time the patients start to complain again, it will be morning and by then the doctors will be awake,"

But Allison was too afraid.

Four hours later, when the same thing happened again, Allison was close to tears. She pulled me away from the desk and into the medication room. "Half my people are crying in pain again, and it's still an hour before I can give them anything. Mr. Rigny, my terminal cancer, and Mr. Winkle, the man with all the fistulas, are in real pain. Could you do it for me?"

So I did.

Mrs. O'Reilly and I were standing at the desk discussing a patient one night when a call light went on. Almost immediately, we heard a loud thump.

"Sounds like somebody in 344 just hit the floor," I said, and we both ran down the hall.

As we flew into the room, Mr. Tallahee, a cardiac patient, was lying on the floor and thrashing like a fish. Mrs. O'Reilly switched on the light. Mr. Tallahee's face was a bloated bluish red.

From the next bed, Mr. Hein's voice quivered when he said, "I think he swallowed a sour ball."

Mrs. O'Reilly tried to hold Mr. Tallahee down as I stuck my finger toward the back of his throat to see if I could feel anything. I couldn't—it was too far back. Mr. Tallahee's eyes were beginning to roll to the top of his head and he was losing consciousness. Mrs. O'Reilly ran out to call Dr. Laki to do a tracheotomy, but as I looked at Mr. Tallahee, now quietly lying blue on the floor, I knew we didn't have time.

I was getting pretty frantic, feeling totally helpless, when I remembered one of the lessons Allison and I had learned from a nursing journal: *Always carry a wide-lumened needle in your pocket or purse. When someone is in respiratory distress and there is no time, use it. It will create a sufficient airway until the doctor arrives.* I had studied the picture showing how to insert the needle through the neck and into the trachea.

I rummaged around in my pocket under my good-luck elephant and found the needle. I had carried it every night for months, hardly remembering why.

Then I held my breath and tried to push it through the skin, but it wouldn't go. *This is no time to be chickenshit,* I hollered at myself; *push hard.* And I did. Through the tough skin and between the cartilage ridges of Mr. Tallahee's neck. Instantly there was sucking hiss, and the bluish tinge began to fade from his face. By the time I looked up, Dr. Laki and the emergency team were at the door. "Oxygen," I heard somebody say as I tried to get up and out of the way. Several large orderlies were hoisting Mr. Tallahee onto a stretcher as I left the room.

Later that night, Mrs. O'Reilly offered to have coffee with me for the first time. We went into the nurses' lounge and she thanked me for thinking so quickly that it probably saved Mr. Tallahee's life. Then she confronted me with the issues that made her uncomfortable as my supervisor. I knew she meant my telling patients their diagnosis before the doctors were willing to; and my sometimes giving drugs at shorter intervals than ordered when the patients were in extreme pain.

She started by explaining, "You're a good nurse, Daley, that's not the problem." She smiled when she admitted, "I'm even beginning to believe you're a good person." She looked down and stared into her cup. "But it's not only the business of your personal life that makes you difficult to deal with. You're headstrong–a lot for a supervisor to handle. You often make independent decisions that I have to be responsible for."

I broke in. "But how often have I been wrong?"

"That's not the point," she explained patiently, as though to a child. "So far you've been right. But what if we let every smart young nurse make independent decisions—how well will it work as an organization?"

"So what am I supposed to do?" I answered defensively. "Let the patients croak until I get an okay?"

She stiffened just a little and stared me right in the eye. "That's one alternative. The other is to go back to school and get an RN degree so you can run your own show and take your own responsibility." When she saw that I was really listening, she said firmly, "You're not going to do anybody much good if you behave in a way that gets you fired."

I could see her point. Besides, being called headstrong was not an alien experience to me. My father, mother, husband and teachers throughout school had often said the same thing. But it was the same as being five feet tall and one hundred pounds, as far as I was concerned: I didn't see how I could change it.

I promised her I would look into getting a degree, and when she left the lounge that night she seemed pleased.

CHAPTER 10

In the next year, I started to take evening courses at the local university in two subjects, anatomy and English literature, that I could eventually apply toward a degree and licensure as an RN. Lil enrolled, too: just for knowledge, not for a degree. Three nights a week we went to class and rushed back just in time to get to work. During that year Mrs. O'Reilly covered for me several times when I slipped and made a decision. She also floated me to Intensive Care on occasion to help me learn. I found it a disappointment.

"Not enough action," I told her one night while we sat in the lounge having coffee. "All everyone does is watch monitors and write on charts. The patients aren't much sicker than on the floors."

She shook her head and smiled. "You're wrong, Teri. You haven't been nursing long enough to know what an H-bomb a bad heart can be, and how much knowledge a good critical-care nurse has to have. Most of the attending doctors in a community hospital are away from the hospital most of the time. A critical-care nurse can't call and say, 'Doctor, the screen on the monitor is making funny lines.' That won't help him or the patient. That kind of nursing deals in minutes, so she'd better know as much as the doctor; she'd better be able to translate and identify the pattern into which part of the heart is dysfunctioning. According to her observations, he orders the medication. And if the patient's heart stops while the doctor is on the telephone, the nurse is the one who has to put the paddles to the patient's chest to try to bring him back."

"But what about the house doctor?" I asked her, thinking about Dr. Laki and almost knowing the answer to my question.

Mrs. O'Reilly raised her eyebrows slightly, but answered

seriously, "Community hospitals don't have more than one or two house doctors on, especially at night. From my experience, I *know* they're not as good as my critical-care nurses. Even if we get a good one, he can't be in more than one place at a time. In a hospital filled with sick patients, is it inconceivable that two patients could arrest at one time? How far can we stretch that doctor?" When I shrugged she added, "While he's trying to save one patient, who's keeping the hearts of the others going? Nurses, Teri, that's who."

I understood better then, but I still didn't want to work in Intensive Care.

A loud thump at the bedroom window startled me out of a sound sleep. I lay paralyzed, afraid to move, when another *bang-splat* hit. Then I slowly crept out of bed and peered through the corner of the frosted pane onto the driveway. I jumped back and almost screamed as a shower of white snow exploded directly in front of me. A snowball? I thought. At this hour? Shivering, I threw on my jeans and sweatshirt. Then I walked downstairs and turned on the porch light.

"We had a boy!" I heard Joel's voice through the door before I saw him. His coat was covered with melting snow.

"Throw on your clothes, little girl," he said enthusiastically. "Let's make our footprints in the snow."

I looked at my watch; it was 3 a.m. "Joel," I said, laughing, puzzled, "who had a boy and where are we going?"

He stood, dripping, smiling ear to ear, as he said, "Well, remember Mrs. Phan, my patient who had three miscarriages? The one who I put to bed six months ago?"

I nodded. The woman he was talking about had desperately wanted a baby, and Joel had tried everything.

"One fat little eight-pound boy! Perfectly healthy, and she was awake to see the whole thing!" he said ecstatically. "And it was some bitch of a delivery." He bent down to kiss me gently. Then, seriously, he said, "Come walk with me."

It was the first snow of our second winter together, and as we walked down the middle of the deserted street, Joel in his black cashmere coat looking terribly doctorly and I in a ski jacket and jeans, we stomped hard to make our footprints deep. We walked, talked and laughed our way down the entire block.

"You know, girl," Joel said, smiling fondly, "you are company, everyone else is presence." He reached down and grabbed a handful of unpacked snow to throw at me. Big, fat, wet snowflakes started to fall again.

By the time we turned to walk back to the house, new snow had all but erased our footprints. "I can't believe how quickly that happened," I said, amazed.

"I can," he said, looking unusually sad.

My teeth were chattering, so I ran ahead, calling, "Come on–hurry up." But he continued to walk slowly, silently. I waited for him as I watched the snowflakes flying past the street lights. When I stuck my tongue out to taste them, Joel turned toward me and smiled.

"You look like the Abominable Snowman," I said as we reached the door.

"And you look like the Little Match Girl." Joel shook some of the snow off himself, then brushed some off me.

Inside, he made us tea while I put the opera *Norma* on the stereo. "Hey, Teri?" Joel called from the kitchen. "How about something quieter? I want to talk to you."

"What's wrong?" I asked when we sat at the table.

Joel stared down into his cup. "I'd like to see a marriage counselor for me and Catherine." He looked to see my reaction before he continued. "She has been so miserable lately. I can't stand to see her like that."

"I never wanted to hurt her," I said, "and I really don't want you to be miserable."

Joel reached across and held my hand. "You do know that I love you, don't you?"

I nodded, teary-eyed. "So what happens now?" I asked. "You just ride off into the sunset and I go back to selling matches?"

He made me laugh by covering his face with his hands and moaning melodramatically, "Oh, God! Don't do that. It's terrible. And stop looking so tragic."

Afterward, as we both lay in bed, Joel said, "Maybe you should think about meeting someone your own age, whom you can have a total relationship with."

I leaned over and placed my finger over his lips. "Forget it," I said. But from then on I thought about it.

"How would you like to work as second nurse in the Emergency Room?" Mrs. O'Reilly asked as I signed into the office the following week. "Gloria Ainsley will be the RN on with you."

"Great," I said, sitting on the corner of the desk. "When do I start?"

"As soon as we have a cup of coffee and I finish talking to you," she said, winking at me. I watched her as she got up to walk over to the coffee machine, and thought how much older than forty she looked. It wasn't only the white hair, or the matronly figure. There was something in her expression that made me think life had done a job on her. Maybe it was having six kids to take care of before you come to work, I thought, with the compassion I usually save for my patients.

"Gloria is good," Mrs. O'Reilly said, "and she doesn't mind teaching you." I knew Gloria from the few times I had been floated down to the Emergency Room when it was busy. She had short black hair, a boyish build, wore no makeup over her weathered skin, and moved like the gym teacher she was before she became a nurse. She was compulsively efficient and a little too machinelike for my taste, but she was a good technical nurse.

After we finished our coffee, Mrs. O'Reilly walked me over to the Emergency Room, where Gloria was filling the glass cabinets with suture material. Gloria smiled and then handed me a carton of needles, saying, "Stocking the cabinets is the best way to learn where everything is."

She walked away and wiped the stretchers with alcohol, polishing their chrome side rails. Then she cleaned the large rectangular room. She knew every corner of the place intimately.

"Is this what you do every night?" I asked her. I hated housecleaning.

"Teri," she explained, "this isn't like a teaching hospital's Emergency Room. Most of the cases we get are people who would go to a doctor if he was available. They come here when the doctors are off—Wednesdays, Saturdays and Sundays, or during the night. It cuts down on the attending doctor's work load tremendously to have us evaluate a patient and only call them if the patients are in real trouble."

"But what about the bad stuff?" I asked. "The car accidents, the heart attacks, the real emergencies?"

She laughed. "Oh, you mean the real blood-and-guts stuff? We transfer all of those to Barrenfield Medical Center, the county teaching hospital."

The only patients we had during that night were a small child with croup, whose doctor called to have him admitted by the house doctor, and a young boy whose mother had slashed his hand with a cleaver for disobeying her. Dr. Laki put a few stitches in his hand and told him to listen to his mother from then on.

When, after a few weeks, I complained to Mrs. O'Reilly that it was so slow I wouldn't learn anything, she encouraged me to try it for six months. "It will keep you out of trouble anyway," she said, laughing.

She was wrong. Within four months, I made another decision that almost got me executed.

One night Gloria called in sick when Mrs. O'Reilly was off, and the alternate supervisor, Mrs. Pousley, put me into the Emergency Room alone.

Mrs. Pousley made me gag, although I had really tried to like her out of sympathy for the way she looked. She had wiry, tightly permed lilac hair that barely framed her large, wrinkled face, and small black eyes that squinted and darted when she played with the several long white hairs that grew from the black mole on her cheek. The top of her very heavy body was overpowered by pendulous breasts, but her legs were so short that she looked as though a cement boulder had fallen from a crane and hammered her into the ground. Whenever I thought about her, I imagined a fairy tale in which an evil princess had been turned into a frog, but after I got to know her I thought her appearance was a treat compared to her personality.

I sat at the nurses' station reading for most of the quiet night, until 4 a.m., when a middle-aged black man ran in. He introduced himself as Mr. Baron.

"Please help me, ma'am," he said anxiously, pulling on my sweater sleeve. "Ma woman thinks they's bugs crawlin' on her, and she's goin' out of her mind from the itch."

He indicated that I should follow him outside, and on my way I grabbed a wheelchair. The security guard who had been sitting by the Emergency Room entrance followed us out to the parking lot and over to the car.

"Alva," Mr. Baron called through the closed window. Over his shoulder I could see a frail, obviously terror-stricken black woman curled into a fetal position on the front seat of the car. Mr. Baron pulled on the door handle.

"She's gone and locked it," he said, looking helplessly at the guard.

"Try the back door," I suggested, hoping she had forgotten those locks. Luckily, the back door on the driver's side was open. Mr. Baron and the guard tried to pull Alva Baron from the seat, but she hung on tight, her knuckles turning pale from clenching the plastic covers. Finally her husband lifted her and carried her, thrashing, into the Emergency Room. He tried to lay her on the stretcher, but she jumped off and paced restlessly at top speed, oblivious to any of us. As I phoned Dr. Laki I watched her: her arms twitched and jackknifed, her tongue thrust in and out of her mouth constantly. In between the tremors, she scratched and muttered, "Them bugs . . . them bugs . . . I seen them before and they has to be burned off." With that she muttered some more to unseen characters as her eyes cogwheeled.

Mr. Baron tried to pacify his wife by hugging her, but Alva just got more agitated. Dr. Laki hadn't arrived yet, so I paged Mrs. Pousley. Elmwood General was affiliated with a psychiatric complex, and I wanted her to request that one of their psychiatrists come over and evaluate the woman.

As I waited for her to call back, Mr. Baron explained that they had come up from Virginia to visit relatives and that an hour before, when he was on the parkway, Alva had tried to set herself afire and throw herself out of the car. He was too frightened to drive any farther without help.

I asked him if she had been sick before or if she had taken any drugs or drink, and he tried to answer, but Alva made a dash for the door and he had cut her off.

"Them bugs is eatin' my babies," she screamed as he talked soothingly to her.

Dr. Laki, sleepy-eyed, came in to examine her, and she finally sat, fascinated by him, for several minutes. All her frenetic activity had stopped.

When I turned around, Mrs. Pousley was in the doorway. "Move them out as quickly as possible, Daley," she said. She pulled me over to the corner of the room. "I want this place cleaned up before the day shift comes on."

I could hear a lot of shuffling behind the closed curtain where Mr. Baron, Alva and Dr. Laki were talking loudly. She was going on about the bugs again; Mr. Baron was trying to reason with her.

I looked back at Mrs. Pousley, who was now tapping her fingertips on the top of the desk. "That woman is too troubled to send back out with only her husband," I said slowly, as though she was more stark raving mad than Alva. "He can't control her."

She shook her head. "I can't believe you are so naive. He probably wants someone to watch her while he goes to a party; they always pull those tricks." Now I was sure she was crazy.

Dr. Laki came out to the desk and smiled as though he had accomplished something. "She will rest now," he said. I looked down at the medication sheet. He had given her five milligrams of Valium. That was like trying to stop a mad tiger by pouring salt on its tail. If Mrs. Pousley hadn't been in my way, I would have tackled him as he left.

"Stop getting so emotionally involved and act professional—if possible," she said. I could hear Mr. Baron still struggling with his wife; she was crying.

"This has nothing to do with being professional," I hissed at Mrs. Pousley. "If they came to my door at home, I would be able to do more for them. I could at least ride in the car with him over to Barrenfield."

"What's the matter with you, Daley?" she said, breathing heavily, spewing droplets. "Are you too dumb to comprehend that a hospital is a business? That it isn't a charity ward?"

"What has that got to do with anything?"

"This is like teaching the ABCs," she muttered, exasperated, as she pulled me outside into the hall. "Let me see if I can make this clear for you. Number one, they are from out of town. Number two, they have no hospital coverage."

I tried to reason with her. "They need help . . . they have nowhere else to go." I sounded a little hysterical even to myself when I finally exploded with "I thought hospitals were to help *sick people!*"

She grabbed my uniform, pulled it tight around my neck and screamed, "Birdbrain! What I'm saying is that those people are *indigents!*"

I pulled her hand off my uniform and bent her thumb back. "You do what you have to. I'll do the same," I told her.

I walked back, leaving her fuming in the hallway, and told Mr. Baron I would get him help to transfer his wife to Barrenfield. Then I called the local police and asked them if they would escort Mr. Baron to the county line, where Alva could be handed over to Barrenfield's chief psychiatric resident and told him that the doctor in charge of Elmwood's Psychiatric hospital was unable to admit Mrs. Baron and would appreciate his help. He accepted her immediately.

When the police arrived, Alva went numbly with them, still mumbling and scratching. Mr. Baron came over to thank me.

"She's a fine woman," he explained, "but when she has them spells—ever since the babies died—it's hard to know what to do. I would have drove her myself, but she kept trying to throw herself out the car. I was afraid to hit someone walking, trying to hold her down."

I smiled and touched his arms. When he reached out to shake my hand I could see heavy calluses on his palm, and when I felt his hand in mine I knew they had been roughened by many years of very hard work.

Before I left in the morning, the directress of nursing called to tell me I would no longer be allowed to work in Intensive Care or the Emergency Room. She made it quite clear that as long as I was an LPN and needed an RN to take responsibility for my decisions, and as long as I continued to be insubordinate, I would be used strictly as extra help on the floors.

"May I come to the office and explain what happened?" I asked.

"There is no need for any more discussion," she said. "The issue is closed."

"But my nursing—" I protested.

"Your nursing ability is not the question," she said, cutting me off. "It's your judgment and your attitude, my dear, that pose the problems." Then she hung up.

By the time I met Lil at the car, she had already heard all about it. "Would you come to work with me at Barrenfield?" I asked her as we drove home.

She smiled sympathetically, fluttered her eyelids, and said, "Great idea, except . . ."

"Except what?" I asked with an edge to my voice, worried that she would refuse.

"Most of the patients there are *indigents*, " she whispered, rolling her eyes, "just like us."

So I took my dented ideals and almost three years of nursing experience away from Elmwood. I tried to convince myself that I had used up that small community hospital, with all its arrogant administration and temperamental attending doctors. At the time, I didn't realize that the problem wasn't just Elmwood . . . or me.

CHAPTER 11

Barrenfield Medical Center looked from the outside like an upright stack of gargantuan dominoes, and inside, it looked like an ancient tomb. Narrow tunnels, caverns and corridors spread like spider legs in every direction from the immense front lobby.

Lil folded her arms across her chest and said, her voice echoing, "Now for a quick review of history." Her eyelids fluttered and she made a half-circle sweep with her arm. "This archaic monument was transferred as is from Mesopotamia after its fall. Its only renovation consisted of the ritual pouring of enormous amounts of gray paint, made from crushed dinosaur skins, down the hallowed walls of the entire establishment in a futile attempt to seal the cracks caused by shipping." Lil always used five-legged words and an exaggerated voice to make fun.

"Depressing," was all I could manage. I had to breathe through my mouth to keep the smell of disinfectant-covered mold from singeing my nostrils. I was beginning to think I should not have been so hard on old Mrs. Pousley.

The wooden elevator creaked and groaned as it pulled us slowly up to the fourth floor, where the personnel office was.

The tiny room was cluttered with high-piled papers stacked on two end tables. They spilled over onto the orange plastic couch and chair. Some had dropped to the floor. Across one wall was fixed a large cork bulletin board covered with ads, handwritten, offering to buy or sell various items. I picked a blue mimeographed sheet from a stack on the table. It was a directive ordering nurses and other hospital personnel to cut down on the amount of wasted material in an attempt to lower hospitalization costs. I picked another; this one heralded the arrival of hot lunch for thirty cents to all employees, cost to be deducted from every paycheck. Lil began studying some of the memos. Eventually we sat, waiting for someone to notice us. There wasn't a soul in sight.

Fifteen minutes later, the directress of nursing, a very imposing woman dressed in flawless white, her brown hair curled tightly in small ringlets, appeared and indicated we should follow her into her office. There she sat down at a huge wooden desk covered with more mimeographed papers, and pointed to a chair each for Lil and me.

After reading over our applications with raised eyebrow, she turned to me and said, definitely, "Burns."

"But I've never worked burns," I protested. "I've worked medicine, surgery, obstetrics and geriatrics. I've even worked some orthopedics and helped out in Intensive Care. Oh, and Emergency Room. But I've never done burns."

"Fine, dear, fine," the directress answered absently. "You'll have an adequate orientation." She shuffled through the papers on her desk, then handed each of us a schedule, explaining, "Orientation starts tonight and will last two weeks."

Lil was sitting paralyzed in her seat, awaiting sentence, obvious fear of execution in her eyes. When the directress motioned to Lil and said, "Oh . . . you, my dear, will work Medicine," it sounded like an afterthought. Lil slumped and sighed with relief.

"Now, that wasn't bad," I said on our way out. "Was it?"

"I'm terrified just by the sight of the place," Lil said, shaking her head.

"It pays more than Elmwood," I pointed out, hoping to cheer her.

"That's what's so frightening. Hospitals *never* pay more than what they have to. You better believe we'll be working ourselves to death in order to earn it."

"Don't be such a pessimist, Lil," I said. "Maybe they just realize how much responsibility there is in nursing, and have finally decided to reward us."

"Ah, child," she said, looking amused. "So naive, so much to learn."

I laughed at her, feeling good that we had gotten jobs. I was certain now that I wouldn't have to deal with so much bureaucratic bullshit.

Barrenfield was grossly understaffed and undersupplied, and "clean" was not a word I could use in its description. In spite of that, the medical center did hold the promise of experience—and the prospect of hordes of unattached interns and residents to spice up our lives.

Within the first week, Lil and I realized that Barrenfield was so large that we could have worked in different hospitals and been closer. She worked on 6D, four floors up and five units across from the second-floor Burn Unit.

The Burn Unit was at the very end of Two South: two rooms and a nursing station, severed from the surgical floor by a heavy set of swinging metal doors.

My first night on, the evening nurse showed me around. Harriet Blumencrass was tall and thin with stringy brown hair that hung limply over the shoulders of her long-sleeved gray cotton isolation gown. She reminded me of one of those old schoolmarm's without glasses—until she spoke. "This unit's sterile, Sweety," she said nasally as she handed me a gown.

As I struggled to climb into it (it covered me down to my ankles, up to my chin and over my wrists). Harriet leaned against the locker in the small closetlike locker room behind the nursing station and continued, "Do you know what that means, sweets?" Without waiting for an answer, shaking her head the entire time, she explained, "That means that we try to keep every goddam bacterium off these patients. Every single little one." Harriet adjusted the straps on a green filter mask and slipped it over my head to my face. "We don't go into a room and even *breathe* without a mask on. "And," she went on, handing me a pair of rubber gloves, "we never touch a patient without these on."

I nodded, understanding everything she said, then asked, "Does it work?"

"Honey," she answered, leaning against the locker again, "you *did* learn the skin is the body's first line of defense against infection?" When I nodded, she continued, "All these people are upward of thirty percent burned. Of course it doesn't work." Then she patted me on the shoulder. "But every little bit helps."

She slipped her mask back over her face and grabbed my hand, dragging me past the nursing station and into the hall toward the ward. It was one large gray-stucco-walled room without dividers, and from where we stood in the hall I could distinguish six beds. The ward was already darkened and the patients were asleep. From the doorway I could see outlines in two beds and at the far end of the room, on top of another bed, what looked like a cloth-covered Quonset hut.

"What's that?" I whispered to Harriet, not wanting to wake anyone.

"A bed cradle to keep the covers off the burns," she whispered back. Then she pulled me across the hall to the other room. Much smaller.

"VIP room," Harriet announced, speaking in her regular voice now, because this room was unoccupied. As I looked around at the grungy gray walls and the dark-stained floor tiles, I wondered aloud what important person would ever be willing to stay here. With a look of disdain, Harriet said, "Not like in your little hospital, honey. Not to *spoil* people. This room's for very severe infections. Or a private death watch." I was as horrified as she had planned for me to be.

The nursing station was also small, with most of the room taken up by a long white metal desk, a silver metal chart rack and three aluminum chairs. Under the one large unadorned window an old-fashioned white radiator posed like a caterpillar.

Harriet and I sat at the desk. She lowered her mask and said, "When Triumph gets here, I'll show you the solution closet." She pointed to the swinging doors. "It's out on Two South. I don't want to have to ungown and then gown again." I looked puzzled, so she explained, "The shower for scrubbing the patients is also out on Surgery."

"I thought you told me everything had to be sterile coming into this unit?"

"True," she said, looking slightly amused again. "But I also told you that the theme is, Every little bit helps."

"That means that I have to take the patients out onto a surgical ward so they can shower? How come that doesn't infect them? It doesn't make any sense."

"I know that, honey, and now you know that, but the big chiefs say that's how it's to be done until this place is rebuilt," Harriet said calmly.

"Why do they have to shower? Why can't we just give them bed baths?"

Harriet pulled a mirror out of her pocketbook to put some red lipstick on her faded lips. She didn't look anywhere near as upset as I felt. "They're not put into the shower to clean them. It's to debride them," she said slowly.

"To what?" I questioned, suddenly feeling very warm.

Harriet stared at me as she said deliberately, "Honey, here, to remove the dead burned tissue–skin–we take the patients into the showers and scrub them down with Betadine and a scrub brush."

"You mean we have to scrub their skin *off?*"

I must have looked shocked, because Harriet immediately asked, "Where did they get you from, sweets? And why did you want to work Burns?"

I ignored her jab and just answered, "They told me, 'Burns'; it wasn't my idea."

She nodded and began to comb her hair.

I sat silently for a minute, wondering if Lil was doing better than I. Then I remembered something Harriet had said. "What's Triumph?" I asked her.

"Not *what,* Sweety; *who,*" she answered, tucking her mirror back into her pocketbook. "Triumph is the nurse you'll be working with on nights until you're trained. Then she leaves."

"What's she like?" I asked Harriet, who had turned her attention to the narcotics book.

"Want to help me count?" she asked, walking out into the hall. I followed her, wondering why she hadn't answered my question.

The medication cabinet was a large wooden fixture built against the wall outside the nurses' station but still inside the unit. It looked like an old-fashioned china cabinet, complete with glass doors on the upper half. Before Harriet unlocked it, she opened the bottom doors and showed me the gauze and the rubber gloves. Then she opened one of the glass doors on top and indicated a tiny metal safe on the shelf. She held up a key clearly marked "No. 1" with adhesive tape, and inserted it into the lock on the front of the tiny safe. Inside there was a second metal door with another lock. She held up a key marked "No. 2" and opened the second door.

Harriet warned, "Be careful the count is correct, because Bradberry, the day nurse, will have Security checking your fingerprints if anything's missing."

I nodded. Lil and I had both been fingerprinted the day we were hired.

Harriet and I counted the vials and pill containers together, wrote everything down in the narcotics book and each signed our name and rank.

As we walked back into the nursing station Harriet said, "Triumph's crazy."

"What does that mean?" I asked as I pulled up a chair alongside hers.

"Hard to put a finger on," she said, shaking her head as she scribbled short notes on the charts. "Nobody's been able to figure her out, except that she's crazy."

"Is she married?" I asked, as though that was an indication of mental health.

"Sometimes she says she is, sometimes not," Harriet said, laughing. "Anyway, she lives in the nursing residence and claims she needs every third weekend to go up to Boston to visit her husband, Edriando, who she claims is married to another woman also."

"Will it be just the two of us?" I asked, not liking the prospect of being taught by a nut.

"No," Harriet reassured me. "There's an aide, Granshaw, who's been here for years. Pain in the ass, but knows what she's doing."

Just then I heard the creak of the swinging doors, and in lurched a tall, skinny black woman whose too small white uniform exposed long gangly arms and legs. Her head was thrust forward from her shoulders, her small starched cap perched on kinky black hair which stood out perfectly straight. Her protuberant eyes were primarily white except for pinpoint-black pupils; her nose was so flattened that it blended into her cheeks, hardly noticeable, and she had an enormous set of beautiful white teeth which shone against her jet-black skin.

Harriet stood when she introduced us. "Triumph O'Hara, this is Teri Daley, the new nurse."

Triumph smiled and almost scared me to death. When her skin wrinkled in a smile, she looked like a shrunken head. She moved toward me and thrust out her hand, saying in a soft, beautifully clear voice, "I'm so pleased to meet you, and very happy to find another 'Irish' here."

I looked at Harriet, puzzled, and she explained, "Triumph's father was Irish." When Triumph turned to grab a gown, Harriet winked at me. Despite what I had heard from Harriet, I didn't dislike Triumph. In fact, the warmth of her smile and her voice were comforting after Harriet's sarcasm.

We walked outside the unit, and Harriet showed me the lateral metal cabinet on Two South which held and heated the solutions needed for the patients' dressing changes. She pointed to one of the long glass two-liter bottles labeled "Sterile Saline" and said, "Use one of the hot ones and take one off the shelf in the unit. Pour half of each in a sterile basin and it should be just about the right temperature. Also remember, the acetic acid can't be heated, so that should also be mixed with half the hot saline."

I thanked her for her help. When Harriet left, I walked back through the swinging doors into the now-darkened Burn unit. The only light Triumph had left on was the small overhead desk light in the nursing station. I caught Triumph racing out of the ward with the thermometers in her hand and stopped her long enough to ask, "Who's under that thing?" pointing at the quonset hut.

"That's O'Donnell," she said. "His old lady threw boilin' oil on his balls when she caught him doin' no good." Triumph raised her eyebrows warningly. "Granshaw ain't comin' in tonight, sick again," she added, and then, as she put the thermometers into the metal tray to soak, I heard her mutter, "She's sick all right, sick of this place, sick of all the rest of these sickos." She giggled and turned to see me just standing there.

"Don't pay me no mind, girl," she said, a quick smile crossing her face. "Jest thinkin' out loud." I smiled back. For the entire time I worked with Triumph she carried on lengthy conversations with herself, always apologizing afterward for 'thinkin' out loud."

I told Triumph I was nervous about doing dressings. "There's only three patients," she said. "I'll do em, you can watch."

"What's with the other two?" I asked as I helped her insert fresh pages of notes into the chart.

"One of them is Driscoll. Arms burnt in a barbecue fire," she said, neatly lining and dating some pages, then charting the temperatures with red pen. "The other fella is Andrew Hamilton, a black man who scalded his back. He's the only one we have to shower in the mornin'. The others have dressing changes every four hours."

I worked alongside Triumph for most of my training period. Granshaw had hurt her back and wasn't expected back for an undetermined period of time. I learned a lot those first weeks, and I marveled at how quickly and efficiently Triumph could change a dressing without stopping when the patients hollered in pain. "Got to be done," she told Mr. Driscoll firmly one night as she unwrapped his arms and he yelled. But outside the room afterward she turned to me and said, "Don't it get you right in the belly, those screams?"

The next night she let me do Mr. Driscoll, and as I unwrapped the dressing the wet gauze stuck to his skin. "I can't do it," I told Triumph. She took a full bottle of saline and poured it over the dressing on his arm. Then she pulled and cut away the skin until the dressing was off.

Later, in the nursing station, she lectured, "Teri, somebody got to do this to them. It got to be done the same way whether they feel your kindness or not. The faster you do it, the faster it's over for them." She sat back in her chair. "In the morning you scrub Andrew in the shower."

The next four hours flew as I dreaded the thought of doing Andrew's dressing. I had gotten fond of him. He was an athletic-looking young man with beautiful brown skin and a smile that could light up the room. He was shy and gentle, hardly ever speaking above a whisper, his eyes looking down whenever he was spoken to.

At 5 a.m. Triumph prodded me into waking Andrew. "Yes, ma'am," he answered softly when I called to him.

"It's time to shower, Mr. Hamilton," I said, and it sounded to me as though my voice was quavering.

Andrew got up carefully, covering himself so that his genitals weren't exposed. I gave him two gowns—one to put on forward, the other backward. I grabbed one of the scrub brushes from the sink and followed him out through the swinging doors into the shower room on Two South.

After I turned the shower on, I tried to stall, regulating the temperature of the water for long minutes before I signaled the okay.

Undressed, Andrew was obviously embarrassed, and I tried not to stare at his body. But every time I looked up my eyes fixed on his, and the pain in them was more uncomfortable for me to see than his nakedness. In truth his entire body was so sleek and muscular that it was a pleasure to look at. I had never seen a young black man undressed, and I thought that though he was well built he didn't look any different from the white men I had seen. More propaganda.

He stood under the running water, droplets tearing at the skin on his back until it bled. He braced himself, uncomplaining, and when I tore at his raw back with the hard plastic bristles of the brush, his only response was to hold tight to the soap dish. I tried to be gentle, but in order to eliminate the green exudate and expose the clean pink tissue underneath, I had to press hard enough to scrape the tissue clean. Fresh blood ran in rivulets down his back. I was practically in tears and my mouth watered constantly, the bitter taste making me want to vomit. Between the hot steam and my own anxiety, by the time I turned the shower off I was as soaking wet as Andrew.

"Thank you, ma'am," he said softly as I blotted his back with a sterile towel. His entire body was covered with gooseflesh, and he was trembling from the pain and the cold. I covered him with a sterile gown and we walked back down the hall, through the swinging doors into the unit. Then Andrew got into bed and lay on his stomach, still shaking, while I put fresh gauze on his back from shoulders to butt and wrapped him in a stretch-gauze jacket.

Triumph had finished everything else, including the charts, by the time I was through. She smiled at me from the desk and said, "The harder you scrub him, the quicker the old skin'll come off and new skin'll grow."

I nodded. My mouth felt as though I had eaten sand. I couldn't remember when I had ever felt so whipped before.

Almost as though she had read my mind, Triumph asked in a very gentle voice, "You goin' to be able to take it, girl?"

"Sure, Triumph," I said with forced cheerfulness. "I'm sure I'll get used to it."

She handed me a cup of coffee and sat me down, looking concerned. "If ya don't," she said, "your insides is gonna look like Andrew's outsides."

CHAPTER 12

"I think it's time to hit the singles scene," Lil said, looking up from the bright-green sweater she was knitting for me. I had been lying around for days, after I had decided to go back out into the world and try to find a man I could develop a *real* relationship with. Joel and I had seen much less of each other since I started working at Barrenfield, and the relationship between us wasn't enough for me anymore. I knew we would always be friends and I really cared about him, but I was healed and needed more.

Lil, with needles clicking, continued, "What do you think about going in to the city? One of the books I read said there's a swinging singles strip on the Upper East Side just crammed with available young men."

Working nights at Barrenfield, I hadn't even seen an intern in the last month. Lil's floor had fifty patients; most nights only she and three aides had to take care of them. She had seen a few doctors but had never had the time to introduce herself. So I figured she was right: the singles scene was our only alternative.

"Where should we start?" I asked her, sitting up for the first time all day. It was a Friday night; both Lil and I were off, and my mother had my kids.

She moved slowly off the couch and rummaged through her pocketbook until she pulled out a wrinkled piece of yellow paper.

"There's a place called Maxwell's Plum," she said, smoothing the crumpled paper on her lap. "One of the girls in my anthropology class said it's full of junior execs." She dropped the paper and picked up her knitting again. "They should at least be fairly intelligent."

"How come you haven't met anybody at school?" I asked.

"How come *you* haven't?"

I laughed. "Most of my classes are filled with nurses. Women, anyway."

"Besides," Lil said, looking amused, "you know I'm chasing knowledge, not men. Aside from *sex* I haven't much use for them, after that creep I was married to."

"Okay," I said, dragging my body off the couch. "Let's go."

Lil walked into the bathroom to run a bath while I called my mother to talk to the kids and tell her that I was going in to New York . . . to see a play.

When I hung up Lil was already lying in the water, bubbles up to her chin. "I hate having to do this," I said to her as I sat on the john to keep her company.

She blew bubbles off her chest and said, "Well, if it wasn't for *your* need for one of those creatures, we could stay home, read and relax."

It was true; Lil did do much better without a relationship than I did. "Why don't you need one?" I asked, getting up to set my hair.

"I am much more complete," she drawled, and then laughed. "Besides, you didn't have a husband who made you chase rubber balls down a hill in Japan."

I stopped rolling my hair long enough to turn around and ask, "What are you talking about?"

"When we were stationed in Japan," she started, then was quiet for several minutes while she dunked her head underwater to wet her hair and pour shampoo on it, "just after we were married, the creep figured I wasn't getting enough exercise, so he would sit in a rocking chair on the porch where we lived and throw a ball down the hill. Then he would scream at me until I ran after it to bring it back to him."

I was horrified. But when I opened my mouth to tell Lil, she had dunked her head underwater again to rinse off the shampoo.

"How could you take that?" I asked when I saw her head surface. "I would have killed him."

"Umm," she said. "I know you would have. And I wish you had been there, but as it was I just ran away again and spent the night sleeping in the rice fields." She sighed. "When the creep finally found me he screamed at me for two solid days."

"So why didn't you scream back? Or run home and leave him?"

"I can't scream back when someone is screaming at me. My brain goes dead." She sat up and let the water out of the tub, adding, "And I couldn't go home because my mother, who was still alive then, would have been disappointed."

"But after she died," I asked, handing her a towel. "Why didn't you leave then?"

Lil moved slowly out of the tub. "*You,* my child, have been spared the knowledge of the moves a woman cannot make when she is economically impoverished." I had always noticed that she used highbrow sentences when anything had an emotional content, and then she giggled, as though that helped her pull distance.

We went to Maxwell's Plum, and from the frenetic, smoky, desperate atmosphere of that magnificent singles bar another knight in pinstriped armor appeared. He had done battle with the bartender to get me my sloe gin fizz, and instead of my handkerchief he wanted my phone number.

Greg Schmidt was tall and blond, every hair in place as though he brushed it one hundred strokes each day, his round face was clear and unblemished, and by midnight he still had no five-o'clock shadow. The shine on his upturned nose and the clear, sincere blue eyes that promised intelligence made him appealing. He spoke with a Midwestern accent–not even that to offend. He smelled of English Leather and said he was a marketing-research manager for a drug manufacturer in New York City, the youngest they'd ever had. The only thing that convinced me that he wasn't a mannequin was his chewed fingernails. I noticed them immediately when I was supposed to be looking at his college ring.

"What do you think, Lil?" I asked on our way home.

"He's everything a girl *should* want," she answered, giggling.

On our first date Greg and I went with his friend, Thad, and Thad's wife, Roberta, to a high-class restaurant on the North Shore of Long Island. Thad was taller than Greg, over six feet; he was a spiffy dresser, like Greg, but he spoke with affected speech and winked at me constantly. Roberta was a tiny woman whose clothes hung on her thin frame, and throughout the entire meal she didn't say one word. Not that I blamed her; her husband kept licking his lips whenever he looked at me. Most of his hoity-toity language was punctuated with obscene gestures.

Halfway through the meal I whispered to Greg, "Take me home, please. I hate your friend."

Greg's eyes popped open like an animated cartoon, and he whispered back, "Kitten, I can't just abandon him."

"Sure you can," I said, pretending I was nibbling at his ear. "Tell him I have a splitting headache."

I put down my fork as though I couldn't eat another morsel and grabbed my head in preparation, holding it tight with both hands.

Greg apologized several times before we left. I could see by his blush that he was humiliated.

"Yuk!" I said outside, "How come you like him? He's awful."

We stopped by the dock alongside the parking field and leaned on the white fence to watch the sailboats sway in the cool breeze. The smell of the salt water made me feel better. Greg looked pensive now. Slowly he said, "You're right, Kitten, he is boorish, but he's the only guy I know who has the right connections and the capital to make a new business work." He explained that Thad was a respiratory therapist who was funding a distribution company for the sale of disposable oxygen supplies—masks, tubings of polyethylene and plastic containers. He had offered Greg a partnership.

"You're young," I said. "What's the big rush? There has to be someone better, if you take the time to look around."

He put his arm around my shoulder. "I'm twenty-six now," he said, looking past me into the water. "I'm going to be rich or dead by the time I'm thirty."

"Ah, what ambition!" I murmured as I snuggled into his shoulder. "Another John Paul Getty!"

"I'm serious," Greg said, standing up straighter. With his arm still around me, he led me to the car.

After we had gone out a few more times, Greg asked me back to his apartment. He parked his black Cutlass in front of a neat yellow Cape Cod house complete with white shutters and white picket fence, and we walked slowly across the neatly mowed lawn toward the side entrance. When he stopped to check his mailbox before he unlocked the door, I thought, he's not exactly consumed with passion.

We climbed the tweed-carpeted steps, and from the top I could see most of Greg's apartment. It was spotless. The narrow hallway was covered in beige grass paper, and on the wall a single small wooden plaque staked the claim "Home Sweet Home." I got depressed. Down two steps on the right was a good-sized living room. In it was a long Colonial couch with at least a thousand flying brown eagles, and one chair–more flying eagles. The brown-and-tan braided rug was either new or just vacuumed, and the one wooden end table held a lamp–another flying eagle. . . .

At the threshold of that room, I had visions of myself sitting on the couch, eagles coming alive–staring at me and nibbling at my shoulders as I tried to carry on an intelligent conversation. I suddenly had the mad desire to place my right hand over my heart and recite the Pledge of Allegiance, to pacify those damn hook-beaked birds.

"What do you think, Kitten?" Greg asked as he walked down the steps to stand proudly, smoothing a brown, eagle-covered patchwork quilt that lay on the back of the couch.

I nodded slowly. "As Mother would say, 'You could eat off the floors,'" I said, trying not to be insincere. Then a silly voice inside my head jabbered, you'd have to eat off the floor or the birds would get your food. I tried to quiet my imagination.

"Real American," I added, smiling with what I'm sure was the same expression I saw on the faces of people who were shown an ugly baby and could only exclaim, "Wow! That's some baby."

"Wow!" I said. "this is some apartment."

Luckily Greg was satisfied. I really didn't want to hurt his feelings. The apartment smelled of air freshener, and as he moved along the kitchen, opening drawers and cabinets, I noticed that the dishes and the silver were stacked at attention. There were no dirty glasses in the sink or on the drain board, and his dish towels were folded. My mother will forgive me anything I do if I bring this man home, I said to myself.

Greg put his arm around me and led me up the stairs toward the bedroom. At the entrance I thought, Thank God, no eagles! Then I looked again–anchors! The bedroom was decorated in sailing motif, red, white and blue. Ropes, life preservers, a captain's hat and a barometer hung on the walls. There was even a bed with a headboard labeled PORT and STARBOARD.

"Was this apartment furnished when you rented it?" I asked, hoping with all my heart that it was.

"No," Greg said, smiling, and then, as he ran his hand fondly over the high lacquered steering wheel which passed for a lamp, "I bought most of it myself, a little at a time, over the last two years." He walked away from me, to the far side of the room, and like a plantation owner asked, "Do you really like it, Kitten?"

I moved toward him and put my arms around his neck. "I really like *you*," I said, trying to evade the question. He bent and kissed me. A nice warm dry kiss. Not bad, I thought, as he drew me closer to the bed with another kiss.

"Port or starboard?" he whispered.

I couldn't believe he'd say anything that corny. Impulsively I covered my face with my hands and wailed. Then, because he looked crushed and confused, I pulled him down on the bed with me, tickled him, and teased, "Both, Greg."

Within minutes we were in a clinch. Greg started to make love to me. At first he was so stiff that I was afraid I'd have to say, as he touched me, "Excuse me, sir . . . a little to the left, please?" And when he reached up and turned off the light I was horrified. Shades of Shawn, I thought.

After we had finished, I lay in bed in the dark, missing Joel and telling myself that it would get better. Greg was sincere and gentle, he smelled delicious, and aside from not being innovative, I thought, it wasn't a bad screw.

Turning sideways, I could see Greg, a shadow, sitting up on the side of the bed. In the dark he looked like the statue of Rodin's *Thinker*, his back hunched, his head in his palm.

"What's wrong?" I asked softly.

"It wasn't fair of me to put you in this position," Greg said, without turning around. He hunched lower.

"Hey, Atlas," I teased, "it was no position for me." I put my hand on his shoulder, and to reassure him I whispered, "I've done it before, you know."

"I don't want you to think that you're just another girl to me," Greg said as he turned and ran his finger down my cheek. "Just another cheap date . . ."

"Why not?" I said, teasing him because he looked so serious. "What's wrong with a cheap date?"

He switched the light on, and because it hurt my eyes I pulled the sheet up over my head.

"I'm not that kind of a guy," I heard him say, "and you're not that kind of a girl."

"How do you know?" I said, talking through the sheet.

He pulled the sheet away from my face and said, very seriously, "I feel very bad about this, Pumpkin."

"Oh, God!" I wailed. "Spare me this! It wasn't that good that you should feel this bad." He looked so crushed that I felt guilty, so I got mad. "Stop being such a sissy," I hollered. "We didn't do anything wrong. We didn't hurt anybody."

I couldn't deal with it. Exasperated, I jumped up and dressed. Greg walked past me into the bathroom, obviously upset. I stomped into the living room and sat among the birds. Furious, I listened to the shower running. By the time I heard the electric toothbrush, I couldn't stand it another minute. I tore up to the bathroom, flung the door open and screamed, "Don't forget the *Raid!*"

The picture Greg made, standing naked, leaning over the sink, foam coming out of his mouth and running down his chin, made me laugh. As soon as I did, he laughed, too, and everything seemed okay.

He dressed and took me home in time for an early breakfast before I had to pick the kids up at my mom's. When he kissed me goodbye and said he'd call later, I felt a new intimacy. Not because of the sex; because of the fight.

CHAPTER 13

"**J**ust watch to make sure the damn stuff doesn't eat through a main vessel," Harriet warned me at report the first night I was on alone. She was talking about Mr. Driscoll, who had so much eschar, or scar tissue, on his arms that the doctors had decided to try a new cream to debride him as an alternative to cutting. No one knew yet how aggressively the escharotic that had been smeared over both arms would work. "Just watch for the spurting of frank blood," she said. "Both arms are wrapped and won't be undressed for several days. If there's any trouble, call the resident." I wrote everything down on paper. I was terrified without Triumph.

I had never had to deal directly with the resident or the intern; I hadn't even seen one. But I had heard that the plastic surgeons who covered the Burn Unit were excellent. Egomaniacal, sadistic, perfectionistic—but excellent. According to rumor, Dr. Zaccara, the chief resident, was the finest doctor and the most miserable person. I had been told that he was bright and attractive in a short, dark, Italian way. Everyone said that he slept with a different girl every night, so I figured he hated women. I dreaded dealing with him.

As Harriet collected her belongings she said, "O'Donnell is almost healed, so the only real treatment is Hamilton to shower in the morning. You should be fine if Driscoll is stable and you don't get an admission."

After Harriet left, I did exactly as I had seen Triumph do and went into the ward to take temps. All the men were awake. First I walked over to O'Donnell, whom I liked least. He was as surly as Andrew was gentle. He frightened me with his arrogant looks and his smart-ass statements. Even with the bed cradle over him,

O'Donnell seemed to take as much trouble to expose his genitals as Andrew did to cover his.

As I tried to place the thermometer under O'Donnell's tongue he grabbed my hand and said, "Sugar, the skin on this here injury is gettin' tight. How 'bout puttin' some cream on it?" Every time I had to deal with him I found myself being happy that his wife had fried his balls.

Andrew warned, "Hey, man, cut it out," as I handed O'Donnell the ointment to apply himself. O'Donnell teased for a few more minutes, but by then he had worked himself into an erection which was so painful that he rolled over, howling. I couldn't help laughing.

I took Andrew's temp and then poured some fresh saline on his dressings to keep them wet. "Don't mind him, ma'am," he said, looking embarrassed. I tousled his kinky hair with my rubber-gloved hand before I walked over to Mr. Driscoll, who was lying in bed with his eyes closed.

"How's it going, Mr. Driscoll?" I asked him as I examined the dressings on his arms. No bleeding yet that I could see.

"Damn stuff sure burns when they rub it on," he answered, irritated.

"Would you like a pill?"

He opened his eyes. "Those pills aren't any better than aspirin," he said, but then added, "Thanks anyway."

After the men fell asleep, I walked through the darkened unit into the nursing station. One small lamp with an uncovered bulb burned brightly over the desk; the overhead fluorescents were off so that they wouldn't shine across the hall into the patients' rooms. I sat, listening to the sound of snoring, and charted my temps. Then I dated new graph sheets and arranged the desk drawers and the closet, which left me with six more hours until daylight . . . Anything could happen.

I jumped when I heard the creak of the heavy swinging doors, but when I turned there was no one around. I shivered. It seemed a very dark night, no stars, when I went to the large bare window which overlooked the Psychiatric Unit of Barrenfield. There also I could see only one small light.

I hated being on alone. The Burn Unit was isolated from the rest of the hospital, and because it was sterile not even the security guards came to visit. The prospect of spending hours by myself depressed me. I sat down again and pulled a book out of my night bag, but the clanging and groaning of the steam heat made me too nervous to read.

I heard some scraping in the hall, and as I raised my head, I saw a small mouse slide under the swinging doors leading to Surgery. I sat hoping he had no sisters and brothers, because I was deathly afraid of mice. I pulled my mirror out of my bag, freshened my makeup and nervously combed my hair.

"Excuse me, Mrs. Daley," I heard Mr. Driscoll say, before my comb flew out of my hand, "may I use the bathroom in the hall?" I hadn't heard him walk into the nurses' station.

"Having pain?" I asked, because he was frowning. His wrapped arms were folded across his chest and I could see no bleeding through the dressings. I handed him a Darvon, the only pain medication we used after the initial period of admission in the Burn Unit, and propped the swinging doors open.

Then I watched in horror as Mr. Driscoll hobbled down the hall, a milky red liquid falling from underneath his bandages in large-enough amounts to splash as it hit the floor. I had a picture of the cream eating its way through the scar tissue and into an artery like a piranha. I hoped the dressing, like a dam, would hold the bleeding back until I called the doctor.

I ran to the one phone in the unit, praying Mr. Driscoll wouldn't exsanguinate while I was talking.

"Listen, Dr. Zaccara," I said without preface, "I've never worked with this cream before and Mr. Driscoll's arms are dripping blood."

His husky clipped voice, instantly alert, asked, "What do you mean, dripping?"

I repeated as I stood rocking back and forth nervously, "Dripping onto the floor." By now I could picture Driscoll lying in a huge red puddle.

Zaccara asked, "Any spurting?"

"No," I said, wishing he would just come up and look at the patient for one minute and take the responsibility for whatever happened.

THE NURSE'S STORY   149

I knew Zaccara was getting annoyed when he asked testily, "Streaming? And if not, could you describe the drainage as to color, amount and consistency a little more accurately?"

"Okay," I said, trying to get it just right. "It's plopping, and it's the consistency of Sacramento tomato juice. You know, plop, plop, plop . . ."

Dr. Zaccara hesitated for a minute. Then, "Hey, kid," he said sharply, "it's four o'clock in the morning. What the hell are you doing, auditioning for *The Ed Sullivan Show?*" He hung up.

I was furious, but I wasn't sure enough of myself to call him back. I felt dumb because he apparently didn't think the information I had given him important.

Mr. Driscoll got back to the unit intact, but for the rest of the night I checked his dressings constantly. He didn't bleed out, and though Triumph told me later that Zaccara had a fit, I felt better about having called him to cover myself.

Triumph couldn't know how thrilled I was to see her back in the Burn Unit the following night. I wouldn't have been able to stand the stress of working another night alone.

After I changed into my gray cotton scrub suit, I sat at the desk next to Triumph to listen to Harriet give report. When she had finished, on her way out the door, Harriet mentioned, "I think there's a patient in the ER who may be admitted. Some kind of a hot-water spill. Just the back, so it shouldn't be too bad."

Triumph, shaking the thermometers, mumbled. "Then why is he comin' here?"

"Hey," I said, laughing, "Don't bitch about it. We have only three patients. Without the admission they'd probably float me to another floor."

Triumph nodded and grumbled her way into the ward. I heard her say as she approached O'Donnell, "We ain't gonna be missin' nothin' when you leave, man." Harriet had told us that he was ready for discharge.

After temps, the ER called with our admission, and Triumph told them to bring him right up. Triumph explained admitting procedure and told me he would be my patient. His name was Bobby Rao.

The chart had the patient's age listed as sixteen, but the boy whom the ER nurse wheeled through the swinging doors, on a stretcher, looked no more than ten. He was a small black child whose enormous eyes strained open wide as the nurse explained what had happened.

As his mother boiled water for spaghetti Bobby had been standing in front of the stove eating a sandwich. Bobby's dog, a German shepherd, jumped up to grab the food. Seeing that Dober was headed straight for the pot, Bobby moved between his dog and the stove. When Dober hit him, the pot overturned, spilling the water down his back.

I looked at the boy as she spoke; he never moved or reacted. He just lay on his side, curled up, his right arm outstretched so as not to dislocate the slowly dripping IV. His back was covered with sterile towels; the nurse told me he had second and third-degree burns.

I leaned down next to Bobby and asked, "Are you in a lot of pain?" There was no response for several minutes; his eyes were staring, clouded over. Then I noticed an almost imperceptible sideways movement of his head.

The nurse pulled me aside and whispered, "We don't know whether he's mentally retarded or emotionally handicapped. When we asked his mother, she acted as though *we* were crazy. She said he never talks much, that there was nothing wrong with him. "Personally," she added conspiratorially, "I think there's something wrong with her too."

When the ER nurse left, Triumph helped me get Bobby into the bed next to Andrew's. Then she helped me put wet dressings on Bobby's back, which I noticed was at least as badly burned as Andrew's. Afterward, when I wrote his admission note, I added that Bobby had not spoken; I also wrote that it was almost impossible to keep him off his back because he didn't seem to understand he was supposed to stay off it.

Once Bobby was settled, there wasn't anything to do until Andrew's morning shower. O'Donnell applied his own ointment and we had instructions not to touch Mr. Driscoll's arms. They were still oozing the same milky red liquid, but the doctors had seen it and assured us that it was normal; still, his dressings smelled awful to me, like bad meat.

As Triumph and I sat at the desk, I asked her what burn psychosis was. I had heard the term thrown around the unit but had only a vague idea what it was. I knew that some of it was the result of an electrolyte imbalance caused by the weeping of body fluids through the open damaged skin, but I wondered whether that was all that created the confusion and madness that some of the burn patients seemed to suffer.

Triumph frowned and shook her head. "We just hurtin' them too much, Teri," she explained sadly. "The other stuff, the fancy talk about blood chemistries, is okay, prob'ly true; but if all the time you was bein' cut an' tore at, and nobody gave you nothin' for the pain, you'd go crazy, too."

Triumph leaned back in her chair, and began to hum a long soulful tune as she gazed out the window into the dark night. For as long as I worked with her, whenever she was troubled, if she didn't mutter, she hummed. At first it drove me crazy, but after a while I found it comforting.

I knew that the theory of weaning burn patients off narcotics quickly was to keep them from becoming addicted because of the length of treatment. Still, like Triumph, I thought it foolish. If I had my choice, I would have given them enough medication to take the edge off the pain and worried about treating their addiction later. To my way of thinking, the kind of psychological scars caused by the brutal medicine we had to do were certainly as crippling.

At the time I hadn't considered the issue of drug tolerance, the fact that after a certain period of time a drug will no longer work to relieve pain, but as I look back now I still believe different medications could be rotated in order to keep the pain level bearable.

In the morning, while Triumph did Bobby's dressing, I showered Andrew again. I had begun to wonder if Andrew could feel pain, because he never complained.

"Am I hurting you?" I asked as I scrubbed his back bloody.

"I'm okay, ma'am," he answered softly while water pounded the raw area I had just scrubbed.

He held tight to the soap dish when I poured more disinfectant on my brush and continued. Most of the dead tissue was gone, exposing clean red muscle that was starting to heal, turning pink along the edges. But in the deeply burned areas under his shoulder blades I now saw the yellow beginnings of an infection.

I held my breath and tore deeper into Andrew's back with the sharp plastic bristles, using more pressure than ever before.

Andrew stiffened. The soap dish broke off in his hands. When I realized how much I had hurt him, I dropped my brush and backed away from the shower.

"Teri," he said sharply, calling me by name for the first time, "please finish." He looked directly at me.

I shook my head and looked down.

Andrew called my name again, then bent down and picked the brush up from the bottom of the shower. As water ran down his face he held the brush toward me and smiled. "Please finish," he said again, in a softer but still firm voice.

I took the brush reluctantly. He turned his back.

"Harder," he ordered as I gingerly scrubbed. "I said *hard*," he repeated, and I started to cry. "I have to get home to Sabrina," he said, so intensely that I began scrubbing as hard as I could while blinking back tears.

When we finished, Andrew thanked me. Then, to help me understand, he explained for the first time how he had gotten burned. Sabrina, his wife, had cerebral palsy. One morning while he was bending to fix the foot rests on her wheelchair, she had inadvertently knocked the electric coffee pot over. He had been stopped from jumping away from the steaming coffee as it spilled from the table onto this back, because he had gotten caught between the chair and the table leg. While he was in the hospital, his ten-year-old daughter was the only one home to take care of his wife. And because the child had to stay home from school, time was essential. "I have no time for an infection," he said.

The entire time he spoke to me, he looked right at me, and for the rest of his stay, whenever he talked to me, he never again looked down.

It was later than usual when I got back to the unit, and so the doctors were making rounds. Triumph had finished report, and she waited for me while I got dressed.

"Who's who?" I asked her as we stood watching from the door.

There were about eight of them. The chief of plastic surgery, Dr. Blake, was dressed in a dark suit covered by a white lab coat. Next to him stood a young man about five foot five with curly Vitalis-greased black hair and dark horn-rimmed glasses. By his look of arrogance, I knew it was Zaccara. He looked a little too heavy to be a lady killer, but Triumph said, "You can't tell by jest lookin'." Behind Zaccara stood a taller, light-haired man who looked nervous to me. "And him?" I asked Triumph again. She made a funny face, shrugged her shoulders and said, "That's Muscio, first-year resident. Wasn't bad when he started, but now he's practicin' to be as bad as Zaccara." I laughed.

As we turned to go, the group cut in front of us and stood in the way of the swinging doors, discussing Bobby. Triumph and I excused ourselves, and several of the guys smiled and winked at me. Zaccara looked straight ahead, as though he didn't see me.

Greg and I spent a lot of time together, and several times a week he would eat with me and the kids. It was a nice feeling, after Joel, to be able to do family things again. But one Tuesday night, convention reared its ugly head and forced me to think about what I was doing.

Greg helped me set the table after I cooked, and then I called the kids down from upstairs, where they were supposed to be doing their homework. I knew they were probably watching TV; I didn't haunt them about that, because Niki's marks were good and Spinner was so young I didn't take his schoolwork seriously.

They both ran downstairs, Spinner with a clomp, clomp, jump, on the last three steps, and Niki walking demurely behind him. Niki chose the chair closest to me while Spinner climbed all over Greg.

"Hi, little man," Greg said, tousling Spinner's hair. "How did it go today?" When he turned to Niki, winked and asked, "How's my favorite little lady today?" she cringed.

Spinner chattered incessantly, telling Greg, "I met a girl today. She winds me up, turns me on, and makes my music play."

"You don't say." Greg laughed. I didn't dare ask Spinner what that meant because I was afraid I couldn't handle the answer.

Then Greg gave the signal, and we all lowered our heads for grace. I glared at both kids with my kill look while they made funny faces. By the time Greg finished, all three of us were ready to burst out laughing . . . but we knew better.

Dinner went well until Greg began to correct the kids' table manners. I restrained myself from defending them until he made Niki so nervous with his "Keep your elbows off the table" that she spilled her milk.

"Cripes," I screamed, "this isn't the Army!"

Both kids excused themselves and headed for upstairs instantly, hoping not to get caught in the crossfire that they knew would follow. Then, rather than hitting Greg with the full force of my exploding fury, trying to spare myself some grief, I yelled up to the kids, "Hurry up! Get undressed for bed."

After I drank my coffee through clenched teeth, Greg tried to explain how much easier it would be for my kids if they would learn some of the social amenities. I was back home again, listening to my mother. Everything he said to try to make it better made it worse. All I kept thinking was how much damage I could do by spitting hot coffee at him.

While I did the dishes in silence, Greg pulled out his worksheet and busied himself at the kitchen table. Within minutes, I heard the stomping of small feet and my kids landed back in the living room.

"What a sexy little lady you are in your peignoir," Greg said to Niki. Humiliated, she ran back upstairs, locked herself in her room and barred the door with a chair.

"Why did you do that?" I asked Greg after several frustrating attempts to talk to Niki through her closed door.

"I was only trying to make her feel attractive as a female," Greg answered defensively.

Spinner was sitting on a chair very close to Greg, scribbling on a piece of paper, imitating his every action. "Greg's really nice, right, Mom?" he said, smiling up at Greg.

I ignored Spinner and hollered, "She's just a kid, why would you want her to feel like an attractive female?"

Suddenly something inside me pulled back and looked at the whole scene, all of us trying so hard, and I felt terrible.

CHAPTER 14

The seasons changed, and Lil and I hardly noticed. Every night at Barrenfield was like a game of *Beat the Clock*. We'd get in at 11 p.m., the next time we looked it was 4 a.m., one more look and it was already past time to go home.

During that year, Lil and I ate bottles of diet pills so we could work double time. Not two shifts, just twice as fast. Amphetamines weren't illegal then, and a prescription wasn't hard to get. We wondered why, on our days off, when we didn't eat the pills, we couldn't get out of bed. We were constantly exhausted, and irritable too, but it was the only way to cope with the tremendous work load at Barrenfield.

Triumph worked only three days now, and Granshaw was out on a leave, so often I was on alone. I had adjusted to the treatments, so they went more quickly, but I had a very hard time getting used to the pain I had to cause. O'Donnell and Andrew had been released. Bobby was waiting for more grafting on his back, and we had gotten two new admissions: Amy Martin, an old woman who had burned her legs and buttocks getting into a scalding bathtub, and Scott Silk, a young man who had fried his arms by hanging on to a hot wire as he fell from a tall tree. Both his arms had to be amputated in the Emergency Room the night of his admission. He was twenty-four years old and the lead guitarist in a band. He had been trying to rescue a trapped kitten.

Bobby still had not spoken. He would just lie in bed, eyes open like big wet saucers, and stare at the darkened ceiling. Several times, rather than sit in the nurses' station by myself, I had pulled up a chair and sat next to him, just holding his hand. Every once in a while I would ask, "Bobby, what's the matter?" But he never answered.

Sometimes, in the dark, Scott would speak to me. His bed was next to Bobby's, so I began sitting between them.

One night, I heard Bobby crying. I had been sitting in the nurses' station doing charts, and before I could get to him I heard Scott talking. As I listened from the doorway, I could hear him reciting poetry in a soft soothing voice. I was certain that Bobby hadn't understood a word Scott said, yet he had managed to figure out that Scott was trying to comfort him. By the time I walked over to them, Bobby had fallen asleep.

When I sat in the room that night, I sat next to Scott.

"I broke up with my girl today," he volunteered. His voice was hollow in the night.

"How come?" I asked. I could see only his shadow in the bed.

"She finds me repulsive now," he said, and even though I couldn't see his face I knew he had been crying.

"Scott," I said, "you're a beautiful man. How can anyone say you're not?" He had white-blond curly hair, a thick mustache and a small, well-cared-for beard. His skin was clear, and his features were so fine they were almost girl-like.

"Nobody would say that to me," he answered softly, "but I can see it in her eyes when she stands at the foot of my bed." There was a long silence before he added, "You should have seen how she looked when she first saw that my arms were gone. She tried, but she couldn't hide what she felt."

"Give her time, Scotty," I said, my voice almost inaudible because of the mask, and the tightness in my throat.

"I love her," Scott said, his voice raised now. "Why would I want to give her time? Why would I want her to have to settle?" He took a deep breath and I knew he was trying to compose himself. "I don't want her to spend her life taking care of me," he added more quietly.

"No one is going to have to take care of you, Scott," I said, trying reassure him. "There's enough of your arms left to wear artificial arms. In no time you'll be able to do things for yourself."

"Hey, Teri, how would you like someone to touch you with a

hook when he was making love?" He laughed a small sad laugh. "Could you handle it?" Without waiting for me to answer, he offered, "I couldn't."

I had nothing to say that could make it better, so as I got up I just reached over in the dark and touched his cheek with my gloved hand.

A couple of hours later, Bobby woke up screaming.

I ran over to the bed and saw that his whole body was trembling. "Bobby, what's wrong?"

"I want to die," he sobbed. It was the first time I had heard him speak; his words were slurred but understandable.

"Why, Bobby?" I asked, wiping his forehead with a sterile gauze and tucking the covers around him to help stop the shaking.

"I just want to," Bobby repeated.

"Common desire in this place," I heard Scott say from his bed.

"Come on, guys" I said, more to Scott than to Bobby, "give me a break. Even a good shrink can only handle one potential suicide at a time."

Scott sighed loudly. "Don't worry about it," he said. "Without arms, the only way to kill myself in this place would be to throw myself out of bed." Then he laughed his sweet regular laugh, and I knew he was making fun of himself. I was certain that once he had mourned the loss of his arms, he was the kind of person who could make the adjustment. He was bright, talented and had a good sense of humor, which I had found was the one thing that saved most very sick people.

Amy Martin was shouting and mumbling because we had awakened her, and even though it was a little early I decided to do her dressings. That way, when she was finished, everyone could go back to sleep. I never did figure out whether she was senile or just had burn psychosis, because I had never known her to make sense. I changed my gloves and mask, poured the solutions into the basin and readied myself to do her dressings. Then I took a deep breath. She weighed almost three hundred pounds. When Triumph was off, I had to rest her leg on my shoulder in order to wrap it. And every time I did, I swore each of her legs weighed more than me. By the time I had finished, she was asleep and my back was broken.

That morning I had to wait almost an hour for Lil. As she

walked into the front lobby, where I was reading a book, she looked destroyed. I could see that she had been crying; her usual sparse makeup was completely gone, her hair was disheveled and her uniform was a mess.

"Welcome back from the war," I said, but when she didn't even smile I knew something terrible must have happened.

She couldn't speak as we walked to the car. She just kept blowing her nose and stuffing the tissues up her sleeve. Finally, as we approached the house, she said, "They found Mr. Brown dead on rounds this morning."

"Was he supposed to die?" I asked, not knowing who he was.

"Not without me knowing it," she said, crying quietly. "By the time they discovered him, he was already . . . stiff." She blew her nose again.

"How come you didn't find him earlier?" I asked her. Lil usually was very conscientious about making rounds. She had checked her patients constantly whenever I worked with her.

"I was the only nurse on last night," she explained as we walked into the house. She sat on the couch with her coat on while I started cooking bacon and eggs. "And my three aides were hiding in a closet as usual," she added. We had talked about that many times. Though Lil was an excellent bedside nurse herself, she was not a good leader. It was too difficult for her to handle the anger of the aides when she told them what to do. I handed her a cup of hot chocolate, and she continued, "I did okay until after two a.m. meds, even though I had to suction Mr. Winslow constantly and try to stop Mrs. Harrow's rectal bleeding. But then I got an admission–an alcoholic in active DTs. He was huge and very strong."

"Why didn't you call the nursing office for help?" I handed her a plate. She was seldom too upset to eat.

I sat at the table across from her and listened as she went on, "I did call, but they told me they had no one to send me. Finally I called again and they sent up a security guard, but I still had to give the patient tranquilizers and monitor his blood pressure constantly because the doctor had ordered so much stuff to try to quiet him."

"Did you explain that to the day people?" I asked, thinking they had given her a hard time.

She wiped her mouth daintily with her napkin, and her eyes

filled. "No one said anything to me," she explained. "I had to make out an incident report, but even the head nurse was nice when she told me it was just a formality. It's really that I feel so bad that poor Mr. Brown had to die *alone*."

"That is sad," I said, knowing how she felt. Anytime someone's pain went unnoticed when he was my responsibility, I felt exactly the same as when I hadn't watched my kids closely enough and they hurt themselves. Guilty as hell . . . and no one had ever died without my noticing. "What did he die from?" I asked Lil. Sometimes facts help get your mind off your emotions.

She shrugged, still sniffing as she answered, "The resident had been too busy to do an admission note. They'll have to autopsy Mr. Brown." Lil sat quietly, shaking her head constantly.

I walked over and put my hands on her shoulders. "There was nothing you could have done differently," I said. "The place is a disaster, and until they get enough staff it won't change. No nurse can even watch fifty patients, never mind take care of—"

"Logic is no good today, Teri," she said, getting up and walking toward the bathroom to splash water on her face. "Because if it were me I would hate to be alone. . . ."

I knew just what she meant. Whenever I took care of a patient, I gave him everything *I* would want in his position. I struck a bargain with the fates. If I give . . . can I have? It always made me wonder what nasty nurses used as logic, just in case there was justice.

It took both of us longer than usual to fall asleep that day. I lay awake thinking of ways I could help Bobby and Scott as Lil went over and over her night, examining it . . . wondering in her heart if there was a valid reason for Mr. Brown to have died alone.

Both Triumph and I jumped when we heard Bobby's hair-raising scream. As I got up to go into the ward, Triumph muttered, "Somethin' more happened with that boy than he's sayin'."

For at least two weeks, every night I had been on, Bobby had awakened terrified. As I approached his bed, he looked so frightened that I knew he'd had another nightmare. And as I got closer the smell of urine signaled that he had wet the bed.

I changed the sheet underneath him, and then, as I was washing his bottom with a wet towel, he got an erection. I placed the towel over his penis and continued to wash the top of his thighs with another.

"That's what happens with my dog sometimes," he said, slurring slightly. I was startled that he was speaking and confused by what he was saying. He closed his eyes and sighed, "That's good."

"What, Bobby?" I asked, still not understanding.

He pressed his hand down over the towel, eyes closed, and sighed again. "Wet and warm . . . like Dober."

After Bobby was dry, I went back to the station and told Triumph that he was talking. Then I tried to repeat exactly what he had said. She raised her eyebrows comically as she listened, and immediately went in to Bobby. From the hall I could hear her ask, "Your dog lay on you, boy?" In the shadows, I could see him nod.

"Lawd," Triumph muttered as she walked back to the station, "sure is a funny world."

"You mean to tell me you think he's really sleeping with his dog?" I asked, surprised. "Sleeping as in screwing?"

"Seems to be what he's tryin' to say, ain't it?" Triumph said, still shaking her head. "Fur ain't wet–unless he's bein' licked, an that ain't no better." Triumph shrugged and added, "No sense askin' his mother, from what I hear."

I was still mulling over Bobby when the phone rang. It was Lil, and she sounded as though she was in a panic. "Teri, can you run up for a minute? There's this lady who keeps complaining about having to urinate. I tried inserting a Foley catheter, but nothing comes out."

"Who's on call?" I asked her.

"Wally," she said, then quickly added, "but he's been on for thirty-six hours, and I can't wake him up."

Calvin Wolansky, who by his own request was called Wally, was an intern. He was intellectually brilliant but emotionally a mess; he spent his days and nights off eating Valium and drinking alcohol so that he could handle his nights *on*. He was tall and good-looking, with a boyish face. Lil had a crush on him because she found him *sensitive*.

He's probably knocked out by the booze and the Valium, I

thought, but to Lil I said, "I'll be right up."

Everything was under control, so Triumph didn't mind my leaving. The elevator was empty, the halls on the units I passed were empty, and as I walked across the four corridors to Lil's floor I didn't meet one other nurse. I heard several buzzers and saw several call lights, heard a lot of moaning patients, and finally assumed that the rest of the hospital was as short staffed as the Burn Unit and Lil's floor. God, spare me this fate, I bargained, if I'm a very good nurse. Since I'd begun working in hospitals my fear of being admitted as a patient had multiplied a thousandfold.

Almost every call light on Lil's floor was on. As I walked down the long gray hall I saw her fly from one room to another, but when I reached that room she seemed to have disappeared. The four patients in the room were old and barely conscious; two of them were trying to climb over the bed rails, while the other two just lay moaning loudly. I walked back down the hall, calling for Lil, and on the way past the linen closet I noticed the light on inside. I pulled open the door and there three aides sat, reading *Modern Romance*. I was enraged, and before I could gather together my logic my emotions exploded and I screamed at them, "Get off your asses and get out here. You're getting paid to take care of these people."

Two aides were black and one was white. The white one spoke first. "Hey, I've got two little kids to take care of at home, and I ain't running my ass off for nobody."

Then one of the black girls got up, excused herself as she walked past me, and went to answer one of the buzzers. The other black woman just stared at me as I reached over to grab the white aide by the collar. I warned her one more time, "You've got only two minutes before I call the supervisor, and if she does nothing I'll take it to the head of administration in the morning." All the aides were civil-service workers and it was almost impossible to have them fired. But my eyes must have been blazing, because when she finally got up and decided to leave she sidled carefully around me.

The one black woman who remained said arrogantly, "You can report to anyone you like, and I'll turn you over to the NAACP."

More furious than I remembered being in a long time, I moved right up in front of her, nose to nose, and shouted, "Don't you dare imply that I'm prejudiced. I've never been–not *for* or *against*–and as long as my little white ass is flying around this place trying to get things done, I'll be damned if you'll be allowed to sit on yours just because it's black." When she stood up, I thought she was going to knock my head off, because she was at least a foot taller than I, but to my surprise she just shrugged and left.

As I called to Lil, I saw the aide going into the room with the old people. "God help them!"I said as I followed Lil's voice down the hall until I found her.

The woman Lil was trying to put a Foley catheter into was almost blue by the time I saw her. She gurgled rather than breathed, and looked to me as though she was in respiratory distress; that would account for her wanting to void, but placing a tube in her bladder would certainly not get the fluid I could hear out of her lungs.

"Where's the doctor?" I asked after I had pulled the Foley out of Lil's hand and told her to take a blood pressure.

As she fumbled with the cuff she explained, "I called him once, but he never came. I didn't have a chance to get back to him because this poor woman was trying to climb out of bed, and the man across the hall just yelled because he dropped his IV all over his bed, and I had to suction the old man in 688 . . ."

I stormed down the hall to the doctors' lounge, where Wally lay asleep, his hand in his pants, his cock erect. "Goddammit," I shouted, "there's a woman down the hall who needs you in order to breathe and you're lying here with your hands in your pants. Get out of bed and give her some Lasix before she croaks on you."

I had heard from Lil that many of the nurses, especially the young ones, hated to wake Wally up because he had a strange habit of playing with himself as he was coming to. Before anyone could cut through his foggy brain, they'd have to deal with his erection. It was at the very least embarrassing.

He sat up as though he had been ejected, his hair standing straight up. Still not fully comprehending, he asked, "Wha . . . what's up?"

I felt like a crazy woman; I wanted to grab him by the throat and choke him like a chicken. "Hurry up, goddammit," I hollered. "There's a woman who has so much fluid in her lungs she's going to need oars!"

He rubbed his face and jumped off the bed. He ran down the hall after me without even putting his shoes on, and he was still struggling to arrange the strings on his green cotton OR pants as he skidded up to the patient's bed.

Running his fingers anxiously through his matted hair, he asked the woman softly, "Having trouble breathing, Mom?" Lil had also told me that he called all old ladies Mom and all old men Pop.

She couldn't speak, so she nodded. Now I could see some fine brownish foam, like the foam from a breaking wave on the sand, around her mouth. Wally was working quickly, starting an IV with shaking hands but all the time soothing the woman. "You'll be fine, Mom, in just a few minutes," he said as he drew up the medication to inject into her IV tubing. After he gave it, he sat next to her and held her hand, telling her, "I'll take care of you, Mom . . ."

I had to admit, while watching him work, that Lil was right: there was something special about the way he handled his patients. Then I noticed Lil. She was staring directly ahead, looking stunned. "Lil . . ." I whispered.

She looked apologetic as she asked, "Will she be all right?"

I nodded yes.

Wally stayed with the woman until her lungs started to clear. When she could breathe more easily, the need to urinate seemed to pass. As she laid her gray-haired head back on the pillow, she looked lovingly at Wally and said, "Thank you, young man. You really saved my life."

He patted the hand he held. After several more minutes, when he was sure she was doing well, Wally left the room and walked slowly, head down, back to the doctors' lounge.

The old woman turned to Lil and me. "Isn't he a fine young man?" she asked, smiling now, "and a wonderful doctor?"

Lil smiled and nodded, and I said he certainly was. What I thought was: A fine young man whose doctoring is killing him . . . and God knows who else.

Everything was quiet when Lil and I walked back to the nurses' station. The aides were seated at the desks doing the charts, and the call lights had been answered.

"Thank you," I said to them as I sat down at the desk next to Lil. All three of them nodded. Lil looked exhausted and it was only 5 a.m. "You have to tell them you need more help," I said. "It's impossible to do any kind of nursing with the work load you have. There's just no way to get to all of them."

She nodded wearily. "I told them. I told the day nurses, I told the supervisor, I told the doctors. Everyone says the same thing: 'Do the best you can, and if you can't do it, quit.'" She slumped in her chair and sighed. "But if we don't do it, who will? And what about all these poor souls?" She motioned toward the rooms.

As I walked back down to the Burn Unit, I thought, I'd rather work burns; it's very difficult, but not impossible. Lil's floor was absolutely impossible.

While I was gone, Triumph had gotten a new admission: Dick Fox, a roofer, who had burned his hands tarring a roof. He had withstood the pain all day, but in the middle of the night he had found it excruciating, so he had come to the ER and they had admitted him. Forty, with freckles and red hair, he was pleasant and talkative. After having Amy Martin, Bobby and Scott for so long, both Triumph and I were glad to have Dick's company. She had put him in the bed next to Scott.

That morning, Triumph and I did Amy together, then Bobby, then Scott, and then we took a coffee break. "They goin' to graft Scott's stumps this week," Triumph told me. "It's time to take the pigskin off again and use his own." She told me that they would take squares of skin from the front of his thighs, with something that looked like a cheese slicer, and place it over his wounds to try to speed the healing. Zaccara wanted him grafted as soon as possible in order to get him fitted for his prostheses before too much time passed.

"He ain't talkin' as much lately," she added. When she started to hum, I realized that I had noticed a change in him myself the last few days. He seemed angrier. And now, when I focused on it, it worried me too.

Lights from the two tall buildings across the courtyard shone through the window of the darkened ward, casting eerie shadows over Bobby's bed.

I sat in the high-back metal chair, listening to the sound of

Scott's quiet breathing. He had just fallen asleep after spending the last three hours screaming his outrage at life, violently thrashing his legs on the bed until he was exhausted. Both he and Bobby had been taken to the operating room several times during the past few weeks for grafting; between the anesthesia and the pain, Scott had finally reached the end of his endurance. He fumed at any of us whom he had to be dependent on.

"I hate being fed, I hate being washed. I can't stand your hands in my mouth brushing *my* teeth . . . I can't even scratch my ass by myself," he raged. Because he couldn't throw things, he kicked anything he could reach with his feet, then he tore at the sheets with his teeth.

Bobby had stared wide-eyed and frightened, while Dick, whose hands were healing well, had occasionally approached Scott to try to quiet him. Then, as suddenly as Scott's tantrum had begun, it ended. He struggled to turn on his side, and when he couldn't he just lay back and fell asleep.

I wished I could have done something to reach him, but the morass was too thick for me. His problems were overwhelming, and I wasn't sure I wouldn't have reacted the same way. He would never be able to play guitar again, and that had been his life since he was a child. His vulnerability and sensitivity had made him a loner until he had met Shelly, the girl whom he now loved enough to refuse to see. His body image was destroyed by the thought of artificial arms, which he referred to as "hooks" no matter how many times someone tried to explain the improvements that had been made in prostheses.

The night before, Scott had told me for the first time that when Zaccara stood next to his stretcher in ER and said, "Those arms have to come off," he thought they were talking about someone else. When it finally seeped into his awareness that the doctor meant *his* arms, he had fainted. His voice had been shaking when he asked me, "Why did he say *those* arms? Why didn't he say *his* arms?"

Bobby's whimpering took my mind off Scott.

"What's wrong?" I whispered, pulling my chair closer to Bobby's bed.

"My mother won't come," he said, softly slurring words through his tears.

"Maybe she's awfully busy. I'm sure she loves you," I said,

trying to comfort him. I smoothed the wet hair off his forehead.

He nodded and then curled over on his side facing me. He reached for my hand. "But she won't let Dober sleep with us," he added sadly.

No wonder, I thought to myself. "Who's us?" I asked, because I didn't remember him having sisters and brothers.

He looked puzzled for a minute but then repeated, "When I sleep with her, Dober can't sleep there." He turned onto his back again, put his hands under his head, and stared at the ceiling. "She's warm, too," he mused, "like Dober."

"What do you mean?" I asked, trying to keep my imagination from running wild. I thought it peculiar that a sixteen-year-old boy was allowed to sleep with his mother, but I tried not to jump to conclusions.

Bobby turned, leaned over on his elbow and faced me. Very slowly, as though he was trying to help me understand, he said, "*You* know, like the other night . . . wet and warm. Remember?" He looked very young and he spoke with the total candor of an innocent child.

I heard Scott whistle. A long low whistle. Jesus, I thought, he must have gotten the same idea, as unfathomable as it seemed. I sat with Bobby until he fell asleep, and then I went over to check Scott. His eyes were wide open.

"What are you thinking, Charmer?" I asked him, smiling.

"Kid's got some setup," he whispered. As I bent closer to see if there was any drainage on his dressings, he said sarcastically, "When I get home, I'm going to have to settle for wet dreams."

"Unless," I said teasingly, "you get rid of that shit attitude you have. Then *maybe* someone will love you."

I pulled down the sheet to check his graft sites; both thighs had been used. The scarlet-red gauze covering, a six-by-six area on each leg, was intact. Scarlet red was a mercurochrome based powder used to stop bleeding and dry the new wounds. "I have to go to the bathroom, while you're down there," Scott said.

I took the urinal off his bedside stand, and rather than laying it between his legs and contaminating his graft sites I held it over him. Then I gently lifted his penis and fixed it in place while he voided.

"I have no feeling down there," Scott said. He sounded worried when he asked, "Why haven't I had a hard-on since I've been in here?"

"Hey, Charmer," I said seriously, "give yourself a break. You've had a lot of other things on your mind, not to speak of the amount of pain you've had. Or the depression." He looked relieved, so I teased, "Besides, the outfits we wear in this place are not exactly conducive to erections." He smiled and seemed to feel better. I tucked a new flannel blanket under his butt because he had perspired.

"Shelly came to see me today," he said. I nodded. Then he added, "I sent her home again."

I stood at the bottom of his bed. "Don't make any big decisions until you get out of here, Scotty," I said gently. "Things might look different when you're home."

"What's going to happen to the kid?" he whispered, indicating Bobby with a movement of his head.

"I don't know," I said. "I don't know how reliable the stuff he says is. But don't you worry about it," I reassured him as I moved up to tousle his hair, "I'll check into it."

I did. . . . Another monumental error.

During morning report, I mentioned it to Mrs. Bradberry, the day charge nurse. She was a stocky woman who reminded me of an aging cheerleader: Her straw-colored hair done in 1950s style and her red lipstick carefully applied to thicken her lips; they always looked cutely pursed. Also she drew a fake beauty mark on her upper lip. She had been working in the Burn Unit for seven years and was overly impressed with her own importance. She was a good technical nurse, but she was also a doctor's handmaiden; anytime a patient's pain got in the way of a procedure, she continued the treatment and sacrificed the patient. She hardly ever called a doctor, and when she did she apologized so profusely for bothering him that they loved her. The patients didn't. I didn't.

After I told her what I thought Bobby had said, repeating it exactly as I remembered, I told her I might have misinterpreted what he meant, but she said dryly, "Not likely; those people are like that." Without looking up, she added, "I'll have Social Service check it."

As I got up to leave, I could see that she had smeared her beauty mark across her upper lip; Hitler's mustache, I thought, amused. I kept a straight face when I said goodbye, hoping no one else would tell her until the patients saw her.

Two days off a week were never enough while I worked at Barrenfield. I always came back on duty still tired, so when Harriet told me at report to get set for another hairy night, I snapped, "What now?"

"I have no idea, sweets," she said, making a face. "Bobby's ole lady came in today, and by the time she left he was hysterical. He screamed for over an hour, then climbed back into his shell and refused to talk. I can tell you one thing, she'll never be nominated for Mother of the Year by me."

"What's she like?"

"Evil-looking," Harriet said thoughtfully. "I'd hate to be stuck in a dark place with that woman, honey." For Harriet that was a big admission. I wondered whether she knew what Bobby had told me when she said, "Bradberry asked me to tell you Social Service was up to see the kid yesterday, then called in the mother." She didn't ask any questions. "By the way," she added, "the kid is pre-op for his last grafts tomorrow."

After Harriet left, I wrote out some of the charts and drank a cup of coffee slowly. Instead of taking the chance of waking Bobby by going into the ward to do temps, I decided to wait until someone called or until I had to start my 2 a.m. dressings. That way my bad night would be shorter.

But Bobby woke screaming before long, soaking wet and trembling. When I ran in and tried to pet him he turned away and curled on his side.

"Bobby?" I asked softly. "Do you want to tell me what's wrong?" I could see from where I stood over him that he'd shut his eyes tight, and was biting his lip. When I put my hand on his shoulder, he started to sob.

"Scott," I said, turning around, "do you want to tell me?" Scott was lying on his back, his face solemn and angry. He shook his head.

"How can I help, then?" I asked them both.

Bobby's whole body was shaking as Scott answered, "You

can't."

I walked over to the other side of the bed and bent, almost kneeling, in front of Bobby. "I'll try my best to help, if you can tell me why you're so unhappy," I said as I watched big tears run down his face.

"She *killed* my dog," he sobbed, chest heaving. I must have looked puzzled, because he repeated, "She killed Dober." He was crying more softly as I looked toward Scott for verification.

"That's right," Scott said angrily. "She gave the kid some cock-and-bull story about having him put to sleep because he got sick."

Suddenly Bobby was quiet. He turned on his back and looked straight ahead. "Tomorrow I'm going to be with Dober," he said, in a voice so clear and cold it gave me the chills. I bent, lowered my mask and kissed his forehead. "Yes," he said with certainty and too much composure, "tomorrow I'm going to die and be with my dog."

"Bobby," I said, trying to comfort him, "I know you loved Dober, but you can't just die . . ."

With that he let out a scream that curled my hair. "I *can* too die . . . I *can* die," he cried. "I want to be with Dober." He sat straight up, leaning on his elbows, and kept screaming the same thing over and over. Dick Fox had gotten out of bed and walked toward him; Scott was trying to talk to him. But nothing stopped his screaming.

I ran quickly out to the nursing station and called the doctor. Muscio was on, and when I breathlessly explained what was happening he said, "Hysterical patients don't need hysterical nurses." Then he hung up.

Jesus, I thought angrily, Triumph was right: he *is* practicing to be like Zaccara. Suddenly I heard Dick holler. I ran back into the room just as he shouted, "My God–cut it out, kid!"

Bobby had jumped out of bed and was rubbing his back along the entire length of the rough stucco wall. Pieces of dressing and bits of flesh hung in one long bloody line. Dick was trying to grab for him, but his hands weren't healed enough to have any strength. When Dick tried to get him in a bear hug, Bobby hit one of his hands hard. I saw him wince. I ran up to Bobby and threw my body against his—back first, so he wouldn't smash me in the face. Lucky for me that he was small. Between Dick and me we held him pinned until he quieted down a little. Scott was staring at us, helplessly.

Finally Bobby slid to the floor, and whimpered, "I *hate* her . . . I *hate* her."

I lifted Bobby from under his arms and walked him back to his bed. Then, instead of showering him, I poured several bottles of saline over his now shredded grafts and redressed his back.

Dick stood next to the bed and talked to him.

"Hey, Bob boy," he said softly, "how about getting well enough to get out of here, and I'll talk to your mother. Maybe if she gives the okay I'll buy you another dog–just like Dober."

But Bobby just stared blankly ahead, insisting with an eerie intensity, "Tomorrow I'll see Dober."

When I went out to the nurses' station to call Muscio back again, Dick pulled up a chair and sat next to Bobby. Every time Bobby's eyes closed, he'd start to thrash and scream again. Several times he tried to jump out of bed, but Dick kept pushing him down.

Muscio was exasperated when he answered the phone. "Why don't you just calm him down?"

"I need some kind of medication," I told him. "He keeps threatening to die, and I can't keep him quiet for more than a few minutes before he gets wild again."

"He's going to the Operating Room tomorrow," Muscio said, as though I were retarded. "That's only a few hours away, I'm not ordering anything now."

"Then at least come up and see him," I begged. "His back looks like a mess." I heard another scream from the ward. "Goddamn," I hollered, "what do you want me to do with him?"

"Sit and hold his hand till morning," he snapped, and hung up again. I promised myself that if I had to, I'd talk to Dr. Blake. I was pretty fucking furious that every time I called a doctor for help he hung up.

When Muscio sauntered into the nurses' station that morning, Bobby had finally fallen asleep. Dick was sitting next to him, as furious as I. "I'm going to give those doctors a piece of my mind," he had told me earlier, "and then I'm getting out of here." I had reassured him that I would take care of it.

I was sitting at the desk, eating a doughnut and reading over Bobby's chart, when Muscio stood over me and said arrogantly, "I see that you finally managed to get things under control."

I don't remember the doughnut leaving my hand, but the next minute there was cinnamon all over Muscio's green scrub coat.

"What do you think you're doing, young lady?" he asked, horrified.

"I'm trying to get you to act like a doctor," I shouted. "When I call you because one of your patients is hysterical, screaming that he wants to die, I don't think you have the right to hang up!"

"It was the middle of the night—" he began, but before he finished whatever he was going to say I screamed, "Goddammit! If you didn't want to be *on* in the middle of the night, you should have been a taxi driver, not a doctor. Then you could have turned your sign off!"

"Hand me that chart," he shouted, his face red.

I threw it at him and walked in back to get my clothes on.

"I'll have your license for this," he hollered as I walked past him through the swinging doors.

I waited for Bradberry by the shower room, and there I explained what had happened.

"I'm certain there was a better way to handle it," she reprimanded. "Maybe he didn't understand what you were so upset about." She said it as though she was having difficulty comprehending it herself.

"Well, Bradberry," I said slowly and emphatically, "maybe you can help him. Listen carefully. It's my opinion that it is wrong for Muscio to take the kid down to operate on him today. If he does, please tell him that I think his judgment stinks, that the boy is not going to make it because of the state he's in."

She smiled as though I was a lunatic, a real certifiable nut.

"I'm not coming in tonight," I told her, then added, "Have someone let me know what's been decided about my license."

At eleven-thirty that night Lil had gone to work, the kids were in bed asleep and I lay on the couch listening to Tchaikovsky's Fifth. I was dozing lightly, enjoying my extra night off and wondering what I would do if by some fluke Muscio could manage to have my license revoked, when the phone rang.

"This is Matt Muscio, Teri," he said quietly. "I called to

apologize for this morning."

"Okay," I said coolly.

"I shouldn't have insulted you, or threatened you . . ." he continued, but his voice sounded nasal and more subdued than usual.

"Doctor?" I said, my voice still cool with reserve. "I'm having a hard time figuring out what moved you to this bit of compassion. It's unlike you." Try as I might, I was still not able to forgive him.

"Please don't, Teri," he said. "I had no idea . . ."

Suddenly my head started to swim and I had to sit. Dropping my sarcasm, I asked, "How's Bobby, Matt?"

There was a long silence and then an audible sigh before he answered, with cracked voice, "We lost him."

The rest of the conversation sounded as though I were listening in a tunnel. No matter how hard I had fought this morning, I hadn't really believed it would happen. Muscio was telling me how Bobby's heart had been fine, how suddenly he had started to fight the anesthesia, how six orderlies had helped hold him down . . . "Then he just went out on us. Nobody could figure out what had happened. We tried everything," he said weakly. Then, "I'm sorry."

The next night I sat in the oppressive silence of the nurses' station, stalling, not wanting to face Scott. Harriet had said he was taking Bobby's death very badly. He had ranted and raved all day, gotten out of bed and kicked apart the room. Dick Fox had signed himself out, his hands well enough healed that he could be seen on an outpatient basis. Amy Martin was too far out in left field to know what was going on. I knew I wouldn't be able to stand the guilt if Scott accused me of having started the whole thing by telling Bradberry what Bobby had said.

I kept doing busy work on the charts until I thought I heard someone cry out from the ward. I sat up straight and strained to hear; I wanted to make sure I wasn't imagining Bobby's cries after all those nights. But I clearly heard it again–a soft moaning.

I tiptoed across the hall and into the room, squinting through the darkness to try to see. Amy, filling the whole bed, was sleeping peacefully. Bobby's bed was glaringly empty.

As I looked at Scott, I wasn't sure . . . I moved closer very quietly. Then I stood at the foot of the bed and didn't say anything because I was afraid I would startle him.

He was lying on his stomach, moving slowly up and down. I heard him moan again. "Scott?" I called softly, and he immediately flipped over onto his back.

I walked over to the side of his bed.

"Go away," he said, and I knew he was crying. When I reached to straighten his sheet I saw that his thighs were bleeding profusely. And that he had a huge erection.

"What were you trying to do, ruin your graft sites?" I asked softly, pulling on a clean pair of gloves.

"I can't do it, Teri," he sobbed, a grimace on his face. I knew he was in pain, but I wasn't sure from what.

I tried to stop the bleeding on his thighs as hard as I tried to ignore his erection.

"I'm scared, Teri," he cried, "and I can't get it down. I've been trying . . ."

I stared at his swollen penis as though it was a foreign object. "Really?" I said, because I didn't know what to do with him.

He threw himself over onto his stomach again and started moving, but within seconds the pain was so bad that he had to stop. When he flipped over again, his thighs were a bloody mess.

"Oh, God help me," he wailed, "I can't do it myself."

I stared stupidly at him, then quickly grabbed a pillow and held it over his penis but away from his thighs. "Try that," I said, biting my bottom lip and putting as much pressure as I could on the pillow. He tried moving frantically up and down for several minutes. Finally, winded, he stopped. When I pulled the pillow away, his penis was as big as before.

I thought about calling the doctor, but Zaccara was on and I was sure that he wouldn't be any help, would probably humiliate both me and Scott with some sarcastic response. I had no medication order for Scott, and he was obviously in pain.

"I think I have an idea," I said to Scott, and I ran out to the solution closet. When I ran back to his bed I said, "I'm sorry," and then quickly poured a liter of cold saline over his penis. I tried not to get his graft sites wet. He hollered and then lay shaking in the wet bed, but his erection stood as tall as before.

After I tucked a clean blanket under him I started to dry him off. "Touch me, Teri, please," he asked in a soft cracked voice. "Just this once . . . please help *me?*"

I drew back as though his body was boiling hot.

"Goddammit! Don't look so horrified," he cried. "I can't do it myself. You've washed me a thousand times; you've stuck your fingers in my mouth and up my ass for medicine. Just once . . . Just touch me once . . . for me? "

I quickly threw sterile towels over his thighs, said a prayer that no one would walk into the unit and that Amy was really senile, and grabbed his penis.

"Teri," he whispered, "take the glove off. I haven't been touched since I've been here." I shook my head.

"Listen," he pleaded, "I can't touch myself. Look at me, dammit! I have no hands!"

I was crying when I pulled my glove off.

Later that morning, lying in bed, I told Lil. And she did one of the things I loved most about her: she bombarded me with logic.

Lil sat up in bed, puffed two pillows behind her, folded her hands in front of her and said, "Common battlefield phenomenon, Scott's erection. Didn't you ever read stories where when a guy's buddies get shot down right next to him, the same thing happens?" I was lying on my side and shook my head. "God, girl," she said, smiling, "your ignorance is abysmal. Well, anyway, from what I've read, fear closely resembles sexual excitation."

"How come?" I asked, not getting the connection.

"Probably has something to do with the survival of the species," she answered matter-of-factly. She reached over and patted my head. "Let's see if I can come up with something less theoretical for you so that your Italian Catholic guilts don't get you." She held her chin and sat thinking for a few minutes before she said, "From the beginning, in nursing, we're taught to use our hands as tools; that means that we have to separate our actions from our emotions, right?"

I nodded, but I was still suffering too much from the events of the past days to pay total attention.

"You eat a sandwich with the same hand that you use to dig feces out of a patient's rectum, don't you? It's merely a tool, child, when we work. And besides, who ever questions what a gynecologist feels when he's got his hand up someone's vagina?"

"It was different," I said to her. "This was more like sex."

"For whom?" she asked, raising her eyebrows. "From what you tell, it sounds more like Scott felt scared after Bobby died. And lonely. Did he make a pass at you afterward?"

"Don't be silly," I said. "We just cried together and then he thanked me."

"Well, did you get pleasure out of it?" she asked gently.

"Sure, the same kind of pleasure I get when I give a shot of pain medication and the patient stops hollering."

"Would you have felt better if he had let you keep your glove on?" Lil asked me seriously.

I nodded.

"I think I understand that," Lil said softly. "The glove protects you. It lets you touch, but you can't be touched. It leaves you in charge. When you took that glove off, you and Scott were equals. You became as vulnerable as he was because then you too could be touched. The guilt comes, I think, from admitting your humanness while you're in the uniform of the healer."

"Human to human, you mean, exposes my impotence?" I asked Lil, still not fully understanding.

"Sure," she said, smiling again. "You know doctors and nurses are never supposed to let a patient know that they're just human beings. And you know also that many times when the patients find out that we're as human as they are, they feel betrayed."

I was beginning to feel better. "Well," I said, "I don't know whether anyone else would believe your explanation, but I like it much better than the idea of any sexual implications, perish the thought!"

Lil laughed and slid down in bed, pulling the covers up to her chin as she said, "God! One of these days your conditioning is going to totally ruin your compassion if you don't watch it."

CHAPTER 15

I had been working in the Burn Unit nine months when I met Melody. It was Christmas night, a real bummer to work.

As Lil and I drove to work I sat quietly, feeling guilty about leaving Greg and my kids. It was different for Lil: she hated Christmas. "It sure is a miserable day for poor people," she said, pulling onto the parkway faster than usual.

"Are you feeling bad because you didn't get your kids a lot of presents?" I asked, sighing.

"A lot is one thing, nothing is something else," she said softly, biting her bottom lip. Although she almost always worked double shifts, she was usually broke because she helped me with the house bills, paid to support her kids and gave whatever was left to any poverty-stricken strangers she happened to meet throughout the year.

"What did you get your kids?" she asked.

"Nothing much," I answered uneasily, "but you know my family. They always have great holidays, in spite of the fact that I'm usually in mourning for myself." Lil laughed. I still felt bad, remembering the morning. I had so badly wanted to play Santa for my kids, but, as usual, Christmas had been at my parents'. My whole family had helped me pick up the pieces, and the tradition of Christmas went on even though I was broke.

I began to feel sloppy sentimental. Even the tinsel on the decorated trees reminded me of sad silver tears. Lil interrupted my depression by saying, "I wonder how many kids didn't have a tree this Christmas, didn't get any presents." She pointed accusingly at the car radio and added, "They had to listen to some jerk shout, 'Ho

Ho Ho, this is Santa, and if you're good little boys and girls you'll get everything you want for Christmas'!" She shook her head. "I'll bet a lot of those kids thought they hadn't been good enough just because their parents were poor."

"And *I'll* bet," I told her as I tried to find a channel that wasn't playing Christmas carols, "that hundreds of parents, just like us, spent the last few weeks racing frantically over to their radios to slam the damn things off before that terrible ho-ho-ho." By the time we reached the hospital, we both hated the society that would sell its children down the tubes just to sell its merchandise.

The sky was black and starless, with several thick snow-laden gray clouds, as Lil and I walked from the car. It was freezing. In the lobby, the first thing that hit us was a people-sized poster of Santa Claus with a red-sequined HO HO HO underneath.

"Sadistic bastards," Lil said. As we got into the elevator she dropped a small package she was carrying, a gift for one of her older patients who didn't have a family. "Hope it didn't break," she mumbled. "I can't replace it."

"What is it?" I asked.

"Holy water from Lourdes," she answered.

"I thought you didn't believe that stuff," I said, surprised.

"I don't, you dope. But *she* does. Besides, it has to work better than what they're giving her here."

Harriet was waiting in the nurses' station, stone-faced. The shoulders of her long thin body were stooped and her mousy brown hair looked more wilted than usual. Her pinched nose had a high shine and all the lipstick had been chewed off her thin lips.

"You're late," she said, looking at the wall clock. God! I thought, what a tight-ass.

"I'm here and I'm depressed," I snapped, "so don't hassle me." I walked into the back room to hang my coat in the locker.

"You're breaking my heart, Sweety," Harriet said when I came back. "You won't know how depressed you can be until you see what we got." Suddenly she looked triumphant.

"Bad?" I asked seriously, but I already knew the answer. Harriet was a real smart-ass, but she was also extremely accurate in her assessments.

"Worse," she said as she pulled a chair in front of the desk.

I sat down. Granshaw, the night aide, back from leave, sat on a chair near the door. She was a heavyset woman with curly gray hair. She wore bright-red lipstick and had thick eyebrows penciled in black. Her corrugated face was covered with powder too light for her olive skin, and her rouge was the same color as her shocking-pink uniform.

Harriet started to read aloud from the Cardex. "'Melody Lee. Seven-year-old female. Eighty percent burned. Admitted from the ER last night. Christmas tree fire. Brother, four years old, dead on arrival.'"

"Ugh," I said. "Dead kids. There's nothing worse in medicine as far as I'm concerned."

"Dying kids are worse," Harriet answered dryly. "Wait till you see this one."

"What's burned?" I asked, and Harriet looked at me as though I had a piece of my brain missing.

"Didn't you hear me say she was an eighty percenter?" she asked slowly. When I nodded, she continued emphatically, "The *untouched* area goes from below her waist to the top of her thighs. The bottoms of her feet are also clean. The rest is burned. Third-degree, I bet." Then, with a look of satisfaction, Harriet said, "I did her dressings twice tonight. It took me three hours each time." Her expression softened when she said, "The guys say she has only about four days."

"Who's covering?" I asked.

"Zaccara," Harriet answered, "and he's had a rough day, so he left word that he's only to be called if it's 'imperative'."

"Christ," I said, "Zaccara's all I need tonight. If he gives me any grief, I swear we'll come to blows."

"You'll never win, honey," she said, smiling weakly. "With him you won't have a chance."

"That may be true, Harriet, old girl," I said, weary already. "But I too have been known to hammer a person to death with words when necessary." Pure and utter bravado.

"Well, I want to wish you luck, Sweety," she said. "And now I'm going home. I'm beat." Harriet pulled her coat on as she walked through the swinging doors, and now that I was alone with Granshaw and the patients I didn't feel nearly as brave as I had only a moment before.

The census in the unit was low. All but two of the patients had been discharged. One was Allito, a drug addict from the county jail, whose needle site had gotten infected and needed grafting; he was always handcuffed to his bed. And the other, Amy Martin, was still waiting for placement in a nursing home. Scott had gone home, complete with two "hooks" as he still insisted on calling them. And Harriet told me that Shelly had come to pick him up.

As I made rounds, I could see that Allito and Amy were quiet for a change, so I decided Granshaw could handle them easily. She was trying to intimidate me into not overworking her by looking annoyed again.

"How about taking temps on Allito and Martin while I check the kid?" I said, ignoring her stare. She stomped away toward the ward as I went toward the VIP room.

The child looked like a small mummy doll lying in bed. She didn't even fill half of it, despite all her bulky dressings. I stood in the doorway, panic-stricken. Aside from Bobby, I had never seen a burned child before.

Melody was almost completely wrapped in gauze bandages. They went around her head, across her face, down her neck and over her chest. Both arms and legs were covered. She had tan patches on her eyes. Only her lower belly and her feet showed. They were black. Intravenous bottles hanging on stainless-steel poles, plastic tubes going into her body and coming out, plus the three wire monitor leads, added to the clutter of the room and to my confusion. The bubbling from the large green oxygen tank and the constant regular beeping of the heart monitor added to my anxiety. It was like an alarm which poked fun at me, while the small monitor screen drew something that looked like . . . a hill . . . a mountain . . . a valley . . . a hill again . . . straight plain; I had never before been totally responsible for interpreting a cardiac monitor. Even in Intensive Care at Elmwood, there had been other nurses to consult. I considered calling the nursing supervisor, but when I remembered that her specialty was obstetrics I was certain she wouldn't be able to help. And I know that on Christmas Night there would be no extra critical-care nurses on.

So, armed with the guilt over my ignorance and inspired by my panic, I made the monumental decision to call Zaccara. This seemed at least "imperative." I walked quickly out to the nurses' station and dialed the phone. After several rings, a husky sleepy sound, not quite a word, came across.

"Did I just wake you, Doctor?" I asked, stalling. I wanted to make sure he was conscious enough to understand me.

"Don't be silly, honey," Zaccara drawled, "I was just sitting by the phone waiting for you to call."

"I hate to bother you, Doctor," I said, trying not to sound shaken by his sarcasm, "but I can't read a monitor, so I won't know when this kid's in trouble." Then I held my breath.

Zaccara screamed, "Teri? Dammit! Don't be an idiot! Most of the girls up there can't read a monitor." I held the phone away from my ear, but I could still hear him yell, "Disconnect the damn thing if it makes you nervous." Then I heard a click.

Oh no you don't! I said to myself, not again. I was furious. I could hear my heart pounding in my ears as I redialed the phone.

"Dr. Zaccara, that is absurd," I said sharply. "And from now on, if you decide to scream at me, scream instructions with the insults. That way I'll learn something and you'll accomplish something."

To my surprise, he laughed. Then, in a much more reasonable voice, he said, "Teri, listen to me. That kid is already in trouble–big trouble. The monitor is only there to indicate any irregularity in rate. Look for longer spaces between beats or much shorter ones." He continued to explain some basic rhythm irregularities until I felt safer, and by the time we hung up I almost liked him.

I waved to Allito and Amy on my way back to Melody. The room she was in was even grungier than I remembered it, and I hated the look of the large black stains on the gray tile floor. When I first saw those spots, I was sure somebody had bled out, that the room was the site of some gory emergency death. "Not so," Harriet had explained. "Just silver nitrate, a chemical treatment that was used before you got here. As soon as the sunlight hit anything it touched, it turned black." Still, I thought, it looks ominous to me.

I didn't know where to begin. I did know that in a couple of hours I'd have to do Melody's dressings, and the thought paralyzed me. Underneath those clean white gauze bandages, worn like a newly laundered suit of clothes, was incredible damage to a real human being. When the suit was removed, I would have to deal with my own reaction to that human being. Gauze gone, there would be nothing between us anymore . . . nothing to protect *me*.

As I walked into the room, I spoke, so as not to frighten the child, "Hi, Melody. My name is Teri and I'm going to be your nurse. I know you can't call for me, so I'll come in every five minutes to make sure you're okay."

Melody nodded almost imperceptibly, up and down, and as she did her chest began to heave erratically and I knew she was crying.

"Melody, listen to me," I said softly, touching the cold wet dressings over her arm. "The reason you can't talk is because you have a tube between your vocal cords that keeps them from vibrating." I tried to remember what it was like to be seven and decided that my explanation was too complicated for Melody to understand. So I tried again. "Melody, I know it's scary not to be able to tell me what you need, but I'm a good guesser. That tube that helps you breathe," I touched it, "the one in your neck, stops you from talking. Don't worry; your voice isn't broken for good. When you get better and the tube comes out, you'll be able to talk again." I pulled down the sheet and touched the clear plastic tubing which was draining her urine, and said. "Don't worry about wetting the bed either, because this," I tugged gently on her catheter, "pees for you. Okay?"

Then I touched the fingers on Melody's left hand and said, "When you have pain, I want you to wiggle these two fingers up and down. We have medicine we can give you to take away some of the pain, but you have to help me by letting me know. Okay?"

Melody shook her head side to side, indicating no, and I was confused.

"Do you understand what I said, Melody?" I asked.

The child moved her head up and down.

"Move your fingers, then, when I ask, 'Do you have any pain.' Okay?"

Melody again moved her head slowly side to side. I thought she didn't understand. "Do you have pain?" I asked, trying to test her. Melody made a very definite movement of her head, up and down.

"Well then, to get medicine, just move your fingers. Okay?"

Melody shook her head from side to side.

I was getting frustrated, so I said, "This is a hell of a time for you to get stubborn, Mel; you can't just shake your head for everything or it will take forever until we go through the list of everything you could need. We have to figure out signals. Got it?"

Melody nodded up and down, and I thought we had it made.

"Now move your fingers for pain medicine," I said again.

Melody's chest started to heave erratically again; she was crying.

"Don't cry, Mel," I said, patting her arm gently. Then, like a brick, it hit me. "Melody, *can* you move your fingers?"

The child's breathing slowed and she shook her head from side to side.

Oh Shit! I thought, as I touched her fingers. They were colder than they should have been, but I had figured that was from the wet dressings. Now it occurred to me that Melody might have nerve damage or circulation damage or both; or even brain damage from smoke inhalation. "Melody," I asked, "can you move your toes?" I touched her big toe on the left foot, then the right. All her toes wiggled. Not brain damage. "Whoopie," I said as I patted the little girl's foot. "We can use the toes on your left foot, okay?"

Melody nodded up and down slowly and then wiggled the toes on her left foot without any prompting. She was a very bright little girl.

"You can't see me because of the bandages over your eyes," I said, "but I'm smiling." I patted Melody's arm again, and then stopped and patted her head gently. "I like you," I whispered.

Through the small space in the gauze on her face, I could see her try to smile. It was eerie because I couldn't see her eyes. "Be back in a couple of minutes," I told her as I walked out of the room.

In the nurses' station, Granshaw said, "Those two are fine. How's the kid?"

Granshaw had worked in the Burn Unit for years. I didn't particularly like her, but she knew what she was doing so I respected her and treated her politely whenever I could. She was brusque and sloppy, about fifty years old. She had a chip on her shoulder that was more like a boulder, because she had to take orders from younger nurses who had been in the unit much less time than she. Still, Granshaw was kinder to me than she had been to any of the other nurses. In Granshaw's words, "You maybe don't know everything, but you don't seem to think that cap on your head means you ain't supposed to get no shit under your fingernails, like some of them." From a woman like Granshaw, that was some compliment.

"The kid's name is Melody," I told Granshaw, looking up from the chart I was reading, "and she's a mess."

"Think ya can handle it?" she asked with raised eyebrows and a crooked smile.

"If I can't, I'll ask for help," I answered, determined not to be baited. I continued to read Melody's chart and came across "Eyes: Unable to assess" on the history and physical sheet. "Wonder what this means?" I asked, showing the chart to Granshaw.

"Prob'ly means that jerk who admitted her didn't want to say she can't see no more. Kid prob'ly got her eyes burned out."

I just stared at her; any display of emotion on my part would have been reported to all the other aides as weakness, and then they'd start testing me. "Crap," was all I managed to say.

"No sense gettin' yourself bothered about her bein' blind. Where she's goin', she ain't gonna need no eyes," Granshaw said loftily.

"Shut up, Granshaw," I snapped. "I can't think while you're talking." Then I heard Allito call from the ward, "Nurse . . . nurse?"

I looked at Granshaw, who was sulking, and asked pleasantly, "Do you want to take the ward while I do Melody or would you rather we work together?" I had found her much more cooperative when I gave her some choice, and usually I didn't mind doing it either way.

"Na," she said, standing, "tonight I'd rather work by myself." As she walked away to answer Allito's call, she glanced over her shoulder and said, "If *you* ain't scared to take care of the kid alone."

"I'll be okay," I answered as I pushed myself up from my chair. "If not, I'll ask you for help."

When she left, I went to check Melody. "Hey, Mel," I stage-whispered from the doorway. Her chest was moving up and down, regularly, and she didn't react when I called again, so I knew she was asleep. From where I stood, I could see the urine drainage bag and the fluid level in her suction bottle. Everything appeared in order, so I stayed out of the room. If I had gone in, I would have had to glove and mask.

"What did he need?" I asked Granshaw as she came out of the ward. We walked back to the nurses' station and sat at the desk. "Pain med," she answered lightly. Then, challenging, "I gave him a Darvon."

"Jesus, Granshaw!" I hollered. "You're going to have my ass in a sling someday if you don't stop doing that." Even though I was annoyed, I understood that she took liberties handing out the small meds because she resented her position. As an aide, she was often forced to accept added responsibility when a new nurse started, only to be limited again before long. She tolerated the difference in pay, but it was the status she missed more. She hated having to say to a patient, after she had done everything else for him, "I have to ask the nurse to get your medicine." It diminished her.

Granshaw stiffened in her chair and said, "I ain't never gonna give a pill again; even if you're in shit up to your elbows." She waved her finger at me. "You can just listen to them damn patients scream if you don't trust me."

"Dammit, Granshaw," I shouted back, "who the hell is talking about trust?" I took one deep breath and added indignantly, "I'm talking about getting my ass in a sling. I'm talking about losing this damn job and not being able to feed my kids." I've always worked myself up into a tornado whenever I've hurt someone else's feelings. "And what's so goddam great about giving a lousy pill?" I continued, wheeling my chair closer. "And you will too give a pill if I'm up to my elbows or I'll see to it that you're up to yours, while I sit and have coffee, put my feet up and give a lousy pill." By now I couldn't be stopped. "And if you think being a goddam nurse and taking all this responsibility and giving a few lousy pills is such glory, why the hell didn't you go to school to be a nurse yourself?"

"I had eight kids I had to support, smarty," Granshaw said, with less conviction than I expected.

"Well, you can't have everything," I said sternly, knowing I was stretching it. But the argument was over and both of us knew it. Granshaw's anger had been totally diffused by my own self-righteousness.

We sat in silence for a few minutes, Granshaw cleaning off the white Formica counter tops with alcohol, and I charting my medications.

Granshaw was the first to speak. "You gonna do that kid up soon? Them guys are sleepin' and I can help ya if ya like."

"Thanks, Granshaw," I said, acknowledging the woman's move toward me as well as her offer to help, "but I'd be more comfortable if knew you were out here in case of anything. I'll try alone, and if I get stuck or need help lifting, I'll let you know."

I liked not having anyone watch me the first time I took care of a patient. I liked the time to explore and discover without having to pretend I was surer of myself than I was. After the first time, I enjoyed the company and the help.

I walked the short dark hall toward Melody's room, quickly grabbing a sterile gown and a couple of packages of sterile gloves on my way. Outside the room there was a long cabinet, grungy gray also, that held the sterile basins to soak dressings in, the sterile suction catheters, the irrigation sets to wet the old dressings before pulling them off, and the bottles of cold solution that I would have to use. All this equipment had to be kept outside the room, wrapped, in order to keep it sterile.

I struggled into another too large, wrinkled, faded-gray cotton gown and reached around to the back of the neck to tie the strings. Broken. I pulled the gown off, discarded it into the large plastic hamper alongside the door and walked back to get another, this time checking the strings. I gowned again, gloved and then put the mask on. The unit was kept especially warm because the patients couldn't tolerate gowns or sheets against their skin. They were often cold because of the wet dressings. Nurses, on the other hand, could tolerate the gowns, but by the time our hands sweated underneath the rubber gloves, and we put the mask over our faces (a mask which all salesmen swore didn't impede air flow), every nurse in the place was ready to die of heat stroke. The nurses who wore glasses were the worst off; they had to fight their way through the thick mist accumulating on their glasses every time they breathed out.

I walked into the room carrying two wrapped basins, gauze and solutions, struggling to hold all of them in my arms. I placed the equipment on the long narrow table which reached over the bed like an arm, and pushed it with my foot, away from the bed.

I stood next to Melody's bed and said, "Hi, kid, it's me again,

Teri." She moved her head in recognition, so I said, "It's time to do your dressings." Melody's feet started to move and her toes were wiggling frantically. "I'll give you pain medicine before I start," I said, trying to reassure her, "and I'll be as gentle as I can." The little girl was terrified. "I'll try not to hurt you. Honest." I patted Melody gently on her belly. She quieted down as I gave her a shot of morphine. She was the first patient I had seen it ordered for. She moved her leg over to the side of the bed to touch me. I really liked Melody; it would be much harder to take care of her now.

I found the Burn Unit particularly difficult. Unlike many of the other services where I could *relieve* pain, here, in order to help, I had to cause pain. Also, I had always refused to work pediatrics, because sick kids undid me. Kids don't understand when you say you have to hurt them to help them; they just believe that you don't love them. So they hate you or forgive you, and either way it's intolerable. Words can't fool kids, and if to reassure them you put your arms around them, there's a good chance that you'll get caught in the lasso of *their* arms. And if you tell a child that she can trust you, and then you hurt her, she acts betrayed. Though I can intellectually understand why I have to do it, I *feel* as though I betrayed her. For me, seeing a child's vulnerability is like looking straight into the sun.

While I waited for the medicine to take effect, I tried to decide where to start. Melody had one intravenous solution running into her right ankle; she had another inserted into a large vein in her neck, and a bottle of plasma was infusing through tubing inserted into her right upper arm. She had a long thin plastic tube through her nose, which was hooked to a suction machine to drain the contents of her stomach. Another tubing came out of her urethra to drain the urine from her bladder. All of these tubings, plus the tracheostomy tube, through which she breathed, had to be left intact during and after the dressing change. The three leads to the monitor hung from their positions on her chest, over the bed rails, and down across the floor to the heart-monitoring machine.

Wishing I were an octopus, I unwrapped one of the basins, poured the solution, and began. The medicine should be working now, I thought. I started to lower the bed rail, and as it stuck on the old chipped enamel bed I said to Melody, "Hey, Mel, you should see this bed. It looks so ancient that I'll bet they built the whole hospital around it." Through the crack in her dressings, I could see Melody trying to smile again, but as she did I noticed that only the right side of her mouth moved and I wondered why.

I walked to the top of the bed and said, "Melody, I'm going to start unwrapping your head first; then your face, ears, neck, chest and all the way down." The child's chest started to heave and I added, "Melody, listen to me. Let's figure out a signal so you can ask me to stop for a while if it hurts too much." Melody's chest slowed and her breathing became more regular.

"For medicine," I told her, "you wiggle your left toes, and for 'stop,' your right. How's that sound?"

Melody nodded and wiggled the toes on her right foot.

"Okay," I said, "here we go." Her head was bandaged like a wounded army veteran's. I started to unwrap the gauze slowly. The few scattered clumps of hair left were singed to about half an inch. The spaces between, that the fire had gotten to, felt soft and mushy like a too ripe banana. I squirted saline, with a syringe, onto the gauze constantly to try to keep it from sticking, but it didn't always work. My mouth watered each time it stuck and I had to yank it off. "Am I hurting you, Mel?" I kept repeating, but she just shook her head from side to side, and my stomach dropped as I realized most of this was third-degree. No matter how careful you are with second-degree burns, they hurt. Third-degree burns don't hurt because all the nerve endings are destroyed. No pain, no chance of regeneration. Shit! I thought, as I walked over to the window, stalling before I continued, looking out into nowhere.

The face dressing was the most difficult and I had to stop several times because Melody was wiggling her toes madly. There was only half an ear left on the right side, and several pieces of gauze had to be placed between her head and the ear to keep them from growing together during healing, if it ever took place. As I removed the bandages from the child's face, I had to walk away again. Melody was a black child, I finally figured out. At first, I had thought it was burned skin. Now I could see that so much had been burned away that she looked like a patchwork quilt. White on black. Through the cheek closest to me, as I removed the dressing, I could see Melody's bottom teeth. Skin gone . . . burned through.

I wet and pulled; wet and pulled gently. Some of the skin came off and the tissue underneath bled. All the time, Melody just lay there unmoving, as I kept asking, "Does it hurt?" In response, Melody would shake her head from side to side.

As I was unwrapping her neck, I held Melody's head up with my gloved hand and the glove stuck to the soft skin and slid. I had to walk over and look outside again. I started making noise, pretending to be doing something and then chattered to Melody about the kind of day I had had; all the time, making a racket with words and sounds so that I wouldn't have to think or feel, defending myself with conversation and activity.

After a few minutes, I went back to the bedside and unwrapped Melody's chest. The child seemed unbothered even by the removal of some of the gauze that adhered hard to her skin. Her lack of emotion made it much easier for me. Now it was only when Melody started to choke and cough, only when her chest heaved erratically, that I felt any revulsion to what I was doing. Only when she felt pain did I react.

Granshaw had finished the dressings on the other two patients, so she stopped outside Melody's room and stuck her head in the doorway. "Hey, Daley, there's a man out here who wants a pill. Wanna get it?" she goaded me. But as I turned to answer, and she saw my face, she stopped and offered, "I'll get ya some coffee. Ya look like you can use it."

I nodded, removed my mask and walked over to the doorway. Moments later, Granshaw returned holding the coffee. She held it so I could sip it without ungloving. She was outside; I was inside the room. "Thanks," I said, feeling really beat. "Hey, you feel like giving a pill?"

Granshaw laughed and said, "So now ya trust me?" She winked as she turned to go.

Back to Melody. I unwrapped her arms. One and then the other. The skin, especially on the left arm, felt different. It was very cold and leatherlike. I rewrapped them quickly; they were stiff and awkward to move. Then I rewrapped her chest; a vest of clean white gauze. Dressed as though for church. Her head rewrapped again, wounded soldier . . . and only her legs to go. Amazingly light little-girl legs. . . .

"Melody, Melody, I'm going to take the patches off your eyes now." And as I touched the first patch I said, "This one first, okay? It'll be real easy."

But it wasn't real easy. I poured saline over the dressings on the child's eyes constantly, but still the patches stuck. After twenty minutes of gentle peeling, both patches were off. One of Melody's lids was gone, the other only half. Her eyes clouded over, staring. I refused to believe what I knew was true, so I took a flashlight and shined it into the girl's lidless eye. "Can you see anything, Mel?" I asked. Her head moved from side to side and her chest started to heave again.

"Melody, don't cry. Don't worry about it now. Please." I replaced the patches as I talked. "Give it time, Mel," I said, but my voice sounded flat even to me.

Then I fixed her bed, turning her gently from side to side, making one side of the bed at a time as I leaned her small body against the side rail of the bed. I concentrated on not dislodging the tubes, as carefully as I had on wrapping Melody's dressings so neatly that it took some of the edge off my hopelessness.

When I finished and Melody was resting, I said quietly, close to her ear, "I'd like to kiss you, kid, but I'm not allowed to give you germs." Melody's foot moved over to touch me again.

It had taken me over three and a half hours and I was supposed to do her dressings every four hours. "Shit! I'm not doing that kid again tonight," I said to Granshaw as I flopped into the chair in the nurses' station. And what I thought was, I don't want to ever do her again. I folded my arms across my chest. I was freezing. I wanted to go home.

Granshaw was resting on a metal chair, head leaning back on a bath blanket. She opened her eyes and asked in a quiet voice, "Daley, do ya believe in God?"

"Sure," I said. "Who else could think of a reason to do that to a little kid?" I never had been able to kick the God habit, but at that point I had no respect for Him. I hoped the fact that I was furious with Him was enough homage.

"Her mother," Granshaw said, pulling me back with a jolt. I must have looked as puzzled as I felt, because Granshaw volunteered without any prodding from me, "I got here early. I heard the guys say somethin' 'bout her bein' shoved in a oven."

In the morning, as I was leaving after report, I bumped into Zaccara on my way through the swinging doors. He actually smiled, "Hey, Dr. Zaccara, what's this about Melody not being burned under the tree?" I asked.

"Had a rough night, kid?" he said, patting me on the shoulder.

I nodded and waited.

"Nobody knows the real story yet, Teri." He shook his head. "We filed a report just in case." Then he smiled, a big beautiful smile, and said, "Call me Ben. I'm glad you're not pissed over last night." He went into the unit, and the door swung shut behind him. I stood without moving, thinking about Melody. I was exhausted and my back was killing me. I dreaded the thought of coming back to work that night. But then, I thought, maybe it won't be so bad. And I smiled when I found myself hoping Zaccara would be covering.

That night, after I did Melody's dressings, Ben and I sat for hours talking over coffee in the nurses' station. We had a lot in common: Italian mothers, Catholicism, guilts.

"Every New Year's Eve, wherever I am," he laughed, "I call home and say, 'Mom, this is Ben. I'm calling to wish you a Happy New Year.' And every year she says, 'You're a good boy, Ben, and I hope you're having a better time than your father and me. We're sitting alone.'"

I laughed knowingly and felt myself liking him. His hair was shiny, black and curly. And he always called his mother. I figured he couldn't be all bad.

He told me he would be on duty until New Year's Eve, so for the rest of the week we worked together. After report, I'd call him and he'd come upstairs to talk. We laughed a lot. And he'd help me with Melody.

One night, as I was doing her arm dressings, I felt her fingers. They were hard as wood.

"Do passive exercises on them," Ben said, wrinkling his

forehead.

I tried to move them and they wouldn't budge. "I can't," I said, "they're too stiff."

"I said exercise them," he ordered. "I told all the girls to do that at least three times a shift."

I was angry with him. He was absolutely charming one minute and a miserable bastard the next. I looked him straight in the eye as I held Melody's fingers in mine and tried to bend them. They were curled over and I couldn't straighten them, even with a lot of effort. I held her arm up to show him.

He just glared at me and said, "Don't be such a sissy. Bend them."

I took two of Melody's fingers between my thumb and forefinger and bent them up, hard. They broke off in my hand like dry twigs. I dropped them almost instantly, as though they were hot, onto the clean white sheets. I didn't know what to do next. My teeth were clenched; I was furious at Zaccara, and I was horrified by Melody's brown fingers lying on the stark white sheets. There was no bleeding where they had come off her hand, and she hadn't reacted at all. I looked up. Zaccara reached over and with a dry piece of sterile gauze lifted Melody's finger off the bed and wrapped them up. "Just send these to the Pathology Lab," he said.

I was afraid Melody could hear him when he added, "That arm will have to be amputated, if she lasts." He went downstairs to bed without saying anything else. It was Melody's fifth day and she still could respond to questions, so I knew she was alert. But every time I suctioned her, big thick clumps of gray lung tissue would come back through the tubing. And I had to suction her often, because she was having more and more difficulty breathing.

The following night, Melody's sixth night, I almost fainted as I unwrapped her arms. There were large slits down each arm, baring the bloody tissue beneath. "Escharotomy," was what the doctor called it when he took a scalpel and sliced open the skin to allow for better circulation. Burned skin shrinks and compresses tissue and blood vessels. Melody's left arm was charred to the bone in most places. As I stood next to the bed, I started to pray to that God I was pissed at to scoop her out of the Burn Unit and put her up on a cloud. Before I left that morning, I wished everyone a happy New Year; even Bradberry. I had been barely civil to her since she had spent an entire report chastising me for giving Andrew a Darvon and a Benadryl at the same time. Darvon is a minor pain reliever and Benadryl acts as an antihistamine to help stop itching; healing burns itch like mad. But Benadryl also had a sedative effect, which I figured could do Andrew some good, but which threw Nellie Nurse Bradberry into such a fit you would have thought I was a junkie. The most unkind thing I could think of to say to her at the time was a takeoff from my mother's words "I hope you have children just like you." In times of extreme frustration, I resort to the same tactics. "Bradberry," I had said, "I hope that if you ever get sick, you have a nurse just like you." After that confrontation, we kept a polite distance from each other. We talked only about necessary things. I had decided she had no heart and there was no Oz to take her to, so I had given up on her.

"Who's on tonight?" I asked her now. I was scheduled to be off New Year's Eve, and Greg and I were going to spend it together; but Triumph was still visiting Edriando in Boston.

"They'll float somebody over from Surgery because the census here is so low," Bradberry answered as she patted her straw-colored hair. It must have been a nervous gesture because a hurricane couldn't have moved a hair in that head, she had so much spray on it.

Crap! I thought, I just can't leave Melody at the mercy of someone who doesn't know her. Especially since Ben is off, too. Matt Muscio would be covering, and I had discovered over the last months that he was less smart, less ruthless, less talented and generally less of a doctor than Zaccara. And Melody needed more, not less.

"If the kid's still alive, call me," I said. "I'll come in." I walked away through the swinging doors.

I had a particularly bad day. Each time I tried to fall asleep, I'd see Melody, a broken, torn teak doll. I called the unit several times to check her condition. Bradberry told me that her blood pressure was going down and her pulse was irregular. The skin across her chest was tightening, making it harder for her to breathe, and her kidneys were probably shot, because she wasn't putting out any urine. I crossed my fingers and prayed to the God of children that he would let Melody start the new year somewhere other than the Burn Unit.

Finally, at about 2 p.m., I swallowed a Valium and fell asleep until almost eight. The first thing I did when I woke up was call Harriet.

"The kid's still going up and down," she answered, "just barely." She sounded exhausted as she added, "Crazy Muscio's doing everything possible and I'm running my ass off. He's even pushing fluids so fast to try to get urine that the kid's lungs are filling and she's gurgling. But I can't stop him. I can't even talk to him."

"I'll call again before I come in," I told her, and hung up.

The time between eight and ten dragged. Greg and I sat on the couch. He petted and hugged me. "I'll be happy to sit in the lounge tonight," he offered.

"Thank you," I said. His support helped me feel better.

At five minutes before ten, when I couldn't wait any longer, I called the unit again. A strange voice answered, giving a name I didn't recognize.

"Where's Harriet?" I asked.

"Some kid in here arrested and I'm watching the unit while they work on her. Harriet's in there now," the woman said.

I hung up. I couldn't believe it. "Some jerk actually jumped on that little kid's chest," I screamed at Greg. "Some miserable fuck with a heavy hand for power just couldn't let her go." I was furious, and for once Greg didn't say anything, though he looked upset. He just drove me to the hospital. The whole ride there, I kept trying to figure out why anyone would want to bring Melody back. Then I wondered if they had succeeded.

I showed Greg the lounge and ran through the swinging doors onto the unit. It was a mess–equipment, bottles and gowns thrown all over the floor. But I didn't hear any voices, so I knew that whatever had happened was already over. I looked in the nurses' station for Harriet; she wasn't there. Halfway down the hall, I heard it and I knew. Hiss . . . hiss . . . hiss . . . came the regular sound of a respirator.

I stood at the doorway to Melody's room, watching Harriet clean up the mess. I didn't say a word, but in a few minutes, when she stopped and lifted her head, I knew by the expression on her face that she wasn't the one who had called the code.

"Who did it?" I asked her without any introduction.

"The good doctor," she answered sarcastically.

"Muscio?" I asked, puzzled. "Doesn't he have two kids of his own?"

Harriet nodded. "Yes".

I tore into the nurses' station and dialed the phone. "Would you have done that to one of your own kids?" I screamed at him. "Is that what you would have wanted for them?" Then, more softly, I asked, "Jesus, Matt, *why* did you do it?"

"I can't play God," he said sharply. "When God calls . . ."

I cut him off; I couldn't let him finish. "God *called*, you lunatic," I hollered at him. "In fact, He screamed and yelled, but you couldn't let her go." I was so mad I wanted to hit him. "You snatched her right out of *His* hands. And as long as you did, you can come up here and work with me, or I'm going home. We'll do your bidding–while we wait again for God's."

His kind of reasoning has always killed me. And if a doctor insists on using a God sword, the only thing you can fight him with is another God sword. Dr. Matthew Muscio and I worked together that night.

I walked over to Melody's bed, after I got myself together, and called her, "Mel?" No response at all. I pinched the top of her thigh. No reaction. I looked at the cardiac monitor. Her heart was beating regularly. Her IV was running very slowly.

I walked out to the nurses' station, where Dr. Muscio was sitting by the desk. "How come only one IV left?" I asked him.

"The kid's veins are all blown and the others infiltrated," he answered softly, not looking at me.

I walked back to Melody. I had to remove the respirator several times to quickly suction her. The tissue I got back from inside her lungs was now blood-tinged and gray. I picked up the stethoscope and put is against Melody's chest to listen to her breathing. Her lungs sounded as though someone was running a dry finger on the outside of an inflated balloon. Squeaky. She didn't respond to stimuli. Still, her blood pressure was holding and her heart rate was slow but regular.

Out at the nurses' station, Muscio sat with his head in his hands. "When are you going to do her dressings?" he mumbled.

I couldn't believe he was serious. What were dressings going to do for an almost-dead kid? Maybe next time I see Bradberry, I thought, I should tell her I hope Muscio will be her doctor if she gets sick. Then, as I watched him run his fingers through his sandy hair, I thought, And *she* can be his nurse. But all I said to him was, "Later, Matt."

I heard the buzzer go off on the respirator. The alarm, I thought, maybe her trach is clogged. So I went in and tried to suction her. She was almost dry. No mucus; not a lot of tissue. She was clear. Still, the alarm sounded again. I checked the gauges on the machine. It clearly indicated some kind of resistance.

Muscio stood in the doorway as the alarm kept sounding. Suddenly I knew what it was. I took the small bandage scissors and cut a line down the middle of her gauze vest. The skin on her chest was thick and tight—a swollen leather band, constricting her breathing . . . stopping her breathing. Her heart rate was slowing as I looked at the monitor.

I didn't see him come up to the bedside. I was rubbing Melody's belly and thighs, the only parts that weren't damaged, trying to comfort her in case she had any consciousness left. I never saw him unwrap the scalpel. What finally broke through my concentration was the spurt of Melody's blood as he dug the scalpel into her left shoulder and cut down to her right hip. Then he cut from her right shoulder to her left hip. An enormous bloody X crossed Melody's chest. The thick skin pulled back, leaving spaces, widening the X, giving her lungs room to expand and letting her breathe again. The alarm on the respirator stopped.

"Escharotomy," was all Muscio said as he left the room. He looked as though he was in a trance.

Melody looked like she should be hanging on a hook in a butcher shop. I just stared at her.

It was almost 6 a.m. I walked into the nurses' station and caught Muscio with his head in his arms, leaning on the desk. When he lifted his head, I could see he had been crying.

"The kid's last IV has stopped," I told him, putting my hand on his shoulder. "Do you have to start another one?" By this time I knew he couldn't get out of the way of whatever was riding him.

"Yes," he said, so softly that I could hardly hear him.

"Where?" I asked. "She's got no veins left."

"Femoral," he said, sitting up, taking a deep breath.

Oh no, I thought, not that. Not there. The femoral runs through the crack in the groin. The only place on Melody that hadn't been touched; that hadn't already been hurt and butchered. No! I thought, I'll *never* let you do that to her. And then the horror of the last seven days almost knocked me out.

"First do her dressings," he said, and I knew he was stalling for time.

"I can't do her dressings while she's on the respirator," I said, challenging him. I knew he knew that was bullshit, because Harriet had just done them the shift before. I looked directly at him.

"But you know what will happen if you . . ." he blurted with undisguised horror. Then he rubbed his hand over his face and shook his head.

I watched him, wondering what was going through his mind; trying to understand what he was attempting to save. What kind of a life could Melody possibly have, even if some miracle pulled her through? She was definitely blind. She would have only one arm, if she was lucky enough to keep that. Most of both ears were gone; her face and body would be so horribly scarred that everyone would be afraid of her. If they sent her home, her mother, who might be a nut, could fry her this time. The alternative was that she could spend her life in an institution, where strangers would take care of what was left of her.

I was really puzzled. When Melody was still conscious, he and Zaccara cut her into pieces. They pulled her skin off, punched holes in her little body for tubes; when she could feel pain, they hurt her constantly, and never seemed to wince. But now, when there's no indication that she exists except for the beating of her heart, not as a real person, I say, "Let's stop butchering her," and he looks at me as though I'm crazy.

"I can't do her dressings while she's on the respirator," I

repeated. "I won't."

"Do her dressings," he said. He looked so troubled that I knew it was the most he could offer me. "I'll wait here," he said as he looked out the window, "in case you need me. . . ."

I walked back into Melody's room and closed the door behind me. I turned off the alarm on the respirator. Detached her and started blindly to do her dressings. I refused to look at the monitor. And then, for the first time, I held her small body tight against me. I hugged her, rocking. After I had laid her down and fixed her bed I straightened the entire room. Finally, I looked at the monitor. Straight line.

My hands trembled as I rehooked the respirator to the trach on her body. I turned the alarm back on and listened to the regular hiss . . . hiss, all the way back to the nursing station. Muscio was waiting in the doorway. I nodded; we didn't talk.

He went into the small room, and when he came back to the nurses station I handed him the chart. He wrote a note and left the unit.

I sat down. Numb. I opened the chart to see what Muscio had written. It read: "Patient died while on respirator. Pronounced at 6:45 a.m."

The day shift was due any minute, so I knew I wouldn't have to wrap the body for the morgue. I gave report, and for once Bradberry didn't hassle me. She just opened the chart, read Muscio's note and nodded.

CHAPTER 16

In the burn unit, with my cheek on the cool metal desk, and the only noise to divert me from my thoughts the sound of my three sleeping patients, I began to cry. What was I going to do about my life? The weeks since Melody's death had been hell. I had been sick almost constantly with stomach cramps and nausea; I couldn't sleep worth a damn; I had broken off with Greg and begun sleeping with Zaccara. What was happening to me?

The night after Melody died, I had tried to explain to Greg about Scott. He had been sitting on the couch, cross-legged, dressed in his brown tweed suit, tie slightly loosened at the neck.

"You mean to tell me that you actually masturbated him to completion?" Greg asked, red-faced and tight-jawed.

"What would you have done?" I asked defensively, "Call in some special forces?"

"Kitten," he said, his voice strained, "how did they suggest you handle a situation like that in nursing school? There must be a precedent."

"Jesus Christ, Greg," I shouted, "no one said anything about anything vaguely resembling sex in school. As far as they were concerned, as soon as a patient got sick his sex organs fell off!"

"What about the element of exploitation?" Greg asked, constantly taking deep breaths.

"Whose exploitation?" I asked, not understanding.

"Scott's," Greg said solemnly.

"Goddammit!" I screamed. "You act as though I ran into work, ran over to his bed, grabbed his cock and jerked him off—just for fun." Then I took a deep breath myself, tried to see how difficult it must have been for Greg to understand while he sat with clean hands and no blood on his Rogers Peet suit, and started to explain what Lil had told me.

After another hour, Greg still sat shaking his head. It was then I said I thought I should date other people, and Greg agreed, saying he needed some time to try to adjust to my way of thinking.

That had been over a month ago, and though Greg had loosened up and seemed to be getting better, I still was angry at him.

And bed with Zaccara . . .

Through the Emergency Room he had admitted a young woman, twenty-nine years old, whose clothes had caught fire. A pretty blond girl; Daisy was her name. She was a very bad burn, and the nurses in the Emergency Room said that they had worked on her for hours before they even brought her up. They told me Zaccara had stayed with her from the minute she had been carried off the ambulance.

By the time she reached the Burn Unit, she was losing consciousness. But Zaccara and I knocked ourselves out all night to try to keep her alive. Around five-thirty in the morning, she arrested. And this time neither Zaccara nor I could let her go. We pounded on her chest and breathed for her, for hours. We started IVs and pushed heart medications; and finally we put her on a respirator. Her heart kept stopping. The next time we pounded, we prayed. But she died anyway.

The sound of our impotence bounced off the walls, and the blank monitor screen mirrored our images. Zaccara and I walked out of the cluttered room, stepping over the used tubes and the bloody gauze. We put our arms around each other's waists. "You did the best you could," I said.

"You too. Thanks," he said. We had both done our best . . . and failed.

It wasn't far from the hug around the waist to the hug around the neck . . . and it kept us both from going under.

Still, I knew there could be no relationship with Zaccara, and sleeping with him was no solution for my life. It only indicated my confusion and added to my depression.

The night passed slowly, and while everyone slept I examined my alternatives.

Finally, when one of my patients called, I lifted my head off the desk. By the time I started dressings that morning, I knew what I had to do.

"Wexon division of Wexthon," the secretary answered in a mechanical voice.

"Greg Schmidt, please," I said, imitating her.

"Mr. Schmidt is in a marketing meeting at present," she answered, as though I should have known. "May I give him a message?"

"Yes, please," I said as I pictured her sitting prissily in her tailored suit and dark-rimmed glasses. "Just tell him I'm *mad* about him."

"Whom shall I say called?" she inquired without hesitation.

"If he asks that, tell him I take it back." I laughed and hung up.

"Kitten," he said, chuckling when he called back, "with a message like that, you'll ruin my reputation."

"I think I love you," I said happily, ignoring his reproof.

"Then how would you like to have dinner with me at the Top of the Sixes Saturday night?"

"Great," I answered. "We can finish discussing our differences there." I was laughing.

Greg hesitated. He sounded more remote when he said, "Seriously, Kitten, the next time you call, please just leave your name and I'll get back to you." When I didn't respond, he added apologetically, "They're a pretty conservative group here."

I also called Dr. Davidson at Meadowland and made an appointment. I had seen him a few other times when I needed help dealing with my mother or not destroying my kids, but this trip was strictly for me.

There was too much of my life I didn't understand, too much I wasn't in control of, and I kept getting sick. The other times he had helped me enormously; I was hoping for some more of the same magic.

As I walked into his office, I noticed that his hair was as messy as the first time I saw him, he wore the same clothes and he had the same compassionate look in his eyes.

"How can I help you, Teri?" he asked when we were seated across from each other at his big wooden desk.

"I don't' know," I said, and then for the next hour and a half I poured out all my tears and outrage, exactly as I had when I first met him.

He rubbed his forehead thoughtfully and said, "Okay, let's take this one thing at a time. First, let's examine your relationship with Greg. What do you expect from it? And what do you feel you're getting?"

While explaining it to Dr. Davidson, I realized that what I wanted from Greg was the very thing that drove me crazy. His intellectual rigidity, his predictability and his conventional morality felt safe. I always knew what to expect. No surprises. It anchored me in a world where everything else was hectic, emotional and changing. And our arguments also gave me an outlet for the fury I felt, which covered my fear.

"Now Barrenfield," he said firmly. "Why did you begin nursing?"

"To help people with their pain. And to learn, so I could save lives," I told him.

"Save lives?" he asked, smiling gently. "Are you able to do at Barrenfield what you wanted?"

"No . . . I'm not." My voice cracked and I started to cry again.

He was calm, his voice was soft, when he said, "You must stop working in the Burn Unit. You must stop taking care of burn patients."

"I don't know if I can," I answered unhappily.

"I think you're becoming a victim of the pain that you cause them," he explained, "and I think that's why you've been so ill lately."

"I won't have any money if I quit my job," I protested weakly.

"Apply for a grant to go to school. Go on welfare. Do private cases," he said firmly. "But stop working at Barrenfield immediately."

And so I did.

CHAPTER 17

"Tomorrow we can go see Mrs. Dayton, the woman who runs the registry for private-duty nurses," Lil said as we sat eating breakfast the following week. When I had told her that I was quitting Barrenfield, she told me that she had stayed only to keep me company; so she quit, too.

"It will feel pretty strange working in the daylight and sleeping at night," I told her. "I don't know how my body will adjust." I had decided it would be better for the kids to sleep home, now that I would have a choice.

The next day, Mrs. Dayton ushered Lil and me into the basement of her large split-level house. She walked energetically and talked with a big smile. Her gray hair was shiny and curled carefully; her housedress was spring garden. As she sat us down on her floral sink-in couch she went to her desk, looked through her crowded files, and told us a little about each of her "girls."

"One of the advantages of private duty," she said, smiling, as she poured us tea, "is that there's much less politics. My girls are directly responsible to the families and the patients who pay them. As long as they do their work, nobody complains. The pay is as good as or better than hospital pay, and no hospitalization insurance or meals are deducted. The amount of work isn't impossible, even in the most difficult cases, so my girls don't get exhausted or sick as often. The girls tell me they love the relationships they can have with the patients and their families. They have the time to read the charts carefully, so the doctors stay happy with them; and they have time to explain procedures and treatments, so the patients are happy. The only problem the girls ever complain about is that sometimes they get a little stale. And I just tell them to study the monthly nursing journals."

Lil and I sipped our tea and smiled at her. It sounded good to me.

Then Mrs. Dayton asked us what shift we chose to work, how many days, and what kinds of cases. I told her I would be willing to work on any patient as long as I could work days, and Lil said she preferred fewer technical and more nursing-care cases. She didn't like to have to make any big decisions on her own, or to chance taking a case where she could make mistakes. Also, she asked for evening or night assignments. She still needed extra money, and hoped to get a job working days at Elmwood's Baby Cottage, caring for retarded and physically handicapped children.

After we filled out applications, Mrs. Dayton talked some more about the registry. She made it sound like a sorority that she had invited us to join.

Outside, Lil and I raced each other to the car. "Why does it sound like a whorehouse when she says 'my girls'?" I asked Lil, laughing.

"Imagine Mrs. Dayton a madam," Lil said as she fluttered he eyelids and giggled.

From then on, for as long as I did private duty, I never again saw Mrs. Dayton. Instead, we talked for hours on the phone each time she called me with a case; we exchanged gossip about ourselves and the rest of the "girls." And from where she sat, she helped me through the next years of my life.

"Would one of you girls like to take care of a nice man who's had a little stroke?" Mrs. Dayton asked when she called the first time.

Lil accepted the case. The man's name was Artie Holleran, he was sixty-eight years old and his only complications seemed to be a weak right side and an irate wife who strongly objected to his lady friend. It was a long-term assignment, and Lil was in her glory. No more hairy shifts trying to save a thousand too sick patients.

When Mrs. Dayton called for me and I asked her what kind of case it was, she answered with her usual cheerful, optimistic voice.

"It's some kind of a rash. But, dear, it's not contagious." Then she added, amused, "Her regular nurse wants relief. She's been working the last three days." Some little warning bell tinkled in my ear, but I managed to ignore it.

"The woman's name is Rachael Simms," Mrs. Dayton told me, "and I'll bet you two will get along just fine." So I accepted the case and inherited Rachael.

I have always loved Mrs. Dayton. The way she ran her registry saved nurses' lives, kept them from being put into jail for bills they couldn't pay, and got all of us loans for cars and houses we never could have gotten if it wasn't for her heroic lies about our income. But every hero has a flaw—and Mrs. Dayton's, I learned, was that she was never too accurate on diagnosis.

It was seven o'clock on a beautiful Saturday morning and I was only half awake when I walked up to the desk in Elmwood's Rehabilitation Center. I had gotten up at 5:30 a.m. in order to take a shower, wash my hair and put on my makeup. After much struggle to get out of the house, I reached the hospital. There I stood and waited for the young blond nurse at the desk to notice me. Her name was Evette. After a few minutes I said, "Hi, can you please tell me what room my lady is in?"

Evette looked up from writing charts. "Are you here to take care of the mycosis fungoides?" she asked.

Instantly I was wide awake. The words alone struck terror in my heart. I had never heard of anything that sounded like that. Certainly no disease. It sounded weird and frightening.

I could hear Mrs. Dayton's voice saying, "She's got some sort of an allergy." I should have known better. Why would someone with a rash need a private-duty nurse?

I grabbed the chart Evette handed me and leafed through it trying to find out as much as I could before I ventured anywhere near her room. Then I threw questions, like a lifeline, out to everyone around the desk. Some of the girls shrugged, some snickered. Evette, who looked serious and sympathetic, finally said, "It's some kind of an autoimmune disease, or a lymphoma. It's a systemic disease, as near as I can understand, but the most obvious symptom is her skin. It seems to just slough off—as though she's allergic to it." Evette looked apologetic when she added, "She's on reverse isolation."

Rachael was in the last room at the very end of the hall, and in front of her door I could see the isolation cart. It held sterile gowns, gloves and masks, very much like the Burn Unit's, except these were disposable. I unwrapped one of the long bright-yellow paper gowns, and as I watched it unfold I was certain it had been specially made for the Jolly Green Giant. It was one of those one-size-fits-all garments—apparently, all at the same time. I removed my cap and plunked a large ugly green paper shower bonnet on my head, completely covering the hair I had just spent one precious hour fixing. This is no time for vanity, I told myself, and then placed the beak-like green filter mask over my fresh makeup. When I rolled the bottoms of my too big sterile white plastic gloves over my hands, I told myself, "No matter how bad she looks, you'll look worse."

I was wrong. I may have looked like a Martian in drag, but I couldn't even believe Rachael was a real person.

As soon as I walked into the room, the smell hit me. Poured all over me, encased me. It burned my nostrils and I could taste it in the back of my throat. I coughed and tried to mouth-breathe; then, when it didn't work, I tried to hold my breath. It was sicky-sweet and pungent like burns, but I could also smell infection, like a rotting potato or a chicken left too long in the trunk of a car. The floral fragrance of hospital air-freshener, stronger and sweeter, ineffectively battled the odor. I almost gagged. I was sure that I would smell just like Rachael's room for all time, and that as I walked anywhere, afterward, no matter how hard I had scrubbed, people would notice and ask each other, "Where has she been?"

I moved toward the side of Rachael's bed. Throughout the years I had developed some calluses over my feelings—or rather, over showing my feelings—so I was able to look noncommittal as I said, "Hi, Rachael. My name is Teri Daley and I'm going to be your nurse."

Rachael looked like a scaly fish monster when I first saw her. Patches of skin, like postage stamps curled around the edges, stuck and peeled all over her face. Dry scales and oval lesions covered her entire body. The whites of her eyes were yellow-tinges and gooey, as though they were melting. She had no eyebrows, or eyelashes, and only an inch of wheat-colored hair covered her head.

Until I met her, the worst-looking patients, the hardest to take as far as appearance goes, were burn patients. But the moment I laid eyes on Rachael, I knew they couldn't even compete. When she smiled—and, to her credit, she did—her face cracked and bled. She was the most terrible-looking patient I had ever had to take care of, but I still wound up loving her.

Rachael tried to force open her crusty, sticky eyes, but managed only to get them half open. She stared vacantly past me and said, "Scared you, didn't I?" Her smile looked more like a leer.

"Well," I said, trying to scoop something sage out of my panic, "you'll never be Miss America. But scare me? No."

"Go ahead," she taunted harshly, "tell me this doesn't shock you. Tell me you've seen other patients who look like me. Tell me I look terrific for what I've got, and then with a smile and your best professional manner pretend again that you're not frightened."

With that barrage of words, Rachael set the tone of our relationship. I knew now that she wouldn't tolerate any bullshit and that platitudes made her angrier than she already was. I would have to give her as much truth as I could so that she would believe me if I ever had to lie to her in order to prevent her from feeling totally hopeless. I no longer smelled anything.

"Actually, Rachael, you look awful," I said softly, frowning. "I've never taken care of anyone with your disease before, so I can't make comparisons." With a firmer voice, I told her, "I haven't the time for the bullshit you describe, and more often than not I've been accused of *not* having the best professional manner, so we don't have to deal with that." Then I reached up and lowered my mask so that she could see me smile as I said, "But no, Zelda, you don't scare me." She looked thoughtful, so I crossed my eyes and stuck my tongue out at her. I had called her Zelda automatically; at the time, it was a name that Lil and I teased each other with. A pet name.

Rachael's look softened. She was too stiff to turn her head, but her face wrinkled in an attempted smile again. It was like the crumbling of the side of an old building. Flakes of skin fell to the pillow around her.

A little bit disgusting, I thought, but now I really wasn't frightened. Once I had heard her voice, it had sunk in that she was a real human being. Her body, then, was like a costume—a terrible one she couldn't remove.

"Help me take my arms out from under these sheets?" she asked, barely moving her lips.

"Sure," I said, and for one of the rare times in nursing I was glad I was wearing gloves. Their primary purpose was to keep *me* from contaminating *her*, but, as far as I was concerned, this time it was nothing short of a blessing for me. I had totally accepted her as a person in *concept*, but sometimes it takes me a little longer to adjust to the stark realities. And the feel of Rachael's skin, even through gloves, was one of those realities.

I reached under the covers to pick up an arm: sandy dry skin and, in the cracks, sticky brown gel, like sap from a very young tree. Rachael's arm stuck to the sheets; she couldn't bend it, and when I tried to lift it I had to pull it away, hard. I had the same sour taste in my mouth as when I had worked burns. Actually, the Burn Unit was like boot camp for my active duty on Rachael. And luckily I had been desensitized by horror movies, or I still would have been wiped out.

Finally, after much more pulling, I managed to get both arms over the sheets, though I winced inside my mask because I was afraid I was hurting her. "It's all right, Teri," she reassured me. "It doesn't hurt that bad." There were skin flakes all over the bed.

Shortly, a smiling, cheerful young nurse stood outside the door holding Rachael's breakfast tray. All disposable dishes and cups. I pushed the over bed table toward the door, and the girl almost threw the tray onto it, saying, "Let's eat a good breakfast this morning, Rachael."

Rachael's lips tightened as she said in a harsh whisper, "Patronizing bitch." Then she turned her eyes away from the food.

I figured this was no time to play supernurse. I was sure she knew more about her treatment than I did, so I asked, "What would you like me to do first?"

"Well," she said irritably, "if you pull the covers down, you'll see that in several places my skin is much thicker. In the cracks, I have lesions. They have to be soaked off before I can move or bend anything."

I did as she asked. When I pulled back the covers, I could see large oval scabs in all the crevices of her body—in the bend of her elbows, under her breasts, in the cracks of her groin. As the air hit them, they turned color almost instantly, from a light to a dark brown.

Though I didn't look at her, I could sense Rachael watching my reaction. This was another of those "no bullshit" times, so I said gently, "These really are the worst lesions I've seen."

Instead of being upset, Rachael just said, "I know. We'll have to soak them to get them soft." I poured some saline onto a four-by-four piece of gauze and placed a pad over each lesion. She told me that after about twenty minutes we could put some nitrogen mustard ointment on the scabs to keep them from returning so quickly. She said it also would stop some of the itching that she suffered from.

While Rachael was soaking, I sat next to her and looked around the room. The bed and the overbed table were new, as was the nightstand. The white-on-white wallpaper was accented with freshly painted deep-blue woodwork, the floors and drapes were sparkling clean. Nothing like Barrenfield, I told myself, and then when I focused on the bright-red plastic isolation hampers, when I counted the peroxide and saline containers on the windowsill and when I looked into Rachael's eyes, I suddenly knew it was not that different.

Anytime I had to leave the room for anything, I had to dispose of everything that covered me except my uniform. Then I had to scrub my hands with a brush and not touch anything in the room as I left. If the door was closed, I had to use a piece of paper as a barrier. If Rachael dared to ask for a glass of water after I had ungowned, it was some pain in the ass. And if, God forbid, her phone rang, it was a disaster. I'd have to scramble into the entire getup before the damn thing stopped ringing.

If someone wanted to speak to me outside the room, or at the nurses' station, after I had regowned, I'd have to strip like a banana, go out, come back and redress before I could do anything for Rachael. I gave up going to the bathroom unless I had to be out of the room for another reason. I had decided that a human body which insists on functioning is a distinct disadvantage to a nurse whose patient is in isolation.

As I continued her dressings, Rachael talked to me. I concentrated so hard on not hurting her that it was like looking through a telescope backward. All the chaos seemed to fade around me.

Once I had put gauze to her lips so that they wouldn't crack, she could speak more easily. She told me that she was married to a gentle man who happened to be an alcoholic and was presently drying out at Elmwood's Detoxification Center. Her one son was married and had two children, but Rachael seldom saw him, because they had never gotten along well. I felt worse knowing that Rachael had so little support from her family. Even though I could understand it. I was willing to bet that Rachael played a real heavy at home—a tough matriarch. She told me that she had been sick for five years; that she had had several remissions and at times been symptom free; even looked like everyone else. But when the lymphoma hit again, it turned her into a space monster.

This time her skin was worse than ever before, she explained, and so she had quickly gotten infected. The physical pain was worse also, but she suffered most from the emotional pain of her imposed isolation. No matter what her doctor had tried to do, he was unable to halt the course of her disease. Her only stroke of luck was her doctor.

Dr. Leonard Diamond was absolutely magnificent; he was one of my hero doctors. He was brilliant, kind, soft-spoken, and had a sense of humor. He always took time to sit and talk to his patients, and, contrary to most doctor tactics, he explained to the nurses he worked with the rationale for his treatments. Not having to follow orders blindly was terrific, because then I didn't have to call and haunt him with a thousand unnecessary questions. A great boon to medicine, doctors sharing information with nurses. If I ever develop a "Build a Doctor" kit, he'll be one of my models.

Dr. Diamond also wrote long informative notes—legibly. The man was almost a saint. It didn't hurt, either, that he was good-looking. Tall, with brown curly hair and aviator glasses. He could have been a real operator, and yet he wasn't. He was a sincere, good-guy doctor who cared about his patients and really cared about medicine.

That day, before he came into Rachael's room, he put on one of the yellow gowns. When he looked down at himself and laughed, I knew he felt silly. He walked right in and sat on Rachael's bed. "How are you today?" he asked, smiling. I could see he was fond of her.

Rachael looked him straight in the eye and answered, "Terrific, Doc."

Without cracking a smile, he said dryly, "Glad to hear it."

I knew it was all a big con when his voice softened to ask, "Is it very much worse today?"

"You're doing all you can," she reassured him without answering his question. He sat for a while, relaxed, treating Rachael as though she was the only patient he had to see that day. She was pleased, and so was I as I listened to them chat. I moved toward the window to allow them some privacy, when I heard Rachael ask, "Got any miracles in there, Doc?" She was pointing to his black bag.

He shook his head, lowered his eyes and said apologetically, "Rachael, the only thing I carry in here is a Linus blanket. And that I need to comfort *me*."

It seemed such a paradox: he was so imposing, but this was one of the most human interactions I had ever seen between a doctor and a patient. Its dignity etched itself into my brain.

Outside Rachael's room, Dr. Diamond explained to me what each medication he had ordered was meant to do, then how he wanted her dressings done, and why. When I said I understood, he asked if I would consider being Rachael's full-time nurse. "Her response to you seems positive and she seems more cheerful than usual."

I thanked him for his vote of confidence but then explained, "I hate the thought of bouncing a fellow nurse off her case."

"I'll take care of that by requesting officially that you take care of Rachael," Dr. Diamond said, and patted my shoulder. "It's the least I can do for her. . . ."

Back in Rachael's room, I began to change her bed. That was some feat: her skin stuck so badly that in order to change the sheets I had to change her skin. Yuk! It was not a great feeling to see her peeled, and three minutes after I had finished, the bed was as flaked with skin as before I started.

During the next weeks, although I found myself washing more

than usual, I really learned to like Rachael. She never whimpered. If she was going to yell, she yelled.

One afternoon as I tried to get her into a chair by the bedside, I held her under the arms. When I pulled away, some of her skin stuck to my glove. "Goddammit! Don't you do anything right?" she screamed.

I started to get angry. She has some guts screaming at me like that, I thought. Especially since she's almost totally dependent on me. But in a moment, when I thought about it again, I found myself smiling at her courage and said, "Not the first time, maybe, but you can try to tell me what makes it more comfortable for you."

After I got her back into bed and started her dressings, she began moaning.

"How can I help make you more comfortable?" I repeated.

"Stop using that word 'comfortable,'" she snapped. "Nothing makes me comfortable."

"I can understand that," I said patiently. "Would you like some pain medicine?"

"No! Absolutely not!" Rachael yelled. "I definitely do not want any drugs. You know that makes me confused, and the one thing I didn't need around here is not to be able to watch all you people to make sure you don't kill me by mistake."

I understood her point. Sometimes, between her silent frustration and her screaming anger, I'd catch a look that was so pained it could freeze me, and I'd remember how frightened she was. I'd feel embarrassed at having seen something I knew she didn't want me to see, as though somehow I had invaded her privacy, so I'd chatter and clean up the room. I worked with Rachael nineteen days in all, and toward the end she almost stopped being gruff with me.

One afternoon as I finished her soaks she said, "You know, Teri, I'm not lonely anymore." Her face cracked as she smiled and added, "You're more company than I've ever had."

I thanked her. Genius that I was, I had never paid much attention to the fact that, in all the time I had been with her, not one friend had visited and no one had called.

Another day she was really miserable over a fight she and her son had had on the phone. Rachael had called to ask him to visit, but he had refused. I tried to explain that it was difficult for her son to see her so sick, but she shushed me quiet and was depressed for the rest of the afternoon.

After that day, I spent hours telling her the details of my relationship with Lil and the kids, occasionally including the arguments Greg and I had in order to spice things up. I tried to make her feel as involved in my life as I could.

Then one morning I found her crying. She had gotten frightened the night before when she had tried to reach me and found my phone had been disconnected.

"Why couldn't I reach you?" she asked me frantically.

"Well, Zelda," I explained, embarrassed, "Lil and I ran up our bill again and neither of us gets paid until the end of the week. We explained that to the New York Telephone Company, but they cut us off anyway."

She looked relieved and indicated with a shaky movement of her hand the nightstand next to her bed. "Open the drawer," she ordered. "In the back right-hand side you'll find my checkbook. Take it and pay your telephone bill so I can call you when I need you."

Boy, did I feel guilty. There have only been a few times in my life when I've wished I was a more conventionally responsible person, and this was one of them. I was all this woman needed, with her other problems.

"Zelda, I can't do that," I said firmly. "You've already paid me extra this week."

"So I should have to suffer for your pride?" she fumed. "That's fair, according to you?" For just a moment she looked frightened again, then she turned her face away from me and said, "I *have* to be able to reach you."

She looked so upset that I conceded. "All right," I said quietly, "I'll take your money." I sometimes marvel at my technique. I take the poor woman's money and make it sound as though I'm doing her a big favor.

"Consider it a Christmas present if it makes you feel better," Rachael said, turning toward me again.

"Zelda," I said, laughing, "it's only August."

"Money should never be an issue between friends," she said seriously. I had started to do her dressings, so her arms were more flexible than usual. "Promise me that you'll stop on the way home and pay that bill?" she asked, and for the first time she touched my arm.

Then she was quiet for a long time and I wondered if her mind was wandering, as it sometimes had been lately. I finished her dressings without saying anything.

"Would you do one more thing for me, Teri?" she asked as I sat on the bed.

I winked at her. "Ask me anything."

"I'd like to give you power of attorney," she said, and when she saw me stiffen she added, "Please let me finish before you decide. I'd like you to pay the nurses for me and take care of some other business. It shouldn't be too much, my lawyer will help." When I didn't say anything, she continued softly. "I need someone whom I can trust to sign my checks; someone I know cares about me, who's available when I need them." She frowned and held tight to my arm again. "I'm getting tired, too tired to do everything myself." She hesitated, then closed her eyes. "I have no one else . . ." she said quietly.

I wanted to ask about her son; I wanted to tell her not to build up resentments, but as soon as I opened my mouth to speak, Rachael began to shake and tremble so badly that I managed only "Okay, Zelda, I'll do it." I patted her head, as I would a child's, to reassure her. Then, petting and soothing, I whispered, "It's okay. I'll work it out."

From that day on, I took on more of Rachael's responsibilities. I spent almost no time at home, and the time I did was spent thinking about Rachael. My kids stayed at my mother's. Greg balked when I couldn't see him, though he claimed he understood. Niki and Spinner hollered "neglect," and only Lil worked around me without complaining. My whole life revolved around taking care of Rachael; being there for her.

One bright day, Rachael's dressings went more quickly than usual. We had gotten it down to a science. It was lunchtime before we knew it. Most of the time, I'd leave Rachael to eat in the cafeteria. More to get away from her pain than from the smell or responsibility. I hated to see her suffer. She could separate from her pain when she got confused; I wasn't so lucky.

"Lunchtime," I announced as the diet aide dropped Rachael's tray on the overbed table at the door.

"Would you just this once. . .Sit here. . .and eat with me?" she asked haltingly. "It's been so long since I've eaten with another person," she explained, looking directly at me. "Couldn't you have them bring you a tray?"

I could see by the way Rachael was looking at me that she understood what she was asking. The window in the room was open and the slight warm breeze was blowing flakes of her skin, like dust, all over the place. I waved away several flies. Another monumental dilemma! I knew she was dying of loneliness as much as from anything else, but I wasn't sure I was ready to be another Father Damien. I was certain, now that I knew how lonely she was, that I wouldn't be able to eat downstairs, so I took a deep breath and said, "This, Zelda, is above and beyond the call of duty." Her face dropped and she looked so miserable, so I added, "But, if you promise that you won't shake the covers, that you won't jump around alot, and that you won't flake all over my food. . . I'll sit and eat with you."

She smiled, and as I sat down on her bed she pulled herself up and hugged me. My mask fell; her cheek was against mine. When Rachael pulled away, some of her skin stuck to my face.

After I told her that I had to order my tray, I excused myself and walked into the bathroom. As soon as I had closed the door behind me, I looked into the mirror. Pieces of Rachael's skin hung from my cheek. I bent over the sink, poured some Betadine into my hands and scrubbed my face.

When I raised my head to look again, her skin was gone but my face was a pale Chinese yellow from the iodine solution. I rinsed again. No change. To get out of the room, I knew I would have to pass Rachael, and I didn't want to hurt her feelings by having her know I had raced right into the bathroom to wash after she hugged me. I needed some greensoap.

I heard Rachael call my name. "Just a minute," I answered cheerfully, "I'll be right out." Then I pulled the cord to the emergency buzzer which signaled the desk.

"Can I help you?" the anonymous voice from the nurses' station asked through the intercom above the sink.

I stood on my toes. "Please send someone in with greensoap," I hissed quietly into the machine. "Quickly."

As soon as I heard footsteps coming down the hall, I stuck my head out the door, grabbed the container from the aide, and signaled her not to say anything about my yellow face.

"Teri," Rachael asked from her bed, "is something wrong?" My back was turned to her as I slid into the bathroom.

"No, Zelda," I answered pleasantly. "I just want to fill the soap dispenser and I'll be right out." She seemed satisfied.

I scrubbed my face hard with the greensoap. All my makeup had disappeared. Some of my skin rubbed off, but finally the stain was gone. Everything came off but the memory that at one point Rachael and I were so connected that I even wore her skin.

A few days after this, I walked in later than usual. Rachael was lying in bed moaning in a weak and quivering voice, "I'm dying of thirst, I'm dying of thirst.. . ."

"No, Zelda, that's not what your dying of," I said teasingly as I tiptoed up to the side of her bed. She hadn't seen me because her eyes were still stuck shut, but as soon as she heard my voice her whole body relaxed.

"I was afraid you weren't coming," she said nervously, struggling to open her eyes. "I can't see."

I immediately soaked her eyelids and when they could open, put drops into her eyes. As she fluttered her lids, she smiled and said, "Thank God you're here."

We finished the morning bath and dressing ritual just before lunch. I ate in the room all the time now, and as I pulled my chair up alongside her bed Rachael asked, "Could you do me one last favor?" I was going to tease her about final wishes, but she looked so serious that I just nodded.

Rachael was propped up in bed, her overbed table across her lap. Leaning forward on it, she said, "There are no children here. My son won't bring his to see me, and you know I haven't seen a child up close for years." She hesitated and bit her bottom lip before she continued, "I need to see a child. Find me one and you can tell him I'll give him ten dollars just to stand outside my window where I can look at him."

"Zelda, I wailed, "I don't believe you. I'd give ten bucks to get a kid *out* of my sight, and your going to pay to see one?" This sounded like *Mission Impossible* to me, and as I looked at Rachael the emptiness of her life seemed to echo.

"Please?" was all she said for the rest of the day.

That afternoon when I got home from work, I talked to both my kids. Niki, now a very grown-up twelve year old, was trying to teach Spinner, now a playful nine, how to read. They were sitting at the kitchen table as I walked over to hug them. "Hey, kids, want to make ten dollars?"

They both looked up warily. I sat next to Spinner first. He was my best shot, a compassionate mercenary. I laid the deal on him. He looked me straight in the eye, put his hand on my shoulder and said without hesitation, "Nope, Mom, not this time."

My children always knew the patients Lil and I were taking care of. They, and the extent of their diseases, were our dinner-table conversation.

I got up and moved over to the chair next to Niki, a real long shot, since she couldn't even stand the sight of a cut finger without getting sick to her stomach. She slowly shook her head from side to side.

"Come on, you little creeps," I said. "The lady needs to see a little kid."

Niki smiled at me and said, "Not your little kids, Mom."

"Not even for ten whole dollars," Spinner said, shaking his head ferociously.

My God. I was crushed. Bunch of little bastards, I thought. By that time, they had both learned to protect themselves from my overwhelming compassion for *other* people.

I was awake most of the night trying to think of alternatives. I dreaded having to tell Rachael that I couldn't get her what she wanted. She had been much weaker lately, her eyesight was failing, and she was frequently more confused. I was certain she couldn't live much longer. And how could I live with myself if I failed her on her last request? What a downer.

As I waved goodbye to Lil in the parking lot of the Rehab Center the next morning, as she trotted toward the Baby Cottage, I got an enormous brainstorm. *Maybe*, I thought. . . just maybe. Later, when Rachael was asleep, I decided to give it a try.

The narrow cement walk cut through the beautifully manicured lawn like a scar. I walked it, under the huge shade trees, going almost completely around the building before I found the door. Locked. I tried the buzzer. Soon a grandmotherly woman, who was passing across the hall, saw me and came to let me in. I asked if she knew where Lil worked and she pointed to an L-shaped corridor ahead.

As I walked down the hall past semi private rooms with open doors, I saw several small bedridden children. Some were hydrocephalics, their huge heads pinning them to the mattresses of the metal cribs; others were armless or had twisted limbs. Most were making animal sounds, so I assumed they were retarded. Though the place was immaculate, and the children were obviously well cared for, the place still made me shudder.

In one of the rooms I found Lil. I told her Rachael's wish and watched her eyes blink like computer lights before she finally said, "So, You want to borrow a child?"

I nodded. She gestured for me to follow her into one of the far rooms. There she pointed to a small red-haired child who was Mongoloid. "Will Rusty do?" she asked, smiling at the child. She walked over to his crib and picked him up. "He can be propped and taken out."

Lil dressed him quickly, struggling with his floppy legs and arms, stuffing them into his clothes. He smiled adoringly at her, and when she had finished she hugged him hard before she tied him into the child-sized green wheelchair that stood next to his crib. After she placed a pillow on each side of him so he wouldn't keel over, she quickly wiped his freckled face with a washcloth. She stood back to judge the effect of his brown plaid cotton shirt and then fixed his collar.

"Spiffy!" she said, and winked at him. I have to admit he looked sweet; I couldn't wait until Rachael saw him.

Lil and I raced through the corridor with Rusty, laughing and trying to duck the other nurses and aides. We didn't want to answer any questions and take the chance that someone would try to stop us. Lil ran Rusty across the lawn and parked just outside Rachael's window as I ran up the front steps, down the hall and into her room. I unglued Rachael's eyes as quickly as I could, without saying a word, and then I raised the top of her bed so fast that I almost ejected her.

"Teri," she growled, "what the hell are you doing?"

"Hang on a minute and you'll see," I told her as I ran over and pulled open her drapes.

"There's your kid," I said, pointing out the window. Rusty's wheelchair was behind a bush, so it looked as though he were standing, and Lil was hidden by a shadow from one of the trees. I saw her lean over and grab one of Rusty's hands so he could wave, but Rachael's sight was too poor for her to notice Lil. When I turned to say something to her, she was waving back, big tears streaming down her cheeks.

From that day on, Rachael deteriorated rapidly. She was so weak that it was almost impossible to turn her. Her responses had gotten much slower and she was confused most of the time. Her skin was so bad that Dr. Diamond ordered oatmeal baths, but Rachael dreaded the pain and effort of walking to get into the tub. The only bathtub was across the hall, and normally I would never have tried to convince her at this stage of her disease. But whenever she didn't take the treatment, the itch was so bad that in her confusion she would scratch hunks of her skin off.

"Hey, Zelda," I cajoled one day, "come on, kid, for me." When she shook her head I added, "I've done things for you." Guilt is great; it can even cut through confusion.

That day she was so stiff and curled up that I had to ask the large male orderly to help me walk her across the hall. It took us a half hour to get there, and once inside the room he had to pick her up in his arms to lower her into the tub.

While he stood behind, holding her, I knelt on the floor next to the bathtub. I was certain her mind was wandering when I asked her a question and she did not answer.

Suddenly she looked directly at me. Raising her arm out of the bath, all hanging flesh and clinging oatmeal, she grabbed my hand and said softly, "Teri, I'm going to let Rachael go."

"Why?" I asked, instinctively frightened by what she said. Her eyes lit up and her expression became inappropriately euphoric. She smiled and said slowly, "Because *Zelda* is getting bigger and more beautiful every day."

We managed to get her back to her room by using a wheelchair; back into bed by carrying her.

After the orderly had left and we were alone, Rachael said softly, "Well I hope that bath made you feel better, Teri, because I feel like hell."

The rest of the afternoon, Rachael slipped in and out of consciousness, but whenever she woke up she panicked until she realized I was right there.

"I'll stay with you tonight," I said, after one very bad dream. "I won't leave you."

Sometime around three in the morning Rachael stopped breathing. I stood next to her bed and watched for a minute, then checked her heart with my stethoscope. It had stopped. Without thinking, automatically, I put the stethoscope to my own chest. And as I listened to the regular beat of my own heart, I began to cry.

CHAPTER 18

Gallbladder, hysterectomy and colostomy patients filled the weeks after Rachael died and gave me great satisfaction without any pain.

Then, one evening in early spring, Mrs. Dayton called and said, "Dear, I have a young man who needs a nurse to keep him comfortable." She flattered, "I know that you don't mind giving pain medicine as much as some of the other girls."

"What's he got?" I asked warily, because usually a doctor won't order enough pain medicine to cause a nurse any difficulty unless nothing else can be done for the patient.

"Some kind of cancer," she said softly. "Dr. Pavetto is his doctor, and he told the directress at Rehab that Dr. Diamond suggested you."

Dr. Pavetto was another of my favorite doctors, very different from Dr. Diamond, not as much a stickler for medical details, but a wonderful human being.

Yves was at Elmwood's Rehabilitation Unit, in Rachael's old room. Evette smiled when I approached the desk on the first day, and said, "You're lucky this time, you have Yves." She told me he had a massive Spinal-cord-compression tumor and leukemia. He was thirty-three years old, a Frenchman from Brittany; he was married. . . and he was terminal.

Still, nothing prepared me for the *man* he was.

When I first saw Yves he was sitting bolt upright in bed and he looked just like a toy soldier: painted pale, short light hair and enormous brown eyes with tan broomlike lashes. He sat stiffly because the tumor had left him paralyzed, unable to move anything but his head and one finger of his right hand.

"Hi, Yves," I said, smiling tentatively. "My name is Teri Daley and I'm going to be your nurse." I didn't know whether he would greet me with anger or with tears, or whether he'd just ignore me.

But Yves looked up slowly with a shy smile and spoke with hesitation. "I am happy to have the pleasure to meet you. I hope I will not be too much trouble."

As I moved closer to the bed, he apologized, "You will excuse that I cannot shake your hand, but I am not now able to move." He spoke without pity for himself, so I was able to say, "Well, I can do that," as I lifted his hand and held it in mine. I expected to feel sorry for him, but nothing in his presentation allowed for that.

After I fed him, while I was giving him a bed bath, he started to wiggle his nose and blink his eyes fast.

"What's wrong?" I asked, soaping the washcloth.

"The nose, it begins to itch," he said, shaking his head. By the time I had frantically dried my hands in order to scratch it, we were both laughing hysterically.

He spoke only a few more minutes before he began to frown. His face looked drawn and I could see he was tired. He hadn't complained of pain, but still I medicated him, and he fell asleep almost instantly.

The girl walked so softly I didn't hear her come into the room. "Hi," she said as she stood next to my chair, and extended her hand. "I'm Liz, Yves's wife." Then, looking over at the bed, "How is he today?"

While I told her how the day had gone, I noticed that her blond curls had wilted and that she had worry lines around her light-blue eyes. Her voice was soft, like her walk, and incredibly sweet.

Yves woke up and, with the smile of a little kid whose mother has just come back from a day away, greeted her. She quickly walked over and kissed him.

"And how were the children today?" Yves asked.

"Oh, fine," she said, pulling a straight-back chair over to the bed. She held Yves's hand and told him, "French isn't their favorite subject, but we're making some headway. Twenty-three restless seventh-grade students aren't easy to keep interested."

"Do you have children of your own?" I asked Liz.

She bent to lean her head against Yves's arm and gazed at him lovingly. "No," she said to me. "We were always enough for each other. We feel complete in ourselves." To see them together made that believable.

Liz stood up and got the basin and some other equipment out of the bedside stand. She began to shave Yves, and then I understood why he had refused when I had offered earlier. She talked to him about their house, her day at school, and their cat, Frimousse, and told him in great detail about their garden.

Afterward, while Yves slept again, Liz talked to me. She told me that they had been married for nine years and that for most of the last eight Yves had not been well. They had spent an enormous amount of time and money going from one doctor to another to try to find out why he was always so tired, so listless. Not one doctor in America could find the answer. So they flew to France, where the doctors knew no more. When they returned, one of the doctors here suggested the possibility of psychosomatic disease.

For many more years, Yves saw a psychiatrist. Still his symptoms persisted. He began, like a man possessed, to keep records and diaries, day and night, hoping not to miss a clue. Liz looked terribly sad as she admitted that she had prodded, supported, encouraged and finally badgered Yves to try harder.

Then one morning, nine months ago, when Yves had tried to get out of bed, his legs refused to hold him and he had toppled to the floor. He was transferred almost immediately from the Emergency Room of the local community hospital to one of New York's largest hospitals. There he was diagnosed by a young resident who looked especially disheartened when he told them, "Malignant spinal-cord tumor." They both sat, held each other and cried. It was worse than either of them had imagined. Liz smiled when she told me that after Yves had composed himself he had said, with his usual optimism, "Well, at least we see I am not crazy."

The months that had followed Yves's diagnosis were extremely difficult. He had undergone all possible radical and aggressive treatment in the finest cancer hospital in New York City. All available current treatment, including chemotherapy and cobalt, was used . . . without success. Then Yves's leukemia had been discovered. Each day for months, Liz traveled in to the city after work to be with him, and each night she came home more discouraged. "I felt so terribly impotent," she told me. "I would have done anything to help him." She had tears in her eyes when she said it.

That day, as I was leaving, I saw Dr. Pavetto standing at the front desk. "Hi," I said, walking over to him. "Is there anything special you'd like me to do for Yves?"

He was a very attractive man in his forties, impeccably dressed and always pleasant. He shook his head thoughtfully and played with his salt-and-pepper beard. "Try to keep him smiling for as long as you can, he said, putting his hand on my arm, "and then keep him comfortable. Don't withhold his pain medicine for any reason." Dr. Pavetto was shaking his head as he walked away.

Evette, who was sitting at the desk, looked after him and suddenly began to smile.

"What's so funny?" I asked.

"He's really something," she said. "One of his patients, a Mrs. Ragen, had been very depressed lately and I was concerned about her. So I called him to see if he would order an antidepressant. He insisted on coming in to talk to her first, and by the time he left she was in great spirits."

"How come?" I asked.

Evette pulled off her cap and ran her fingers through her curly blond hair before she answered. "He told me it was the easiest case to solve in years. Because I didn't know what he was talking about, I went in and asked Mrs. Ragen. She looked like a Cheshire cat. She had told Dr. Pavetto that she had been depressed because she couldn't pay her mortgage. So he told her not to worry, he would pay it."

A few days later, as I was bathing Yves, he looked particularly thoughtful. When I turned him on his side to wash his back, he said, "I will not get well, will I?" He made it sound factual, a rhetorical question, so I didn't answer. Dr. Pavetto had said that the doctors in New York had told Yves he was being sent to Elmwood for rehabilitation; now I knew he had never believed that.

When I turned Yves over on his back, he looked expectant, but I didn't know what to say. I finally tried. "Yves there are many things medicine can do now to help you."

He frowned and took a deep breath before he asked, "If I refuse all treatment . . . how long will it be before I die?"

As outrageous as it sounds, the first thing I felt was betrayed. I wanted to shout at him, "How could you ask me a question like that? You know I'm not allowed to tell you." When I got myself together, I felt confused, then helpless.

I really believed he had a *right* to know; a *right* to do what he wanted with his own life. But at the time, I would have gotten pulverized if I were the one to tell him. That was a doctor's responsibility, and I knew for sure that Dr. Pavetto would never tell him.

I stood there, wet washcloth in hand, thinking how unlike the movies this was. Yves's eyes were fixed on me and I was afraid. As an abstract concept, I believed in informed consent. But with Yves staring at me, how could I tell him the doctors had said he had less than two weeks to live? I can't tell him, I won't destroy all his hope, I swore to myself. Also, I was afraid that in some way my telling him would make me responsible for whatever happened. Besides, I thought as I watched his white cheeks flush, I love him already. He was one of the finest people I had ever met, and though I knew he was going to die, I didn't really believe it.

The next time Yves spoke, my resolve evaporated. He looked at me compassionately and said in a very firm, very soft voice, "Teri, please allow me the dignity to know. No one else will. I must have time to prepare. We have only each other, Liz and I, I must be there for her at this time. She will be frightened."

The lump in my throat was choking me. I was angry again at God, angry at fate, angry at medicine and more angry at my own limitations.

Yves smiled at me. "It is not so hard if you just nod. I will say it." Then he began, "I will die in one month if I refuse all treatment.
I didn't nod.

"I have maybe . . . three weeks?" he asked, his voice still firm.

Some remnant of my own voice returned. I breathed out hard as I answered, "Maybe three weeks, Yves." I could no longer look at him, because I was crying.

Yves shook his head and said very quietly, "It is not so long, three weeks; it is not so long . . ." Then he raised his head, looked at me and said with determination, "I have much to do."

Time passed as he tried to absorb what he had already known, and then he said, "First we must tell Liz. You will help me, please." Another fact, no question.

I was more composed now, and as Yves and I spoke about his dying it was as though we were both talking about someone else. Liz was the priority now, he emphasized: this would be very difficult for her. Just two days earlier she had insisted on getting a new hospital bed with pushbutton controls. That way, Yves could arrange his bed in whatever position he wished. One finger could allow Yves some control; a little bit of independence. Liz had never stopped hoping.

That afternoon, before we called Liz, Yves asked, "Is there a way to remove the pain but I do not sleep so much?"

I explained that because of the intensity of his pain, a large dose of medication had to be given or he would get no relief. Unfortunately, one of the side effects was that it put him to sleep.

He thought about that for only a minute before he said, "I have not so much time, and I must be more awake. You will give me just enough medicine so I can bear it." Then Yves's eyes filled for the first time as he said, "I wish to see the green one more time."

Although it was spring, the weather was still cold, and I understood he was waiting for the grass and the trees to turn. As we both looked out his window we could still see some dirty, scattered snow covering the spare bushes and barren land.

I was standing next to the bed, my hand on his, when he continued, "One morning I will say, 'It is beautiful today; it is very green,' and you will know I must have medicine to take away the pain. I will want never to have any more pain." He lowered his head. "Can you understand?"

I looked at Yves and understood how brave he was and how much he loved life.

"Do you believe in God?" I asked. "In heaven?"

He looked at peace when he told me gently that neither he nor Liz believed in any religion that promised fulfillment in a "hereafter." "We are, what you would say, Existentialist," he explained. "Do you know of that?"

"It's a belief in today?" I asked him, trying to remember what Lil had read me about Camus and Sartre. What I did remember was that at the time it had seemed terribly depressing to me. Now it caused me some difficulty. Liz and Yves seemed to have nothing that could make this experience easier for them.

I tried to remedy it by teasing Yves. "According to Johnathan Livingston Seagull, you will be *recycled*."

He wrinkled his nose and made a terrible face as he asked, "What is this 'recycle'?"

I explained that I was sure he would return after he died, possibly as someone or something else. That we all came from a main energy source, and that energy could be neither created nor destroyed. It just changed form.

He laughed and I knew he didn't believe it. I didn't, either, but I thought it would offer some salve for wide-open wounds.

The following afternoon, Liz brought in three huge posters of flying seagulls to hang on the wall as an inspiration. We all laughed as she taped them up, and then Yves told me how much he had always loved the sea.

Yves had postponed his talk with Liz for several days until he decided it was time. When I tried to call her at home, there was no answer. I was nervous about it, but Yves reassured me, saying, "She is in the garden. She has a love to see things grow. We will try later."

When Liz did come, Yves immediately asked her to sit on the bed. His tone warned her, and before he had said a word she already looked frightened.

He turned to me and said, "We will begin." I moved to the side of the bed, close to him.

"Liz," he said gently, "I have much to say. I will not live too long . . ." She leaned her head against his chest and began to protest, and he soothed and silenced her before he continued. "I must thank you first for all the years; I regret only that there was not more time." When Liz began to cry, her body trembling, Yves turned to me and said, "Please place my hand on her head, so that I may comfort her." As he continued to speak, Liz hugged him, her head still on his chest.

Then, when her sobbing subsided, she made Yves a promise. "America hasn't been kind to you," she said. "I'll take you back to

Brittany and bury you by the ocean, under a mimosa tree."

He spoke firmly but kindly. "Liz, we have lived like old people for years because of my sickness. You will take what money we have and you will *live*. You will do all the things we could not do. . ." I watched as she argued silently; I knew she would take him back to Brittany. Then they hugged for a long time, letting the reality of their situation penetrate, and sharing while they could.

About two weeks later, I woke up to birds chirping and the sun shining arrogantly through my curtains. The warm breeze forced me out of bed with more enthusiasm than I usually felt in the morning. I sang while I dressed, and as I walked outside I was elated. It was such a beautiful day.

Suddenly my stomach lurched. Everything was green, vibrant and alive. I remembered, then, what Yves had said.

I drove to work more slowly than usual, sadness washing over me in waves. I didn't want Yves to die–not yet. Even though he had been struggling with more pain lately.

As I walked slowly into Yves's room, he was sitting up in bed, beads of perspiration rolling down his face. A pitifully emaciated man had been moved in with him during the night. Yves's face was drawn and he was tight lipped as I had never seen him before.

"What's wrong?" I asked.

"It is just that I have been sitting too long in this way," he whispered.

"Is something wrong with your finger?" I asked. "Couldn't you lower your bed?"

He motioned with his head to the man in the next bed. "He, my friend, had much pain last night. And this bed, it makes so much noise. I didn't wish to wake him." I knelt at the foot of the bed and lowered it by hand so that the sound of the motor wouldn't disturb the other patient.

After a few minutes, when he got his breath back, Yves smiled and thanked me. Then he said softly, "It is beautiful and green out today. I wish to sleep. . . ." He looked exhausted. All his bones protruded through the almost transparent cover of his drained white skin, evidence that his disease was eating him alive. The dark circles that hollowed out his eyes and the deeply carved lines around his mouth indicated the price he had paid to stay awake these last weeks.

I drew up his pain medicine and called Liz. When she arrived, the medicine had already begun to take effect. She sat next to him, holding his hand, crying quietly, and just before he closed his eyes he mumbled, to reassure Liz, "Maybe there is something with this 'recycle'!" He had a half-smile on his face.

Liz quickly bent down, her cheek against his, and whispered, "Yves . . . promise me, if there is *anything*, anything at all–you'll send me a sign, something that I can recognize. Promise me, please?"

Yves promised and went to sleep. Liz stayed with him, but he never again awoke.

Two nights later, at three o'clock in the morning, a hospital administrator called me at home to tell me that Yves had just died. The administrator was troubled because Liz, who had never left Yves's side, was insisting now that she be allowed to wash and shave Yves. He implied that he thought it in some way unnatural. "Could you come up and get her?" he asked stiffly. I tried to reassure him that what she was doing was healthy and necessary for her to deal with her grief, but I couldn't convince him, so I went to the hospital.

As soon as Liz saw me, she turned to come out of the room. "I'm sorry, Teri," she said. "I know you loved him, too." We left the hospital with our arms around each other, and because I didn't want Liz to be alone, I asked her to come home with me.

We parked our cars under the trees by the side door and walked slowly through the backyard to the canal. For a long time both of us just sat staring. A warm fog had settled over the black water, and everything looked hazy. It had been a long difficult ordeal, and now that it was over, there seemed nothing to say. I felt empty. Finally, when Liz started to shiver, we walked back to the house without speaking.

Inside, I laid Liz on the couch and covered her with a blanket. I put some tissues on the end table and went upstairs. I knew she wanted to be alone. From bed, I listened for Liz to cry. I was afraid that in trying to be brave she would bottle her emotions inside, and I knew that that would cause her more difficulty. Later, when I heard her sniffling, I fell asleep.

I awoke before six and quickly went downstairs to see how Liz was. She was sitting on the couch and had opened the window behind her wide, to get some fresh air. It was a beautiful warm day. I sat at the table across from her and we talked. Behind her, I could see the sun shimmering off the clear blue water of the canal.

As I watched, a large white sailboat came gliding through the water. It was very close. But I could hear no motor...the sails were down...and no one manned it. That puzzled me. That day there was no breeze, even the leaves on the trees were motionless, and I wondered how the big boat was moving; then I wondered why it was coming in rather than going out of the canal at that hour.

"Liz," I interrupted, "look at that."

She turned her head to see, and said incredulously, "My God! That's Yves!" Before I realized what was happening, she had grabbed my hand and we were running out the door toward the canal. All the while, Liz was laughing and crying, "That's Yves. . ."

I was sure she was having a hysterical reaction. But when we reached the water we had a complete view of the end of the canal. I strained to see, and couldn't believe my eyes: no boat! I was stunned. There was nowhere it could have gone, and yet it clearly wasn't there!

Liz was euphoric. She was talking about Yves's funeral, her traveling plans, what she would do with the house. I kept trying to question her. "Please, Teri, come with me," she said excitedly. "But don't ask me any more questions yet. Just come."

I was puzzled, but I followed her. I kept trying to figure out what had happened to the sailboat I knew I had seen. No explanation I could think of satisfied me.

When we got to her yellow Volkswagen, all she said was, "We're going to my house, then you'll understand."

She lived in a small wooden cottage across from the fishing canals. There were several vendors hawking "Fresh fish," across the street as we ran up the front stairs.

Inside, she took me to Yves's study. It was small, sparsely furnished, with one brown couch, a TV and several cluttered bookshelves. "Yves spent most of his time in the last years here," Liz told me. In the far corner of the room I could see a large architect's drawing board covered with a sheet. Liz immediately ran over and yanked the sheet away. *The boat!* I stood and stared at a sketch of the sailboat I had just seen on my canal: an exact replica. I still couldn't understand until Liz explained, "Yves spent years planning this boat. He always said, 'When I am free from pain, I shall sail'. . . ."

CHAPTER 19

The taxi was backed into the driveway, trunk open, when I came home from dropping the kids at school. I smiled, wondering what Lil was up to, and thought how pleased I always was to pull around the corner and find her there.

I called to her as I walked into the living room, and when she didn't answer I ran up the stairs to our bedroom.

Lil's back was to me as she emptied her clothes from our closet into two paper shopping bags.

"Hey, what's up?" I asked, flopping onto the bed.

She turned for a minute to look at me, then turned back quickly and continued to slip the clothes off the hangers. "I've got to leave," she said quietly.

"Why?" I asked, puzzled. "Is something wrong with your Dad? Or your kids?"

"No," she said, moving away from the closet and walking over to our dresser, "they're okay." She began to empty her drawers.

"Did I do something wrong?" I asked her as I sat up and moved over to the edge of the bed.

"No," she said softly, "you didn't." She picked up her loaded shopping bags and walked downstairs. In the kitchen she grabbed a plastic bag to take into the bathroom. She quickly dropped her shampoo and makeup into the bag and then lifted the bathrobe from the hook in back of the door.

Just before she reached the front door, I stopped her and shouted, "Goddammit, Lil, you can't just walk out without some kind of explanation."

She sat down on the bottom step, still hanging on to the handles of the shopping bags. Eyes down, she told me, "Look, Teri years ago, when we first met in school, we were both a mess. After I left that creep I was married to, I could barely think. And I couldn't really function. Since then you managed to get your life together and I'm finally getting undepressed. It's every child's birthright to have a mother," she added, smiling slightly. "I have to go back to my father's and make a home for my kids." She took a deep breath, stood up, kissed me on the cheek, and walked past me out the door.

I watched the yellow taxi pull away. After several minutes, I walked slowly down to sit by the canal. Funny, I thought, as I watched the fish swim through the murky water, it's the first time since I've known Lil that she kissed me. . . .

Greg and I had another fight. This time it was over my not wanting to go to church Sunday morning.

"The children must have some kind of example, something to believe in," he insisted at dinner Saturday night.

Both my kids scrambled away from the table and ran for the stairs. Niki stopped at the bottom just long enough to say, "Don't worry, Mom, I can go to church with Grams and Poppy."

Spinner ran back down and hit her. "I'm going with Greg," he said, frowning at her.

"Get out of here!" I hollered. "Both of you will go with who I tell you to."

"Can't you see the damage you're doing?" Greg said, looking after the kids. I wanted to hit him on the head with the meatloaf pan. I knew he was concerned about them; I knew he wanted to try to make us a *real* family, as he put it. But I had been working several private-duty cases lately. I was tired, and Sunday would be my first day off in eleven. I wanted to sleep late. But each time I stood for my own needs, Greg accused me of hurting my kids. I was afraid if I always gave in I would resent them. Resent them, nothing; I would *hate* them.

"Give me a break, Greg," I said wearily. "I'm tired of slicing myself into a million pieces. I want something for me."

"I would like to marry you and help make your life easier," Greg said, "but with all my hangups I'm not sure it would be best for you, Kitten."

My anger flashed and I snapped, "That's what I mean, Greg: you're always doing what's best for me, not, God forbid, what's best for *you!*" Instantly I was standing in front of him hollering, "Why don't you just say, for once, that you don't want it because it's no good for *you?*" As I walked over to the stairs I added sarcastically, "You're just too *good*, Greg."

He stood up, grabbed his coat and moved toward the door. "It's not that I don't love you enough," he shouted back. "It's just that I don't want to marry a gladiator. It scares the hell out of me." He walked out looking beat.

Upstairs, I tucked the kids in, and after Spinner fell asleep I lay down next to Niki. From under the covers she pulled a small perfume bottle with "Love Potion" scrawled on tissue paper taped to the front. "It's for you and Greg, Mom," she said as she kissed me. "I hope it works so you won't be unhappy ever again."

I laughed and hugged her. "What's in it?"

"Holy water," she teased, ducking under the covers.

"What a brat!" I said, slapping her playfully through the blanket. Then I kissed her again and told her, "Thanks for the sentiment anyway, kid."

When I went to bed, I took the bottle Niki had given me and hid it in my night-table drawer. We already are a *real* family, I said to myself.

Somewhere around two in the morning, I heard knocking at my door. I jumped into a pair of jeans and ran downstairs to see who it was. "Greg! What happened?" He looked miserable.

After what seemed like a very long time, he softly asked, "Do *you* want to marry *me*?"

Two weeks after the wedding Niki ran away. One afternoon I came home to find a long yellow note hanging on the front door:

Dear Mom,

I guess by now you know I'm gone. Well first I want you to know it's not because of you or the family. Actually, I don't want to say exactly why it is. I'm going to miss you and Spinner but I need time away from home to work out some things in my head. I'll be okay. You really have been a great mother and friend. Also, I want you to know I'm not pregnant or anything.

Tell Spinner I'll miss him and I'll be back. I know I can't expect you to just sit around, I know you'll call the cops and stuff, but I need time.

Please try not to worry too much, I'll call when I can. Please forgive me. I'm sad I had to go. I love you more than you know. Tell Grams not to panic and tell Poppy I love him.

Love ya,
Niki

P.S. Greg, she (Mom) wasn't too free with me and that's not why I left. It's me and my head. Make Mommy happy. She deserves it.

For six days I lay on the couch in a heap while Greg ran around like a madman calling the police, handing out photographs and checking all Niki's friends for leads. Mother kept dropping off spaghetti for me to eat, instead of chicken soup, and Spinner kept saying, "Niki said she'll be back."

And for six days, whenever I acted as though I understood, whenever I made excuses for Niki, Greg paced up and down in front of the couch yelling, "Why aren't you angry at her? Why can't you see she has no right to do this to you?"

"I can only handle one big emotion at a time," I answered quietly, "and right now I'm paralyzed with fear."

I was worried that I'd get a call from the police saying that

Niki's body was found crumpled like a broken doll at the side of the road somewhere, and while I pondered how I would handle that, Greg yelled, "Don't you care about her? How can you look so complacent?" That's when I learned that paralyzing anxiety sometimes passes for apathy. Actually, I was so depressed that I didn't even get mad at Greg until after I heard from Niki.

On the seventh day, the phone rang and I heard Niki's voice. "Mom?"

The first clue I had that I *was* angry was that I answered, "Who is this, please?"

"Mommy, please be serious," she said. "I'm stuck in Palm Beach and I have no money to get home."

"How did you get there?"

"My girl friend Candy's grandfather told her anything he had was hers, so she took some money out of his safe . . ."

I groaned, thinking of Niki behind bars as an accomplice, then asked, "Why did you do it, kid?"

"I was trying to be independent," she said softly.

"If you used Candy's grandfather's money," I told her firmly, "then you were *not* being independent. You were just transferring your dependencies."

There were a few moments of silence before I could hear Niki say seriously, "Maybe everybody's first attempt at independence is sloppy."

Then her first statement finally dawned on me. "Palm Beach where?" I asked.

"Florida," she said, taking a deep breath.

"Oh God," I said, forgetting that she had managed to survive the last six days without me. "Stay where you are. We'll fly down right away and get you."

And that's what we did. "I want to come, Mom," Spinner insisted, and when I said it wasn't a pleasure trip he turned to Greg and asked, "Why is Niki always rewarded for being bad? I never get to go anywhere."

Spinner had played it just right. We all hopped the first plane out of Kennedy Airport that night. And it was in the Palm Beach bus terminal that Greg and Niki officially declared war on each other.

I ran up to her and hugged her, while Greg, directly behind me, said sternly, "I hope you know how much, young lady, this has cost us, both emotionally and financially."

Niki stared at him and answered coolly, "I never asked *you* to come." His anxiety had been at a peak for days; he hadn't gone to work and had honestly been worried about her. Niki's indifference infuriated him, and before I could stop him his hand flew out and hit her in the face. I knew by the look in her eyes that she would never forgive his presumption.

When a year had passed, there was still only an uneasy truce. Greg tried hard to be the father that Niki hadn't had, and she resented him for it. "I have a father," she told me one night, sitting on her bed. "And if he's not around I have Pops."

Shawn had also remarried, and his wife, Marie, a very kind, motherly woman, invited the kids to Ohio each summer. They had gone for the last three years, and though Niki's relationship with her father couldn't be considered good, he was crazy about her. She hadn't forgiven him for leaving but still felt a certain loyalty, which intensified her resentment toward Greg.

Spinner didn't seem bothered by the same kinds of conflict. He was as charming and easygoing as ever. He loved Greg, and his father. After one summer vacation spent with Marie and Shawn he had told me, "I could live with Marie, she's terrific."

"And Daddy?" I had asked, sitting on the couch next to him. "How do you like Daddy?"

"I don't know him that good," Spinner had said, wiping his turned-up nose on his sleeve. When I poked him, he shrugged his shoulders and added, "I know Greg better, so it would be easier to ask him for what I want."

As much as Spinner's reaction bonded us, Niki's separated us; and while I could understand her feelings, Greg's inability to handle them always made me angry at him.

I began to think that maybe if I were home more it would be easier for all of us to adjust to being a family. In truth, I also needed some space away from my patients' pain.

So I decided to apply to college. At the rate I was going in evening school, it would take me eight years to get my RN; full time, it would take only two years. As Mrs. Dayton had warned, I did feel

I was getting stale working private duty, and I knew how much more I had to learn to do nursing really well. Often I felt as though I were sitting on a keg of dynamite; and if I had the job, I wanted to have the knowledge.

CHAPTER 20

Most of the college nursing program was a repeat of my LPN training. But whereas most of that had been clinical practice, most of this was theory. We had only two mornings in the hospital a week.

The philosophy, anthropology, English literature and psychology were a breeze for me after Lil's teaching. I took several electives in music and art, making practical use of Joel's instruction, and I even took economics for Greg. It was the only course I got a C in all through school.

I was an ace in the hospital-practice exams, but, as before, I cut most of my nursing classes and read my books at home. The only time I went to class was to challenge an exam. My marks were good.

But there was one class I never missed, "Nursing Process and the New Philosophy in Nursing." The instructor, Ms. Richards, was an intelligent feminist with a Ph.D. And it was in her class that I learned that my frustrations with nursing were not mine alone.

She was a tall thin woman with straight dark hair pulled back and tied. She didn't wear makeup and came to class in jeans all the time. My first encounter with her devastated me.

Fifteen college kids and five of the older students like me were seated in a circle. She sat in the center. To begin the class, she asked that we all identify ourselves and explain what we had been doing before we entered school.

Two of the kids went before me, and when it was my turn I smiled proudly and said, "Well, my name is Teri Daley and I've worked in medicine for seven years."

"Well, Teri," she said, not unkindly but very firmly, "it's time you stopped." When she continued, she addressed us all. "Here, in this program, we teach the profession of nursing. Nobody who gets through this course will be working in 'medicine,' they'll be working in nursing. Here you'll be eating, sleeping and breathing nursing."

I thought she was talking semantics, until she stood to speak. "While I was going for my Ph.D. I had the neat little theory that patients, health-care consumers, were treated badly because most doctors were men. Another wonderful feminist issue! Except now that I've seen more women doctors, I've decided my theory is bullshit. They're at least as insensitive as the men." Ms. Richards walked around the circle as she talked, looking at each of us.

"So I sat around trying to figure it out. And I talked to other professional nurses. Good ones. This is what we came up with: Birds have feathers. Fish don't. And they don't need them, even though they're pretty and soft. In fact, feathers would weigh a fish down and impair his survival.

"So maybe doctors can't have a lot of sensitivity, a lot of compassion. Men or women doctors. Especially the kind of doctor who does a lot of pain-producing procedures. I'm sure it's hard to cut into another person's body and cut out a cancer if you have to picture him as part of a family–if you picture his wife and kids waiting for him to come home from work just like you. Maybe you can't afford the luxury of that kind of identification. Then, as a surgeon, your cuts won't be as deft, or, as a medical doctor, you'll find it harder to shoot people with poisons to try to kill their cancers without killing them. It *is* possible that a doctor has to maintain that kind of distance to function well in his capacity. Okay, let's give them that."

She took a deep breath, stood straight in the middle of the circle and faced half the group at a time as she said firmly, "But I want you to remember this. Medicine, as everyone has been calling it, is more than just body mechanics. Even if we're talking about an A-number-one Mercedes mechanic! Health care is both doctoring *and* nursing. Different, but, goddammit, one is *not* more important than the other."

She unclipped the hair from behind her neck and shook it out, then ran her hand across her face and closed her eyes as though she was thinking. Not one of us made a sound.

Suddenly she said, "Teri, pull up a chair and sit on the inside of this circle, across from me."

I was afraid to refuse, but I hated this kind of role playing and I had no idea what she had in mind. As I pulled my chair up she turned to the rest of the class. "Teri is going to represent the health-care consumer, or patient. And I am going to be the professional nurse. What I'm going to say is *not* to be taken and repeated literally. What I am going to say is going to give you an idea of the role *you* must play, the messages you must transmit to the patient."

She sat directly opposite me and stared right into my eyes. "Back to the theory of a doctor as a mechanic," she said, smiling just a little. "If *your* body breaks down right after the mechanic walks out that door, somebody better know enough to patch it quickly and call the mechanic. And while he's on his way somebody better be there to help you control your panic as you watch your life start to slip away. Somebody who cares enough about you as a *person.* Somebody who's been so intimate with you that they've taken care of you as they would their own children, no matter what your condition. Someone who cares enough about your pain that they *can* cry for you. A nurse."

Ms. Richards got up and began to talk to everyone again. Thank God! I thought; I was a wreck.

She began to pace as she told them, "I'm not putting doctors down. They have a hell of a lot of responsibility; more, in fact, than any human being deserves. *But, we have it, too*–for at least eight hours at a time. Every day. And we have to take responsibility for the body and the *person.*"

She was very serious when she sat opposite me again. And without her telling me, I was the health-care consumer again. I knew that because my heart started to pound again when she spoke. "*Your* mother, *your* father, *your* child. The people who are more important to you than anything else in this world. And *we* know that. That's who we take care of. Why is it, then, that we're stacked alongside the bedpans and the gauze pads as part of a doctor's or a hospital's supplies?" At that concept I almost giggled, but then she pointed at me and demanded, "Why don't *you* want to know who *we* are? You're trusting us with the most precious things in your life. Whose responsibility is it to see that we're as competent as the doctors you choose? Whose, if not yours?"

By the time class ended, I was a nervous wreck. I had to admit she had made some very good points, but I was afraid that if she had shattered me with what she was selling, that "health-care consumer" would never be able to handle it. And besides, "medicine" has been around so long the way it is, I thought, people will never believe how important we are even if we do tell them.

Each time Ms. Richards' class met we sat in a circle, and the whole year she paced as she spoke.

"Some of medicine is science, there's no denying that, but a lot of it is art. Some objective data, a lot of individual preference and independent subjective judgment. All the decisions are made in the gray area in between. As a functioning adult, the patient should be allowed to make *his* choices and state *his* preferences. He can do this only if he's given some information. Mystery retains power. Doctors retain mystery. And patients can't argue, because there is no argument with the unknown." She pointed at us again when she said forcefully, "It's *your* job to teach these patients. It's *your* job to give them back the power to make the choices in their lives."

Another day, out on the lawn, sitting in a circle with the sun shining on Ms. Richards' chestnut hair:

"Research has proven that pre-operative teaching increases the patient's capacity to move and deep-breathe after surgery. *We* teach him; he gets home earlier, and in better shape.

"Significant research has also shown that the only real help for dying patients comes from nursing. Remember, a patient is a whole person. We have to consider his physical, emotional, spiritual and social needs." She stood across from one of the other girls and asked, "Do you understand what I'm saying?"

The girl looked embarrassed when she shook her head.

"Okay," Ms. Richards said, beginning to pace around the circle again. "Let me give you an example. Mr. Jones's doctor removes his legs for diabetic neuropathy, they're getting gangrenous and have to come off–body mechanics. While he's in the hospital, we take care of his physical needs, we feed him, bathe him, change his dressings; he heals. His doctor releases him. Now what? If the man is a house painter, we've removed his job as well as parts of his body. We've altered his lifestyle and his self-image. We've changed him from the head of his family to a dependent child. Is that a kindness? He's alive, but will he be able to *live* now?"

We all shook our heads, and Ms. Richards hammered on. "Okay, now let me show you how it can be done. Let me show you the place of *nursing* as a profession. The doctor has discharged his patient, he's done his job and he walks around feeling very self-satisfied.

"Now if, while Mr. Jones is in the hospital, he has a professional nurse, and she does her job, she begins to teach him how to care for *himself*. She helps him *explore* other talents he has, things that it will be possible for him to do even without his legs. She teaches his *wife* how to change his dressings and helps the wife ventilate her feelings. She helps do away with some of the helplessness that breeds anger in a relationship. And she teaches all the family members that Mr. Jones is still a *man*. She does this by her attitude. She *treats* Mr. Jones like a man, she talks to him like a functioning adult and allows him to make many of the decisions about his own care after helping him understand, in terms he uses, the other options for treatment and their consequences. She respects his judgment. And . . . she *touches* him. Touch says more than words can. If you can hold Mr. Jones's hand, if you can rub his forehead, if you can make contact as one human being to another, he'll know he's a valuable human being. You won't have to tell him.

"So Mr. Jones has mourned his legs, and all patients do mourn the loss of any body part, and we've helped him with that. It's time to be discharged. *We* see to it that his wife has help at home, we make available to her the sources, or we recommend she speak to a social worker whom we will work with to get them help. Then and only then have we done our job, and then Mr. Jones can *live*."

Every class with Ms. Richards was an inspiration–and on a beautiful sunny day the expanded role of the nurse seemed like a hell of a lot more work. Yet, little by little, I could feel a change in myself and I could sense that change in the other students. Most of us were beginning to feel proud of our profession; most of us had stopped thinking of nursing as second-class.

But there was one session that was a real bummer. Instead of being energetic, instead of talking from her soapbox, Ms. Richards was subdued. She didn't pace when she talked.

"Okay," she said as she looked around the room, "I've given the *information* you need to do your job well. Now I'm going to tell you that you'll have to fight with everything you have to be able to do it. Change is not accomplished quickly, and all change costs something. The best of you will wind up being burned at the stake, the others will just fade back into apathy. This is the problem, as I see it: Right now, because doctors are an elite group, they have all the money and all the power. They own the hospitals in one way or another. Patients follow their doctors, and so hospitals do all in their power not to aggravate them. The difference in what patients are willing to pay a doctor and what they are willing to pay a nurse comes from their assumption that they are paying for knowledge. Medicine is a big mystery. As long as we keep it a mystery, the doctors will maintain control. They're not going to greet us with open arms as we erode their power and give the patients answers to the mysteries."

After a pause, she softened her voice and continued. "And patients aren't going to be thrilled to find out that they have to make some pretty big decisions, that they have to take the responsibility for their own lives. They don't like the way the doctors are doing it, but while they are dumping the decisions on the doctor for Mom or Dad's life, they can get angry at him and not have to handle the guilt over making a decision themselves. Once we let them know that a doctor isn't a wizard, just another poor slob who's trying his best to add up all the numbers and come out with the right answer, they're not going to be thrilled with the disenchantment. No matter how grown-up we are, all of us like to believe that somebody can take care of us, that somebody has the answers we don't. When the health-care consumer, whether he be a patient or a patient's family, finds out what the health-care system is really like, he's going to feel pretty helpless at the start. Helplessness breeds fear, and a person's response to fear is often anger."

I was so overwhelmed,I interrupted her. "So what are we supposed to do? How are we supposed to handle it?"

She smiled, a little sadly, and said, "The profession we've chosen is that of *patient advocate*. Somebody has to begin change, because the system we have now isn't working, for us or for the patients." She hesitated a long time before she concluded, "And someday, you know, we'll all be patients."

The following semester . . . Autumn leaves crackled under my feet and I had to wear a sweater. Ms. Richards was teaching "Nursing Abstracts." I had taken biochemistry during the summer, because I could never handle all that math and chemistry with any other subjects, and this semester my heaviest subject was microbiology. At least I had finished with anatomy and physiology and gotten the smell of formalin, from my fetal-pig dissection, out of my nose. That poor little pig. It was certainly unfortunate for him that his anatomy and man's were similar; by the end of the course he was an empty closet.

Ms. Richards had gotten her hair cut. She had also gotten married. Those were the only changes. We were all in a circle again in no time and she was back on her soapbox.

"Patients and doctors are now in adversary positions," she began, and started pacing. "The withholding of information by the people in the medical profession is an exertion of power; malpractice suits are the retaliation. Nobody's winning. The whole concept of malpractice is based on a faulty premise, that of a perfect human being. It's the same faulty premise that 'medicine' is built on."

She went on to outline the growing problem: Doctors, in order to cover themselves, were doing more testing than necessary; more X-rays; more blood work. All these things cost the patients more and they still weren't getting the services they expected, because in order to meet escalating costs the first thing hospitals cut was their staffs.

". . . and, worse than that, many patients are being kept alive contrary to their wishes and the wishes of their families. Why? Because a doctor is afraid to say, 'I can't do anything else.'" Ms. Richards voice softened when she added, "Most doctors are competent. Some are better human beings, but most are competent. Even the best make mistakes, because crises are the rule more than the exception, and enormous stress is a constant." She told us that even though the stakes were so high we had to realize that the people who were running the show were still just human beings who were subject to "*human*" incompetence."

When she stopped, one of the girls asked, "Well, what can *we* do about that?"

Ms. Richards smiled. "*Teach*. Give your patients back some of the power. If they don't feel as helpless, they won't be as angry."

On that day I first began to see that the patient held the key that could open up a new door in health-care. If we could give them enough information that they'd begin to ask hospital administration how many *nurses* were on a floor, what the nurse-patient ratio was, then and only then would hospital staffing improve. If we could get them to refuse to enter a hospital if there wasn't enough *nursing* staff, then we'd have a chance to give the kind of care they had a right to expect. If we could get them to insist that hospitalization include third-party payment for nurses, then they could be taken care of properly at home when they couldn't be cured. They had all the power, all the muscle, if only they would withhold their money until their demands were met. The only thing they needed was the information . . . and we would give them that.

On the way to the car that afternoon, I wondered if the health-care consumer knew that at the top of the list of priorities of any nursing strike was the issue of *patient safety*.

At the next class Ms. Richards talked about something called "burnout." She was even more high-keyed than usual, more emotionally involved.

"Burnout. Catchy phrase," she said, and she really looked angry.

"It means that a nurse literally *cannot* work any longer; it means she's forced to stop. Let me explain–first the reasons, then the symptoms. For you as a nurse, there's a tremendous amount of responsibility. The work load in a hospital is usually impossible, the tension of waiting for something to happen to one of twenty patients plays havoc with your nerves. The pay is terrible and that adds financial pressure to your personal life. There's a high degree of accountability. You'll be called to take the blame for almost anything that goes wrong in patient care. If the patient's unhappy, he'll scream at you; if the doctor's unhappy, he'll scream at you; administration will insist you explain every move you've made. If a lab slip is missing or if blood work hasn't been done, they'll ask *you* why. And if the doctor doesn't order the proper medication in the proper dosage and *you* administer it, *you'll* be held *legally* responsible.

"Also, because there is no clear-cut job description for a nurse, you'll be picking up for every other service when they're not available. You'll be mopping floors when your patients vomit or bleed, you'll be making toast and tea for your patients when the kitchen is closed, you'll be transporting to X-ray and back, to the Operating Room and back, when the technicians are off–and you'll also be acting as Recovery Room nurse at night when they do surgery on an emergency. All this, while you still have to care for your assigned patients. You're going to feel depleted from the emotional support you give your patients and their families, and you're going to feel unappreciated because when you can't handle an impossible assignment somebody is going to make you feel as though you should have been able to.

"There is no applause for nursing as a profession; there isn't even recognition for what we do as professionals. . ."

I was stunned as I listened to her. It wasn't that I didn't know all this; it was just that I had never realized in all the years I'd worked that this were *issues*. The realization that *my* problems in nursing, *my* discontents, were not mine alone really shocked me. And now that I knew that even as an RN, I'd still have to deal with them, I felt better knowing I wouldn't have to fight for my ideals alone.

After a break for a drink of water, Ms. Richards continued. "Symptoms of burnout," she said with a voice more controlled than usual. "You stop being able to work to your full capacity. You get depressed more often than usual and for longer periods of time. You start to somatosize, you get sick more often because of the stress. Sometimes you get more irritable, have insomnia, and when you do fall asleep you have nightmares. You lose your objectivity, and one day you find that in order to spare yourself work or pain you sacrifice your patients."

"What can you do if that happens?" one of the men in the class asked. "Can you ever go back?"

Ms. Richards paced more slowly. "If you can see it coming, you can quit your job and work private duty; you can work less often or you can insist on a long vacation. Or . . . you can go back to school for a master's or a doctorate and teach."

Suddenly a light clicked on in my head. Ms. Richards had burned out! No wonder she spoke with such fervor.

One of the other students, who hadn't made the jump I had, asked, "But why would you want to?"

Ms. Richards smiled. "For the same reason you chose it in the beginning: because there is nothing else that is as essential, as valuable. And by comparison to nursing, everything else pales."

Two years had passed. I had filled up on staying home, fixing beds and cooking meals. Even though I had enjoyed being home every night and spending time with Greg and my children, I had missed nursing. The space that I had taken from the pain of my patients had left a big hole in my life. I knew I was ready to go back.

By the time I graduated this time, I had a new set of expectations and a whole new set of weapons.

CHAPTER 21

The noonday sun ricocheted off the bronze-aluminum curtain walls, creating a shaft of light so vivid that I imagined I could climb it to the cloud-filled sky reflected on the gold solar panes. Boldly carved into the gleaming face of the building was the legend BETH SHALOM HOSPITAL.

When I had first seen it, as I rode along the parkway, the hospital had looked like an ancient Aztec sun temple. Blazing, hot and primitive. I immediately whipped up pictures of downtrodden slaves and human sacrifice in honor of the savage god Medicine. Up close, it looked more like a space-age Shangri-la. I expected the workers inside to be wearing gold lamé jumpsuits, preparing to blast off into Tomorrow. As I stepped onto the black conveyor-belt mat, the large glass doors opened so quickly and silently that I felt as though I had been beamed into the front lobby. Sunblind, I stood blinking for several minutes before I was able to follow the cheerfully colored arrows that led to the nursing office.

A tall dark-haired woman, who I assumed was secretary to the directress of nursing, looked up from her desk as I entered the room.

"Hi," I said, smiling at her. "My name is Teri Daley and I'd like to know who I should see about getting a job here at night?"

"Hello, Teri," the woman said as she stood to shake my hand, "I'm Janis Strong, assistant directress of nursing on nights." Her voice was warm but no-nonsense, and something in her manner reminded me of a mother superior. "Why do you want to work at Beth Shalom rather than at Cambridge Medical Center?" she asked, still standing. Beth Shalom and Cambridge were the two finest teaching hospitals outside New York City.

I took a deep breath and told her, "I just got fired from Cambridge."

Even I knew that wasn't a great introduction. I hadn't expected an interview to begin with a question like that, and though I had never intended to lie about it, I had assumed I could lead into it gently after I had first presented all the reasons why I should be hired.

"Sit down," she said, indicating a small vinyl armchair, "and tell me what happened. Then we can decide whether you should fill out an application."

As I sat across from her, I noticed that even though she had introduced herself by her first name there was nothing informal in her affect. She sat up straight and looked interested–nothing more.

"I sent cultures of suspected infections without doctor's orders and argued with the team leader about giving pain medicine before taking a blood pressure on a patient with a possible aneurysm," I answered, with irritation left over from Cambridge.

"Why?" she asked, without emotion.

"*Why?*" I asked incredulously, and then, losing the little cool I had managed to maintain, I answered vehemently, "I took cultures because none of the doctors *would* order them, and all the patients were being cross-contaminated. To save space, they were mixing cases. Instead of our surgical patients getting well, they were all developing massive wound infections."

"Why did you refuse to give the pain medication?" she asked, as though I had been speaking in a normal tone of voice.

Exasperated now, not caring if I got the job or not, I said, "Because the guy's head could have blown off by the time the other team member got around to taking his blood pressure. Pain medication would keep him quiet, but it wouldn't necessarily keep his blood pressure from skyrocketing if he was going to blow."

"Why didn't *you* take his blood pressure?" she asked, as even-toned as before.

"It's *team* nursing. I asked if I could, but the team leader told me that someone else had been assigned that task and everything would be taken care of in its proper time."

"Okay," Mrs. Strong said firmly, as though she had heard enough. Then she asked more softly, "How long did you work there?"

"Only three months; since I graduated as a registered nurse," I answered, completely defused.

For more than an hour she asked me questions concerning my previous experience, and finally she smiled and handed me an application. "If the only complaint that Cambridge and the other hospitals have is that you're a troublemaker, and if I can verify the reasons you give, you're hired," she said definitively.

Now I was puzzled. After my initial admission about being fired, I had fumed and fussed, using Mrs. Strong as a sounding board, not really expecting that I would be hired. "May I ask you why?" I said, laughing.

For the first time, she sat back in her chair and seemed to relax. "At Beth Shalom," she began, "we practice *primary* nursing. What that means is that each nurse is responsible for a certain number of patients–say, five. Ideally, each patient has the same nurse from the time he enters the hospital until he leaves, except, of course, for her days off."

The phone rang and Mrs. Strong stopped to pick it up. As she talked, I looked around the office. It was painted a bright yellow and all the furniture was teal blue or red. Nothing was painted a neutral color; no more dreary gray.

When she hung up, Mrs. Strong continued, "We feel that the advantage of primary nursing is that when a nurse sees a patient day after day, the subtle nuances of behavior which often indicate a change in condition are noticed more than they would be by the usual methods, which fragment a patient's care. We also feel that when the responsibility for a patient is given to *one* specific nurse, there is a better chance that his needs will be met."

"Sounds great!" I said, completely enthralled.

"Before you get too impressed," she warned, "understand that this kind of nursing puts a tremendous burden of responsibility on the nurse. Nothing, including giving a bedpan, goes unsupervised by her. There are a few nursing assistants on each floor, but their purpose is strictly to assist. When we hire, we look for nurses with the ability to make their own decisions; we prefer to have women or men who have not been indoctrinated by other hospitals that use conventional role models. Our nurses and doctors consider themselves peers; and anytime a nurse has a disagreement with a doctor, if it is proven that she has used good nursing judgment, our directress will stand behind her and defend her to the chiefs of staff."

I couldn't believe my ears. Beth Shalom was the place I had always dreamed of–a place where I could think, a place where I didn't have to knuckle under as long as I knew what I was doing. I felt as though I had died and gone to heaven.

"Are we allowed to wear white pantsuits as our uniforms?" I asked, mulling over the other things she had said.

"The nurses here don't wear uniforms," Janis Strong said, smiling. "Or caps." When she saw my look of surprise, she explained, "Mrs. Zamovich, our directress, believes that the absence of color causes sensory deprivation for the patients and therefore depresses them. Our nurses wear pastels, and we prefer pantsuits of washable fabric."

I was stunned. "And no cap?" I asked, thrilled. I had always thought it ludicrous, after my first few years in nursing, that we wore caps, like a wreath of daisies, while we were up to our ears in shit most of the time.

"The purpose of wearing a cap is to indicate servitude," Janis Strong said gently. "Here we understand that a nurse is not the handmaiden of the doctor."

"I find this so hard to believe," I said, taking a deep breath.

"One more question," she said as she stared at me. "Are you married? And if so, why do you want to work nights?"

I was surprised by her question, because I didn't know what difference it could make. "Yes," I answered, "I am married, and I want to work nights because I find it a challenge. The patients are usually more frightened and I enjoy being able to comfort them. Also, to be truthful, I enjoy the patient contact more than I like running around to X-ray, giving bed baths and feeding."

She nodded. "I felt the same way when I worked on the floors. Night is an especially hard time for patients, and, contrary to popular belief, I think a night nurse has to have more on the ball than a day nurse."

As she handed me a sheaf of papers explaining hospital policy, she added, "You'll find that everyone uses her first name here, so I'd prefer it if you'd call me Janis. We've found that when patients are allowed to call a nurse by her given name it reduces the impersonality of the hospital setting. It allows the patient to keep his dignity as an adult and not to be immediately demoted to a dependent child."

She stood again to indicate that the interview was over. "Does Mr. Daley work at night?" she asked pleasantly.

"No," I answered, smiling, "he works during the day in New York City as a marketing-research manager for a pharmaceutical company. Why do you ask?"

Janis looked serious as she told me, "We want to make sure our nurses realize that even in this time of more freedom for women, it usually causes added stress to a marriage when a nurse works the midnight-to-eight shift. We want you to know that transfer to days isn't even considered until after a year."

"That's no problem," I reassured her. "My husband knows I prefer nights, and has agreed that it causes no difficulty for us."

On my way out the door I turned. "By the way, my husband's name is Schmidt–Greg Schmidt. I use Teri Daley because that's the name on my nursing license."

Greg's tan Volkswagen was still parked in front of our new house when I pulled up. I found him in his study, as usual crouched over his cluttered desk, his reading glasses low on his nose.

"Hi," I said cheerfully as I came up behind him and threw my arms around his neck. "I'm glad you didn't leave yet." As Greg tried to extricate himself from my enthusiastic embrace, I rattled on about my interview at Beth Shalom.

"Hold on, Teri," he said. "Last night when you left for work, I could have sworn you were going to Cambridge."

I moved to sit on the chair opposite him. Swiveling his black leather recliner toward me, he lit his pipe.

"Yes, I did, I mean I was," I said excitedly. "I guess I forgot to tell you, I got fired this morning." Even through the thick cloud of smoke around Greg's face, I could see him frown. "Don't get crazy on me," I said defensively. "I was right, and anyway you don't have to worry about the bills. I've practically got another job already."

"I wasn't worried about the bills, Teri," he said, looking amused.

"I was simply attempting to decipher what you were trying to say."

I took a deep breath and started over. After about fifteen minutes, Greg stood without a word, and collected his papers.

I followed him into our bedroom, to watch him put on a fresh white shirt. "What time do you think you'll be home?" I asked.

As Greg knotted his striped brown-and-yellow tie he said, "Same time as usual. About eleven." Then he kissed me absently and headed for the front door.

I made myself a cup of tea, sat down in the paneled living room, and tried to unwind. This was one of those times when I really missed Lil. She had been so busy working and taking care of her father and her kids that we had very little time to see each other. Not living with Lil had created a big space in my life; one that, no matter how hard Greg tried, he couldn't fill.

I finished my tea, walked the long hall into the bedroom, and climbed into the bed that Greg had carefully made. But just as I started to doze, I remembered the cup I had left on the coffee table. If it made another ring, Greg would have a fit. Annoyed, I jumped up, grabbed it and threw it into the sink. As I climbed tiredly back under the covers, I wondered if Greg's and my values would ever grow parallel. Right now they were perpendicular.

The kids and I were eating supper at the long wooden table in the dining room when the phone rang. It was Beth Shalom's evening secretary trying to schedule an appointment for my official interview.

Excited, I hung up and told Niki and Spinner, "Your mother is now going to be working at the finest hospital outside New York City."

"Is our mother going to be able to handle trying to save another entire population?" Niki asked, big brown eyes looking up from her plate. She was smiling, but she sounded concerned. "You look really tired, Mom."

"Work can do that to you, kid," I said, reaching over to touch her long brown hair. Somehow she had bypassed the gawky teenage stage and grown into a very pretty fifteen-year-old. She had inherited all of Shawn's fine features, but her coloring made her look like an American Indian maiden. I enjoyed looking at her.

"Mom," Niki said seriously, "why can't I quit school and go to work? Then I could help out. You wouldn't have to work so hard, and Greg wouldn't have to pay for everything."

"Don't start that again, Niki," I said, more sharply than I should have. "I can't go through it again."

Spinner pushed his sandy hair out of his eyes and said, "I better go do some homework or something before you guys start hollering."

"We don't holler at each other," Niki said sarcastically, "unless Greg is around."

"Niki, *please*," I said wearily.

The morning of my interview, I woke before the alarm and was dressed before I had my coffee. Though the ride to Beth Shalom was long, the day was so pleasant that I didn't mind. I kept rehearsing the answers to the questions that Janis Strong was sure to ask me.

As I walked toward the building, squinting because of the glare, I noticed several women dressed in pastel pantsuits. Last time I had assumed they were visitors, now I knew they were nurses. I smiled, picturing myself dressed as they were.

Janis Strong wore the same blue suit, impersonal smile and professional manner as before when she said, "Everything checked out. So now the question seems to be, where would you like to work?"

"What areas are open?"

"Nights, even here, usually has several openings," Janis answered ruefully. "This time we need nurses for Pediatrics."

I shook my head. "No."

"Obstetrics?"

I shook my head.

"Geriatrics?"

I shook my head again.

"Psychiatry?"

I still shook my head.

Then Janis asked somewhat sarcastically, "Where would you

like to work?"

"Medicine," I said. "Surgery, or Intensive Care."

She shook her head as she glanced down along the list of openings. Then she asked, "I don't suppose you'd like to GWYN?" I frowned, and Janis explained, "GWYN is short for Go Wherever You're Needed. In other words, float." She knew as well as I did that floating is a nurse's nightmare.

"What does the job entail?" I asked.

Janis answered seriously, "It means a different floor with different patients every night. The work is very much like troubleshooting; also very nervewracking. Even our regular floors here are filled with serious cases. If a nurse works on the same floor each night, she begins to know which patients she can relax about, but for a GWYN each patient is new each night and all symptoms are serious."

"Anything else?" I asked, smiling; she had made it sound awful.

"On some of the floors, the staff nurses are very helpful and will give a GWYN the easiest district because they're grateful for the extra help." Janis leaned forward to make her point. "On other floors, the girls are so whipped by their own patient load, they're not only no help, they often use a GWYN as a scapegoat, dumping the patients they don't want to handle."

"Okay," I said, smiling at Janis, "why are you trying to make this position sound so unappealing? It pays more, right?"

She laughed. "No, it doesn't pay more. And I try to make it sound as it is because I supervise the GWYN team and if you take the job I don't want any whining."

When she said "the GWYN team," I got pictures in my head of the Olympics–Rah! Rah! Rah! "I'll take it," I said enthusiastically, "and I won't whine."

Janis looked surprised and then smiled. "At the beginning, you'll be sent to the regular floors; after we see what you're capable of, we'll move you to some of the specialty areas. Remember, this is a teaching hospital, so many of the patients will be more challenging than in the smaller hospitals. You'll only be sent to floors that are especially heavy or short-staffed."

Janis then told me that I would have a one-month intensive orientation on days, with another group of new nurses. After that, I and another new GWYN, Erin Shapiro, would be required to "buddy" with other experienced GWYNs until it was judged that we could be sent out on our own. Just before I left, Janis asked, "Why do you choose to GWYN?"

"It will keep me from being bored; teach me more than I would learn under normal circumstances," I said seriously. "And more important, it will keep me from getting too attached to any one patient."

By the time of my interview at Beth Shalom, I had been a nurse for nine years. I had stopped fooling myself about my ability to stay uninvolved with patients. My own needs prevented me from keeping the kind of distance that could protect me; no matter how hard I tried, some of them always managed to worm themselves through the thin veneer of my defenses.

So at the moment when Janis asked where I wanted to work, I knew that the only hope for controlling my emotional involvement was to try to control my physical setup. It worked . . . . but not perfectly.

During the month of orientation, Erin Shapiro and I stuck together like adhesive tape. When it was time to practice drawing bloods for lab work, we chose each other as partners. Beth Shalom was no small-time operation, no sticking oranges for experience as we had done in nursing school. Here, while learning, we wielded our unpracticed syringes against each other. Each of us felt the powerful impact of an inept shot or the pain caused by torn tissue from sloppy entry into a vein. This method of learning, it was explained to us, not only helped develop proficiency; it taught empathy. Not one of us, after our orientation, ever asked a patient why he didn't lie still while we attacked him with our syringe. We knew.

Though Erin was a few years older than I, she had gone to nursing school later. She had three kids, two of them adopted, and a husband she was fond of. During lunch one day in the cafeteria, when I asked what her husband, Ted, was like, she answered, "He doesn't bark, he doesn't shed, and he doesn't jump on the furniture." I thought she was outrageous. Yet as I watched her work, I knew she was the most compassionate person I had met since Lil. Looking at her, tall, with short dark hair, blue eyes and just a trace of a brogue, there was no mistaking the fact that she was Irish. Erin Shapiro had chosen to GWYN for the same reason I had: patients she loved had blown her away.

CHAPTER 22

Lupus, cystic fibrosis, all the teenage cancers and leukemias that the smaller hospitals couldn't handle, were transferred to Beth Shalom's Adolescent Unit. There were few small fractures here, and no uncomplicated surgical procedures; most of these kids had barely survived Pediatrics. Many of them would die here.

While Erin loved working with adolescents, I found them the only patients who were more difficult emotionally for me to handle than the children on Peds. The older kids knew what was happening to them, so they were angry. In their age of rebellion, they had been forced to be dependent, and they hated it.

The mood of the unit was often frenzied. These kids were going to have fun, no matter what. And we, the nurses and doctors, were their natural targets. The ingenious little bastards used to balance water pitchers on top of the door so that the nurse who made rounds would get soaked as soon as she pushed it open. Rotten little shits, . . . you couldn't even cream them, when most of them were dying.

I remember only two kids from the unit; the rest blur and blend into a composite picture of dreadful diseases. The first one was a beautiful blue-eyed blond girl named Dion. She had gone to a party, gotten drunk and stoned, then decided to drive home. The telephone pole she hit had crunched her head and shattered her body. When I first took care of her, she was in a deep coma with no responses, but over the next few months she started to surface. She hit me whenever I tried to turn or wash her; she spit anything I put into her mouth back at me. And as soon as she got her speech back, she cursed constantly. A conservative description of her would be "totally abominable." Her family told us that she had been an angry girl her whole life and so Dion fought her sickness as she had everything else that had ever tried to hold her down. After a year and a half, she could talk and walk out of the hospital with a cane. Nice isn't everything.

The other kid I remember is Manny. I took care of him only three nights, but I remember exactly how he looked, and I can still feel his too-soft skin against my fingers.

On the night of his admission, he was put in a bed in the hall because all other eighteen beds were filled. One of our kids was to be transferred out the following morning, and Manny was waiting for the bed. He had been admitted for a fractured ankle through the ER and was supposed to have it set in the morning.

During that first night I hardly noticed him. On one of my many trips down the hall to answer a call from another kid, I passed Manny's bed and asked, "Are you all right?" He just shook his head and I thought, Thank God he's only got a broken ankle–he's almost too good. The buzzers were ringing all around him, the kids in the rooms across were jumping and howling, the fluorescent lights were shining directly in his eyes, yet when I asked, "Is everything okay?" he smiled and answered, "Just fine."

Manny was a pretty boy. His brown hair curled in distinct ringlets around his pallid face, which was a bit too cherubic to be handsome. His huge brown eyes had the innocence of a puppy's and his front teeth were still too large for his face. He was chubby–soft-skin chubby, not sturdy looking stocky like browned children who play in the sun.

There were so many really sick kids on the ward that night that I forgot all about Manny until about 4 A.M., when his blood studies came back from the lab.

I sat at the desk and stared at the results, finding it hard to connect the patient with what I was reading. His cell count clearly showed leukemia. But he came in with only a fractured ankle, I said to myself; it must be a fluke . . . I reached for his chart and leafed through to find the history. According to all previous exams he had no known pathology. He had never been sick, not even with the usual childhood diseases.

I dialed Dr. Stewart Gill, the intern, read him the results and asked him what he wanted to do.

"Get a repeat," he answered softly. "Maybe somebody fucked up."

When I left that morning, the second set of blood results hadn't yet come back.

Three weeks later, when I walked onto Adolescents again, I knew it was going to be one of those very bad nights. One boy, an emergency for the Operating Room, had cut his arm off; another was bleeding out from a rectal tumor, his life's blood oozing into a bedpan; two of the cystic kids couldn't breathe, and so one of the nurses was holding them upside down and alternately pounding each on his back. I listened as the wet coughs choked them–and kept clearing my own throat.

During the night, as I was running down the hall to change an IV, I passed Manny's room. He was vomiting like mad, and because his nurse was busy I hurried into his room. The doctors had bombarded him with chemotherapy, and he obviously hadn't tolerated it well. He had lost about thirty pounds since I had last seen him, and he looked dreadful, with transparent skin and dark circles under his eyes.

"Can I help, Manny?" I asked as I grabbed for the stainless-steel basin to empty it. He just shook his head and lay back, staring at the ceiling.

Manny's last night . . . As soon as I walked onto the ward, I knew it was going to be another disaster. It was so quiet that I could feel the weight of the tension in the air like a thick fog. The halls were empty, so I walked directly into the nurses' station. Two of the nurses who worked the floor regularly were slumped down on the old vinyl couch, not talking. Kim, the little Chinese spitfire, had worked the unit for three years and was not easily flustered. She usually chattered as much as I did, but that night she wasn't saying one word.   Jackie, the assistant nursing-care coordinator, comparable to head nurse at the less progressive hospitals, looked shellshocked.

"Who's on with me?" I asked Kim as I threw down my pocketbook and flopped next to her. I could almost tell what kind of a night it would be according to whom I worked with. If it was a "strong" nurse, no matter what happened we'd be all right. If she was a "weak" nurse, no matter what happened it would be a disaster.

"Both the regulars called in," Kim said tiredly. "So it's you and another GWYN."

I had left Erin down in the office waiting for her assignment, and I held my breath as I asked, "Do you know which one?"

"I think you'll be okay," Kim said. "I requested you and Erin Shapiro because the floor was so heavy."

Neither Erin nor I had been on this unit for the past week, so we didn't know all the patients. It was going to be a rough night, and I knew by the look on Erin's face as she walked onto the floor that she understood that. By the time she sat for report, her upper lip was twitching, as it did whenever she was nervous.

Jackie started report. "We've got a lot of sick kids tonight, but all of them will hold their own . . . except Manny."

"Manny?" I asked, surprised. "He's already that bad?"

Jackie and Kim both nodded, and Erin asked, "How bad?" Kim answered this time. "He's going to go any minute."

Jackie interrupted her. "He's not really the problem. He's practically comatose, his fever is spiking constantly, he's bleeding out and can't breathe, the guys are still drawing bloods on him and they put him on a hypothermia blanket to try to lower his fever, but no luck. It's been over 104 for the last six hours. He gets IV Demerol for pain." She pulled a wrinkled tissue out of her jacket pocket and blew her nose before she continued. "Two hours ago, when the guys didn't know what else to do, they hung blood, but the kid's bleeding from every hole he's got, so it's running out faster than we can pour it in. All in all, the boy's a mess, and there's not much we can do. But that's not the problem."

"All right," I said after frantically scribbling everything she had said on my long yellow pad, "I give up. What's the problem?"

"His old man," Kim said as she rubbed her hand across her

forehead. "The guy is ready to kill the first human being who goes anywhere near the kid."

Jackie added, "The mother and the grandmother are resting in the waiting room. The father won't even let them in to see the boy."

"Anybody talk to the man?" I asked.

"Teri" Kim said, leaning her head back, "be serious. We can't talk to him. He won't listen to a word any of us says." She got up and walked over to the bulletin board and stared at it absently as she said, "I tried most of the evening; he wouldn't even look at me." Kim was rearranging the board, squaring the papers, placing them evenly alongside each other. "He's sitting on the cot in the dark, staring into space. He doesn't talk to the boy, but he's made it clear that he's not about to let any of us near Manny."

Jackie was doodling dark clouds and mucky waters on her yellow assignment pad with a black felt marker. She glanced up at Erin and me and said, "The doctors have been doing the minimum, and so have we, but Mr. Abrams had a fit the last time Stew drew blood, and when he hung the platelets Mr. Abrams looked so furious I thought he was going to explode."

Kim looked to Jackie for approval as she suggested to Erin and me, "One of you is going to have to take Manny and the other will have to cover the rest of the ward."

Manny had been moved to a room at the end of the hall. Funny about those rooms, the private rooms at the end of the hall– always saved for the almost dead and dying, as though to ease their way out . . . already separated, isolated.

When Erin looked at me she was frowning. "Want to choose?" I asked, pulling a coin from my pocket.

She shook her head and looked stricken. "Come on," she said, "I'm willing to run my ass off with all these other kids, but I can't handle spending an entire shift trying to comfort another tormented parent."

Two nights before, Erin had worked the Delivery Room. The baby born was a microcephalic (one having an abnormally small head) whose mother knew beforehand that the baby couldn't live. She had volunteered to carry the child full term because the doctors had convinced her that it would be better for her health to proceed with a normal delivery rather than undergo surgical removal of the defective fetus. They had also convinced her to sign the baby's kidneys over for transplant to a good baby with kidney disease. The only hitch came when the woman's husband insisted on seeing his son before the kidneys were removed.

The young man stood watching expectantly as Erin unwrapped the white flannel blanket. Inside lay what looked like a gray-blue frog; eyes bulging, head perfectly flat on top, still covered with the blood and white cheese of birth. The man hit the floor with such a thump that Erin almost dropped the baby. Another nurse grabbed for it as Erin stooped to help the distraught father, and for the rest of the night she fed him coffee and chicken soup, wiped away his tears, and tried to help him forget what he had just seen. Her lip was still twitching as we drove home that morning.

Oh God, I thought, this is going to be another one of those earth-shattering experiences for me. But all I said to Erin was, "Don't worry about it, I'll do it." Then, when I saw how depressed Kim was, I poked her and teased, "*I* will now give it a *real* try."

She never smiled as she said flatly, "Well, you can't do any harm."

As she stood to go, I put my arm around her shoulders. "Hey, cheer up," I said. "You did everything you could." I knew her well enough to be sure of that.

Kim tried to smile, but as she did her eyes filled. "I just wish sometimes that we could do more." Guilt, another occupational hazard.

Erin and I made rounds together, checking all the kids. Then I walked to the end of the hall alone. I gently pushed open the heavy wooden door to the room and saw Mr. Abrams, just as Kim had said, sitting on the cot in the dark, with his back to the boy.

Through the dim light, I could see that the boy in the bed was a mess. But if I hadn't been told, I would never have believed it was Manny. He looked as though a street gang had worked him over. Every inch of the fragile white body he had had three weeks before was puffy, swollen and purple.

I tiptoed quietly into the gloomy darkness and closed the door slowly behind me. The full moon glowering through the small window filled the room with nightmare forms. Projected on the wall and ceiling over Manny's bed, almost obliterating the boy, loomed the enormous shadow of a stooped man, head in hands. The air was thick with the smell of anguish and the sound of Manny's gurgling breaths.

I was concentrating on Mr. Abrams' yarmulka as I walked closer to Manny's bed. But when my shoes squeaked, Mr. Abrams stiffened, stood up and turned toward me quickly. The short, powerfully built man threatened me with his stance but didn't say anything. I noticed his fists clenched tightly down at his sides. He took a step toward me, and in the dim light I nodded a hello. Then I walked to the foot of the bed and checked the gauges on the hypothermia machine. It was placed on the lowest setting possible, and still it wasn't working to reduce his fever. I moved from the foot of the bed up along the side, still not getting too close. Mr. Abrams made a sound low in his throat, like a guard dog. Manny's head jerked to the side. I didn't know whether it was voluntary or a reflex from the effort of his breathing.

I looked up at Mr. Abrams and said, almost asking permission, "I have to adjust Manny's oxygen." The man stared without blinking and didn't move a muscle, but I noticed that his thin lips were held so tight it strained the muscles in his face.

I very carefully checked the green oxygen mask and found that the soft plastic around the edge was stuck to Manny's face. I told the boy's father, "I'm going to put some gauze under the sharp edges to try to make him more comfortable." Mr. Abrams nodded slowly. I moved very slowly and explained every detail before I touched his boy.

Because Manny's eyes were closed, I had no idea how conscious he was. I gently pushed his wet curls off his forehead–his hair was much thinner because of the chemotherapy–and as I did, I noticed how blue his lips were. I knew he wasn't getting enough oxygen, but there was nothing I could do because he was still bleeding: it was no longer a question of saturating his blood cells with oxygen, it was a question of keeping enough blood cells in his body. I reached up and opened the IV line to run the platelets faster. Mr. Abrams moved closer to me as I touched Manny's forehead again. The kid was still burning, probably dehydrating. Mr. Abrams kept watching me, but I never saw him look at Manny.

As I left the room I said to the boy's father, "In a little while I'll be back. My name is Teri Daley, and if there's anything you want, please let me know." I laid my hand on his arm for just a minute, waited for some kind of response, and when there was none I turned and walked out.

Mr. Abrams sat on the narrow cot, and the huge shadow crouched over Manny again.

As I walked back to the nurses' station I thought, This is going to be harder than I had expected. I sat at the desk and leafed through Manny's chart, looking for clues that I could try to use to help Mr. Abrams. I was reading the notes from the last two shifts when I heard heavy footsteps stomping down the hall, fast.

When I looked up, Mr. Abrams was standing in front of me. With an open-handed smack on the counter top, he announced, "My boy has pain."

"Okay," I said quickly, "I'll get the doctor for him." Manny was getting IV Demerol. Because the medication was to go directly into a vein, and because in this case it was a narcotic which could depress respirations if the dosage wasn't regulated properly, a floor nurse couldn't give it.

Mr. Abrams stood stiffly and tapped his fingers while I dialed the phone. I let it ring several times, but Stew Gill, the intern on, didn't answer. Stew was an excellent doctor. I knew if he wasn't in his room he was handling an emergency some where else, or at the very least starting an IV that the girls couldn't get. I hung up and dialed Pediatrics.

Bonnie, one of the few girls on Peds I didn't like, answered "Peds, make it quick."

"Bonnie?" I asked, already annoyed. "Stew there?"

"He's in the unit," she said flatly. "Some kid's going out on them, and everyone is pulling heroics."

"Tell him I need him when he's finished," I said.

Before I hung up I heard her say, "Don't hold your breath."

I explained what was happening to Mr. Abrams, who stared at me stone-faced, nostrils widening, face turning white as he listened. "Call another doctor," he ordered when I had finished.

I rubbed my hand over my face as I tried to think. I knew that the resident, Harvey Entrep, would be in the unit with Stew. None of the Pediatric Intensive Care nurses who could help would be available, because the ones who weren't helping Stew with the kid would be knocking themselves out taking care of the other children in the unit. They were legally covered to give IV meds, because they had been trained and supervised. In fact, so had I, but outside the Intensive Care Unit it wasn't legally acceptable unless a doctor signed.

Mr. Abrams still glared at me. Finally I said, "Let me check Manny." I walked tentatively around him and down the hall.

Manny was thrashing around, semicomatose now, still not responding. His right arm was bleeding, apparently from hitting the chrome side rail, and as he violently shook his head back and forth a small stream of blood ran from his right nostril. I lifted his mask and wiped the blood away. I noticed that each time he moved, his breathing was more labored. He was obviously in pain.

As I walked toward the phone, Mr. Abrams hovered over me. Bonnie answered the phone again and told me she had given Stew the message but he was still too busy to get back to me. "What's the problem?" she asked curtly.

I explained what I could with Mr. Abrams listening to my every word, and when I had finished, Bonnie said, "C'mon, Teri, it's only pain."

Terrific, I thought, and was glad Manny's father hadn't heard her.

"Well?" Mr. Abrams demanded. He looked as though he was ready to tear the place apart. As I watched his face contort with rage, the small veins of his forehead pulsating, I thought about how insane this situation was. The kid is terminal and in pain. I knew how to give the medication he needed, I had done it often. His father was frantic, and no one else was available. And just because of some blind administrative rule, I was going to say to this furious man in front of me, "I'm sorry, but I can't help him." Sheer insanity for any thinking human being.

"I'll give it to him," I told Mr. Abrams, and then went to find Erin. As we walked to the medication room, I told her what I wanted to do.

"Did you call Janis?" Erin asked.

"No," I answered as I drew up the medication. "If she gives us the go-ahead she has more to lose than we do."

"Umm," Erin admitted, holding the syringe up to the light to check my dosage. She too had often worked the specialty units, where she had also administered IV medication. We could hear Mr. Abrams pacing up and down the hall. "I could give it if you like," Erin offered. I shook my head and just asked if she'd come with me for moral support . . . and to be a witness in case something went wrong.

All three of us walked down to Manny's room. Erin watched carefully as I injected the Demerol into the IV tubing. In a matter of seconds, Manny was quiet. When, after a few minutes, he was still breathing, Erin and I sighed with relief.

I turned toward Mr. Abrams, who was standing by the doorway, and asked, "Would you like a cup of coffee now?" He shook his head, but as he followed Erin and me out to the hall I had the feeling that he had something to say. "Is there something else I can help you with?" I asked. He still looked angry, but didn't say anything.

Erin and I were halfway down the hall when I heard Mr. Abrams start to speak. "There is nothing that can be done, and yet they stick my boy with needles; they force blood into him; they move him too often; they bother him constantly. There is no hope . . . There is nothing! And still they will not leave him alone." The last statement was a hopeless wail.

Erin continued down the hall, but I turned and walked toward Mr. Abrams as he went on, "I am his father . . . and I can do nothing." His look was an accusation before he turned away from me and walked to the hall window.

I followed him. "Mr. Abrams?"

He half turned, the strain on his face showing like white chalk lines extending from his nostrils around the corners of his mouth to his chin. "What do you want?"

"You don't want Manny to have the blood?" I asked softly.

With tired eyes and an exhausted shake of his head, he sighed, "No-o-o- . . ."

"Did you tell them that?" I asked gently.

He turned fully and looked directly at me. "Tell who?"

"Did you tell the doctors, or the other nurses?"

"Tell them what? I am only his father," he said, as though it was an absurdity.

"No," I corrected him, "not *only*. You *are* his father. That's *your* boy. Tell them to stop."

He squinted and asked, "I can tell them I want no more? Nothing but medicine for the pain?"

I nodded and he looked relieved for a minute, before, guarded again, he asked, "And if they will not listen?"

"Tell them how you feel," I insisted.

"But if they will not listen?" he repeated.

"You can stand at the door. You can refuse to let them in."

"I *can* do that?" he whispered, and his eyes filled.

"You're his father," I said firmly. "You have to try."

At any other hospital, I would have been crucified for that number, but at Beth Shalom there was a lot of respect for individual judgment. Here, when there was nothing else that could be done for the patient, the family's wishes were always considered, and often observed. I knew that part of Mr. Abrams' rage was caused by his impotence, and I hoped Stew and Harvey would understand that and allow him some control.

"You will tell the doctor first," Mr. Abrams directed.

"Of course," I said, and smiled at him.

As he turned to walk back to Manny's room, he stopped and said, "You have children. . . ." Without waiting for my answer, he walked away.

A couple of minutes later, Stew ambled onto the unit, walked past me quickly and made his way toward Manny's room. I jumped up from the desk to try to catch him. He was holding a needle and a blood-collection tube in his hand. I reached him, and the doorway that Mr. Abrams guarded, at the same time.

"What have you there?" Manny's father asked, pointing at Stew's equipment, real challenge in his voice.

Stew looked at me quizzically.

"Stew," I explained, "Manny's dad wants the blood stopped . . . He wants everything stopped. . . . Except the pain medicine. And no more tests."

Stew looked at Mr. Abrams and asked, "Is that right, Sir?"

Mr. Abrams glared at Stew, ready for opposition. "I am his father, and I want nothing more done to him. It is enough. Just pain medicine."

Stew nodded and walked in to look at Manny, almost tripping over Mr. Abrams. "I understand, sir," he said. "We'll see what we can do."

"Nothing," Mr. Abrams said definitively. "I want my boy to have no more pain."

Stew and I walked to the nurses' station. "Okay," he said. "Where's the Demerol?"

"I already gave it, Stew. I had to. Will you cover for me?"

Stew was one of those bearlike, pleasant-faced young men, so good-natured that you could forget how smart he was.

"Yep," he said, smiling at me. "As soon as I got a look at the kid, I figured you had." Then he patted me on the head and said, "I couldn't ask you to do it and stick your neck out, but I'm glad you did." He got the chart out of the rack and signed his initials to the injection I had given. The pediatric guys were always the nicest doctors. As a rule, the majority of them were gentle men, as gentle as the majority of the surgeons were sadistic. There are always exceptions, but Stew wasn't one of them.

When he finished writing his note, he turned to me and asked, "What do you think about Mr. Abrams?"

"Stew," I said, "what are the kid's chances?"

"Zilch," he said, and pointed his thumb toward the floor.

"So what are we doing?" I asked. "If he's only got a couple of hours."

"But the platelets might help control the bleeding . . ." he said. "I hate the thought of him drowning from all the blood in his lungs."

"Stew, there's blood coming out of his nose. It's already foaming out his mouth. His urine is bright red and he's shitting bloody clots. You ordered platelets, not holy water."

"Yeah," he said, shaking his head. "I guess you're right. I'll call Harvey and tell him." He got up and walked around the desk. "Good luck, kid," he said as he walked away. Halfway down the hall, stopped by an afterthought, he turned to me and asked, "Do you want me to talk to Mr. Abrams?"

"Nope," I said, feeling better. "I think I can handle it. Just come quickly when I call for pain medicine." I smiled when Stew winked and held up his thumb and forefinger, making a circle.

Mr. Abrams was still sitting on the cot when I walked in. The entire room was vibrating with the sound of Manny's breathing. He rattled and gurgled and bubbled as though he were drowning. And Mr. Abrams sat letting the noise punish him. His back was to the boy and he was still slumped over, his head in his hands. I patted him on the shoulder and asked, "Do you want to go out for a while? I'll sit and make sure no one comes near Manny. I'll watch him for you, if you want to talk to your wife."

He looked up at me and smiled weakly but refused.

I left the room and walked down the hall into the lounge, where Manny's mother and grandmother were waiting. They were both sitting in the dark on the blue plastic couch, with pillows behind them and blankets over their legs. The adolescents' playroom which doubled as the lounge had two large pool tables, scattered records and a stereo, pinball machines, torn books, and games spread over broken shelves.

I opened the door and in the dim light from the hall saw the eyes of the grandmother quickly open. I said, "Hello," and the old woman reached up and turned on the light. She looked like an old lady out of an ancient Russian portrait, wrinkled skin with deep lines that time uses to sketch age in a face. She had coarse features and white curly hair, and as she reached to shake my hand I could see that her fingers were stiffened with arthritis. She grabbed hard, a strong, serious woman.

"How's the boy?" she asked.

Manny's mother seemed simpler, not as cunning or bright as the older woman. She had dark hair, black eyes with long lashes, and a very fine nose; she looked at least twenty years younger than Manny's father. She waited expectantly for my answer to her mother's question.

"He's not doing well," I said, trying not to sound morose. Hoping to give them a chance to talk about how they felt, I asked, "Why are you here instead of in there?"

"The father does not want us to bother him," the grandmother said, with some bitterness in her voice. "He does not want the boy disturbed." And then, quickly, as though the issue was closed, she reached for her pocketbook, rummaged through it and pulled out a stack of photographs. "Sit here," she said, pointing to the seat on the couch next to her.

"Can't I get you some coffee or tea first?" I asked.

"Nothing now," she said. "Just sit." As she straightened up on the couch, her blanket fell to the floor. I reached for it, but she firmly motioned me away and patted the couch again. When I sat next to her, she began to show me pictures, holding each a long time before she handed it to me, fingering every one fondly as she did.

The photos were of a boy who only vaguely resembled Manny. They were taken at his Bar Mitzvah, she explained, when at thirteen he had gotten to be a man–six or eight months before. He attended yeshiva, she continued, and they had had hopes that he would become a lawyer. His father, she told me, had been in a concentration camp and the only member of his family to survive. This boy was to be the last to carry the family name. "There are no other boys," she said, "only one daughter. Manny would have been . . ." She stopped and blew her nose hard on a wrinkled white linen handkerchief which she had pulled out of her pocketbook. Then, gruffly, she asked, "Is he having pain?"

"Not now," I said as I handed back the last photograph. "The doctor was just up and he had pain medicine."

Manny's mother hadn't said anything, had taken the pictures as they were handed to her by the older woman and stared at them blankly. "He was always such a good boy," she said suddenly, without looking up from the photo that was still glued to her hand.

I hear that line from mothers all the time, and often it makes me laugh because it's so stereotypic. Murderers' mothers always say that. But when she said it I thought, Yep, that I believe. He probably was a good boy. And for a reason I couldn't explain, I found myself angry at him for being that good, for not fighting harder . . . as though that would have made all the difference.

I reached over and patted her hand. She asked, "How is my husband? Has he spoken to you?"

"Some," I answered.

"He loves the boy," she said, glancing over at the old woman, who just looked away.

"Yes, I know," I said. "I can see that."

"He's a very good father," she said. She looked at me, but the words seemed to have been thrown at the old woman.

"Yes," I said. "I know that too." I bent down and picked up the blanket to cover the old woman's legs, and as I left I told them to call or come to the desk if they needed anything. I turned off the light and closed the door.

I searched through the rooms looking for Erin. Everyone seemed quiet and settled. I found her in the medication room mixing some of the morning IVs and helped her finish by fixing the piggybacks (smaller medication bags that hooked into the large IV bags). Afterward, Erin and I wrote the necessary charts. Things on the unit were quiet, no buzzers, all meds given out and most of the kids asleep.

I walked back into Manny's room to check him, past Mr. Abrams, who was standing in the doorway. Manny was still burning up; blood still trickled from his nose . . . and anywhere else there was an opening. I padded the bed rather than change it, and made a few minor adjustments before I left the room. I was finding it very difficult to do nothing except watch Manny struggle to breathe.

Outside the room, Mr. Abrams was waiting for me. "He has had his shot," the boy's father snapped. "Why is he uncomfortable?" He moved from one foot to the other, hands behind his back, deep lines across his forehead.

I placed my hand on his arm. "He's still having trouble breathing . . . and maybe he's a little frightened."

Mr. Abrams raised his head to look at me, his black eyes pained and squinting, and said, "This is a very hard thing."

"I could put a cold washcloth on his forehead," I said. "Maybe that would cool him and make him slightly more comfortable. And even wet his tongue and lips. . ."

"No," Mr. Abrams said quickly. "I do not want him disturbed again." Looking around frantically, an animal trapped, he said, "This is a very hard thing for him. . ."

"Why don't you sit by the bed and hold his hand?" I asked. But he looked instantly angry.

"I do not want to disturb him," he said in a voice that sounded as if he had told me too many times.

"Often, when doing a very hard thing," I said, knowing that I was pushing, "it helps to know that someone you love and trust is close to you. Touching you. It sometimes helps take some of the fear away . . . and that takes some of the pain away."

"I do not want to bother him," he rasped. Backing away from me, shaking his head quickly back and forth, his breath coming more quickly now, he moaned, "I *can't!* . . . I can't."

"What is it, Mr. Abrams?" I asked him. He looked panicky. I put my hand on his arm again to try to reassure him as I asked again, "Why can't you talk to him? Why can't you talk to your boy? What *is* it that you're afraid of?"

He stiffened, throwing my hand off his arm, as he said, "And then if he should awake . . . if he should . . ." He stopped and took a deep breath as he tried to contain himself.

"If he should *what?*" I asked. If he could only express his fear I was sure I could help him deal with it.

Mr. Abrams, whipped, bowed his head and said, in a croaking whisper, "I am the boy's father . . . And if he should ask me how I could let this happen to him . . . ?" Then he started to cry–a lifetime's worth of tears.

It had never occurred to me that he would feel responsible for his son's death, his sickness. I should have known it, but I didn't. I wish I could say I thought of something magnificent, but I was demolished. Without thinking, I put my arms around him. And he allowed it.

Within a very short time, he straightened up, sniffed a few times and with a pensive nod and an embarrassed look said, "So now you see. . ."

"You truly could do nothing about his sickness," I said. "You can do nothing about his death. But you can help him be less afraid. You are his father, and whether he is conscious enough to see you or hear you . . . if you hold his hand he will know you are there. Touch him, tell him how you feel about him." By this time I was crying, too, trying to brush the tears away.

I looked at Mr. Abrams and knew that he was the kind of man who had felt so much and held it in for so long that he was ready to explode. I could see how he felt about the boy, and I was willing to bet that Manny had never heard it.

"Mr. Abrams," I said, "you've done as much as any man could have. You stopped the doctors from sticking him with needles. You've been there with him to make sure he gets his pain medicine. All of this after you've spent weeks in the best hospital in the area, trying the latest treatments for him. No father could do more . . . and now you can go in there and help keep him from being afraid. You can hold his hand and you can tell him all the things that you would have wanted to tell him later on. You can tell him how proud you've always been of him . . . and you can tell him how much you love him." I stopped to catch my breath. Mr. Abrams was really listening; he hadn't tuned me out. So I added, "And don't underestimate the importance of that. It's a hell of a lot better than a doctor or a nurse can do most of the time."

He looked at me for a long time, then patted me on the shoulder, turned around, walked into the room and closed the door behind him.

Two hours later I saw Mr. Abrams come out and walk down the hall. Behind him, through the window, I could see the red morning sun coming up in the sky. He nodded solemnly as he walked past me.

"How's Manny?" I asked.

"The same," he said, and then, "but much quieter . . . much easier now."

He walked into the lounge and stood in front of his wife and Manny's grandmother. Through the glass windows of the playroom, I watched him help the old woman up from the couch, and as they all walked past me down to Manny's room I heard Mr. Abrams encouraging them to touch and talk to the boy.

I checked Manny once more before my shift was over. His coma had deepened and his breathing was less regular, but both mother and grandmother were holding his hands and talking to him, and Mr. Abrams no longer looked angry or afraid.

CHAPTER 23

After three years at Beth Shalom, I dreaded hearing my assignment because I dreaded knowing for sure that I was going to have to work in PCU (Progressive Care Unit) again.

One night, as Erin and I came into the hospital, we heard everyone talking about an eleven-car accident on the Long Island Expressway; some of the passengers were in our Emergency Room.

In the office, Janis said, "Several of the patients were moved out of Intensive Care to PCU to make room for the emergency admissions, so PCU's short-staffed."

I almost stomped out of the office, grumbling to Erin, "If they keep sending me there, I'm going to quit. I could have worked *staff* if I wanted to spend every night in PCU."

Erin nodded. "I know what you mean. I was up there every other night for the past two weeks, worked myself to death and went home in the morning feeling as though I'd accomplished nothing." Then she shook her head and said indignantly, "I fell asleep dreaming of those *sick things*, hanging from the ceiling, tucked into corners, growing like cauliflowers out of a vegetable patch of white sheets. Rows and rows of them."

I laughed whenever Erin said something crazy, because no one was kinder or gentler or gave better care to the sickest, most dependent patients. Erin was the one who sang to comatose patients and took all the white-haired oldies out of their rooms and sat them around the desk just to talk to them all night. "*Sick things*" was her defensive endearment.

In PCU there were so many comatose patients who had to be constantly turned, suctioned and tube-fed that as soon as I finished

THE NURSE'S STORY 273

one round it was time to start over again. The only criterion for being there was that the patients required four hours of nursing care out of every eight. Each room, except one, held four patients, and each nurse had one whole room to herself. Simple addition would tell anyone but hospital administration that four patients at four hours each equal twice as much as any supernurse could possibly do, even if she loved her job.

It wasn't the amount of work that bothered me; the unit threatened my sense of ethics. It seemed to me that we were bleeding the families of these patients, emotionally as well as financially not to speak of what we were doing to the patients. Most of them were irreversibly brain-damaged, and what we did was keep them alive on machines while the interns and residents practiced medicine on them.

Erin and I took the elevator upstairs together. She had to work PIC (Pediatric Intensive Care), which was no bargain, either. "You still need a degree in horticulture instead of nursing," she explained. "Only there we have 'sick *little* things' and Brussel sprouts instead of cauliflowers."

I winced whenever she said that stuff where other people could possibly hear; they didn't know her as I did and I was afraid that they'd perceive her words as cruelty. During many of the most critical times in nursing, I found myself and others saying things that were so outrageous I realized it was a form of hysteria, a form of distance pulling, to separate *us* from *them*. To help us forget that those *sick things* could be us.

When I walked into the locker room, most of the evening nurses were already in various stages of undress. In the specialty units we wore scrub gowns. With all the patient drainage we should have been wearing hip boots and plastic raincoats.

"Hi, Teri" Rena called from across the room. She was a tall blond GWYN from evenings, an efficient, caring young nurse who was bright and not unreasonably compulsive about technical details. "I think you've got my patients tonight," she said.

I looked up at the board. She was right. I threw my stuff into one of the lockers, and as I pulled my sweater over my head she said, "Shouldn't be too bad. Loads of meds, but both the guys are no CACs."

"Terrific," I said, pulling on the gray-blue scrub suit. "What are they?" I sat down on the long bench next to her and placed my pad on the Formica lunch table.

"One is a twenty-seven-year-old man with melanoma, black lumps sticking out through the skin all over his body. It's infiltrated into his brain. Brother and father died from the same kind of cancer, obviously some kind of hereditary predisposition. Anyway, he's gone except for a reluctant heartbeat. I had to suction him every ten minutes to keep the mucous plugs from sounding the alarm on his respirator." Rena got up and pulled on her jeans. "I signed for all the meds, but I only gave the anticonvulsants because I didn't want to have to handle a seizure. The interns ordered a barrage of blood tests, but I hated to stick that poor guy, so I just told them I couldn't find a vein. None of them were ambitious enough to try, thank God! You can do it if you like, but I don't see the sense if when the man goes out on us nobody's going to jump on his chest anyway."

Makes perfect sense to me, I thought as I copied the details from the Cardex. The man's name was Roy Turner, and the list of medications and treatments covered the entire card. "Why did you say it shouldn't be too bad?" I asked Rena, laughing and shaking my head.

"Well, it's only two patients, and both of them are 'no heroics.' You can actually lock yourself in the room and do nothing most of the night and nobody will squawk."

Rena handed me the next card as she sat down next to me on the wooden bench. My second patient, Dr. Jules Rosen, was a forty-one-year-old dentist.

"What happened to him?" I asked.

"Some kind of a brain bleed," Rena explained. "Came in this afternoon, heart stopped, and they brought him back in the ER. Then they transferred him up here, where his heart stopped again. Brought him back again, but this time it looks like his brain's shot. He's been throwing seizures on and off for hours."

"What kind of a history?" I asked, noticing he was so young.

"None," Rena answered. "Just came back from a vacation in the islands, got up in the middle of the night to go to the bathroom and keeled over. Wife called an ambulance, but he never regained consciousness." Rena took a deep breath and shook her head. "I gave him all his meds," she said apologetically, "just because I had the time. He's had no response to even painful stimuli."

"And he's a no-code, too?" I asked.

Rena bent over to tie her shoelaces. "The interns, the new guys, said they're waiting for two EEGs to see if he's brain dead; the old interns and resident whispered, '*No code*,' and Steve, our smartest resident, said to make it a slow walk thirteen."

Each hospital has a different way of saying it, but the same concepts run throughout. A "code" or "CAC" means that if a patient's heart stops you call for a team and jump on his chest to try to bring him back. The success rate rises or falls according to the efficiency of the Code Team. We had a very good Code Team at Beth Shalom, but any saving that is done has to be done quickly or there is irreversible brain damage.

In a "slow walk thirteen," or variation, the idea is to give a patient the chance to finish his dying *without* somebody jumping on his chest. The nurse doesn't call a code; she calls the intern on thirteen . . . after she walks to the phone . . . slowly. Then he comes up to the floor . . . walking slowly. With any luck, all this takes enough time to let the patient with terminal disease or irreparable brain damage finish dying without extraordinary measures being instituted. In a few cases it's written on the Cardex, but more often it's passed by word of mouth so that no one can be sued for malpractice.

In reality, no one but the person who finds the patient who has stopped breathing can decide what to do. No matter the propaganda on the power of the doctor, if the nurse is the one to discover the patient, she's the one to decide on the biggest God move of all. She can start to pump–or she can walk away.

Rena was combing her hair in front of the long wall mirror. "Want me to show you your patients?" she asked.

"No," I said as I watched her put on fresh lipstick. Then I asked, "Going out tonight?"

"Yep," she said as she started to walk out the door. "Some of us are going drinking for a couple of hours. Need to get the taste of this place off my tongue." She smiled, and the door slammed behind her.

Now that the locker room was empty, I took a deep breath and walked onto the unit toward my room. Before I got there, I could hear Dr. Rosen's ring hitting the chrome side rails. By the rhythm, I knew he was still convulsing.

I just glanced at him as I passed his bed to get to Roy, who was in the bed by the window. He was choking. Roy had a large gauze bandage wrapped around his head and, as Rena had said, grotesque black lumps like mushrooms sprouting out of his skin. He was propped on his side with a large pillow holding him there, and mucus was bubbling out of his nose and mouth. I picked up a piece of gauze to wipe his mouth, but his saliva was so thick and tenacious that I only managed to smear it all over his face and my hand. "Yech!" I said aloud.

In all my years of nursing, I had never gotten over my aversion to mucus. I'd rather have shit up to my earlobes, or blood filling my shoes. Ever since I'd seen it under a microscope, I'd always pictured an army of rotten little bacterial animals slithering around with lousy yellow glue guns, stuffing up air cavities and snuffing out breath. It frightens me–the idea that one of their crawling spies can invade *my* body and snuff out *my* breath.

After I suctioned Roy and took his blood pressure, I pulled back the covers to do a rectal temp. Shit! More shit than a quagmire, pooling in all the cracks of the plastic raft that we used as an air mattress to prevent bedsores. I pulled on a pair of gloves and began to clean him off.

The noise from the two respirators alternately hissing, the bubbling of the oxygen, the clattering of Dr. Rosen's ring while it kept hitting the side rail, and the slurping of the suction machines were all competing to drive me crazy. As it reached a crescendo I wanted to scream, 'Okay, you guys–shut up!'

I felt like Alice in Horrorland . . . Machineland . . . Deadland. All my nerve ends had developed little sensors, like microphones, which exaggerated every already strident note. I thought about throwing myself against the wall with my hands up . . . I thought of waving a white flag . . . I thought of tossing myself on top of one of those beds . . . over one of those loxed-out men who were part of the machines that were hissing and hollering at me to do something–but what?

I walked over to Roy and lifted one of his eyelids. "Hello. Hello in there," I whispered, but the dull glaze told me there was no one home; no sense pouring more goop down his feeding tube so that it could erupt out of his nose and mouth–or immediately shoot in a brown stream out his rectum. "Why are we doing this?" I asked myself. "Is this nursing?"

I left Roy as he bubbled and wet-farted, and walked over to Dr. Rosen. He was lying on his back, respirator tube coming from his long straight nose, his whole body shaking and vibrating in seizure. Oh God, I thought as I pushed his curly black hair off his forehead. It was soaking wet. His large eyes, fringed with long dark lashes, stayed closed; underneath the lids they twitched. A line of small sweat beads ran along the top of his full lips. Rena must have shaved him, because his velvet tan skin was smooth and hairless. Between seizures, when he lay still, he was very handsome.

I ran my hand over his furry chest, and as I did, his black hair curled around my fingers. Automatically, I ran my hand over his chest again. I tried to push the hair down, like fresh-cut blades of grass, but as soon as my hand rested, the hair curled around my fingers again.

I knew then that I was sunk–that I'd have to work my ass off all night. I'd have to do everything possible for Dr. Rosen, because when I pinched his tan skin, it bounced back fast . . .because when I bent down to smell him, he didn't smell sick enough . . . but mostly because the hair on his chest wouldn't lie flat, wouldn't act dead; because it curled around my fingers . . . and it shined.

On the way home that night, I looked so exhausted that Erin teased me about being a compulsive nut. "Would you have jumped on his chest and tried to bring him back if his heart had stopped, in spite of what they had said?" she asked.

"I don't know for sure," I told her. "I'd have to decide at the time."

And that was the truth. For as many years as I've been nursing, I've never been able to develop a general rule.

In the silent space between a stopped heart and the call for help lies everything I really am. That's where I practice my morality; that's where the strongest of my beliefs is tested.

Almost instantly, as I stand at the side of a patient's bed, the witness to Death . . . each time I raise my arm with the dagger of hope in my hand . . . all the information I have about this man, his family, and myself . . . the philosophy I've learned, the religion which still terrifies me . . . everything I know medicine to be, and not to be, computes.

Before I can lower my arm, before I can bring my hand down to sever the cord that stops the hands of time, a panoramic view of my own life passes before me. I have only a minute or so to separate myself from this other . . . and at the same time, I have to put myself in his place. . .

It is then that I do battle with death–or surrender–using another person as the field. And I don't for a minute think that I've always made the right decision. I have sometimes been too depressed to fight, and often too happy to relent.

A week and a half later, on a night when by some stroke of luck I was working on Medicine, Erin called me from PCU.

"Are you sitting down?" she asked.

I sat down. "What's up?" I asked apprehensively.

"Guess who I'm taking care of tonight?" She sounded amused.

"How the hell would I know?" I asked, getting annoyed.

"I'll give you a clue," she baited. "We just had a cup of coffee together."

There was no one I had taken care of in PCU for several weeks who was capable of having coffee, so I said, "Okay, I give up. Who?"

"Your friend with the shiny hair," she laughed. "Dr. Rosen."

A month later Dr. Jules Rosen left the hospital; he had totally recovered. The only indication that he had ever been ill was a slight limp.

CHAPTER 24

Beth Shalom was taking a terrible toll on my family life. On the two nights a week I was off, I tried to straighten the house and cook, but the rest of the time Greg did most of the housework, shopping and cooking.

"You don't take enough interest in the house," he accused one night as we got into bed. "I work *and* do most of the chores."

"But, Greg," I defended, "I do a different kind of work. On my nights off, I'm exhausted."

"Then stop working nights," he demanded. "Work a shift that is compatible with family life."

"I can't do that," I insisted. "Day work is too heavy for me. I'm not that big." And that was partly true. Though I had more patients to care for at night, most of the physical work that had to be done was due to emergencies; with the added adrenaline, it was easier to pull and lift. But more important, there was counseling to do and additional fear to control. And because I understood it, I was better at reassuring patients than a lot of the other nurses.

Greg tossed and turned in bed, still obviously upset. After several minutes, he got up and continued with his complaints, this time ranting about our latest problem. Niki had a new boy friend, Lynch, who drove Greg out of his mind. He had long blond hair and worked in a gas station. His presence alone was an affront to Greg's whole value system, and each night he came to pick up Niki, Greg swore he got grease all over the house.

"There are footprints on the living-room rug," he shouted pacing up and down our bedroom, "and greasy fingerprints all over the refrigerator door."

"I'll make him wash as soon as he walks in the front door," I said as I lay in bed watching him fume.

"No," he said, challenging me now. "You'll tell Niki to have her friends come in the back door."

"That sounds a lot like 'Sit at the back of the bus,'" I mumbled, but when Greg stiffened I said I'd tell Niki in the morning. I had just worked a six-day stretch at Beth Shalom, most of the time on Adolescents, Pediatrics and PCU, and I was just too tired to fight with him.

Finally, a little calmer, Greg got back into bed. He reached over and put his arms around me, but I automatically stiffened. He turned away from me.

"I'm sorry, Greg," I said. "It's just that I'm really tired. Can't we let it go for another night?"

"What night?" he asked. "You're working all next week, aren't you?"

"But I'm off tomorrow. I can sleep with you tomorrow night," I said quickly. But even I knew that one night a week wasn't fair to him. I knew I should call Dr. Davidson again. No matter how hard I tried, I kept getting angry with Greg for the way he acted toward the kids. I had been trying to avoid making love to him for months . . . and that used to be the best part of our relationship. I lay awake for a long time, wondering what I could do to make things better.

At breakfast the following morning, I told Niki about Lynch. She nodded and didn't say anything until Greg had gotten up from the table. Then she whispered, "Mommy, why does our house have to be like this now? Everybody used to be welcome when we lived with Aunt Lil."

"That was then, this is now," I teased as I patted her head. She looked at me, but she didn't smile.

Greg started spending more time locked in his study. There were several reasons for that, he explained, but the most pressing one was that Lynch had started eating with us several times a week.

"You shouldn't have to leave your own table for us," Niki said in an unusual moment of compassion for Greg. "I'll make sure that on the nights you're home Lynch doesn't eat over."

And she kept her word. Greg came back to the table but still spent an enormous amount of time closeted away from the rest of the family. Niki stopped spending as much time at home, and when she came in one evening, without Lynch, she announced, "Mom, I can't do it anymore. I have to quit school and go to work."

Greg stared stone-faced, waiting for me to react, but I had just worked a week in PIC and was too depressed and tired to whip myself up into a fury over a kid who wanted to drop out.

"You'll have to get a job first," I told her. "I can't have you hanging around doing nothing."

She hugged and thanked me, then ran happily down to her room to call Lynch and tell him the good news.

Greg was glowering at me. "You're the one who's supposed to teach her the value of commitment," he said sternly. "As long as you've tied my hands by asking me not to interfere."

"What are you talking about, Greg?" I asked wearily. I hadn't been able to fall asleep during the day because I was getting more and more depressed by the patients at work. They were so sick, and there were so many of them; they seemed to move through the wards of Beth Shalom on conveyor belts. I was finally giving up the hope of stamping Death and Disease out of the Western world. . .

"I'm trying to explain that unless you insist that she finish what she starts," he said, exasperated, "she'll never know the value of commitment."

"But it wasn't *her* commitment to go to school," I explained patiently. "We can lay that on her if she tries to quit the job she hasn't gotten yet."

As I watched Spinner and Greg start to clean off the table and do the dishes, I couldn't help thinking of all the sick kids I had been working with lately. Niki wasn't sick; she didn't have a terminal disease. I wanted her to have fun in her life. There was too much pain already for me to try to force her to do something she didn't want to do. When I explained that to Greg, he got twice as furious.

"You keep treating these kids as though they're not going to have a tomorrow," he said. "They have to have an education, they have to prepare. You keep wanting them to enjoy *today,* but don't you understand how miserable their *tomorrow's* will be if they're not prepared?"

I understood what Greg was so desperately trying to explain to me. I just didn't agree with him; there were simply no guarantees on tomorrow.

I got up and went into my study to read. Later, Niki bounced in to kiss me goodbye. She and Lynch were going to a movie.

"Honey," I said, thinking I should at least give it one try, "maybe you should finish school. You only need three more credits to graduate."

"I can't, Mom," she said earnestly. "In my opinion, I did finish it; I used it all up. I'm bored by it."

"Honey, school is important later on," I said, figuring that if I warned her about the pitfalls in what she was doing I wouldn't feel as guilty afterward if it worked out badly.

Niki smiled her happy teenager smile. "Then I'll go back to school *later,*" she said, "like you did."

Two nights later when I rode to work with Erin, she told me she was thinking of quitting. "Why?" I asked, crushed. The thought of working at Beth Shalom without her horrified me.

"Ted's starting to bark," she teased, but then she admitted that the work at the hospital was wearing her down, physically and emotionally. "We spend so much time catering to the demands of the dying," she mused, "that I can't stand the demands of the living. My family, to be more specific." She laughed when she added, "Every time I come home from working PIC, I can't stand my healthy children, and at the same time I'm so grateful they're not sick that I let them get away with murder. Ted's going to be convicted of child abuse if I don't shape them up soon."

Janis didn't look at either of us when she assigned me to PIC and Erin to PCU. Erin told Janis that she was leaving before she walked out of the office.

As I forced myself into the unit that night, I was aware even before the shift had begun that I was exhausted. I dropped my bag into the hall locker and walked into the large brightly lit room of PIC.

A doctor I didn't recognize sat on a chair next to a little boy on a respirator. He must be one of the new interns, I thought as I watched him look toward the child and then back at the chart he was writing. He was a very thin, pale young man, with thinning brown hair and a hunched posture which made him look much older than the other interns. There was something strange about him; something sad and intense.

The little boy was lying motionless. The only discernible movement was that of his small chest, caused by the pressure of the respirator, which was breathing for him. Up and down . . . hiss . . . hiss . . . with unnatural regularity. The child was beautiful. His blond curls were wet from the effort of his breathing, and long brown lashes resting on clear pink skin made him look porcelain-figurine perfect.

I looked around at the other children. The same three as last week, I noted. The newborn baby in the corner bassinet who stops breathing if you don't watch her carefully . . . the apnea machine attached to her chest sounds an alarm when she forgets . . . if you flick the bottom of her feet, she remembers and starts to breathe again. In the bed across from the baby, Tanya, a four-year-old dark-skinned girl who just had open-heart surgery. I looked at her monitor. Regular rhythm . . . she'll go home in a few days. Nice little kid.

And in the third bed there's Timmy, one of my very favorite "little things," as Erin would say. God, I love that kid, give him more kisses than either of my own . . . he touches something so deep in me I didn't even know I had it before now.

Timmy had fallen into a lake and drowned. He was three years old, with smooth brown skin and jet-black eyes. His father took him fishing, turned his back for a minute, and Timmy was gone. Poor man was frantic, groping and struggling around underwater trying to scoop the kid out . . . sputtering, gagging and crying all at the same time. Would have been happy to drown himself if he could have gotten Timmy back quicker . . . but by the time he reclaimed his son from the muddy water . . . the kid hadn't been breathing for a long time. The water was cold, too, so Timmy was almost as blue as the water by the time his dad got him to the Emergency Room. The doctors worked on Timmy for hours . . . finally got his heart going again . . . but his brain was shot.

He couldn't move, couldn't talk, couldn't eat, and we didn't think he could understand. Yet somehow I even managed to get past the gunk that flew from Timmy's trach as I bent to kiss him. I was never able to do that with anyone else; maybe it was because sometime, in the dead of night, when I'd sit next to his bed, I'd see a look of horror contort his face and I'd watch his big eyes widen in terror. It was as though he was always waiting for the water to engulf him again.

I walked over to Maureen, the young nurse who was taking care of Timmy. "What's with the new kid on the respirator?" I asked.

"Leukemia," she whispered, and shook her head. "Real bad. Won't make it home this time."

"You sure?" I asked, bending down to kiss Timmy. His dazed eyes stared straight ahead.

"Yep," she said. "He's had it for a couple of years, so he's on borrowed time. Had one run of chemo, and was in remission for more than a year." Maureen wrinkled her nose as she stuck her hand inside the diaper that Timmy wore. He was wet again. "He can't tolerate another run of chemo," she continued, "and his leukemia is back–twice as virulent as before."

I fixed Timmy's oxygen and then glanced over at the other child. "Pretty kid," I said. "How old is he?"

"Just six, I think." Maureen answered as we worked together making Timmy's bed.

"Any other kids at home?"

"No," she answered as we pulled Timmy up in bed and turned him on his side. Propped with several pillows, he still fell over because he had no muscle control.

"New doctor?" I asked, nodding toward the intern.

"Yep," she said as she ran over to flick the baby's heel because the apnea monitor rang off.

Tanya's heart monitor was beeping like mad, too, while the scope was showing what looked like a TV Telstar game. She had playfully removed all her lead wires while we were changing Timmy. I glued them back on her zippered chest while the monitor raced in jagged mountains across the scope until the beeping stopped.

After I changed her diaper and took her temperature and blood pressure, I hugged and kissed her.

"Night, Nurth," she lisped. "I'm thleeping now."

"Want me to help with the new kid?" I asked Maureen. She nodded.

"What's he writing? And how long is he staying?" I whispered, nodding toward the tired-looking intern. Maureen shrugged.

I walked over to him. The doctor was patting the child's arm. He had been sitting in the same position, holding the boy's hand, since I got there.

"Hi," I said. "Aren't you going to sleep tonight?"

He looked up and smiled sweetly. "No," he said, "not yet. I'll stay here for a while. . ."

The boy still hadn't moved. "Is he comatose?" I asked.

"No," he said, and then, as he held out his hand, "My name is Luke." Motioning toward the boy, he added, "His name's Chris."

I smiled at Luke and introduced myself. Then I asked "Why isn't he moving at all?"

"Pavulon," Luke answered as he stood to wipe Chris's wet forehead with his own handkerchief.

"Pavulon?" I was surprised. Pavulon was a drug used as an adjunct to anesthesia. "Doesn't that paralyze him?"

"Yes," Luke answered softly, "it does paralyze, temporarily."

"Why are we giving it to him?"

"Because he kept thrashing around and fighting the respirator," Luke explained patiently.

"Why do we have him on a respirator anyway?" I asked frowning.

"He wasn't breathing well," the doctor answered, stroking the child's face.

"Is he as bad as they say?" I couldn't understand what was going on.

"Yes," Luke almost whispered as he bit his bottom lip. Then he sat down again.

"Then why do we have him on a respirator?" I persisted. I was trying to keep the pitch of my voice down, but we didn't usually put kids who were hopeless on respirators. Extraordinary measures were instituted for viable kids, and from what I was hearing, Chris couldn't be saved.

The little boy's eyelids started to flutter slightly. "Hi, Chrissy," Luke said.

Just then the fire alarm went off and I jumped. "Luke," I said urgently, "help me move the furniture out of the halls. They have to be clear."

Luke bent down and whispered into Chris's ear, "Don't worry, Chris. It's only a fire drill. You know about fire drills, right?"

Luke and I quickly cleared the hall, and he immediately went back to Chris. The Pavulon was wearing off, so the little boy could open his eyes and look into the eyes of the man. Luke bent down and kissed Chris on the nose.

There is something definitely strange about this young doctor, I said to myself; I wonder how long it will take for his compassion and dedication to wear thin.

He startled me when he said, "Teri, please get me the Pavulon. I want to remedicate Chris. He's starting to move."

"Why can't we give him morphine or something else that will relieve his pain and relax him as it sedates him?" I asked, frustrated. "You know that stuff leaves him conscious with his pain–and just paralyzes him." I was upset.

Luke tapped his foot but again patiently explained, "Narcotics will depress his blood pressure . . . that's why they weren't ordered."

I felt as though I were back in nursing school. Everything Luke was telling me I already knew. I wasn't asking why; I was asking *why?* "But I thought this kid is terminal . . ." I persisted, "Why are we . . .?"

Luke cut me off, speaking a little more sharply than he had been. "Give me the medicine to give him."

Just then one of the floor nurses from Peds, Bonnie, stuck her head into the doorway of the unit and cried, "Fire's for real this time."

I looked at Luke, he looked at me . . . and we both looked at Chris. He was struggling to keep his eyes open. I knew by the expression in them that he was afraid he would be trapped by the fire.

The respirator began to hiss erratically and the alarm went off as Chris started to thrash. Luke ran over to the medication closet and drew up the Pavulon himself. Almost immediately after Chris got the drug, his eyes closed and even his slight movements stopped. The regular rhythm of the respirator resumed and the alarm stopped. Then I watched as two big tears rolled down Chris's cheek. Luke bent over and soothed, "It's okay, Chris, I'm here. I'll stay with you."

I had decided that Luke was crazy. I was still furious with him when the alarm for the all clear sounded. "Fire's out," Bonnie shouted.

I walked over to Luke and pulled at his blue scrub shirt. "Come with me a minute?" I asked with a moderate amount of control. I didn't want Chris to hear us; I didn't want to frighten him more.

"Doctor, listen," I said, dropping the familiar, "the kid only has a few days . . . if we give him the benefit of the doubt . . . he only has that long. That junk paralyzes him, and the respirator just prolongs his suffering. His mother can't hold him or kiss him while he's hooked up to all those damn machines." I took one breath before I stormed on, noticing as I did that Luke was getting paler. "Why can't you call the doctor who ordered all this heroic nonsense and ask him to cut it? This is like burying Chris in cement. He can't move anything . . . He's going to die with fluorescent lights in his eyes and the sound of a respirator hiss and a monitor beep as the last sounds he hears . . . he should hear his mom's voice . . . and have her arms around him." Luke was rubbing his eyes and stooping lower as I pleaded, "Call whoever ordered that stuff. Please ask if we can just give Chris medicine to keep him comfortable . . . Please tell him we want all the heroics stopped. . . ." I begged Luke with my eyes to understand what I was trying to say.

He looked directly at me. His face was implacable: jaw set tight, immovable. "No," he said.

I couldn't believe this. Luke looked so kind, so caring. Why would he do this? I tried one more time. "Is that little boy hopeless?"

"Nobody's hopeless . . . until they're dead," Luke answered wearily.

I was more exasperated than ever. Another damned egotist having a tug-of-war with God, I thought. I tried to stay calm, but instead I erupted. "Would you like somebody to do that to you, Doctor? Paralyze you so you're buried in your own body before you're dead? He can't even scratch his nose, *Doctor* . . . Would *you* like that?"

Out of control, I ran out of the unit into the hall of Pediatrics. Janis was making rounds, and I almost plowed into her.

"What's wrong?" she asked, looking concerned.

I pointed to the open door of the unit, where Luke and Chris were clearly visible. Through tears of frustration, I asked, "What's wrong with him? I sure would like to know what the hell his problem is."

Janis looked at me quizzically. "He's got leukemia," she said softly.

"Not the boy, Janis. The doctor."

"He's got leukemia," Janis repeated, this time more gently.

I turned back. I looked at Luke bending over Chris, talking to him, touching him. . .

That afternoon, I called Dr. Davidson to make an appointment. It had been almost a year and a half since I had last spoken to him, and I really needed to see him again.

When his familiar voice answered, I could feel myself grinning. "Hi," I said. "When can I see you?"

"Sorry, Teri," he answered, his voice sounding sadder than I. remembered it, "but I'm not seeing patients any longer."

"Why not?" I was horrified.

"I just don't believe in it any longer," he answered matter-of-factly.

"You don't believe in what?" I asked, thinking he wasn't telling me the truth about something; that maybe he was going to die or something equally terrible.

"I don't believe psychiatry works . . . I don't believe it really changes anything," he explained patiently.

"What do you mean?" I argued. "Look how much you helped *me*. Look how much I learned from you."

I heard him chuckle. "Teri, you learned from life, I didn't do anything but listen." He sounded so convinced that I knew nothing I could say would change his mind.

"What are you going to do instead?" I asked, feeling shaken.

"Move to the West Coast. California. And live the rest of my life . . ." he said softly.

"Tell me why one more time?" I asked.

"Because the people who needed the most I was able to help the least," he said unhappily.

When I hung up, I had the same feeling in the pit of my stomach that poor Samson must have had when good old Delilah took the scissors to his hair.

CHAPTER 25

In a desperate attempt to try to make our home life bearable, Greg and I made plans to take a four-day vacation in Montauk. We loaded the dice and made reservations at the same motel, same room, where we had spent our honeymoon. I took a Valium in the bathroom before we left, in order not to haunt Greg while he drove Sunrise Highway as though competing in the Indianapolis 500. I was always scared to death with him at the wheel because he looked like those cartoons of the Aggressive Driver: hunched forward, jaw jutting, wrinkled brow, and extra stones in his shoes as he pressed down on the accelerator.

He had optimistically packed our wicker picnic basket with wine, crackers and caviar; and I had packed my pocketbook defensively with aspirin, Maalox and some more Valium in case that didn't work. I gave the kids my last-minute warnings and told them that if they didn't behave I'd hang them by their thumbs when I got home.

Once we had arrived, I lay in bed, staring at the ceiling, while Greg unloaded the car. He was chattering happily, as he never did at home, and I was quietly listening as I never did at home.

"Hey, Kitten," he shouted from the terrace, "come look at the surf, it's great!" I was exhausted; I didn't want to move. "Kitten," he called to me again, "come look at these seagulls."

I dragged myself off the bed and across the room to the balcony. "Great surf," I said, trying to smile, "great seagulls . . ." My Valium talk is laconic. Greg put an arm around me and pulled me close. Then he turned me around and kissed me passionately. Because we were in a motel and I didn't feel married, it felt good. Greg popped open a bottle of champagne that he had brought to surprise me, and we lay in bed drinking and eating cheese, crackers and caviar. Then we made love. Long, good love, another thing we never did at home. It always surprised me how sensual I found Greg to be during sex; somehow passion didn't seem a facet of his character, except in bed. Relaxed, we both fell asleep.

When Greg woke up he asked, "Want to go down to the beach for a walk?" It had begun to get dark and the breeze blowing into the open door was wet and cold. "Throw a sweater on," he suggested pleasantly. I watched him get dressed, then I dressed myself and followed him outside.

I first noticed I was feeling strange when I tried to walk down the narrow steps leading to the beach and found it extremely difficult to aim my feet so that they hit the iridescent white steps solidly. The stone seemed to wave and melt under me. I blinked my eyes, trying to see more clearly through the thick damp air. Maybe I should have worn my glasses, I thought. Greg was walking right in front of me, and because I was moving slowly and uncertainly he reached back to grab for my hand. It felt as though he was tugging at me, and I was afraid I'd fall, so I pulled my hand away. My body began to tremble and I wrapped my sweater closer around me.

As we reached the bottom of the long flight of stairs, I looked across the dark hazy beach. Suddenly, all the white wooden beach chairs turned into small rectangular tombstones . . . arched slabs in long rows . . . markers for dead soldiers in a military cemetery. I stopped short and stood horrified.

When Greg turned, the moonlight shining on his face made him look like a cadaver. I almost screamed. "What's wrong, Teri?" he asked. He tried to come closer, but I recoiled in horror. My head started to spin and his voice echoed as though through a tunnel. Then there was a deafening flapping noise from overhead, the sound of swarming buzzards, circling, waiting to sweep down on some unseen carrion. I felt myself falling.

"Kitten? Kitten? What is it?" I heard Greg call from far away, but I couldn't answer. I felt my body turning cold. . . I saw my lips turn blue. . . . I heard the hiss, hiss of the machine. . . . Then nothing.

When I woke up, I was shivering. Greg had carried me back to the room and tucked me into bed. By his expression, I could tell he was worried sick. He sat on the bed next to me and smoothed the hair off my forehead. It was several hours before I felt normal and could talk again. And even after Greg was again chattering reassuringly, I was still worried.

What Greg didn't know was that something similar had happened two other times in the last few months. The only person I had told about it was Erin, because I thought I had a brain tumor. She had smiled compassionately and said, "Look, I think you need to stop working for a while. I think the pressure of taking care of sick and dying patients plus all the other pressures of daily living are just getting to be too much."

"Hey, come on," I had replied, "all of us at one time or another have to face our own mortality."

She had laughed when she told me, "Facing your own mortality is different from having it shoved down your throat like a grapefruit each night."

Later that week, I had gone to Dr. Pavetto and gotten a checkup. "No sign of any neuro damage," he had told me kindly. "Maybe you just need a rest."

As I lay in bed in Montauk, listening to the sound of the surf, I told Greg what had been happening. He listened intently. Then, anxiety straining his expression, he asked, "Well, what do you want to do?"

"Maybe I could just stop working for a few months," I said, feeling guilty. "Then, if this doesn't happen again, I can go back."

Greg frowned and bit his bottom lip. Without a word he got up, walked over to the dresser and lit up his pipe. When he sat again, it was on a chair across from me. He spoke softly but very deliberately. "You know that I want you to stop working at the hospital, Teri. I've asked you to do that for quite a while now."

I wasn't sure what was bothering him, but it looked like more than my not feeling well. "Is something else the matter?" I asked.

Greg sat up straight and took a deep breath. "How much do your bills add up to?" he asked softly, frowning. Early in our marriage, when we couldn't agree on how to spend our money jointly, we had drawn up a verbal contract on how we would split expenses. I was supposed to take care of all entertainment, medical bills, car payments and repairs, house renovations, and clothing. All the charge accounts plus the gas credit cards were my responsibility. All the basic living expenses, mortgage, utilities, and insurance were Greg's.

I made a quick tally in my head. "About four thousand dollars," I said, and then held my breath waiting for the screams.

Greg shot up from his seat involuntarily and started to pace back and forth. He didn't say anything for quite a while, but when he did his voice was hoarse. "I had no idea it was that much. Why didn't you tell me? What did you manage to spend all that money on?"

"Greg, don't get so upset," I said softly. "It's not as bad as it sounds. They're all time payments. We can get away with sending them each twenty dollars a month."

He stood at the bottom of the bed, clouds of smoke from his hard puffing separating us. "What the hell did you spend all that money on?" he repeated, but without waiting for an answer he went on, "Time payments eat up more money in interest than the principal. Where are your brains, Teri?"

"Stop getting so hysterical," I said angrily. "I spent the damn money on sheets and rugs to make your house more comfortable for you. The kids' clothes, your clothes and dentist's bills ate up most of it. How was I supposed to know that I would fall apart?" I started to cry with frustration, and Greg slammed out the door for a walk on the beach.

By the time he came back in, I knew that I would go on working. "Don't worry about it, Greg," I told him. "I can always do private duty. That can't wipe me out in the same way . . ."

"Kitten," he said, turning toward me, still looking distraught, "it's not that I don't want you to stay home. It's just that we can't use up what little money we have in the bank."

I didn't really understand Greg's panic over money, but I did know that I had given my word when we got married and bought the house that I would help him carry it. If he didn't release me from that promise, I couldn't stop working.

"Don't worry about it," I said again, putting my arms around him. "I'll work it out. I'll be okay."

As soon as Greg and I got home, I called Janis Strong and applied for a leave of absence. "Rest and recovery?" she asked sympathetically.

"Something like that," I said. "I just need to be away from the hospital for a while." We agreed on a year's leave, and Janis told me she would label the application "Educational." Before we hung up, she wished me luck and thanked me.

That afternoon, I called Mrs. Dayton. She sounded thrilled to hear from me and promised to get me light private-duty cases for a while. Everything arranged, I felt much better by the time I called Erin that night.

I was surprised that when I told her what had happened in Montauk she was more than a little irritated with Greg. "Doesn't he know it's a husband's job to carry things for a while if you're in trouble?" she asked sarcastically.

"Come on, Erin," I said. "You know I asked for independence and equality. We can't use that helpless-female shit when it suits us."

"I'm not talking male-and-female nonsense," she countered. "I'm talking friend in need. If I had the money, I'd give it to you."

"I'll be fine," I reassured her. "Most private duty is a cinch."

And the next months were practically painless as far as work went. Mrs. Dayton got me cases for no more than two days at a time, and that way I couldn't get involved with my patients. At home, because I was less of a crazy, the situation between Greg and me improved some. There was still cold war between Niki and Greg, but I tried to stay out of it as often as I could. The only problem was that I didn't like myself as well. I felt as though I had abandoned her. I told myself that Niki would have to deal with frustration in the outside world and that this was practice; I couldn't protect her forever.

Once Niki had gotten a job, Greg insisted that she pay rent. I hated the idea. I offered to pay her share. Greg kept saying that I was doing her a terrible disservice by not preparing her for adult life. I couldn't make him understand that I had never charged anyone who lived with me rent; how could I charge my own kid? Niki pulled me aside and told me not to worry, she'd pay rent.

When she asked Greg to give her a ride to work one morning, he told her, "I'm not going to help you do this thing." He made it sound as though she was going to work in a brothel instead of a fast-food joint. I kept my mouth shut because I knew Greg was really afraid that without an education Niki would be trapped, totally unprepared to handle life outside the house.

Also, I was getting worried about Spinner. The fighting seemed to be taking a real toll on him. His schoolwork was horrible and I knew, as I watched him try to do homework, that he was beginning to feel dumb, which he definitely wasn't. Though he didn't fight Greg the way Niki did, the added frustration of Greg's pressure on him was making him an angry boy. He had a shorter fuse than I did, and because he hadn't had my father to teach him all the Spartan-youth tricks he seemed to have none of my endurance. I hoped as I watched him struggle with values–Greg's strictness and my permis-siveness–that he would somehow settle in the middle. But each day I could see him identify more with Greg.

I started spending more time in my study because things were so uneasy when Greg was home for supper.

One night when Niki and Lynch had gone out and Spinner was doing his homework, Greg came into the study to talk to me. I was lying on the couch, and he pulled up a yellow director's chair across from me.

"What's up?" I asked with my eyes closed. I was depressed again, and that always exhausted me. Tonight I didn't even know what I was miserable about.

"I'm worried about Lynch's potential for violence," Greg said quietly. "The boy comes from a bad home, and Niki may not be prepared for what happens when he eventually erupts."

I was up like a shot, standing, shouting, "The kid hasn't done anything wrong! I think it's *my* potential for violence you should be talking about; I'd just as soon kill you as not when you start laying all that fanatical stuff on me."

Greg got up and left. I lay on the couch shaking. What the hell does he expect from me? I asked myself. I'm her mother; I want to respect her choices. Niki and Lynch seem to enjoy life together, and she doesn't seem nearly as lonely as I feel. As I lay there, tears running down my cheeks, I though Goddammit! I can't believe I keep trying to stop him with a torrent of words that not only rains on him but practically drowns me.

I felt totally empty as I got up, walked over to the study door and locked it. For the first time since we had been married, I spent the night on my couch.

CHAPTER 26

It was the end of the summer, the days were still warm and long, when Mrs. Dayton called and asked me to take care of Robin. She was a twenty-five-year-old girl with terminal cancer. Mrs. Dayton explained that she wasn't sure where the cancer was, but she was sure that this would be Robin's last trip in to the hospital.

Within a couple of hours I had my hair washed and my uniform pressed and was in the car on my way to Mary Vincent Hospital. It was one of my least favorite places to work—so backward technically that they hadn't yet introduced disposable needles, and so conservative philosophically that most of the skills I had could not be used. Also, they were usually so understaffed that I often found myself in a position where I felt I had to help other patients—a real taboo when one patient's family is paying for individual care. I had sworn that I'd never work there again, but now I thought, what the hell, I can't just leave a twenty-five-year-old kid to anybody.

In the nursing office, when I checked in, I was told that Robin was in the old wing. My stomach dropped. That section of the hospital was ancient even in comparison to Barrenfield. As I got out of the rickety elevator, I searched the hall for Room 308, the room number I had been given. I couldn't find it, so I kept walking until I found myself in the hall of one of the new units. When I saw the number 300 I was elated. "She must be here," I said aloud. The older parts of a hospital seem so much more hopeless to me, as though too much death and disease have been smashed into the floors and squeezed into the cracks in the walls.

I landed at the nurses' station, where a group of very efficient-looking night nurses had already gotten report. I stood directly in front of the first of two desks and spoke to the woman who was obviously in charge. Her badge read "Mrs. Privost, RN." She had large dark-rimmed glasses worn low on a long straight nose, and a very starched cap planted firmly over her brown bun. She looked at me over her specs, as though she had a fly on her nose, and asked in a shrill voice, "Yes?"

"I'm here to take care of Robin," I announced, smiling as a down payment. I figured I might need her help later. She stared at me blankly as though I was speaking a foreign tongue.

"The young girl with terminal cancer in 308," I said pleasantly, trying to help her out. I figured that she was one of those disease-oriented nurses: if you say "the gall bladder in 706," they catch on, but you have to be very careful not to confuse them with a person's name. I shouldn't have been angry–especially since I knew it was a form of protective distance-pulling. But I've always wanted the people in medicine to be perfect. And my capacity for accepting healthy people who go into a helping profession and then don't want to get involved is limited.

"Oh," Mrs. Privost said, brightening, "you mean Robin Zapp, the blind girl."

I was hoping that she was mistaken, but before I could ask her any questions she had dismissed me with a wave of her hand and a "Talk to Kathy."

Kathy was a small blond nurse, much younger, who luckily had an easier manner. She smiled and motioned me over to the other white Formica desk. She sat and pulled up a chair for me. "Do you know Robin at all?"

"No," I told her. "I've never taken care of her before."

"Are you an RN?" she asked, flipping through the Cardex.

I nodded and pulled my red pen out of my pocket. "Why?" I asked. "Is she a real heavy case?"

"It's not that," she explained. "She needs to be catheterized, and in this hospital only an RN can do it. If you weren't, I'd have to cath her before I went home." More insanity, I thought; I learned to cath when I was an LPN, and even then I was better at it than most of the RNs. In fact, most of the practical nurses were excellent with bedside care because they had more practice there and less at the desk.

"I don't mind cathing her," I told Kathy, though in truth I would have preferred a different way to meet her. Sticking a tube up someone's urethra before I said hello seemed like a terrible invasion of privacy. But I was good at it, so I didn't mind the procedure. "How long has it been since she voided?" I asked.

"It's been almost eight hours, but we couldn't reach the doctor until a few minutes ago," Kathy said apologetically. Another disadvantage of conventional hospitals. In Beth Shalom a nurse could have done it without asking a doctor.

I heard a loud buzz at the main desk, and as I looked toward the intercom Kathy said, "That's Robin again. I'll have to give a quick report. She's pretty uncomfortable."

"Sure," I said, turning the Cardex toward me. It read: ROBIN ZAPP. 25 yr. old. MULTIPLE MYELOMA.

"By the way," Kathy added, "she's blind."

"By the way?" I said, laughing involuntarily at how much working in hospitals changes perspective. "Is it from the cancer?"

"I don't think so," Kathy said, looking puzzled. "I think she's been blind a long time."

A twenty-five-year-old blind girl with terminal cancer. Talk about short straws . . .

"So you better say something as you walk into the room, Kathy continued, "or you'll frighten her."

"Anything else I have to know?"

"Yeah, she's got an IV running to keep the vein open, and her belly looks as though she's got a watermelon in it. She can't breathe well because the cancer's filling up her lungs and closing her throat, and that belly pushing up against her diaphragm doesn't help. They say it's filled with fluid, but my guess is that it's tumor too." Kathy stopped to take a breath and pulled her cap off. "If you have to cath her more than once, leave the Foley in so that she can drain; she doesn't need the added pressure of a bladder full of urine."

"What has she got ordered for pain?" I asked.

"Dilaudid every three hours if she needs it, and she has Compazine ordered for the vomiting, which she does every time we help her turn on her side. Any questions?"

"Only one," I said smiling. She had given a really thorough report. "Does Robin know how bad she is?"

"Not really," Kathy said, starting to close the Cardex and put her pen away. "She thinks she's got bronchitis or pneumonia."

"You mean she doesn't even know she has cancer?" I was stricken. After working at Beth Shalom, it was very difficult for me to accept the idea that a lot of doctors in a lot of hospitals refused to tell their patients the truth.

"No," Kathy said as she stood up. "At least she's not admitting to anyone that she knows she has it." The buzzer sounded again and Kathy left, saying, "I'll get you the cath tray."

On her way down the hall, she pointed out Room 308. On the door a large sign in red magic marker announced, "PATIENT BLIND. PLEASE SPEAK WHEN ENTERING."

I knocked gently on the door as I went in, calling, "Robin? Hi, my name is Teri Daley and I'm going to be your nurse."

She was lying in bed crying–no tears, but her face was all screwed up, and I could hear her whimper: a small child lost. She looked about sixteen, younger than Niki. I walked to the side of the bed and asked gently, "What's wrong?"

Robin held her belly, a huge bulge covered only with a thin white sheet. "My stomach," she cried. "My stomach hurts." She was tipping from side to side, not rolling, never getting off her back.

The dark circles under her eyes were the next thing I noticed. Her eyes weren't as bad as I thought they would be–somehow not as hollow-looking.

"Okay," I said, holding one of her hands, "let's take care of that first. One of the reasons you're uncomfortable is because you haven't been able to pee. There may be a classier way to say it, but you know what I mean. So I'm going to catheterize you and then we can talk about the rest."

She started to cry again. "Oh, please don't hurt me. Please."

"Robin," I said softly, "I'll be gentle and I'll really try not to hurt you. I'll explain everything I do as I'm doing it."

"I'm afraid," she whimpered, squeezing her eyelids tight. "I'm so afraid. . ."

"Robin, listen," I said slowly, holding her small hand firmly. "It's uncomfortable, like an enema is uncomfortable, but not necessarily painful. In fact, it usually doesn't hurt. The tube is very small, smaller around than a pencil, and it's rubber, so it's pretty soft. I'll let you touch everything before I use it."

This was definitely taboo. A cath set is supposed to remain sterile in order not to introduce bacteria into the bladder. But in Robin's case I considered her fear a priority. I was afraid that if I didn't let her touch it she would assume I was going to use a garden hose.

Robin sniffed, then wiped her nose with the back of her arm like a little kid before she said, "Okay."

When I had brought in the cath tray, I asked Robin to move up in bed and spread her legs. She started to cry again.

"Even I have to admit that this is a hell of a way to meet anyone, Robin," I teased. "Now, this is what I'm going to do. I'm going to unwrap all this sterile stuff–here," I said, as I held out the small red tube for her to feel.

"Oh . . . okay," she said as she held her breath and ran her fingers over the tubing. A wide smile of relief broke over her face and she started to laugh. "It really is small."

"I'm going to wipe it off with alcohol and then grease it up good so it slides right in," I told her, and so we managed to get through the cath with very little trauma.

After I had siphoned the urine out of her bladder, she felt better. "Isn't it funny how everything is so much less painful when you trust someone?" Robin asked, laughing and crying at the same time.

After I had cleaned everything away and fixed Robin so she was comfortable, I took her hand and said, "Now let me introduce myself properly. My name is Teri and this is what I look like." I lifted her hand and put it on my face. I ran it across my forehead, over my eyes, down my nose and across my cheeks and lips. Robin started to giggle and then burst out laughing. "I know I look terrible," I teased her, "but I ran out of the house in a hurry. And if I thought you were the kind of person who would laugh at me-"

She cut me off. "No, no," she said, still laughing, "it's not that;

it's just that people don't usually . . . umm . . . introduce themselves like that." She put her hand over her mouth and tried hard to control her giggling. Actually, there's no telling whatever possessed me to do a thing like that except that I saw it once in a Helen Keller movie. I felt a little foolish, but when I looked at it from Robin's position it made me laugh, too.

"I hope I didn't offend you," I said.

"Oh no," she replied, with a big smile. "I liked it. Thank you." Then she laughed again. "It's just that I didn't expect it."

She took some sips of apple juice that I had brought, and explained as I held her head up that any more would make her vomit. When I put her head back on the pillow, she said that she felt better than she had all evening. I sat next to her in the high-back chair and held her hand. It was a very small hand, black and blue from needle punctures, with short fingers and chewed nails.

As I leaned my head back, I looked around. The room was very large, large enough to dance in, but instead it held a single hospital bed, a bedstand and two chairs. The walls were muted beige and freshly painted, the floor a brown-and-white chess board. Suspended from the ceiling there was a large color TV, and over the square bay window cream-colored drapes with orange and brown flowers blew gently in the soft night breeze. On the wall directly across from me was painted an enormous mural–a Roman garden with turquoise flowers growing on magical silver branches, two sculptured cement pillars guarding a fountain spurting aquamarine water, on which tiny colored fairies flew.

I glanced at Robin, pale and still. What a wonderful room to die in, I thought, suddenly angry. Her eyelids were half open, and under them I could see clear blue eyes. I didn't know whether they were real. I remembered that when I spoke to her, her eyes hadn't moved at all, so they were probably glass or lucite of some kind.

We sat silently for a long time before I finally spoke. "Rob?"

She jumped.

"I'm sorry," I said. "Were you sleeping?"

She smiled and whispered, "I don't know." I thought about that and wondered how you tell if you're awake or asleep when you can't see. When dark is all the time.

"Were you dreaming?" I asked.

She shook her head slightly. "I don't know."

"You mean you can't remember?" I asked, pushing her damp black curls off her forehead.

"No," she explained. "I mean I don't know. I don't dream the way you do. I *can't* dream like you do."

"I'm not sure I understand," I told her.

"Well," Robin said, looking very thoughtful, "you know how when you dream, you *picture* a table?"

"Yes."

"Well, when I dream, I have to picture *touching* that table; that's what I 'see.'"

"You never have seen?" I asked her.

"No, not that I remember," she answered, rubbing one of her eyelids roughly. "They had to remove both my eyes when I was about a year old because of retinal blastoma."

Retinal blastoma is a congenital malignant tumor of the eyes. It can occur in one or both eyes and is present at birth, though usually not discovered until later.

After listening to Robin talk for a while longer, I realized how little understanding I had of blind people. Because blindness had never touched me personally, I had never even thought about their problems. I wanted to be able to understand more so that I could be more help.

I turned toward Robin and said, "I never knew a blind person well." I hesitated before adding, "I know this is a hell of a time to ask, but if I teach you everything you want to know about medicine, would you teach me about blind people?"

Robin got a funny, amused expression again. The corners of her mouth turned up and then she shook her head.

"Why are you laughing at me now?" I asked. She had quite a sense of humor for a girl who was dying.

"Well," she said very slowly, obviously trying to control her laughter, "I'll do my best to teach you anything I can about *me,* and some of that will apply to other blind people. Not all of it will."

Then I started to laugh. My question was like asking a black person what black people were like, as though all of them were the same. What a sophisticate! Luckily Robin was very good-natured about it.

She started to doze but was having trouble breathing; she kept clearing her throat. Her eyes were wide open.

I sat looking at her face, staring. Somehow, being able to look at her for as long as I liked without having to worry about her looking back and feeling self-conscious really pleased me. She had very fine smooth skin, pale, and freckles running across her cheeks over her small ski-jump nose. Her black eyebrows were very full, with scattered weeds between, and there were curly, long, thick lashes over those clear blue eyes. I could see the crinkles around her eyes and study the fine little hairs on her upper lip. Her full lips were parted slightly, showing perfectly white capped teeth. She had a cleft in her chin. Her mass of dark curly hair was rumpled, like Niki's when she first woke up in the morning. Robin was very nice to look at.

Then I saw her neck. Above the soft white hospital gown there were several radiation squares of red magic marker, barbed wire setting claim, the skin inside as dark and cracked as parched earth.

I was getting stiff, so I tried to move my arm, loosening my grip on Robin's hand. Startled, she asked anxiously, "Where are you going?"

"Nowhere," I said. "Just trying to get more comfortable."

"Whew!" she said, smiling. "I'm glad. I'm afraid of the dark."

Oh *Jezuss!* I thought.

Robin started to grimace and breathe with a wheeze as though through a tightened drawstring.

"Do you want me to help you turn?" I asked, standing.

"Okay," she whispered, and I put my hands under her butt and helped her slide onto her side. Her belly was enormous, and the weight of it as I turned her made her want to vomit. I lifted her head for a few minutes and as soon as she got settled she felt better.

"Could you rub my back?" she asked. "Down low?"

I took the lotion out of the bedside stand and poured it onto my hands to try to warm it before I touched her. Then I rubbed her back gently.

"Oh," she murmured, "that's great." She coughed, cleared her throat and continued, "This reminds me of the time when I worked in the school for retarded children. I was sitting in the nursing station, when an aide whom I had been looking for came over to me.

I asked her where she had been and she answered, 'I was giving two of the kids back rubs for their bruises.' 'Bruises?' I said. I was horrified. 'Where did they get bruises?' The aide laughed at me and said, 'Not for the bruises on the outside, honey, I was talking about the bruises on the inside.'" Robin smiled as she remembered. I wiped her back with the towel, powdered her and placed a pillow behind her back for support. Then I covered her and walked around the bed to sit again. She reached out for my hand and, holding it tightly, fell asleep. It was spooky to see her sleeping with her eyes wide open.

I stared at her body in profile. Robin looked like so many of the young girls I had taken care of on Obstetrics. Girls whose bellies held babies, not tumors. What a shit life this kid's had, I thought.

I reached with my free hand for the chart, which I had placed on the radiator, and pored through her history. Robin was right. It had been retinal blastoma, at one year old; bilateral enucleation–both eyes removed. I continued to read. Robin had received a bachelor's degree in liberal arts from Oneonta College, and then a master's degree in special education. She had taught the handicapped for a nonprofit organization as a volunteer, and currently she worked teaching English as a second language to foreign students. Brother, I thought, talk about doing a lot with a limited life. . .

As Robin grabbed for me with her other hand, I noticed for the first time a small diamond ring on her left hand. "Teri," she said, laboring to talk, "could I have something for the pain?"

I ran out and got her Dilaudid, and after I gave the injection I rubbed her back, waiting for the medicine to start working. Then I began playing with her hair, petting and stroking her, wondering if she minded all that touching. It's the Italian in me, the mother in me, that makes me do it, but if I'm sick and anyone touches *me* I cringe. As though in answer to my unspoken question, Robin whispered, "Oh. . . that feels so good."

I tried to distract her from her pain with "Hey, kiddo, I see you're engaged."

"Yes," she said, smiling weakly. "Three months ago, to the most wonderful man in the world."

"Oh God, Robin, does that sound soupy," I teased her.

"Really," she said, "he is. Wait until you meet him, you'll see.

We're supposed to get married next . . ." She took a deep breath and then turned her head away. "Next month."

She kept dozing fitfully, in and out of a medicated sleep. I noticed some uncoordinated, jerking movements of her arms and head; occasionally, she raised her eyebrows and I could hear a muffled sob.

"Rob?" I whispered, but still I startled her and she jumped again. "You were crying. Can I do anything?"

"I don't remember crying," she said softly, rubbing her eyes. "I must have been asleep."

"I've been looking at you," I told her. "You have very pretty skin."

"I do?" she said, obviously pleased. "What is it like?"

"It's smooth and light, with freckles," I told her.

She laughed, her nose wrinkling as she asked, "What are freckles?"

"Brown spots," I said.

Robin laughed again. "What are spots? What is brown?"

I realized that she was keeping her part of the bargain and trying to teach me about blind people. "Oh God," I said, "this is going to be impossible. How can I describe what brown is?"

Patiently, she said, "Just tell me how it *feels.*"

I sat back in the chair and closed my eyes, repeating over and over, "Brown . . . brown . . . Oh, I know: like the earth, only not in winter–in summer.

As though I had made things perfectly clear, she smiled and said, "You mean like a warm puppy?"

"Sort of."

"Then I'm glad about the freckles."

She explained there was a book for children called *Hailstones and Halibut Bones,* which describes what each of the colors feels like. "It's a seeing children's book," she offered, "so you can read it."

"Hey, Rob?" I said, interested now. "Could you have someone bring in a braille book so I can see it?" She nodded and promised she would.

As I watched her, she started to scratch herself all over. Pain medicine can sometimes cause itching, but when she asked, "What's wrong with me now?" I had to get her back for her teasing about freckles and brown, so I said, "Maybe you have fleas."

Her face registered that she knew what I was doing, and she laughed as she said, "Then maybe we'll have to spray me with something or get me a flea collar."

"No doubt," I said. I put some cool washcloths over the itchiest parts to try to make her more comfortable

Suddenly she winced and grabbed her right side. "Please turn me again," she whimpered. She vomited from the weight of her belly, and I held her head up until it subsided. "Why does it hurt so much?" she asked weakly.

"Do you want me to call the doctor for more pain medicine?"

"No, not yet," she said. "Let's give it a few more minutes." Then, exasperated, she asked, "Isn't there anything else we can do?"

I felt helpless when Robin started to cry with a child's broken-hearted sobs, saying, "You don't know how frustrated I get . . . or how scared."

I bent down and kissed her forehead. "Hey, kiddo," I whispered, "I wouldn't have made it this far. I'm ninety percent chicken."

"Well," she said, sniffing and trying to smile, "you've got a ten percent edge on me."

I sat down again and hung on to her hand. She mumbled thanks, then her breathing got easier and she was finally asleep.

I medicated her twice more during the night, not waiting until she complained, and before I left in the morning I gave her a bed bath and promised her I'd be back.

The second night I went in to take care of Robin, a large index card was taped to the front of her chart. In heavy definitive script was written: "Under *no* circumstances is the patient to be told of her diagnosis or prognosis." It was such an archaic dictate that had I not cared so much for Robin I would have turned around and walked away. It had been years since my professional hands had been so tied.

When I walked into Robin's room, I could see that she was upset. "How did it go today, Rob?" I asked, walking over to her bed.

At first she tried to keep a stiff upper lip with a lot of conversation about how her guests talked about her wedding all day. When I didn't respond, her upper lip quivered and she asked, "What do *you* think about my wedding?"

I walked around behind her and began to rub her back slowly. I didn't want to lie to her, because I was afraid that if she really wanted to discuss what she felt, my pretending would shut her off. And yet for the first time I wondered whether or not there was any purpose in telling her and destroying her hope. I believed patients had the right to know, I believed she should have the opportunity to talk about her dying to someone– but for once I wasn't sure it should be me.

"What do you think about the colors they should wear?" she pushed.

When I still didn't answer, she started to cry. "Why are they lying to me?"

I paused for a long time before I walked around the bed and sat in front of her. "I don't think they're lying to you, Rob. I think sometimes people want to believe something so hard that they convince themselves that what they want to believe is true."

She looked thoughtful, as though trying to understand. "You're probably right," she said, frowning. "They wouldn't deliberately lie to me; they just don't know." She paused and bit her lip, then added, "It scares me, though, when they talk like that . . . it makes me feel crazy."

I pushed her curls off her forehead. "Sometimes the truth is so painful . . . that you try to protect yourself from knowing."

"Who can I ask if I really want to know?" she asked softly.

I remembered the note on the chart and recognized the writing as her doctor's. "You can ask Dr. King if you need more information," I said, feeling as though I was copping out. But I wanted to give him the benefit of the doubt; maybe he wanted to be the one to discuss it with her.

Robin lay quiet for a while before she told me, "It was very hard after the operation on my thigh when Dr. King removed the lesion that he said was cancer . . . but then he said there were good results from that kind of surgery. When I asked him if it could come back, he said, 'You could get run over by a car tomorrow.'" Robin hesitated before she added, "And because that's what I wanted to believe, that's all I heard."

I was hoping that if Robin asked him he'd come up with something a little better this time. But she didn't want to let me off the hook yet. "What's really wrong with me, Teri?" And then with a catch in her voice, "Will I ever get well?"

I wanted to grab her and hold her and cry with her. I wanted to yell with her and scream about how unjust it was. I wanted to curse God and medicine . . . but all I said was, "I don't know, Robin. So often when it seems impossible for people to get well, they do. . . ." And then, with a lump in my throat that made it hard to talk, "And sometimes they don't. . ."

Robin nodded slowly, then turned her face away. After long minutes, she slept.

The following night when I came in, I knocked gently, not knowing whether she was asleep. She waved, so I walked over and kissed her hello.

"Hi," she said quietly. Her eyes were closed. "I hope you don't mind, but I had one of the nurses take my eyes out. They're in a paper cup in the bedstand. I hope it doesn't frighten you, but they were terribly uncomfortable."

"Don't be silly," I said, tousling her hair, but truthfully I was a bit squeamish about it, as I was about false teeth.

"Sit down and hold my hand, Teri," she said, struggling again to try to get comfortable. "I've just had pain medicine, but it hasn't started to work yet."

I dropped my stuff next to the chair and sat. "And was today better for you?" I asked.

"Oh, it went pretty well," she said in a hoarse voice, clearing her throat almost constantly. "Justin, my fiance, called me, and so did his mother. I never met her and only spoke to her a few times, but she invited me over to dinner when I get out. . . ." She took a deep breath and brushed a piece of hair off her cheek. "That was really nice of her, wasn't it?"

"Yes," I said, playing with her fingers.

But suddenly, in a voice full of frustration, she stormed, "Sometimes I think I'm never going to get out of the hospital . . . that

I really won't get well." She turned her face toward me and asked, "What *is* this I have? What's making it so hard for me to breathe?"

"What do *you* think?" I asked, trying to figure out how much information she had, and how much more she would need to keep her comfortable without destroying all her hope. At this point I wasn't trying to withhold information; my theory was much more like not explaining *everything* about sexual intercourse to a kid who asks where babies come from. They don't need to know it and often they don't want to. Too much information is sometimes frightening, and I have always found that a patient will ask *specific* questions as long as they don't feel placated or lied to.

"Well," Robin began, "when my sister and I went to see Disneyland last year . . . it was fantastic–I began having trouble breathing. We went to an emergency room, where they told me I had a pinched nerve. We had to come home earlier than we planned. After that the doctors here said I had bronchitis or something."

She shook her head and then asked for some apple juice.

Afterward she said, "Please sit next to me and hold my hand. I feel different tonight . . . weird."

"Weird how?" I asked, sitting close.

"Restless . . . uncomfortable. But that's not it. I can't explain," she said sadly, and then wrinkled up her face as though she was going to cry again. "What's really wrong?" she asked aloud.

"Are you asking me why you have so much pain?" I said, choking on the note taped to her chart; still hoping Dr. King would speak to her– and desperately missing Beth Shalom.

She nodded. "Yes, and why is my belly all swollen?"

"The swelling is from the fluid and also from some of the air trapped in your intestines. Because you can't move well, gas builds, and when you're unable to release it, it forms pockets. The pain medicine slows down intestinal activity, which makes it worse." I wet a washcloth with cold water and placed it on Robin's forehead. "Tomorrow we can ask Dr. King to take some of the fluid out of your belly, and for the gas maybe he can drop a tube down your nose," I said softly.

"Okay," she said. Then she went on hesitantly, "But there's something else wrong. . ."

"What are you trying to tell me, Rob?" I asked. "What do you feel is wrong with you?"

"Well," she whispered, shutting her eyelids tightly, "I'd like to think it's from the radiation, because then I can pretend that as soon as it's over. . . the symptoms will be gone." She looked apologetic when she added, "It gives me hope."

"Is the pain medicine you're getting enough to take care of your pain?" I asked.

"Yes," she said, screwing up her face again, "but I'm nervous or something."

"How about some Valium between the pain shots?" I asked.

"That would be good," she said. "I'd like to be able to relax a little more."

"Done!" I said, patting her hand. "I'll go get an order for the Valium, and after I give it we can talk until you can fall asleep." I found myself doing a lot more of the patting, huggy, kissy stuff because I couldn't wink or smile to reassure her.

She stopped me by grabbing my uniform and said, "I'm glad I have you to help me, and I'm glad you're not afraid."

After her shot, I sat in my usual position and held her hand. She was still fidgety, turning and twisting and trying hard to breathe. Short quick breaths.

"Hey, kid," I said. "How about a special game?" As long as we couldn't come right out and talk about all the things in her life that she hadn't done that she would have liked to, as long as she couldn't cry for herself or mourn straight out, I wanted to give her a chance to talk about her dreams in the least threatening way.

"What kind of a game?" she asked, interested but wary.

"A let's pretend game," I said. "Let's pretend that we were told, each of us, that we only had a year to live, and we could do anything we wanted during that time. What would we do?"

She put her fingers up to her lips, nodded and said, "Okay, who goes first?"

"You can go first," I said, and began filing one of her fingernails to keep her from scratching herself.

"Let's travel," she said, wrinkling her nose and forehead, thinking.

"Where to, Captain?" I asked.

"Naturally, Hawaii first," she said, smiling now.

"Why Hawaii?" I asked. "And why naturally?"

"Because of the colors, silly. The scenery is beautiful," she drawled, teasing me. "Anyway, I love the music and the bird sounds."

"Okay," I said. "Hawaii it is."

She looked worried for a moment and then asked, "Can I take Justin? And some of my students?"

"How many?" I asked.

"Six," she said. "It's not going to be too crowded, is it?"

"It is obvious to me, my dear Rob, that you have had little if any experience with wish thinks," I said, with pomposity. "You may bring whomever you like and we will just wish for a larger boat."

"Oh, good." She smiled and asked, "I can have everything I want?"

"Certainly," I answered.

Good," she said again, scratching her nose. "Then you can be my guide and take me places where I wouldn't be able to go alone. You can describe things to me that I couldn't see without you."

"Okay."

"And then we can stop in Japan. Some of my students were Japanese, and I promised if I ever got to Japan I would visit them and have lunch—" She started to bite her bottom lip, and then in a soft, sad voice she said, "Oh. . . I wanted so much to see Japan. . ."

"Well," I said, trying to keep her from crying, "I'll tell you what I'm gonna do. I'll split my eyes with you and we can travel together. You can have the left and I'll keep the right." Even in a wish think, I wasn't willing to give her both, and apparently neither of us thought it possible for her to ask for eyes of her own.

"Thank you very much," she said, smiling, and then, "I'm sorry, I never asked who you wanted to bring."

"That's all right," I said, shifting my weight in the chair. I was getting stiff again. "I'll just come with you."

"Well," she said, sighing, "I'm tired of traveling for now."

"Sleepy?" I asked, standing up and stretching. My eyes were getting tired in the dimly lit room.

She shook her head and asked, "What now? Let's talk more."

"Right," I said. "What was the most phenomenally happy moment of your entire life? Assuming, of course, that you can remember that right off the bat?"

"I can," she said, in a voice that goes with clapping. She let go of my hand, held her left hand with her right and showed her ring. "The day I got engaged to Justin was the happiest time of my whole life."

We didn't talk anymore for the rest of the night. Between the Valium and the Dilaudid, she was zonked. In the morning, as I kissed her goodbye, she reached up, touched me and said only, "Tonight?"

The last time I took care of Robin, I worked the day shift. I had called Erin and asked her to cover nights, explaining that Mrs. Dayton was finding it difficult to get a good evening nurse. If Erin and I worked twelve-hour shifts Robin would be covered. Erin was still great that way. Even though we saw each other infrequently, she was there whenever I needed her.

When I came in that morning, Robin was sound asleep and immaculate-looking. She smelled delicious, and I was sure Erin had given one of her fabulous three-hour bed baths. Everything was perfect.

After Erin gave me report, we chatted about our kids until Robin started to twist and fidget restlessly. Then it took both of us, holding the sheet like a hammock, to turn Robin on her side. Even with the Dilaudid and Valium every two hours, Robin's belly was so swollen, and all her bones were so sensitive, that it was still very painful for her to be moved. She didn't speak at all that morning. Erin mentioned, just before she left, that Justin was supposed to visit about noon.

I had been taking care of Robin for five days now, and because I had been working nights I had never yet met Justin. I was paging through a large braille *Life* magazine, which Robin had asked her mother to bring, when Justin walked in. I was so engrossed, so amazed that braille was an entire code rather than just raised letters, that I didn't hear him until he was standing at the foot of her bed.

He was short, with stocky build, straight light hair over a very high forehead, deep hollowed eyes . . . and a cane. Obviously blind. Robin and I had never spoken about whether he was a seeing or nonseeing person, yet somehow it had never occurred to me that he was blind.

As I pushed back my chair to get up, Justin switched his cane from one hand to the other and introduced himself. "You must be Teri," he said. He had a melodious voice and a very sweet smile. He turned toward Robin's bed and greeted her, "Hi, my pretty." When she didn't answer, he looked concerned.

"I just medicated her again," I reassured him. "That's probably why she's not speaking. . . ." But the truth was that she had been getting less and less responsive for hours.

Justin groped his way along the side of Robin's bed and sat in the chair I had pulled up for him. He leaned over and began to speak in slow, soothing, loving whispers. And as he did, he stroked Robin's entire body, with none of the self-consciousness a seeing person would have. He ran his hands over her face, down over her breasts and belly: a gesture so intimate, but so nonsexual, that I wanted to fade into the woodwork so that they could be alone. As he continued to touch her from head to foot, big silent tears ran down his face.

"I've missed you," he told her. "I've taken the mail in, and I threw the garbage out when I stopped at the apartment." When she didn't respond, Justin pulled back and sighed deeply, his arms falling to his sides.

After several minutes of silence, I walked over to him, put my hand on his shoulder and asked, "Would you like to come outside and talk?"

"Yes," he answered softly. "Thank you very much." I took him by the arm and he hooked his cane over Robin's bed rail, leaving it there.

In the lounge, Justin and I sat across from each other, he in a blue vinyl high-back armchair, and I on the flowered couch. He leaned over with his elbows on his knees, shaking his head.

"She's not going to beat it, is she?" he asked, without lifting his head.

"No," I said softly. I leaned toward him, wanting to touch him, wanting to do something to comfort him . . . but he seemed so pained, so fragile, that I was afraid if I laid a hand on him he would crumble.

"God!" he said, his voice hollow. "I find that so hard to believe. She's beat everything else. She went to Disneyland . . she was on the dean's list . . . she lives by *herself* . . . she's got a wonderful job that she loves . . ." He put his hand over his eyes and said quietly, "You know, Teri, when I first met Robin two years ago, I was crazy about her. I took her number and put it in my pocket that first night. When I got home, I sat for a long time thinking about her. Suddenly I got this awful feeling that something terrible was going to happen to her, and so I didn't call her. Then, just six months ago, I met her again–at a dance. We talked, and when I found out all she had accomplished, all that she had conquered, I felt that nothing could happen to her even if I loved her. I felt we had a real chance. That's when I asked her out, and three months ago we were engaged. . ." He shook his head again. "I just can't believe it. . ."

He started to cry quietly. "She's a magnificent person, you know. I couldn't believe it when she told me she cared about me."

I reached over and put my hand on his arm. "If it's any comfort at all," I said, "the other night, when I asked her to pinpoint the most phenomenal moment of her entire life, she said it was the moment she got engaged to you."

He tried to smile, but his voice cracked when he told me, "It changed my life, being loved by someone as special as Robin."

"What are you going to do?" I asked.

"After Robin dies?" he asked, looking up.

"Yes," I said quietly.

He sat straight up in the chair, held tight to each of his armrests, took a deep breath, and said, in the most dignified voice I have ever heard, "It's a League rule . . . I'll bounce back."

That night Erin called to tell me Robin had died. I wrapped myself in a blanket and stayed on the couch; I couldn't sleep and I didn't want to be in my bedroom alone. Greg and the kids brought me food and I could hardly talk to them. All I wanted to do was hide. Finally, after two days, Spinner reminded me, "Today's Niki's eighteenth birthday, Mom."

Niki moved out the day after she turned eighteen. I wasn't home when she came to get her stuff; I was at Robin's funeral service.

When I came home, I looked at Niki's half empty-room, clothes thrown all over the floor, and tried to decide how I felt. Very grown-up, I decided. Not her . . . Me.

Well, she'll probably come around to finish cleaning up tomorrow, I thought; and somehow all that mess was comforting.

Greg and Spinner seemed very upset that Niki had left. I really didn't feel that bad. It would certainly relieve some of the tension between Greg and me, and I was happy that she would have a chance to live by her rules, not Greg's. Besides, by the time I was eighteen I had been married, and I had survived. And Robin, who had been not much older, and had done everything right, hadn't survived. Niki was just moving in with Lynch–it wasn't fatal.

After supper, because Greg was raging and Spinner was sulking, I went into my bedroom. I lay there for a long time, just thinking, before there was a knock at my door.

"Hi, Mom," Niki said as she opened the door, "I'm here for closure." She kissed me and sat on the bed. "I thought you'd feel bad if I left and you hadn't had the chance to say whatever you wanted to me," she explained. "You know, sort of finish warning me and stuff." She smiled sweetly, but I knew she was teasing me.

"Thanks, honey," I said. And as I looked at her I realized how pretty and grown-up she was–and how much I loved her. I loved her intelligence, her sense of humor, and her zest for living. "I'll miss you," I said, smiling. "And I have no new warnings. Just remember, never go out of your way to hurt anyone, but trust yourself and try to do what makes you happy."

She leaned over and we hugged each other. Suddenly I wanted her to know how much I respected her sense of adventure and how much I wanted her life to go well.

I got out of bed and walked to my closet. There, heaped in the corner, was the uniform I had worn the last day I had taken care of Robin. I rummaged through it, and as I did I could hear Mr. Marcus' voice say, "Katie wanted life on her terms, too." I pulled my little elephant out of the pocket and walked back over to the bed. I handed it to Niki. She smiled but looked puzzled. "What's this for, Mom?"

"It's a good-luck charm, kiddo," I said, and bent to kiss her. "I want you to have it."

CHAPTER 27

It was a dark, winding road, and I almost passed the driveway.

It was hidden between two massive weeping willows, the leaves and branches forming a gauzy curtain that slid across my windshield as I pulled in.

The house was a very large split-level, and the first thing I noticed was that there was a light shining from every window. It looked like a jack-o'lantern. They must be frightened, I thought as I walked to the front door.

Before I had a chance to knock or ring the bell, the door was yanked open and I stood facing a distraught looking middle-aged man. He was tall, with longish pepper-and-salt hair. He wore a white terry-cloth robe and was barefoot.

"Hello," he said quickly. "I'm glad you're here. My wife is upstairs, she's having an attack." He ran his fingers roughly through his hair and motioned toward the stairs.

I dropped my bag at the door and ran up the stairs, removing my sweater on the way. I threw it over the wrought iron-railing as we made a left into a very large bedroom.

The woman looked nothing like what I expected. She had short curly auburn hair, very fine features, and blue eyes. She wasn't thin or emaciated. Whenever I hear "terminal cancer," I think of someone ravaged; she didn't really look sick.

The only information I had gotten from Mrs. Dayton was that she desperately needed a nurse to cover a woman with terminal cancer.

"Why me?" I asked. It was only five days after Robin had died, and I had asked not to be called until I had more time to recover. Mrs. Dayton usually respected my requests.

"Well," she said sweetly, softly, "they're Italian."

"I don't get it," I said, trying to stall. I needed the money, but I was exhausted.

"They're such wonderful people," Mrs. Dayton said, recovering her natural volume. "I just meant that at a time like this. . . they might be more comfortable with one of their own."

Go on, Mrs. Dayton, I thought, appeal to my sense of family. Make me feel as though I'm abandoning a relative. That's one way to get me out of my nightgown and out into the cold dark night. I hated to admit it, but she had a point. Generally, it is better to match a nurse and a patient with the same cultural background. An Italian nurse finds it easier to understand when an entire family, dressed in black, descends weeping on a patient who has had a hernia repaired. She doesn't consider it an overreaction, she doesn't report that the family is being over emotional. She knows they're okay. A German nurse has a much harder time getting through the din.

"Okay," I said wearily. "What's the name and what's the hospital?"

She faltered for a minute, and I knew that meant trouble

"The name is Vitale and–" she tried to slide this past me by lowering her voice– "it's a home case."

"Oh Jesus," I moaned. For as long as I'd worked for the registry, Mrs. Dayton had known I hated to do home cases. I liked the support I got from the other nurses in a hospital setting, and the emergency equipment that was available. And again: it protected me from too much involvement. I had seldom done home cases, and whenever I had, my own family lost me.

I took a deep breath. "What's the address?"

After she gave me instructions, she added, "The patient's name is Jennifer and the husband is Steven."

"Jennifer?" I asked. "Jennifer, for an Italian?"

"Oh no," she said. "I think she's German."

"Well, then, why would *she* want an Italian nurse?" I asked, puzzled.

"She married him, didn't she?" Mrs. Dayton answered.

I stopped trying to figure Mrs. Dayton out. All I knew was that now I was going to have to be cool instead of warm, or I'd turn the poor woman off instantly.

"Who else is on the case?" I asked.

"They only want a night nurse," Mrs. Dayton answered quickly. Then she hung up.

Terrific, I thought as I ran to get dressed. No one to share the responsibility with. I'd have to have Erin cover on my nights off so that we could share observations. It was safer for the patient that way.

Jennifer was sitting on the edge of the bed with her head in her hands, rocking gently back and forth. I instantly forgot that I didn't want to be there. I walked over and put my hand on her head as I asked, "Where's the pain?"

She didn't uncover her face and couldn't answer. I knelt in front of her and repeated, "Is it pain? Or discomfort somewhere?" She just shrugged and whimpered.

Suddenly I felt ridiculous. What the hell difference does it make why she's suffering, I thought, ask questions later. I moved quickly toward the long dresser, where I had noticed a bottle of morphine. I read the label for dosage, drew up an injection and went back to her. As I lifted her legs into the bed, I said, "Turn over," and before she had a chance to object I pulled down her pajama bottoms and gave her the shot.

I waited a few minutes until I could see her relax, then I turned to her husband, who was nervously fidgeting. "Hi," I said, "my name is Teri Daley." When Jennifer opened her eyes, I smiled at her and said, "I'm going to be your nurse."

"Hi, Teri," she said, and smiled weakly. The pain or whatever it had been was almost gone. Her brow was no longer wrinkled and the fingers on her hand had begun to unclench.

"Steven," Mr. Vitale said absently, holding out his hand. He was still glancing toward his wife, looking concerned.

"Feeling better?" I asked Jennifer.

"Yes," she said. "It wasn't really pain . . . I can't describe it . . ." But whatever it was, I knew the morphine had helped, because soon her eyes closed and she began to doze.

After Steven took me through the house and showed me where

all the supplies were, we started downstairs again.

We sat on a blue couch in the large living room; from where we were we could hear Jennifer easily. Steven spoke quietly so that she couldn't hear us.

"She was in the hospital over four weeks," he said. "It was terrible to have to leave her there every night."

"Why was she admitted?" I asked, trying to get some kind of history. I was at a disadvantage without a chart.

"She couldn't breathe," he said as he pulled a small cigarillo out of his pocket and started to chew on it. "They said it was bronchitis . . . but maybe it was the cancer. . ." He sat with furrowed brow and a look of deep concentration. "Anyway, one night she started to cough–a dry hacking cough–then she turned an awful color. When I called the doctor, he said to bring her right to the hospital. . ." Steven leaned toward me. "How does my wife look to you?" he asked.

"Her color is good. And her lips and fingertips are pink, not blue," I told him, trying to explain how I evaluated her condition. I wanted to be honest, but I didn't want to give him any false hope. I kept wondering where Mrs. Dayton had gotten her information. "I don't hear a wheeze, but then I haven't listened with a stethoscope yet, so I can't really be sure."

"What was that attack tonight?" he asked, obviously worried.

"I don't know," I answered. "Maybe she's a little nervous her first night home." From upstairs I could hear Jennifer's even breathing.

"Where did the cancer start?" I asked.

"Two years ago she had a mastectomy," he explained sadly. "She hated that. Then she used to take pills at home–chemotherapy pills. She took them faithfully."

Suddenly we heard her call from upstairs. We both ran up. Jennifer was sitting on the edge of the bed, looking more alert. She was smoothing her hair with her right hand while trying to balance her weight on the left. "I have to go to the bathroom," she said quietly as I walked over to her. I took her left arm; Steven was already at her other side holding her around the waist. When she stood, she was a lot taller than she looked lying down–much taller than I. We walked her slowly into the bathroom, and though she never complained of pain, her whole body trembled with effort.

In the bathroom, it took both Steven and me to turn Jennifer around slowly. I pulled down her pajama bottoms, and she reached up and put her arms around his neck while he lowered her gently onto the seat. Steven walked back into the bedroom, and I sat on the tub across from her and waited, looking up at the cobwebs on the glass chandelier. I can't believe the things I notice when I'm nervous. And why was I nervous? Because it was my first night in a strange house . . . with strangers. Jennifer was in pain, I could see her knees shaking as she leaned on them, and I didn't know any more than the patient for a change, so I wasn't sure what to watch for.

If it was her lungs, then I should be checking her respirations more closely. If it had gotten to her bones, then I should be very careful whenever I moved her–bone cancer cracks bones like brittle chalk. On the other hand, if it had hit her brain, I should be watching for seizures . . .

And so, because I didn't know what to watch for, I had to watch for everything. I always get first-night jitters. By the second night I feel competent, and by the third night I'm so confident that nothing can touch me or my patients. But in twelve years I'd never gotten comfortable with first nights.

When Jennifer said, "I'm ready to go back," Steve was back in before I had to call him. I watched him as he lifted his wife off the toilet, his hands on her naked buttocks, raising her gently but firmly. He held her as she leaned against his body, and walked her very slowly toward the bed. Each step took a very long time. But she was determined to walk back, and he was determined to help her.

Steve lowered Jennifer onto the bed carefully, as though he was afraid she would break. She looked up at him smiling, a shy radiant smile, and said to me, "He's got a special grip– a very special grip." He bent down and lifted her legs onto the bed, then covered her with the sheet. "Thanks, honey," she whispered, and then closed her eyes tiredly.

The following night, after Steve and I were sure Jennifer had fallen asleep, we went downstairs into the kitchen. I wanted a cup of tea. He wanted to talk. I put the tarnished copper kettle on the stove and turned the knob only slightly. I wanted it to take a long time for the water to boil.

Steve sat at the kitchen table with a can of soda. "They told me two months ago, at the big cancer center in New York, that my wife only had a couple of months left . . . she doesn't look that bad, does she?" he asked hopefully.

"Not to me," I said, sitting across the table from him, "but there's really no way to tell. I mean I don't think the cancer will kill her in that short a time . . . but you have to remember that her lungs are bad . . . and her resistance is low because of the chemotherapy." I didn't want to seem too clinical, but I was worried about Steve building up false hopes. I had called her doctor before I got there, and he had told me that Jennifer's cancer had even gotten to her bones. It had metastasized through her whole body. I felt that if Steve could accept her death a little at a time it might be easier for him.

Suddenly he looked upset. "If she asks me if she's going to die, I won't tell her. . ." he said adamantly.

"Why?" I asked.

"All our lives," he said quietly, "I've always been here to reassure her. We've had one of the best marriages going. I've always told her, 'It will be fine,' and then I've worked my ass off making it fine."

I just nodded as Steve toyed with his soda can. He smiled weakly and continued, "I've always been able to pull it off so far; come off as some kind of hero, you know. . . ." He wiped his eyes roughly. "That's what she needs from me, reassurance. And that's what I'll give her, even if I have to lie."

I put my hand on his arm. "Feels lousy," I said, "not being able to make it better, doesn't it? After all the years you protected her and kept things from hurting her . . . and now, the biggest thing, the thing that really matters and you're helpless."

I felt bad for Steve, worse than I did for Jennifer. I could give her Valium and morphine; he had to go it cold turkey.

During the next couple of weeks, I taught Steve how to give Jennifer her pain injections. She didn't want nurses on the other shifts, and he insisted on doing most of the care himself. The first time he stood in front of her, looking over his glasses and measuring the morphine, his hands shook so badly that I teased her, "Jennifer, are you going to trust this man to give you a shot?"

She smiled at me, then looked fondly at him when she said, "I've trusted him for thirty years, makes no sense to stop trusting him now."

Later that night was the only time I ever saw her look really sad. She told me, "I wish I could have seen my sisters in Europe one more time."

One of the nights Erin relieved me, she called me in the morning to give a report.

"The first thing Jennifer said to me," she said, laughing, "was, 'What kind of a name is Erin Shapiro for a girl with a brogue?'"

"What did you tell her?" I asked. Everyone always teased Erin about her name.

"The same kind of name as Jennifer Vitale," she answered.

One morning Erin asked me seriously, "You know who the real patient in that house is, don't you?"

"What do you mean?"

"Steve," she said. "Every night, when he lies next to Jennifer in that bed, all the while she sleeps he stays awake and stares at the ceiling. Last night he was up again eating Gelusil and taking nitroglycerin."

"Yes," I told her, "I know. I tried to get him to sleep in the other room, but he said that Jennifer feels safer with him right there. I think the only thing we can do is keep telling him he's doing all he can."

"I just hope nothing happens to her while he's there alone with her," Erin said.

"I'm sure it won't," I told her quickly. "I think maybe we can keep her alive till Thanksgiving."

"Do you?" Erin said, concerned. "That's months away. Teri, she's dying. You know that with someone like Jennifer you can't even count on tomorrow."

But Jennifer seemed to be getting stronger. She was able to eat more, and several times when I came to work she was sitting up in bed reading, watching TV or knitting.

One night when I walked into the room she was working on a long green and white article. She looked up and smiled. A very pretty smile with even white teeth.

"What are you knitting?" I asked as I pulled a chair next to the bed.

"I don't know yet," she said quietly. When I looked puzzled, she explained, "Whenever I have a problem, I knit as I think. I knit and think and consider. Actually, I knit until I solve the problem." She straightened herself in bed and I fluffed up her pillows. She started to laugh as she told me, "I once knitted a six foot scarf. Every time I thought I was finished, there was something else to consider . . ."

"And if you can't solve the problem?" I asked.

"Then I don't finish what I'm knitting . . . ," she said softly.

Later, after she had fallen asleep, Steve and I sat downstairs again and talked. "She seems to be getting stronger, doesn't she?" he asked, pacing around the living room. "Do you think I should take her to another doctor? Try something else?" He looked upset again. I was sure it was because he had no idea what to adjust to. Was Jennifer dying or was she getting better?

That morning when I talked to Erin I told her how great Jennifer had looked.

"Looks are deceiving," Erin said. "You're not denying that she's terminal, are you, Teri?"

"Hey, Erin," I said irritably, "don't be such a nut."

The following night, Jennifer had another attack. Steve and I were downstairs when we heard a noise that made us both jump. We ran up and found Jennifer sitting, rocking back and forth.

"What is it?" I asked, kneeling in front of her.

"It's not pain," she cried. "It's something else." She looked puzzled. "I don't know what it is, but somethings not right. . ."

I medicated her with morphine and sat holding her hand until she fell asleep. Steve lay next to her, staring at the ceiling.

Later, during the night, I got her up to go to the bathroom. She looked pained as we walked back, but she didn't complain.

I watched as she got into bed and lay down, her back toward me. For the first time, I noticed the graying roots through her auburn hair and how bent her back was. She turned her head and looked over her shoulder at me. Her blue eyes were pale and I noticed dark circles underneath as she waved me away. Impulsively, I bent and kissed her cheek; it was very soft.

The next morning, I was so sound asleep that Greg had to shake me to tell me, "Steve's on the phone. He sounds very upset."

I tried to clear the cobwebs from my brain. "Hello," I said.

Steve sounded hysterical. "Something terrible is happening, Teri. Jennifer's eyes are rolling back in her head."

"Where is she?" I asked, instantly awake.

"In the bathroom. What should I do?"

"Get her onto the floor," I said, assuming she was having a seizure. "Or get her into bed if you can. I'll be there right away."

"Should I give her a shot?" Steve asked, his voice trembling.

"No, don't give her anything. And if anything else happens before I get there, call Emergency," I said, throwing on my jeans.

The whole ride there was terrible. Though Greg and I were speeding, I knew Jennifer would be dead by the time we arrived, no matter how fast we drove.

When Greg dropped me off there were several police cars in the driveway. I rushed into the house, almost falling over the front bushes on the way, then up the stairs and into Jennifer's room.

The only thing I saw was Jennifer's still white body lying on the bed.

I knew– but still I put the blood-pressure cuff on her arm and listened to the sound of her beatless heart with my stethoscope, straining to hear . . . knowing I wouldn't . . . still hoping I was wrong.

She was *just* dead. So newly dead that I wanted to scream her back . . . shake her back . . . hug and kiss her back . . . slap her back. I wanted to get into bed and warm her already cooling body back. But I just stood there saying empty things to the policemen, who were pacing back and forth, looking helpless.

Steve was saying how well Jennifer had been that morning.

"Then her eyes rolled back . . . her expression changed." The struggle was over in minutes. Brutally, mercifully, quickly.

I listened to the sound of his impotence, knew that mine would have been as great, and then tried to convince him that it couldn't have been different. No matter how much distance chemotherapy put between cancer and its target, it was eating away like insidious worms–inside, through breasts, lungs, bones and brain. Nothing could stop it.

But even I had forgotten that. We wanted a quick painless death; we kept saying it would be a blessing. Then, when it happened, we acted surprised and confused.

Steve cried quickly, tears confined by control, and I wanted to hug him and make it better. I called Erin, told her I needed her help. I needed her to come and share the responsibility, the horror and the pain. After she got there, we called everyone for Steve and then spent time cleaning and doing . . . talking about what we remembered of Jennifer . . . keeping what we could of her alive.

She had said she felt fine last time I saw her; in the morning, she had told Steve she felt better than ever. And an hour later she was dead. White now, and getting colder by the minute, and all of us still running around in a frenzy trying to do something, when it was already done.

I chattered a lot, the sound of my own voice making noise loud enough to keep me from hearing the sound of my own fear and pain. It was evening before I went home.

Then I repeated to Greg everything I knew. Finally I was too tired to talk. In the quiet, lying in bed, I could feel the waves of pain start from my feet and move up until they hit my throat and got stuck. Soundless tears and earthquake sadness seemed to shake my whole body, and I moved closer to Greg. I said nothing, but tried almost to climb into his body. It wasn't enough. I couldn't get close enough to hide inside him. I felt too alone.

I started to sob and pushed hard against him; still I needed to be closer. My nose was stuffed and my voice cracked when I asked him to make love to me. Mad, passionate sex, with an intensity I had never felt before. It was brutal and honest. I cried through it, and Greg held me tight.

Afterward, I lay quietly, realizing that usually sex restored my energy. Slowly I remembered that several times during that day when I looked at Jennifer's cold white body . . . I had wanted to climb into bed with her . . . I wanted to restore her energy with mine . . . I wanted to pull her back no matter what.

Four days after Jennifer died, I lay wrapped in a blanket on my couch again. I talked to Steve several times and told him that I would meet him the following week so that we could talk.

Three days later when Mrs. Dayton called and told me she needed me for a pediatric case, I told her to get someone else. When she called back, she said she had tried everyone.

"The child's name is Beth Casey," she said, "and she's got some kind of seizure disorder."

And so that night I went in again. And I tried to take care of Beth. I really did. But there was no way I could. And by the time morning came, I knew I couldn't be a nurse any longer, not for one more night, not for one more case . . . no matter how badly they needed me.

This time, when I crawled into bed, I stayed there. For days at a time, then for weeks. I lay paralyzed, afraid to move in any direction. I tried to understand. When I finally did, I kept hoping the tooth fairy would put a different solution under my pillow. When I knew the answer, when I couldn't hide it from myself any longer, I tried to pretend I was dead.

Then one morning I began raising my straw out of the quicksand again. Not much, maybe two inches or so, but at least that was something. I had certainly been depressed before, but nothing like this, nothing like having my whole body submerged in quicksand, the only part above, a straw held in my mouth so that I could breathe . . . and only an eighth of that straw above the surface.

The first person I talked to was Erin. She refused to stay away any longer, and one day she just landed in my bedroom. "Okay," she said compassionately, "I'm ready to listen."

I propped myself up in bed and started to cry. Not loudly. "You'll think I'm nuts if I try to explain," I told her.

She grabbed a tissue from on top of my dresser and handed it to me. "I already think you're nuts," she said, smiling, "so talk to me."

"It's because of my grandmother . . ." I said. As soon as Erin's lip started to twitch, I started to laugh. "Calm down," I told her. "It's not as wacky as it sounds."

"Well," she said warily, "you better talk fast if you want to bail yourself out."

"I mean I figured out that I thought my grandmother died because I was a kid and didn't know enough to save her. So after Shawn and I split I went into nursing to try to stop separation, right?"

"I follow you so far," she allowed.

"Don't you understand that in order to stop separation in nursing I would have had to stop death?" I asked, as though Erin had been spending as much time as I had trying to figure all this out.

"Okay," she said, "I'm still with you."

"Maybe it was crazy," I said, blowing my nose, but remember I told you Jennifer reminded me of someone? Well, it was my grandmother. And now I was all grown up. I knew what I was doing, right?"

Erin was frowning, trying to listen hard, as I continued. "Well, up until Jennifer died, there must have been enough successes-you know, enough Dr. Rosens-that I deluded myself into believing that if everything was perfect, we could win. Death *could* be stopped. It was only when something went wrong–when somebody made a mistake, when somebody didn't care enough–that death could come when you didn't want it. But with Jennifer, she really wanted to live, they had enough money for good medical care, her husband was crazy about her, her doctor was good and the nurses were just you and me."

Erin was nodding, concentrating, as I continued, "And even if I had any question about you, I was the last nurse on, and I know I didn't make any mistakes. So there it was, clearly in front of me: perfect care, will to live, love . . . and still she died."

Erin got up and started walking around the room. "You spent more time than I trying to prepare Steven for her death . . ."

"I know," I said, "but I was totally unprepared. And then when I knew that death couldn't be stopped, even by me, that death is inevitable, I knew that someday I would die, too. All the knowledge, all the wanting, all the bargaining in the world couldn't stop it."

When Erin raised her eyebrow I told her, "I know it seems absurd, but until now I had no idea that all this had anything to do with me

. . . for twelve years, it was only theory."

Erin smiled at me and patted my legs. "Okay again, I understand that you finally absorbed the idea that we're all going to die, including you. But now that you know, can't you do nursing just to relieve pain?"

I took a deep breath and started to cry. I felt silly as I explained, "All that time, my delusion protected me. It was a magic shield, the mirror I used to ward off the head of Medusa. And now that I have the knowledge that I can't beat it, the understanding that I'm going to die, too, I feel vulnerable. Afraid that I won't be able to protect myself or my patients anymore. Maybe my fear will wipe me out; maybe the only sword I ever had to protect me was the illusion that I could hold death at bay."

Erin leaned over and put her arms around me. "Teri," she soothed, "you're just exhausted. You're just burned out."

CHAPTER 28

I had always said that growth was my highest value. What I hadn't considered was that growth seeks change, causes change and cuts like a scythe through safety, through sameness.

Greg and I spilt. I cried. He cried. But neither of us had the energy to turn the wheels that could make the marriage work anymore. We were mismatched cogs and had worn each other down.

The following year I spent adjusting to being unmarried again. Spinner signed himself up for a vocational program in printing, which he loved. Niki packed all her things in a plastic bag and set out for California–without Lynch. She enrolled in college, psychology her major. When I asked her what possessed her to go back to school, she answered, "It's the only alternative to manual labor."

I spent the days trying to decide what to do with the rest of my life. Sometimes, I'd go for long walks by myself, and just sit watching the squirrels scatter. . .

Now I could see that what I had tried to do when my world fell apart after Shawn and I split was aim for safety. But choosing nursing was like diving into the eye of a hurricane. The cyclone of Death and Disease swirled around me constantly, and from where I stood I couldn't help watching the damage and destruction it caused.

Even in the times when it had passed, when I was away from the hospital, and sickness, when I was home or out with friends, I still had the memory. I had managed to escape without being demolished myself; I was one of the survivors. Still, I walked around knowing it had been a close call. My memory and that knowledge made me feel a stranger, because most people had never seen the wreckage, had never seen an entire countryside ravaged and destroyed as I had. They had no idea that the tornado of Disease could in any way touch them, except in theory.   But because I had that knowledge, I had the fear.

The following winter, lying in front of a crackling fire, I could see even more . . .
Throughout my years of nursing, most people had told me that no physical pain, including that of terminal cancer, had caused them as much suffering as isolation. Loneliness is one of the big killers, as are ignorance and fear. The only effective weapons, the only big guns we have to fight with, are intimacy, knowledge and compassion.
And my nursing had always been my most intimate connection. Sharing someone's sickness . . . someone's death . . . having someone really dependent on me, had connected me more than anything else. After I'd hugged and kissed hundreds of sick and dying bodies, helped wrap and care for another hundred dead ones . . . I'd *really* been touched.

Then one day the following summer, I sat at the edge of an old wooden pier, watching as the bright sun shimmered on the clear blue water like dancing silver fish. After a while I lay back with my eyes closed, daydreaming. . .
Wishing that there was one last Magic Land. One place left where a knight in shining armor could save a perfect princess and slay a huge green dragon with one slice of his sword. Somewhere a brave young prince, with one romantic kiss, could wake a sleeping maiden and have her live forever. . .
Suddenly I remembered Yves, my pale toy soldier; Rachael my scaly fish monster; Melody, my torn teak doll; and all the others in medicine.   And I knew: I'd met heroes *there*; real live heroes fighting the biggest dragons, with dignity. I've touched essence there; bright caring, red passion–and loving.

Finally I had worked out my philosophy. If Death and Sickness were great equalizers, if they treated a black man and a white man just the same, if neither youth nor money was defense–if, naked, a poor man and a President looked the same–then only one thing tipped the scale. I could picture it:

On one side of the scale lay all the people who had died. They were stacked on a plate like the corpses in the trenches of a war. With the same emaciation, the same dark circles under their hollow eyes, the same crushed and broken limbs, the same dead stare.

On the other side of the scale were all the live people I'd met, struggling. And because they were moving, whether they were fighting, loving or screwing–too much or too little–whether they were kind or cruel, because they were struggling the scale always tipped on the side of life. And it was that very movement, the struggle to live, that tipped the scale for those of us who stayed alive, in our favor. That fight, for long as we could struggle, seemed more just to me, more moral. Because the common enemy is Death.

Immoral, for me, was the man who lay still.

Late yesterday afternoon, almost two years after Jennifer died, Erin called. "I have a problem," she began. "There's a fifty-year-old man with terminal pancreatic cancer. His name is Mr. Russell. They threw him out of the hospital three weeks ago because his Blue Cross coverage was up and he's too young for Medicare. He wants desperately to die at home but private nurses cost eighty-five dollars a shift and they're not rich people."

"What about welfare? Medicaid?" I asked her.

"The man worked his whole life. His only real possession is his house. He'll have to turn it over. Besides, there's no time. His wife called me today and I went over to see him. It's pathetic. She looks exhausted. She's been doing all the nursing herself, even learned to suction and set up his IVs. But she's whipped. She's been up constantly for the three weeks he's been home, giving him pain medicine every three hours around the clock. She really can't do it another day."

"Don't they have any children?" I asked.

"They have one daughter," Erin said, "but she's in the hospital.

Just had a baby."

"What about public-health nurses?" I asked, trying to cover all the alternatives . . .

"They can only come in for a few hours a day. That man needs a lot of care– he's terminal."

"I don't know what to tell you, Erin," I said finally.

Her voice was very soft when she asked, "What about you?"

I hadn't even seen it coming. It had been so long since I had worked, I had stopped thinking of myself as a nurse.

"I can't, Erin," I said, feeling terrible, "I really can't."

"But there's nobody else," she said stubbornly.

The front door was ajar. I pushed it open slowly and let myself into the darkened hallway. Overhead, I could hear the sound of oxygen bubbling . . . I could hear him wheezing.

From the foot of the stairs I could smell his sickness, and my nose wrinkled. I threw my pocketbook down and pulled off my sweater, throwing it over the wooden banister.

I climbed the stairs quickly. From the doorway, I could see him propped on several pillows, his emaciated face yellow and strained. Even with the oxygen running full blast, his nostrils were flaring; he was straining to breathe. At his side, his wife sat with her head in her hands. I walked quietly toward them.

"Hi," I said. "My name is Teri Daley, I'm going to be your nurse

Afterward 1997

Nursing's Real Power to Heal

How many of your patients know that you, as a nurse, are the most important link in the Health Care System? How many of them understand that if it wasn't for your observation and intervention, they wouldn't get the care from the doctors they need? How many of you, yourselves, have forgotten how essential you are, have repressed your own need to help and heal, have minimized the calling that moved you toward nursing in the first place? And how many of you have gotten so frustrated and discouraged by the business of Health Care that often Nursing feels like just another job where the magic and meaning are gone!

Well, you are important and if anyone has the power to change the current Health Care System so that it can provide healing for the sick and dying, it's you. It's us! It's Nurses.

The TV dramas ER and Chicago Hope are two of the most popular programs on television. They have a vast audience. People want to know what goes on in hospitals, and they want to know more about the healers who work there. They want the real information, but most of it is hidden from them.

Health Care consumers are told that they have to be aware of what's happening in the Health Care System. They are told that hospitals, doctors and nurses can't be held totally responsible for their care, that they must be "informed" in order to make intelligent choices. But, of course, most of the time, we know that unless they're from Scotland Yard they can't get that information. They don't have a clue because we, in health care, are party to keeping it secret from them. We speak in jargon and tell them only enough to be certain we can't be sued.

Patients, when feeling sick and vulnerable, can't stand for themselves. Even if they understand that the system doesn't serve them. But who can act as their advocates, as their teachers, and help them accept their responsibility to make the correct decisions in order to get the best care?

The doctors can't, because in many cases, they're hired by the hospitals or given staff privileges, and are constrained by the AMA. In the newly developing system of HMO's, if doctors don't adhere to the rules, if they suggest consultations too often, if they spend too much time with their patients, they're locked out of the lists, not allowed to be "participating" physicians, and so they can't work. They can't earn a living. They're becoming powerless.

Hospital personnel have nothing to gain by telling patients about the flaws and shortcomings of the Health Care System. Hospitals are businesses and so those who work for them are generally public relations people, because they want to keep their jobs, especially with the latest mergers and the increased competition between Health Care Conglomerates. Everyone has a stake in keeping secrets.

But we, as nurses, have promised to act as Patient Advocates. Part of our job description is "teaching." Over the past ten years, nurses have fought for more education, more recognition and higher salaries. And we actually have made some headway. But as a result, the new business of Health Care, Managed Care and HMO's, has begun to replace us with unskilled workers – in order to cut their costs. How many patients know the difference between an white uniformed professional RN, or an LVN in a white uniform or an unskilled worker wearing a uniform, who has had only 6 weeks training?

Soon nurses won't be allowed at the bedsides of the patients who need us to comfort them when they're sick and dying. We'll be doing more complicated documentation and charting for the Health Care business. In a very short time, the medical crises that occur will have to be full blown before the assistant can recognize it and call the doctor to see a patient, because we – nurses who have been trained to know – aren't there to intervene, to catch the errors, to evaluate the changes, to know when a situation is life threatening. Historically, it was the nurse who acted as a safety net and called the doctor so he could diagnose, treat or get to the hospital in time to prevent irreparable harm or even death.

In the short run, taking nurses away from the bedside will save the business of Health Care money. It might lower costs. It might help the bottom line.

But eventually, when enough malpractice suits are filed, when the business of Health Care, HMO's and Managed Care, has to pay more for staffing less, we'll be called back.

In the meantime, what can we do to help our patients and to stand for ourselves and those vows that we made? What can we do to honor our calling, heal ourselves and keep the promise of our dreams?

I believe we have to tell our stories! Each of us have them. Stories of patient's who suffered because of bad policy, incompetence or poor staffing. Stories of damage caused, and harm that is being caused now. We, as nurses, are the expert witnesses. And there are millions of us.

And politicians and policy makers don't know more than regular consumers. Their research is done with pen and paper, not with fluttering hearts and struggling breaths. Their policies are decided with impersonal charts and numbers. We have to let them know what we know.

If each nurse tells one story, writes one story, and sends that story to a local or national newspaper, a magazine, a TV station, a local Congressmen, or to the White House, we will be heard! With so many of us telling the truth we might even be able to save some of those patients that we've fought so hard for the right and the knowledge to save.

But as long as we're silent, as long as we're separate, we have no power to nurse, to teach, or to change the Health Care system as it exists today. If we're not with our patients, we can't serve them. And if we don't stand up now, together as one, our patients won't be able to fight to keep us in hospitals. They will continue to be powerless. And we, as nurses, will become as extinct as Unicorns.

Coming Next Volume

THE THREE MAGI

The girl who could be the Kami is kidnapped by a trio of mysterious sages. To save her, Shio must join forces with a former opponent and battle through a slew of ever-more-powerful renegade Guardians!

AVAILABLE NOVEMBER 2009!

1 PROOF OF THE GODS (End)

OOO

THIS IS... REALLY BAD.

ALL THE BONES IN MY LEG THAT AREN'T PROTECTED BY ARMAITI ARE BROKEN.

GLANCE

GRIP

THIS MOUTH...

...HAS CAUSED ME ENOUGH TROUBLE.

THUNK

03

THUD

FOOOM

SWRRRRRL

BOOOM

GOJIN-ZOU ASHA'S ULTIMATE FIGHTING TECHNIQUE!

FIRE DRAGON ROAR!

THOOM

UHA!!!

I'LL BLOW YOU AWAY!

RA

WR

SWIFF

OOPS.

CRUNCH

MUNCH

UHA! SORRY, MR. DEAD MACHINE!

BUT I'M FIGHTING HARD FOR ONE OF YOUR FRIENDS!

MUNCH

IT'S USELESS.

SKUFF

NO MATTER HOW POWERFUL, A SLOW ATTACK LIKE THAT WILL DO YOU NO GOOD.

THIS TIME, WITH MORE SPEED!

CHEEEE!

CRR

DON'T BE MAD AT HIM, PLASTY.

HISSS

THAT WAS DIRTY!

SORRY, BUT FIRE WON'T WORK ON ME!

PHEW!

EXCUSE OUR GAS.

UH HA HA!

MAYBE COPYING DAD WON'T WORK AFTER ALL!

THERE'S ONLY ONE THING I CAN DO!

GLINT

CLANG

EAT !!!

CLANG

CLANG

YOU CAN'T HIT ME WITH THAT.

LURCH

...I THINK HE'S GONNA BLOW.

WHAT?!!

URP!

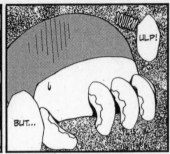

SQUIRM

ULP!

BUT...

BURRP

DISGUSTING!!!

SKFF

FOOOM

GAAA AH

CHOMP

CLINK

PSSSH

LOOKS LIKE THIS MOUTH CAN DO JUST ABOUT ANYTHING!

UHA! HE JUST ATE THE FLAME SWORD!

WHAT?!

HERE HE COMES!

WHAT DO I DO? I COULD'VE SWORN DAD HAD OTHER TACTICS HE USED!

YOU DON'T EVEN KNOW WHY I'M FIGHTING!

YOU SAID YOU'D STOP ME FROM FIGHTING.

THAT'S AWFULLY PRESUMPTUOUS OF YOU.

I JUST DON'T REMEMBER ANY OF THEM.

UH-OH.

THWUK THWUK

THWUK THWUK THWUK

TRY ANYTHING FUNNY AND I'LL SCORCH THE MACHINE.

YOU HAVE **REALLY** GOT TO STOP IT RIGHT NOW!

WSH

NOT SO FAST, LITTLE LADY.

....!

WE TOOK A LOT OF DAMAGE EVEN WITH THE SHIELDS.

I'm on fire!

Hot!

Hot!

I... I'M OKAY, KAMI! I WON'T LET HIM GET AWAY WITH IT!

BFF

BFF

174

-07- FOOD

Waq waq

I DID IT!

BUT IT STILL DIDN'T WORK.

TWIRRRRRRL

UH!

FLAMES JUST SHOT OUT OF HIS BROKEN BLADE!

...EAT STUFF.

THIS IS BAD! LEO HAS COMPLETE CONTROL OVER HIS GOJIN-ZOU!

BUT ALL I KNOW HOW TO DO IS...

HERE I COME!

I'LL BURN YOU ALIVE!

SHOOO

KFF!

NO!

...!!!

THE EARTH GOJIN-ZOU ARMAITI, HM?

NO WONDER HE'S SO TOUGH.

PASH

SWOOSH

GRR

KAMI, TAKE CARE OF PLASTY!

GOT IT!

PHEW!

I HONESTLY DON'T WANT TO FIGHT YOU!

GUARDIAN LEO!

MERGE!!!

ASHA!!!

HUH?!

WHOOSH

KSSH

KSSH

KSSH

KSSH

KSSH

YOU'RE A FOOL.

WHAT USE IS THERE TO MAKE NICE WITH THE MACHINES?!

AND I HAVE NO TIME TO DEAL WITH FOOLS!

THO OM

ZWUNK

HMPH!

AND HE'S MY FRIEND!

HE'S A GOOD MACHINE!

LISTEN, GUARDIAN LEO! THE KAMI HAS THE POWER TO MAKE MACHINES AND HUMANS GET ALONG!

SO WE GUARDIANS WON'T HAVE TO FIGHT ANYMORE!

SHUTTUP! YOU MAKE ME SICK!

THERE'S NO SUCH THING AS A GOOD OR BAD MACHINE! THEY'RE ALL THE ENEMY!

GRR!

THROB

THAT'S WHY I PRESENT MY WISH TO YOU, KAMI!

HELP ME SLAUGHTER EVERY LAST MACHINE WITH YOUR RED BLOOD!

ALL I REALLY NEED IS YOUR RED BLOOD...

I SUPPOSE TALKING TO YOU WON'T HELP.

NOW START WALKING!

YOU'RE ASKING TOO MUCH!

WAIT!

ARE YOU GOING TO KILL ME?

DON'T KNOW YET.

...SO I CAN OFFER IT AT THE ALTAR OF SPIDER'S THREAD.

DESTROYING MACHINES HELPED CALM MY SPLITTING HEADACHE.

SWSSSSH

IT WAS ONLY AFTER BECOMING A GUARDIAN THAT I REALIZED.

THE PEOPLE WERE PLEASED AND THANKED ME FOR MY WORK.

AND SO I STARTED MY UNENDING BATTLE WITH THE MACHINES.

TURNS OUT THE GOJIN-ZOU COULD FULFILL ONLY PART OF MY WISH.

BUT NO MATTER HOW MANY MACHINES I CUT DOWN, MY HEADACHE WOULD COME BACK BEFORE LONG.

MY HEADACHE WOULD NEVER COMPLETELY HEAL UNTIL EVERY LAST MACHINE WAS WIPED OFF THE FACE OF THIS PLANET.

CHEEE...

THEN, ONE DAY, I LEARNED SOMETHING.

AAAH!

AAAH!

AAAAH!!

ANY- ONE!

I THOUGHT FOR SURE THE PAIN WOULD DO ME IN.

AND SOMEONE ANSWERED MY PLEAS.

SO I WISHED FOR SOMEONE TO STOP IT!

A PAIN I HAD NEVER THOUGHT POSSIBLE BEFORE.

AN IMMENSE PAIN OCCUPIED MY BROKEN MIND.

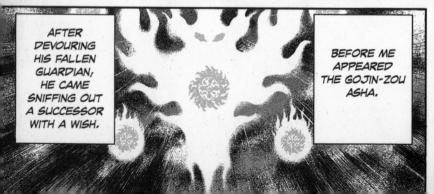

AFTER DEVOURING HIS FALLEN GUARDIAN, HE CAME SNIFFING OUT A SUCCESSOR WITH A WISH.

BEFORE ME APPEARED THE GOJIN-ZOU ASHA.

MY HOMETOWN OF VILLAGE 5 WAS THE WORST KIND OF PLACE.

SO WHEN OUR LAST GUARDIAN AGED AND WAS DEFEATED...

IT WAS SURROUNDED BY SWARMS OF MACHINES, AND WOULD'VE COLLAPSED ON ITSELF IF NOT FOR THE GUARDIANS.

伍

...THE MACHINES FELL UPON OUR VILLAGE LIKE A METAL AVALANCHE.

THKOON

LEO! THERE'S NO HOPE LEFT FOR OUR VILLAGE!

YOU MUST REMAIN HIDDEN IN THE HEARTH!

RRRRUMBLE

STOP THIS INCESSANT MIGRAINE!

KAMI!

EVER SINCE THAT LIFE-CHANGING EVENT...

I'VE BEEN LIVING WITH THE PAIN FOR THREE YEARS NOW.

MIGRAINE?

THAT DAY...

-06- THE BATTLE OVER WISHES

Waq Waq

NOPE.

DID YOU HEAR IT?

SCREAM?

DIDN'T YOU HEAR THAT SCREAM?

I COULD'VE SWORN I JUST HEARD THE KAMI'S VOICE!

K-KAMI ?!

HUH?

EXIT

SCRAMBLE

SORRY BUT I GOTTA GO!

THWACK

SO YOU'RE...

...THE KAMI?

PLASTY!!!

THUD

HE JUST SUDDENLY DISAPPEARED.

AND WE NEVER EVEN GOT TO THANK HIM.

SO WHERE IS HE NOW?

I SEE.

GASP!

FOOSH

KYAAAAH !!!

THOOM

↑ MERGING

THE MOMENT HE ARRIVED AT OUR VILLAGE, HE STOOD OUTSIDE AS BAIT TO ATTRACT THE MACHINES.

AFTER MOST OF THEM HAD GATHERED, HE SLICED THEM DOWN IN A FURY.

THE GOJIN-ZOU LOOKED LIKE FLAMES-- APPROPRIATE CONSIDERING THE BURNING PASSION FOR BATTLE HE SHOWED.

CREAK

A GUARDIAN?

DON DON

DON

HELLO? EXCUSE ME!

IT'S ME, A GUARDIAN!

SO THERE WAS ANOTHER GUARDIAN HERE ALREADY?

YES!

HIS NAME WAS LEO HEDIARD, AND HE HAD A GOJIN-ZOU NAMED ASHA WITH HIM.

LOOK! ANOTHER GUARDIAN!

I'M GLAD TO SEE YOU'RE ALL SAFE!

Totally awesome!

THAT'S AN ANCIENT LANGUAGE!

I KNEW THE KAMI WOULD BE ABLE TO READ IT!

Awesome!

OH! I GET IT!

PLASTY-WHAT NOW?

I NAMED HIM BECAUSE OF WHAT'S WRITTEN ON HIS BELLY.

BE CAREFUL!

WE'RE OFF, ARMAITI!

OKAY!

SOOP

AN ANCIENT LANGUAGE ...?

...

144

THERE WAS PROBABLY A BATTLE WHILE HE WAS TRYING TO PROTECT THE VILLAGE.

ONLY ANOTHER GUARDIAN COULD'VE DONE THIS.

I'M GOING TO CHECK ON THE VILLAGE!

SO THERE ARE OTHER GUARDIANS BESIDES YOU AND ARMAITI?

YUP. SEVEN IN TOTAL.

THE MAN WHO WAS AFTER YOU, QAF, WAS ALSO ONE.

SHF SHF

KILL THE WITCH!

KILL HER!!

STAY THERE UNDER THE TREE'S SHADE.

IF YOU COME WITH ME, THE VILLAGERS MIGHT FREAK OUT AGAIN.

I'LL STAY RIGHT HERE WITH PLASTY!

CHEE! CHEE!

3

UHA! NO NEED TO APOLOGIZE!

ALL RIGHT. SORRY FOR ALL THE TROUBLE, SHIO!

NOOOO

I'M FLATTERED.

LOOK! HE'S FOLLOWING US.

EH HEH HEH!

I THINK HE LIKES YOU, SHIO.

TOK

TOK

WHAT THE--?

...?!

LOOK!

GRIP

BUT WHY?

THAT'S SMOKE COMING FROM THE VILLAGE.

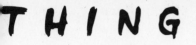

...THERE'S, LIKE, NOTHING OUT THERE.

I MEAN, NORMALLY THERE ARE TONS OF MACHINES WALKING AROUND.

US GUARDIANS ARE USED TO HAVING TO TRAVEL WHILE IN HIDING.

BUT, SO FAR, HE'S THE ONLY ONE WE'VE SEEN.

WHAT ELSE DO YOU EXPECT IN A DESERT?

THROB

...FEELS LIKE A TERRIBLE DREAM.

JUST BEING HERE...

FLOP

LET'S GET OVER THIS DUNE BEFORE THE SUN SETS.

BETTER FOR US THAT THERE ARE NO MACHINES!

OH, WELL!

...SO WE'LL BE STOPPING BY 2 OVER THERE.

WE DIDN'T PICK UP ENOUGH FOOD OR WATER WHILE WE WERE IN VILLAGE 7...

SHLP

THEN WE'LL HEAD STRAIGHT FOR THE SPIDER'S THREAD DOCTOR YOKI TOLD US ABOUT.

HMM.

IT WAS PROBABLY KIKU.

THE SPIDER'S THREAD? HE TOLD ME THERE WAS SOMEONE I MUST MEET THERE.

RIGHT! KIKU'S THE ONE WHO MAY BE ABLE TO HELP ME. BUT...

STILL ...

NO.

IT'S NOTHING.

...

BUT WHAT?

AND MAYBE IF SHE REALLY IS THE KAMI WE'VE BEEN WAITING FOR, SHE'LL BRING AN END TO THE WAR BETWEEN MAN AND MACHINE.

I BELIEVE IT'S THANKS TO THE KAMI THAT I WAS ABLE TO MAKE FRIENDS WITH A MACHINE.

DAD...

CHEEE...!

CHEEE...!

CHEEE...!

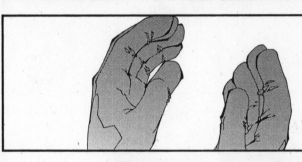

IF THE KAMI'S ABLE TO HELP HUMANS AND MACHINES GET ALONG...

... THEN I KNOW ...

...I'LL DO ANYTHING IN MY POWER TO PROTECT HER.

WHENEVER DAD WENT OUT TO SLAY MACHINES THAT WERE NESTED NEAR A VILLAGE...

THAT'S WHAT I'VE ALWAYS THOUGHT.

...I USED TO WONDER IF MACHINES ALSO HAD HEARTS AND FAMILIES JUST LIKE US. IF THEY WERE JUST TRYING TO SURVIVE.

SPARK

DEAR DAD... I MUST BE DREAMING.

WOULD YOU BELIEVE I'M ACTUALLY FRIENDS WITH A MACHINE NOW?

IF YOU JUST OPEN YOUR HEART AND CONNECT, YOU CAN ALWAYS MAKE A NEW FRIEND.

...

YOU'RE KIDDING ME!

EVEN THIS LITTLE CUTEY?

SWFF

YUP.

YOU MAY NOT KNOW THIS, KAMI, BUT MACHINES AND HUMANS HAVE HATED EACH OTHER SINCE AS FAR BACK AS HISTORY GOES.

THAT'S WHY GUARDIANS FIGHT TO PROTECT PEOPLE FROM THE MACHINES.

FLUMP

JUST HOW LONG ARE THEY GONNA WHIRL AROUND?

CHEEE!
CHEEE!
CHEEE!

AH HA HA HA CHA CHA

WHIRL
WHIRL
WHIRL

HEH HEH.

AFTER ALL THAT HATE, NOW THEY'RE THE BEST OF FRIENDS!

Solar Tree

-05- KAMI'S REALITY AND SHIN'S FAITH

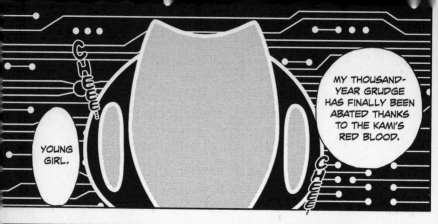

CHEEE...

YOUNG GIRL.

MY THOUSAND-YEAR GRUDGE HAS FINALLY BEEN ABATED THANKS TO THE KAMI'S RED BLOOD.

CHEEE...

...THEN THIS MAY BE YOUR CHANCE TO GET ALONG WITH HIM!

Catch!

SHLUMP

WHAT?!

SWFF

NOW, LET'S SHAKE HANDS!

SQUIRM   SQUIRM

WAIT A SEC. WERE THOSE TEXT MESSAGES THIS MACHINE SPEAKING?

IF THAT'S THE CASE...

BUT IT'S SO SUDDEN!

HOW TWISTED THAT THE KAMI...

...WOULD BE FRIENDS WITH A MACHINE.

GYAAAAH!!!

...!

FLAP   FLAP

SNAP
SNAP
SNAP

SHIO!

BWO-OSH

WOO

KAMI?

OOO

OOO

PHEW!

HE HATES HUMANS, JUST LIKE THE OTHER MACHINES!

GET AWAY FROM HIM!

HEY!

PLOP

CHEEEE!!!

I DON'T WANT TO FIGHT, BUT I WILL, IF I HAVE TO!

DASH

THIS IS WHERE I STARTED!

KAMI! IT'S TOO DANGEROUS GOING OFF ALONE!

...I CAN FINALLY GO HOME!

MAYBE... IF I'M ABLE TO SEE THAT SHADOWY FIGURE AGAIN...

HE'S NOT HERE.

SKUFF

J-Tel
Received Messages

PING-A-LING- PRRRING

NO WAY!

I'M GETTING THREE BARS HERE!

TING- DING-A- LING

PERK EEK!!!

UHA!!!

AND THAT WEIRDO SAID I WAS THE ONE.

THEY SAY THIS *KAMI* IS ABLE TO GRANT ANY WISH.

MY BLOOD MAY BE RED, BUT THAT DOESN'T MEAN I HAVE ANY SPECIAL POWERS.

FOR NOW, JUST TRY TO KEEP YOUR WITS ABOUT YOU.

YOU'RE BEING HUNTED DOWN BY THAT GUARDIAN QAF!

MAYBE, BUT HOW IS THAT A GOOD THING?

BUT YOU'RE WRONG, KAMI! YOU WERE ABLE TO THROW THOSE VILLAGERS INTO A FRENZY!

SKUFF

MACHINES?

I'M REALLY NOT EAGER TO FIGHT ANYONE FOR A WHILE!

IN ANY CASE, LET'S MAKE SURE TO AVOID QAF AND OTHER MACHINES ON OUR WAY.

ARMAITI'S ONE OF THE GOOD GUYS! HE'S NOT LIKE THE OTHERS!

POKE

BUT ISN'T *THAT* A MACHINE, TOO?

JSTLE

RUSH

ONCE THE KAMI'S BLOOD HAS PURIFIED THIS ALTAR AND I OFFER THE LAST REMAINING GOJIN-ZOU...

...THEN MY 2,000-YEAR-OLD WISH SHALL FINALLY BE FULFILLED!

...SURE IS A HASSLE.

SMFF

ALL THIS SAND...

YES, BUT... ...I STILL DON'T UNDERSTAND WHAT ALL THIS MEANS.

SMFF

JUST A LITTLE BIT FURTHER, AND WE'LL BE ABLE TO GET FOOD AT VILLAGE 2.

PLUS, WE CAN GET BETTER DIRECTIONS FOR THE SPIDER'S THREAD PLACE DOCTOR YOKI WAS TALKING ABOUT.

SMFF

SPIDER'S THREAD

I COULD CARE LESS ABOUT THOSE GUARDIANS HAVING THEIR WISHES GRANTED.

ALL I WANT IS THE LAST WINNING GOJIN-ZOU.

VMMM

THAT'S WHY I CRUSH EVERY MACHINE I COME UPON!

I SEE.

ALTAR?

BUT IN ORDER TO DO THAT, YOU'LL NEED TO OFFER THE KAMI'S RED BLOOD TO THE ALTAR.

THEY'RE THE CAUSE OF MY PAIN!

BUT ONCE THEY'RE ALL GONE, I CAN FINALLY BE AT PEACE!

SLORSH

SLORSH

HMPH. SO I HAVE TO OFFER THE KAMI'S RED BLOOD, HM?

THUK

AND ONLY ONE KAMI MEANS ONLY ONE PERSON WILL HAVE THEIR WISH GRANTED.

IT LIES IN THE PLACE KNOWN AS SPIDER'S THREAD, FOUND IN THE VERY CENTER OF WĀQWĀQ.

SHKK

IT'S BACK ALREADY...

THAT IS SO.

NOW, GUARDIAN, FIGHT FOR CONTROL OVER THE KAMI!

SLICE

MEANING THE KAMI MUST BE WHERE I'M BEING DRAWN TO.

OKAY THEN, MONSTER, YOU SAID "THE KAMI" BEFORE.

VMMM

IT'S FUTILE.

ISN'T IT OBVIOUS?

TO GET RID OF THIS BLASTED HEADACHE ONCE AND FOR ALL.

THE RED-BLOODED KAMI, CAPABLE OF GRANTING YOU GUARDIANS YOUR WISH.

INDEED.

WHAT IS IT THAT YOU WISH FOR?

118

SHOOM

SLITHER

SLITHER
SLITHER

BUT IT HAS A NASTY HABIT OF COMING RIGHT BACK.

ONLY THEN SHALL YOU TAKE CONTROL OF THE KAMI AND HAVE YOUR WISH GRANTED!

KILL THE OTHER SIX GUARDIANS!

LOOK, I DON'T KNOW WHO-- OR WHAT-- YOU ARE, BUT YOU'D BETTER SCRAM WHILE I'M STILL IN A GOOD MOOD.

MY MIGRAINE SUBSIDES WHEN I'VE SLAUGHTERED MACHINES.

...

BUT REMEMBER, SHIO. THERE ARE STILL FIVE MORE GUARDIANS IN THIS WORLD WHO ARE AFTER THE KAMI.

AND THEY EACH HAVE A WISH AS POWERFUL AS QAF'S.

MIIII KAAAAA MIIII KAAAA !!

...JUST WHOSE WISH WILL YOU GRANT?

AND IN THE END...

...

WHAT AM I SUPPOSED TO DO NOW?

SHooo

THERE, THE MAGUS KIKU WILL BE SURE TO AID YOU.

IF YOU ARE IN NEED OF DIRECTIONS, I SUGGEST YOU HEAD TO SPIDER'S THREAD VILLAGE.

IT SEEMS I'VE UPSET THE PEOPLE OF THIS VILLAGE.

YOU'VE ALL DONE SO MUCH FOR ME.

THANK YOU.

WHUMP

I'M TRULY SORRY.

I AM PREPARED TO LEAVE.

TMP   TMP

STILL FULL OF SO MUCH LIFE.

HA HA.

YES, YES. I KNOW.

GOONG

DOCTOR YOKI!

LET'S GO, ARMAITI!

THANKS FOR HANDLING MY FATHER'S FUNERAL!

FOOM

THEY DISAP-PEARED!

UHA!

OOOSH

I'LL LEAVE THE KAMI TO YOU FOR NOW.

WOOOSH

Kill the witch!

Set up the ladders!

THE VILLAGERS ARE ON THEIR WAY HERE.

PLOONG~~

AND AS FOR YOU-- GET AWAY FROM THIS VILLAGE AS SOON AS POSSIBLE!

HUH?

AND THE EXISTENCE OF A KAMI ALONE IS SAID TO THROW ANY HUMAN MIND INTO CHAOS.

I BELIEVE THAT YOU ARE *NOT* THE TRUE KAMI, BUT YOUR RED BLOOD DEFINES YOU AS SUCH.

YOU'RE SHIO, RIGHT?

THANK YOU FOR ALL YOUR HELP.

ALL RIGHT.

LEAVE THE REST TO ME.

HE'S SO DARN VIOLENT!

FLAIL

FLAIL

DOCTOR YOKI, PLEASE TELL YOUR FRIEND TO STOP!

QAF?

MAGUS?

DON'T BE RIDICULOUS.

ARE YOU GOING TO KEEP IT UP?

WELL?

AT LEAST, FOR NOW.

VRMM

I HAVE NO INTENTION OF GETTING ON A MAGUS'S AND THE KAMI'S BAD SIDE.

BUT WHO KNEW...

...KHSHATHRA WOULD RESPOND TO THE KAMI'S VOICE?

BWOOSH

WHOA!

103

SHRING

I'LL FIGHT...
BECAUSE I
DON'T WANT
TO FIGHT
ANYMORE!

DAD
...

WHOEVER
HEARD
OF A
GUARDIAN
WHO
DOESN'T
WISH TO
FIGHT?!

THUD

WHOOSH!!

YOU FIGHT BECAUSE YOU DON'T WISH TO FIGHT.

I FOUGHT BECAUSE I WISHED TO PROTECT PEOPLE.

BECAUSE YOU WANT YOUR ENEMY TO REALIZE THAT.

ONLY THEN WILL YOU BE FREE FROM BATTLE.

HOW CAN I FIGHT WHEN I DON'T WANT TO?

DAD... I DON'T UNDER-STAND.

SHIO...

...I'VE ALWAYS WISHED FOR YOU TO LEAD A GOOD LIFE.

I KNOW YOU'LL BE A GREAT GUARDIAN.

THAT'S A MUCH BETTER WISH THAN I EVER HAD.

THUS COMPLETES THE TRANSFER IN FULL.

THIS IS AS FAR AS I CAN HELP YOU.

99

THE KAMI...

...!!

I CAN'T EVEN GET THROUGH TO ARMAITI.

I DON'T WANT TO FIGHT.

ARMAITI HAS TO KNOW THAT ALREADY.

IS THAT SO?

WHAT ...?

HOW CAN YOU CALL YOURSELF A GUARDIAN?!

A GUARDIAN WOULD NEVER DO THIS!

VWOOSH

SKVLEEE

UHA!

THE KAMI!

STOP THIS! PUT ME DOWN!

STOP IT, *PLEASE!*

NOW I NEED TO FIGHT LIKE MY FATHER MORE THAN EVER!

ARMAITI, WE'VE PULLED IT OFF ONCE BEFORE, RIGHT?

YOU CAN'T CONTROL YOUR GOJIN-ZOU WITH SUCH A WEAK WILL!

HA HA HA! "LET'S GET MERGING"?

HUH?

A STRONG ENOUGH DESIRE THAT STEMS FROM THE BOTTOM OF THEIR HEARTS!

GUARDIANS REQUIRE DESIRE.

AND SOON, I WILL HAVE ULTIMATE POWER!

NOW I'M TAKING THE KAMI AND YOUR GOJIN-ZOU!

SO, YOU'RE NOT EVEN AWARE OF YOUR STATURE?

I GUESS THAT'LL MAKE THINGS EASIER FOR ME.

PLEASE, DO YOU KNOW NOTHING?

WHU MP

I DON'T UNDERSTAND.

EVERYONE KEEPS CALLING ME KAMI, BUT IT DOESN'T MAKE ANY SENSE!

EEK!

ARMAITI! LET'S GET MERGING!

RISE

OH, NO! KAMI!

I SAID, MERGE!

PONK PONK

HELLO IN THERE?

...?

ARMAITI?

VWEEN

BLACK.... BLOOD ?!

GRANT WISHES?

THE KAMI WOULD DO THAT?

THE ALMIGHTY RED-BLOODED KAMI, SAID TO GRANT ANY WISH.

WHOEVER CONTROLS IT WILL GAIN ULTIMATE POWER.

THAT'S RIGHT.

HOVER

I SHOULD EXPECT A DUEL OVER CONTROL OF THE KAMI.

EEK!

LUNGE

SNAP

WHOA! WATCH IT!

CRK

CRK

CRK

HUH?

WHAT ON EARTH IS THAT?

Z
W
R

R
L

NOW, IF YOU DON'T MIND...

...I'LL BE TAKING THE KAMI.

UHAA!

YOUR GOJIN-ZOU LOOKS PRETTY STRONG!

Waq Waq

...Z

SPRINKLE

DW OOM

HAND OVER...

...THE KAMI!

HUH?

CREAK

YOKTS ESCAPE ROUTE

MY MIND FEELS AT PEACE NOW.

THANKS.

SHIVER

SHIVER

SHIO MUST'VE BEEN SAFE FROM IT BECAUSE HE'S A GUARDIAN.

THE KAMI OR NOT, THERE'S SOMETHING ODD ABOUT THAT GIRL.

IT TOOK ALL MY CONCENTRATION NOT TO FEEL HATE FOR HER.

THAT'S --!

HM?

HUH?

WHIRRRRR

TWITCH

WHAT?

WHAT ON EARTH GOT INTO ME?!

...Z!

Huff! Huff!

I HOPE YOU CAN FORGIVE THEM...

I KNOW IT LOOKED BAD, BUT THEY'RE USUALLY REALLY GOOD PEOPLE!

TMP

WE'LL BE SAFE HERE.

WITH ALL THE STAIRS BUSTED, NO ONE CAN REACH US!

SHO

KAMI!!!

RA H

WOOSH

AFTER THEM!

DAMN IT! THEY TOOK TO THE SKIES!

WO O

OSH

DWUH ?!

TURN

PLIP

PLEASE...

...OPEN YOUR EYES.

DRIP

DRIP

OUT OF MY WAY!

STOMPSTOMPSTOMPSTOMP

TMP

MURMUR

KILL HER...

KILL HER...

MURMUR

GULP
!!!

BETTER
GET
MOVING,
KAMI!

GRAWR
!!!

THE
GOJIN-ZOU
MOVED
ON ITS
OWN!

WE WON'T
LET THEM
ESCAPE!

WE MUST
KILL THE
GIRL!

KILL
THE
GIRL!

STOMP
STOMP
STOMP
STOMP

IT'S
PURE
HATRED!

IT'S NOT
INSANITY
THAT
DRIVES
THEM!

THIS
IS...

....!

OH,
NO!

WOOSH

UHAAA!!

NOW I REMEMBER.

I REMEMBER WHAT THAT VOICE TOLD ME.

IT MUST BE BECAUSE OF ALL THAT'S HAPPENED.

OOOOW!

THEY'VE LOST THEIR MINDS!

IT'S MY DUTY AS A GUARDIAN!

BUT I SWEAR I'LL PROTECT YOU, KAMI!

WHAT IS THIS?

THE KAMI'S EXISTENCE IS TO BE SCORNED BY HUMANS, AND REVERED BY MACHINES!

WE MUST ...

...KILL HER!!

WE ...

WE ...

I'M ON IT!

CHAK

SHIO, IT'S NO USE!

TAKE THE GIRL AND GET OUT OF THERE!

SHIO!

WAM

WHAT'S GOING ON HERE?!

PLEASE, STOP IT!

SHE'S NO KAMI!

SHE MURDERED YOUR FATHER!

YOU MUST HATE HER, TOO!

I DIDN'T DO ANYTHING!

MY DAD SAVED HER, AND ENTRUSTED HER TO ME!

YOU'RE WRONG!

DRIP

SHE'S IN NO CONDITION TO--

NOW WHERE COULD THE KAMI HAVE RUN OFF TO?

OKAY!

SHIO! CHECK THAT WAY!

KYAAAH!!!

SPIT IT OUT, GIRL!

YOU CARRY OUT THE DEVIL'S WORK, DON'T YOU?!

AND THE FACT THAT YOU CAME OUT FROM THAT GIANT MACHINE IS PROOF OF IT!

A WITCH?

SWISH

SWISH

SWISH

!!!!

GASP!

ARE YOU REALLY A WITCH?

RUSTLE

THANK YOU VERY MUCH.

PHEW

HEY, THAT WAS A ROCK!

BAM

DID YOU PUNKS DO THAT?!

THW ACK

?!!

WH ISH

SHE'S THE WITCH THAT DESTROYED OUR VILLAGE!

WE HATE HER!

THRUST

I REMEMBER A SHADOWY FIGURE...

WHAT ON EARTH HAPPENED TO ME?

AND THEN ...

OOPS!

BUMP

DON'T KNOW WHAT VILLAGE YOU COME FROM, BUT OURS IS A MESS RIGHT NOW.

SORRY IT AIN'T MUCH, BUT PLEASE, MAKE YOURSELF AT HOME.

HEY, YOU'RE THAT NEW GIRL.

S-SO SORRY!

HUH?

WE'S HEARD YOU WAS CAUGHT BY THAT GIANT MACHINE. YOU ALL RIGHT NOW?

HUH?

OH! DINNER, RIGHT?

HUP!

SHIO?

SHIO!

WOULD YOU DO ME A FAVOR AND BRING THE GIRL HER DINNER?

KAMI! I'VE GOT SOME FOOD FOR YOU!

SLAM

EXAMINING ROOM

BUT AS A GUARDIAN, HE IS FORBIDDEN FROM SHOWING ANY SIGNS OF WEAKNESS, IN ORDER TO KEEP THE PEOPLE AT EASE.

HIS FATHER'S DEATH MUST BE HARD ON HIM.

HUH?

PING

WHEEEn

IT'S CLOSE.

THE RED-BLOODED KAMI AS FORETOLD IN LEGEND...

AND THEY ALL SENSE AND ARE DRAWN TO THIS KAMI.

THERE ARE SEVEN GOJIN-ZOU AND SEVEN GUARDIANS IN THIS WORLD.

GUARDIAN QAF.

SHING

...WILL GRANT LIMITLESS WISHES TO WHOEVER CLAIMS HIM.

IS THE KAMI'S GRAVITY ALSO DRAWING YOU NEAR?

WELL, HER BLOOD MAY BE RED, BUT WE DON'T KNOW FOR SURE IF SHE'S REALLY THE KAMI--

YOKI

WHAT? IF SHE'S NOT THE KAMI, THEN WHAT IS SHE?

SHIO

YEAH, SHE LOOKS PRETTY HUMAN TO ME.

VILLAGERS

THAT'S... THE KAMI?

AND WE EVEN FOUND THE KAMI!

Right, The Kami?

NOW WĀQWĀQ CAN LIVE IN PEACE WITHOUT ANY MORE WAR!

What?

WHERE...

...EXACTLY AM I?

IS IT TRUE THE GUARDIAN'S DEAD?!

AND IN THE CONDITION THE VILLAGE IS NOW...

BTAM

DOCTOR YOKI!!

...IF IT WERE ATTACKED BY A MACHINE, WE'D ALL BE DOOMED!

Y'UP! Y'UP!

NO NEED TO WORRY, FOLKS!

LOOK AT THIS! I'VE INHERITED MY DAD'S DUTY AS GUARDIAN!

OOPS!

NO...

QUIET!

NO YELLING IN THE MEDICAL CLINIC!

AND BE-SIDES...

DOCTOR.

TAKE A LOOK AT THE GUARDIAN SEAL.

FWIP

SHE MAY VERY WELL BE THE RINGLEADER BEHIND THE ATTACK.

IT GLOWS BRIGHTER, THE CLOSER IT GETS TO HER.

SEE?

SHING

SO SHE MUST BE THE RED-BLOODED KAMI WHO CREATED THE WORLD OF WĀQWĀQ.

GUARDIANS ARE SUPPOSED TO BE ABLE TO KNOW, OR SENSE, WHO THE KAMI IS.

WHAT IS THIS?

WHAT ARE THEY TALKING ABOUT?

I SEE.

THAT STILL DOESN'T KEEP ME FROM GETTING A BAD FEELING ABOUT HER.

64

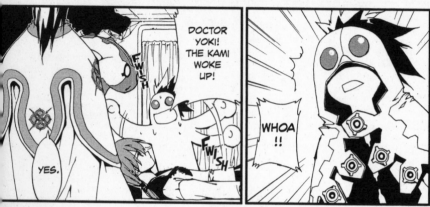

DOCTOR YOKI! THE KAMI WOKE UP!

FWISH

FWISH

YES.

WHOA!!

BUT IT'S STILL A FACT THIS YOUNG GIRL WAS FOUND IN THE CENTER OF THE MACHINES THAT ATTACKED THIS VILLAGE.

HUH? SHE HAS TO BE!

You all right, miss?

ZOOONE—

BUT DO YOU HONESTLY BELIEVE SHE'S THE KAMI?

...SHE'S THE LAST THING MY FATHER LEFT ME BEFORE HE DIED.

WHO'S THERE?

HER BLOOD'S RED. AND BESIDES...

THAT DAY...

...I WAS WAITING FOR MY FRIEND MAY LIKE USUAL.

WHEN SHE NEVER SHOWED UP, I TRIED CALLING HER.

IT WASN'T MAY, BUT A DEEP AND CREEPY VOICE.

COME...

...I HEARD THE VOICE.

AND THAT'S WHEN...

...COME...

COME WITH ME!

COME, LOST SIMIAN!

-02- HATRED

AND THAT'S HOW I ENDED UP...

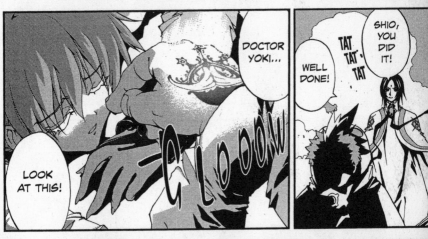

PAT.

SHIO.

A MACHINE WILL DIE ONCE ITS HEART IS DESTROYED.

WHAT...

...DO I DO NOW?

CRUSH IT WITH YOUR LEFT HAND!

ONE OF THE MACHINES SURVIVED!

SHIO, YOU HAVE TO SAVE HER!

HUH?

BUT, WHAT CAN I DO?

SWEAT

MERGE !!!

HURRY!

AL ASKED YOU TO TAKE CARE OF THAT GIRL!

A-ARMAITI!

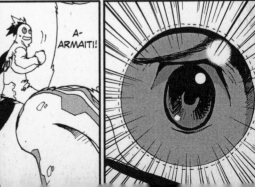

CLANK

CLANK

CLATTER

UH...

I WONDER IF DAD WAS SCARED.

TO THINK THE VERY GOJIN-ZOU THAT WATCHED OVER HIM ALL THIS TIME WOULD...

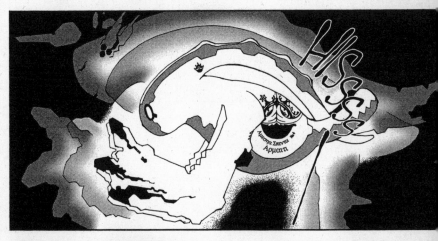

HISSS

BING

INDEED, NOW IT'S SHIO-SIZED.

UHA! IT SHRUNK!

SO, THE KAMI'S POWER IS AS IMPRESSIVE AS I THOUGHT.

KUH KUH KUH.

THUS, MACHINES AND GUARDIANS ALIKE WILL FIGHT OVER IT.

SO BEGINS THE STRUGGLE TO CLAIM THE KAMI!

...MY DEAR CHILDREN.

YES, LET IT BE A BLOODY AND GRUESOME WAR...

GLOOW

A GUARDIAN WILL SACRIFICE HIS LIFE TO PROTECT PEOPLE, AND IN THE END, BE DEVOURED.

...A GUARDIAN SENDS ALL OF HIS SKILLS TO HIS GOJIN-ZOU.

THE TRANSFER IS WHEN...

DAD!

GLOOW

THE NEXT?

OH, DAD...

SHIO, I ADVISE WE LEAVE FOR NOW.

WHAT?! WHY?!

WHAT'S HE MEAN *TRANS-FER?!*

SKOOCH

TRANSFER?

WOMP

WOMP

ARMAITI.

DO THE TRANSFER... BEFORE I'M GONE FOR GOOD!

PERK

I'M SORRY, SHIO.

THIS WILL BE THE LAST THING I CAN TEACH YOU.

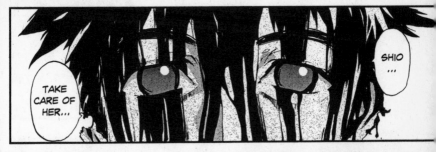

SHIO...

TAKE CARE OF HER...

DAAAD!!!

SKUFF

ARMAITI TOLD ME...

...HE'S CHOSEN YOU AS THE NEXT GUARDIAN.

TWITCH

TWITCH

...

DOCTOR, CAN YOU SAVE MY FATHER?!

SHIO, ARE YOU THERE?

SHIO.

UGH

DON'T TRY TO MOVE, DAD!

THERE'S NO WAY I CAN HEAL THIS.

THUD
THUD

DAD!

HE...

HE DID IT!

!!

IS THAT...

...THE MONSTER'S HEART?!

DAAAAD!!!

VHUMP

I CAN SEE IT...

PLOP

CRACK

CRACK

THIS THING'S ALSO GOT A HEART!

GAH!

BO
O
O
M

TMP
TMP
TMP

PHEW...

PLOP

...

THAT WAS QUITE A BLOW.

GET BACK HERE!

DASH!

PLIK

THANK
YOU!

SLUMP

04

THANK
YOU
SO
MUCH!

HURRY
UP...

...AND
GET
OUT OF
HERE...

39

YOU SHOULD ALREADY KNOW...

...THIS IS MY DUTY AS A GUARDIAN.

QUIT DAWDLING AND GO, SHIO!

I WON'T LEAVE YOU BEHIND, DAD!

GRAB

ROGER.

YIPE!

DOC-TOR!

GET SHIO OUT OF HERE!

CRICK

CRICK

CRICK

UH-OH!

THOOM

GRAA

SHIELDS UP, ARMAITI!

NOW!!

KACHING

GWAK

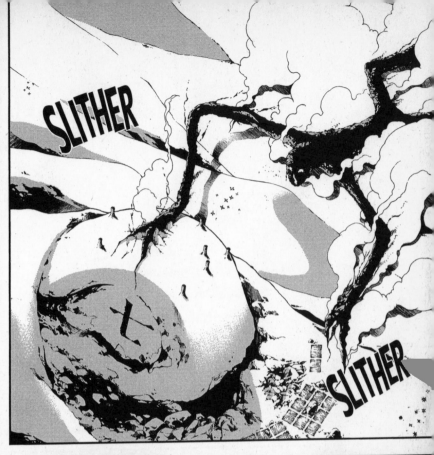

I mean, over there!

Lookie lookie, Doc!

HM?

IT'S LIKE A CLUMP OF... MACHINES.

NO!

DON'T COME ANY CLOSER!

...?

WHAT ON EARTH IS THAT?

AL, WHAT'S HAPPENING ?!

RUMBLE

RUMBLE

DAD!!

RUMBLE

WHAT'S THIS?

THE CENTRIPETAL FORCE'S DISAPPEARED!

SHWEEN

NO!

VMM

VMM

THERE'S DEFINITELY SOMETHING THERE!

SHUUDDRR

AND THE SEAL'S STOPPED GLOWING.

SHIO, YOU BELIEVE IN THE KAMI?

HEH HEH.

HERE, BRING ME FORTUNE.

POINK

CLANG! CLANG!

奉納

(OFFERINGS)

WHAT--?

RRRRR

HM?

RUMBLE

OF COU--

HERE, YOU ARE ALL-POWERFUL.

TMP

AND IT IS FOR THAT POWER THAT THE SEVEN GUARDIANS OF THIS WORLD FIGHT FOR YOU.

WHAT IS THIS?

A SHADOW?

WHAT?

IT IS THE FATE OF THE KAMI!

THE MACHINES HAVE ALREADY GATHERED BEFORE YOU!

HMPH. SEE FOR YOUR-SELF.

FLOMP

FLOMP

AN EXISTENCE SCORNED BY HUMANS, AND REVERED BY MACHINES.

HE'S A KAMI FROM AN ANCIENT LEGEND.

YOU COULD EVEN CALL IT A RELIGION.

AND THE LEGEND SAYS THAT HE'LL COME BACK TO WĀQWĀQ TO SAVE HUMANITY.

What on earth happened to you? You're dripping black with blood!

GLUP GLUP

PEOPLE'S BLOOD IS BLACK, BUT THE KAMI WHO CREATED THE WORLD LONG AGO HAD RED BLOOD.

Uh, I just got attacked by a machine.

ERMM...

SURE, WHAT IS IT?

...

ANYWAY, SHIO. MAY I ASK YOU SOMETHING?

WE NEVER SET OFF A RESCUE FLARE.

AND I'M SURE THERE ARE PLENTY OF OTHER VILLAGES IN MORE DIRE NEED OF A GUARDIAN.

HOW DO I EXPLAIN?

WHY DID YOU AND YOUR FATHER COME TO THIS VILLAGE?

JUST WHAT IS A SCENT-TRIP-PETAL FORCE?

CENTRI-PETAL FORCE.

A POWER THAT DRAWS ONE TO SOMETHING.

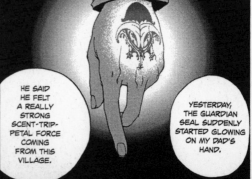

HE SAID HE FELT A REALLY STRONG SCENT-TRIP-PETAL FORCE COMING FROM THIS VILLAGE.

YESTERDAY, THE GUARDIAN SEAL SUDDENLY STARTED GLOWING ON MY DAD'S HAND.

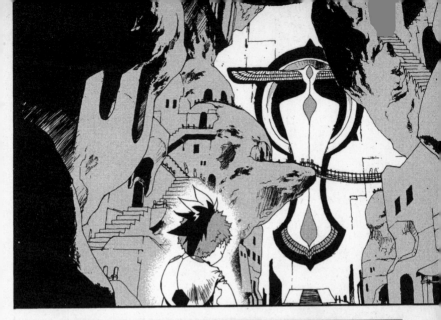

...MAY THERE PLEASE COME A DAY WHERE MY DAD DOESN'T HAVE TO FIGHT ANYMORE.

CLAP CLAP CLAP

DEAR KAMI...

HE SAID HE WAS HEADED OUTSIDE TO STAND WATCH.

HUH? WHERE'S AL?

SHIO!

SKUFF

I'VE PREPARED YOUR ROOM ON THE UPPER LEVELS.

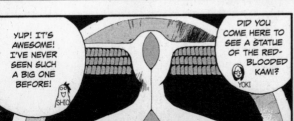

YUP! IT'S AWESOME! I'VE NEVER SEEN SUCH A BIG ONE BEFORE!

SHIO

DID YOU COME HERE TO SEE A STATUE OF THE RED-BLOODED KAMI?

YOKI

AH, NO NEED TO WORRY. THAT'S A GOJIN-ZOU. THEY'RE ON OUR SIDE.

HOW?

TIK TIK TIK

No Boo! fair!

SOLD OUT

Boo!

SOME EVEN CALL THEM ANGELS, BESTOWED UPON US BY THE KAMI HIMSELF.

THEY ARE RELICS FROM AN ANCIENT CIVILIZATION THAT MERGE WITH GUARDIANS AND GRANT THEM IMMENSE POWER.

YOU MEAN THE RED-BLOODED KAMI?

THE KAMI?

WOW!

22

SO IN ORDER TO PROTECT THEMSELVES, HUMANS DIG OUT HOLES IN MOUNTAINS AND LIVE IN HIDING.

ACCORDING TO MY DAD, IT'S INSTINCT FOR THE MACHINES TO ATTACK HUMANS.

LOOK AT THAT!

OH, MY!

WHEN DID YOU GET HERE?

THE GREAT GUARD-IAN!

IT'S THE GUARD-IAN!

RUZZAH

JUST NOW.

BUT THERE IS ONE KIND OF PERSON THAT CAN BATTLE THE MACHINES-- THE GUARDIANS!

THEY'LL SACRIFICE THEIR OWN LIVES TO PROTECT PEOPLE!

EXIT

21

NYUUUM

Separate

神神像
Armaiti

SLIP

HEH HEH.

VERY NICE OF YOU, SHIO.

OH!

DOCTOR YOKI!

No prob.

So much...!

Thanks!

OH, HONORABLE GUARDIAN! THANK YOU!

ANYWAY, PLEASE COME AND REST INSIDE THE VILLAGE.

YUP! AIN'T HE BIG NOW?

PAT

LONG TIME NO SEE, AL!

AND THIS MUST BE SHIO!

YOU MUST BE WEARY FROM YOUR TRAVELS.

YOU WERE THIS TINY LAST I SAW YOU.

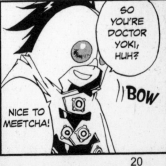

NICE TO MEETCHA!

SO YOU'RE DOCTOR YOKI, HUH?

)) BOW

CRU NCH

KABOOM

CLAP CLAP

DEAR MR. MACHINE, MAY YOU FIND PEACE IN THE AFTERLIFE.

RESCUE MISSION COMPLETE!

TMP

THUD

UPH!!

THUD

POOF

POOF

...

IT'S THE MACHINE'S HEART!

ARMAITI--
MERGE!

VMM

S
WOOSH

復神機
Armaiti

KRIK

KRIK

KRIK

VRIK

NO--!!

IT'S
HIM!

WE CAN'T THANK YOU ENOUGH!

SLINK

BUT THE RADISHES--!

MUTTER

MUTTER

AND I WARNED YOU NOT TO GO OUTSIDE WITH THOSE BIG MACHINES RUNNING AROUND!

I'M A DOCTOR, NOT THE VILLAGE SENTRY!

GYAAAH!!!

WHIP

DASH

DOC--!

OH, NO!

Save us!

BAH

THIS ONE'S GOT A SERIOUS GRUDGE!

THIS IS WHY I DIDN'T WANT TO GO OUT INTO THE FIELD DURING A FULL MOON!

SHUT UP! THE SAND RADISHES NEED CARE EVERY DAY!

HERE COME THE MISSILES!

YIPE!!!

RIGHT BEHIND YA!

SHIO, LET'S GO! ARMAITI, YOU'RE WITH ME!

DASH

THAT GUNFIRE...

七

IT'S COMING FROM THE VILLAGE!

BOOM

BOOM

BOOM

BOOM

PSSHT

CLANG

PLING

サイクルへ

PLING

EEEEEK!!

BANG

BANG

LONG AGO, THE RED-BLOODED KAMI INHABITED THIS LAND.

THEN... HE JUST DISAPPEARED.

THE RED-BLOODED KAMI MADE THIS WORLD, CREATED US HUMANS WHO RESIDE HERE, AND CREATED THE MECHANICAL LIFE-FORMS.

UHA!!

SKUFF

MY DAD SAYS THAT SOMEDAY, HE'LL COME BACK AGAIN AND BRING HAPPINESS TO THE BLACK-BLOODED PEOPLE.

-01- PROOF OF THE GODS

WHERE
...

...AM
I?

-01- PROOF OF THE GODS

THE
FUTURE?

IT LOOKS
LIKE THE
FUTURE
TO YOU...

01 Proof of the Gods

STORY AND ART BY Ryu Fujisaki

ワークワーク

01

Proof of the Gods

Wāqwāq vol. 1

SHONEN JUMP Manga Edition

This graphic novel contains material that was originally published in English in SHONEN JUMP #80. Artwork in the magazine may have been slightly altered from that presented here.

Story and Art by Ryu Fujisaki

Translation & Adaptation/Alexis Kirsch
Touch-up Art & Lettering/James Gaubatz
Design/Sean Lee
Editors/Joel Enos & Ian Robertson

VP, Production/Alvin Lu
VP, Publishing Licensing/Rika Inouye
VP, Sales & Product Marketing/Gonzalo Ferreyra
VP, Creative/Linda Espinosa
Publisher/Hyoe Narita

Printed in the U.S.A.

Published by VIZ Media, LLC
P.O. Box 77010
San Francisco, CA 94107

10 9 8 7 6 5 4 3 2 1
First printing, August 2009

www.viz.com

THE WORLD'S MOST POPULAR MANGA

www.shonenjump.com

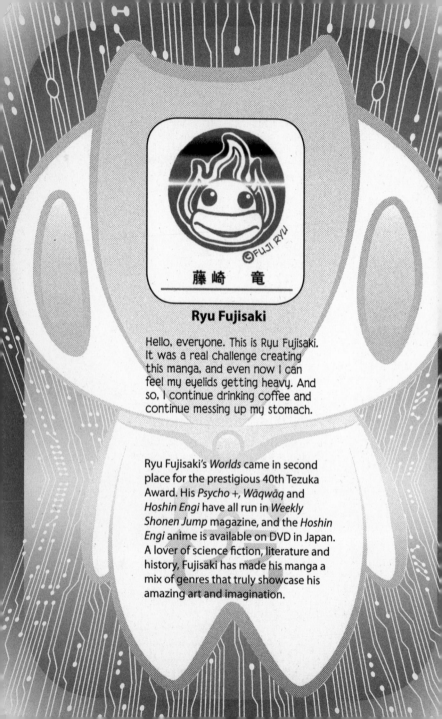

藤崎　竜

Ryu Fujisaki

Hello, everyone. This is Ryu Fujisaki. It was a real challenge creating this manga, and even now I can feel my eyelids getting heavy. And so, I continue drinking coffee and continue messing up my stomach.

Ryu Fujisaki's *Worlds* came in second place for the prestigious 40th Tezuka Award. His *Psycho +*, *Wāqwāq* and *Hoshin Engi* have all run in *Weekly Shonen Jump* magazine, and the *Hoshin Engi* anime is available on DVD in Japan. A lover of science fiction, literature and history, Fujisaki has made his manga a mix of genres that truly showcase his amazing art and imagination.